THE

PUBLICATIONS

OF THE

Northamptonshire Record Society

FOUNDED IN DECEMBER, IN THE YEAR 1920

VOLUME XVII

FOR THE TWO YEARS ENDED 31ST DECEMBER, 1951

This book is published with the aid of grants made by the Society of Authors from the Crompton Bequest Fund, and by the Dean, Canons and Students of Christ Church, Oxford. The Northamptonshire Record Society desires to make grateful acknowledgments for this assistance.

Printed for the Northamptonshire Record Society
by Staples Printers, Ltd., Green Lane,
Kettering, Northamptonshire

BRIAN DUPPA, AS BISHOP OF WINCHESTER
by Hugh Howard after the lost original by Michael Wright (signed)
This illustration appears by courtesy of the Dean, Canons, and Students of Christ Church, Oxford.

Frontispiece

THE CORRESPONDENCE

OF

BISHOP BRIAN DUPPA

AND

SIR JUSTINIAN ISHAM

1650-1660

EDITED WITH

MEMOIRS OF THE CORRESPONDENTS

AND AN

HISTORICAL SUMMARY

BY

SIR GYLES ISHAM BART.

together with a

PREFACE BY SIR GEORGE CLARK
PROVOST OF ORIEL COLLEGE, OXFORD

PUBLISHED BY
THE NORTHAMPTONSHIRE RECORD SOCIETY
LAMPORT HALL
NORTHAMPTONSHIRE

ABBREVIATIONS

(See also List of Authorities, pages 211 to 216 below, for full names of authors and titles of works cited).

Archd. Northampton	Archdeaconry of Northampton.
B.M.	British Museum.
Bodl.	Bodleian Library.
C.S.P.Col.	*Calendar of State Papers Colonial.*
C.S.P.Dom.	*Calendar of State Papers Domestic.*
D.N.B.	*Dictionary of National Biography.*
Firth	Sir C. H. Firth, *The Last Years of the Protectorate,* 1656-1658.
Gardiner	S. R. Gardiner, *History of the Commonwealth and Protectorate.*
G.E.C.	G. E. Cokayne, *The Complete Peerage.*
Harl. MSS., B.M.	Harleian MSS. in the British Museum.
Harl. Soc.	Publications of the Harleian Society.
I.C.	Isham Correspondence at the Northamptonshire Record Office at Lamport Hall.
I.L.	Isham (Lamport) Collection of MSS. at the Northamptonshire Record Office.
Journals H. of C.	*Journals of the House of Commons.*
Journals H. of L.	*Journals of the House of Lords.*
P.C.C.	Prerogative Court of Canterbury.
P.R.O.	Public Record Office.
Rawl. MSS.	Rawlinson MSS. at the Bodleian Library.
V.C.H.	*Victoria County History.*

The spelling of the original MSS. has been preserved, but abbreviations have been extended and the use of capitals and the punctuation have been modernised, except in quotations from printed books. The letter "y", representing the Anglo-Saxon "thorn" in words such as "ye", "yt", is here printed as "th". The method of accenting Greek words throughout is in accordance with standard modern practice.

Dates

Before 1752 the year started on March 25th, therefore, according to contemporary dating, Charles I was executed on January 30th, 1648. In England from 1752 the year started according to modern usage on January 1st. Single dates in this work are given according to modern usage. Where double dates occur the first is in the old English usage and the second in modern, e.g., the date of Charles I's execution—30th January, 1648/9.

CONTENTS

ILLUSTRATIONS

PEDIGREES

BRIAN DUPPA

"To conclude; This worthy Person now gone before us, often professed to Mee, that He desired only Two Blessings in this world, and He should cheerfully sing His *Nunc Dimittis*, *Depart in Peace*; To see the King His Gratious Masters Return unto His Throne, And the Churches happy Restitution to Her Rights.

God gave Him the desire of his Lipps. He liv'd to see Both, And, *in a good old Age*, *full of Dayes*, having compleated *Seaventy and three yeares* . . . . with some few dayes over, He exchanged his Painful Life for an Everlasting Rest. Leaving his Virtues to be Imitated by those that can, And His Loss to be Lamented by All who are left behind."

From the Funeral Sermon preached by Henry King,
Bishop of Chichester, at Westminster Abbey.

PREFACE

ALTHOUGH I wish to draw attention to one particular aspect of the correspondence between Brian Duppa and Sir Justinian Isham, I might be misunderstood if I did not begin by saying something about its value in general. Everyone who is attracted by the English seventeenth century will find something of interest in it. Naturally there are plums for the various kinds of specialists. The historians of Parliament will note that the best friends of the bishop, or rather of the causes in which he was engaged, drifted away from the Convention after their pleasures, presumably their country pursuits, in August 1660. They will be reminded that this was one of the practices Danby tried to check when he stiffened parliamentary discipline fourteen or fifteen years later(1). The allusions to hare-pies sent from Lamport to Richmond may conceivably help Shakesperian scholars to elucidate the jokes about hare-pie in the second act of Romeo and Juliet. And not only specialists but many other readers will respond to the human interest of the letters.

Before the letters were printed much information about the two correspondents was easily available, but in the light of this new material we see that our former sources were misleading as well as inadequate, especially for the character of Sir Justinian Isham. Many readers have formed a notion of what he was like from another correspondence, the famous letters which Dorothy Osborne was writing at this time to William Temple. We must reckon it as one of Sir Justinian's misfortunes that, as a widower of forty, he offered his hand and his broad acres to this lady of half his age, with the mocking pen, when she was already in love with Temple, who became one of the outstanding writers and public men of the time. Sir Justinian's best qualities were not of the kind that could further his suit, but they do come out plainly in his letters to Brian Duppa. The bishop is seen more intimately in these letters than was possible before, and his gentle wit is very attractive. He was already over sixty when he wrote the first letter in this volume, and he could look back on a career of steady advancement from one dignity to another, Fellow of All Souls, Dean of Christ Church, Vice-Chancellor of Oxford University, Bishop of Salisbury, friend and adviser of King Charles I. Now he was only a titular bishop, deprived of his revenues by the victorious Puritans, and straitened in his means; but he was the most active and the least dispirited among the little band of surviving prelates.

The letters begin in the affliction which these two loyal subjects felt when the king was put to death; they run on through ten anxious and eventful years, and end in the sudden excitement and activity of

(1) See A. Browning. *Thomas Osborne, Earl of Danby*, especially i (1951), 166-73, 272-7.

the Restoration. Every one of them expresses the special quality of their friendship, honourable to both men and coloured by the cultivated English and Anglican tradition which they inherited. The older was affectionate, appreciative, kind and candid, the younger respectful, considerate, generous with material help when it was needed. They addressed one another as equally accustomed to exercising authority and equally debarred from exercising it during this enforced suspension of their active lives. It was unsafe to write much of what they thought about Church and State, or anything at all of what they knew about secret plans and projects for the future: even as it was, Sir Justinian was haled off to prison more than once. They fell back on the resources of their learned, and especially their classical, reading. Among their authors they recurred again and again to Seneca, in whom they found the consolations of stoicism as well as a Latin style which it was the general European fashion just then to admire. Of the two writers the country gentleman seems indeed to have taken more trouble to maintain a good literary standard. We must not take him seriously when he writes of himself as scribbling: he drafted and copied fair, and he had his library at hand. The bishop wrote with less study, and he did not always read very attentively. Once in his answer he ascribed a long quotation of Sir Justinian's to Seneca when it really came from the so-different Cicero. Did Sir Justinian falter in tact when he pointed out the mistake? It seems not, for the bishop showed no sign of being perturbed.

All this was altered by the transformation-scene of 1660. The king, Charles II, came into his own again. The two friends were no longer condemned to inactivity: they were needed where there was work to be done. We may smile when we see how promptly Sir Justinian enquired about the possibility of an investment in one of the bishop's leases, and how conclusively, if urbanely, the bishop replied that he had none to dispose of. We cannot approve of the gusto with which the Justice of the Peace set about his local Quakers. The two men did not indeed, if everything is considered, become less admirable now that their responsibilities had returned; but their minds turned from literature to the world about them. The few pages they had time for after the Restoration show how fortunate for us was the accident which provided two such representative men with the opportunity to exchange all these letters. The letters give one more proof that to be impregnated with the thought of great writers is not the worst education for difficult times.

Here arises the point which, as I wrote at the beginning, I specially wish to make. These letters give an insight into an aspect of English country life which is still comparatively unexplored, the part played in it by education and learning. The two correspondents were well-educated men. Neither of them was a scholar or a writer in the narrower sense. Duppa had been a university teacher, but he was no longer a professional student; for a long time he had been applying in practice the charitable but disciplinarian wisdom of his calling. Nothing of his had ever been published with his consent. Isham had studied to good purpose at Uppingham and Christ's, and he was aware of the questioning and innovating elements in the thought of the time. In due course he was to become a Fellow of Charles II's Royal Society, but he did not claim to be either a mathematician or a scientist. Both of them, however, were readers, men who remembered and quoted books. We learn from the letters what new books they heard of, what difficulties they had in acquiring them and how they reacted to their reading. This part of their correspondence does not rise to the level of close discussion, but it is more substantial then mere literary gossip. The older man is naturally less eager in enquiry, perhaps less assiduous in reading what is new; but both express their opinions sincerely and unaffectedly. We see at work the process by which the reputation and influence of books was established, and this at a particularly interesting point of time, —the end of the ages in which conversation and letter-writing were the two available aids to judging a book. The first periodical to publish reviews of books was the French *Journal des Sçavans*, which began in 1665. It was soon imitated in England and the next generation after Sir Justinian Isham's relied, as we do, on reviewers for learned and literary opinions. So this correspondence throws light on various factors in the mind of the educated England of that time.

At least it does so for Northamptonshire. As it happens we do not know very much about the resemblances and contrasts between the different parts of England in this matter of reading. Mr Peter Laslett, who has a gift for asking new questions and finding unexpected answers, touched on this matter in his article on the gentry of Kent in 1640(1). He quoted some words of the noted scholar William Lambarde, who died in 1601 and himself belonged to their number: "These gentlemen be also (for the most part) acquainted with good letters, and especially trained in the knowledge of the lawes." Mr. Laslett indicates the reasons why there was "striking intellectual activity among these county clans" in seventeenth-century Kent, with Canterbury and the seaports at one end and London near the other. He traces the family relationships of the Kentish authors, 'not only poets and pamphleteers but also theologians, mathematicians, geographers, classicists, archaeologists and historians.' But we need to compare Kent with other counties and with the towns. There is much work to do on the history of thought even in the universities, and there is abundant, if difficult material not only for them but for all the other greater or lesser centres of thought. Lamport Hall, as we see from these letters, was in its degree one of these centres. Its famous library is still preserved, and in it are some of Sir Justinian Isham's own books: now and again we can still look up a passage on the page where he verified

(1) *Cambridge Historical Journal*, ix, No. 2 (1948) 148 ff.

it before quoting it to the bishop. I do not know how far it would be possible to go in estimating what the contents of the library were in his time, nor what other country-house libraries there were in Northamptonshire then, how large and of what character. Something can be known about the libraries of parsonages and school-houses, and of the scholarly interests of their occupants. Much might be discovered about the intellectual climate of Puritan Northampton, very different from that of Lamport eight miles away. Information of this kind which local Record Societies are so admirably qualified to provide, can be brought into connection with what is known about the printing and circulation of books, so that the history of ideas may become, far more than at present, an organic element in English history as a whole. Dr. R. S. Bosher has already used the Duppa-Isham correspondence in solving some of the mysteries of the history of the Church of England; there are other chapters of the history of thought for which both the text and the learned annotation will be useful and every further edition in this field will make them more useful still.

G. N. CLARK.

Kings Sutton
Northamptonshire.

EDITOR'S NOTE

In the Appendix to the Third Report of the Historical MSS. Commission (1872), in an account of the MSS. of the late Sir Charles Isham, Bart. of Lamport the late Mr. Alfred J. Horwood noted :—

"1660 etc. A bundle of letters by Brian Duppa, Bishop of Salisbury, and afterwards of Winchester, to Sir Justinian Isham. They contain political news."

There follow a few notes on various letters, mentioning the death of Selden, the death of Harvey, and Duppa's elevation to the See of Winchester.

Of the collection of family letters at Lamport, Canon Augustus Jessopp, writing in *The Norfolk Antiquarian Miscellany* (Vol. II, 1883), stated that "perhaps no mansion in England, except Hatfield, contains a larger collection of private letters than is to be found at Lamport." These letters (and those of Bishop Duppa among them) remained at Lamport till 1929. From 1907 to 1929, the house was let to various tenants, and the letters remained in boxes, safe but inaccessible, in a locked room over the side entrance, known as the Swan Room. In 1929, Miss Joan Wake and I removed the letters and other MSS. to the Record Rooms at Northampton, where my father deposited them in the custody of the Northamptonshire Record Society, of which Miss Wake was then, as now, the Honorary Secretary. My own interests lying largely in the 17th century, I removed the letters of that date for examination.

It seemed to me that the correspondence between Sir Justinian Isham and Brian Duppa had a special importance. First, it dealt with a period, 1650 – 1660, in which the Government was in the hands of persons whose views were directly opposed to those of the correspondents, and it is notorious that the Government's point of view of any period is always better documented that those of their opponents.

Secondly, the letters of Brian Duppa, written in a clear hand and in the dignified prose of the period, had their counterpart in the draft replies of Sir Justinian, written on the spare places of the MS.; they are only drafts, and they are far less legible than the Bishop's letters. But at least they provide, what is rare, an approximation to a two-handed correspondence. There is, however, one grave drawback. The Bishop has dated his letters by day and month only. It was, therefore, my first task to arrange the letters under their respective years, relying on internal evidence, but helped by the various other letters in the family archives. When this had been completed, I had the letters typed verbatim, and began the task of annotation. Owing to the fact that both correspondents were suspect to the Government they were careful to disguise, or to omit, their political connections. But this had another advantage. Politics being largely barred, the correspondents spent much time not only on family news, but also in discussing the contemporary literary scene. As Sir Justinian wrote (Letter xv, April 8th, 1651) "our booke intelligence may be very inoffensive and [I] shall much desire to know what passes in the Republic of letters from your Lordship, so great a Judge in it." Accordingly, there is much of books in these letters. Hobbes' *Leviathan*, Izaak Walton's *Compleat Angler*, Harrington's *Oceana*, are some of the "classics" that appeared in these years, and both the books and their authors (who were personally known to the correspondents) are discussed on their appearance. Nor is their interest confined to England. Descartes, Pascal, and Grotius were distinguished contemporaries in Europe and they receive as much attention as English authors. There is much, naturally, of authors famous in their day, but largely forgotten to-day: Dr. Henry Hammond of Penshurst, John Hall of Richmond, Thomas Vaughan, brother of the Silurist, Sir Henry Blount, and Henry More, the Platonist. I suggest that the "Republic of Letters" seen through contemporary eyes has a value that cannot be gauged after three centuries.

A special interest also attaches to the ecclesiastical climate of these letters. Duppa was a protégé of Laud, and Isham was a devout layman of the same school. This was the period when the Church of England was not only in eclipse, but proscribed. It can be seen, in these letters, that, driven underground and suppressed, Anglicanism gained a strength that enabled her leaders, at the Restoration, to reassume control of the Establishment, and to retain it for good. There were only eight bishops left alive at the Restoration, of whom Duppa was the most active despite his years, and it was his closest friends, many of whom are met with in these letters, who formed the nucleus of the restored episcopacy; Henchman of Salisbury and London, Ward of Salisbury, Sanderson of Lincoln and, above all, Sheldon of London and Canterbury. It is true that some of the leaders of the restored Establishment spent their time on the Continent, like Cosin and Morley, but this is reflected in the great interest shown in these letters in the controversy in the French Church between the Jesuits and the Jansenists. Dr. Robert S. Bosher, who consulted these letters, stated in his recently published book *The Making of the Restoration Settlement**, that they form one of "the chief sources for a study of Laudian activity" during the Commonwealth. It should not be forgotten that the period of suppression was one of considerable literary and scholarly activity, for the Church. Jeremy Taylor's most important work, and Brian Walton's Polyglot Bible were produced under these apparently hostile conditions. Jeremy Taylor, indeed, appears in these letters several times, as does Herbert Thorndike, who contributed the Syriac portions to Walton's work. Lesser lights mentioned include Jeremy Stephens, the coadjutor of Sir Henry Spelman, Anthony Farindon, and Robert Sanderson.

* (1951) p. 295.

Politically, the letters lose something through the unwillingness of the correspondents to enter that field, but Duppa's account of the ending of Barebone's Parliament in 1653 (Letter XXVIII, December 13th) has no rival for gentle satire. It was not to be expected that the republican Governments would be impartially judged by those who had been so adversely affected by them. Indeed, Sir Justinian himself seems to have felt this. When in 1661 he was asked to stand for Parliament, he at first declined, as it might be thought he was a "provok'd person" and it would be better to have a representative unconcerned in "the late unhappy differences". The reasons, however, that led to the triumph of the Royalists, and the use which they made of this triumph, are clearly seen. Deprivation, sequestration and imprisonment weighed most heavily on those, like these correspondents, whose attachment to Church and King was best known. But it was the military anarchy, that supervened after Cromwell's death, which made the Restoration of the King a political necessity. The actual recall of the King owed most, not to the Royalists, but to the Presbyterians and the City, elements that had been most active in opposing his father. But only the Royalists and Anglicans were in a position to profit by the return of the King. It is true that this was Royalism with a difference, and, in fact, only the political skill of Charles II disguised the fact that a limited Monarchy had begun. It was James II's flouting of the spiritual descendants of Sir Justinian and Bishop Duppa that caused his downfall. The second Sir Justinian, son of the first, was a Member of the Royalist Parliament of 1685, but he is found at Nottingham in 1688, bearing, as cornet, the banner inscribed with the words *Nolumus Leges Angliae mutari*, while his captain, Bishop Compton, leads the insurgent gentlemen of the Midlands.

But, apart from books, religion and politics, the letters have a personal side that is not to be overlooked. The old Bishop, with his ailing but devoted wife, creeping, as he says, "into the chimney corner" of his little house at Richmond, and writing to his friend, at first a widower, then a happy husband with a growing family; grateful for a Lamport "hare-pye"; performing "the duties of the time" at the great festivals; visiting the sick bed of the dying William Harvey; the man is vividly revealed in these letters. And his correspondent "noble, just, temperat," is scarcely less clear.

I have felt that, since the published material on the two men is meagre, and sometimes inaccurate, it would be well for the reader to have a firm picture of the two protagonists in this good-natured battle of wits. Therefore, I give short Memoirs of the two men, in the hope that they will illuminate the pages that follow.

Before each year, I have placed a summary of the events, local and national, that affect the letters which follow, using, wherever possible, unpublished MS. material from the Isham letters, but also the works of the historians, both contemporary, like Clarendon, and modern, in particular, Ranke, Gardiner and Firth, to whom all students of the period must forever be indebted. The notes on the books and persons mentioned, the translations and sources of the quotations follow the letters.

Regarding the quotations in the Letters, the reader will notice the number from Seneca. It would, indeed, seem as if Seneca's letters had formed, in some respects, the model for this correspondence. Seneca's letters addressed to a young friend Lucilius, probably written in the last years of his life, tell us something about Seneca's own life, but much more about the moral outlook of a zealous Stoic in the days of the early Roman Empire. If for 'Stoic' we substitute 'Churchman', and for 'Early Roman Empire' we read 'Puritan Republic', this description might serve equally well for Duppa's letters. Indeed, Bishop Duppa himself seems to have felt this resemblance, for in one of the undated letters (see Appendix B) he writes: 'Had not Seneca told his good Friend Lucilius *satis magnum theatrum sumus tu et ego*, we might possibly be at a loss what to write one to the other' (I(D)123).

The staff of the Northamptonshire Record Office have been patient and helpful on all occasions ; and Mr. P. I. King, the Archivist, has been more than co-operative. The staffs of the Bodleian Library, the British Museum, the London Library, and Somerset House, as ever, have made the path of research easy. The Record Office staff at Bedford has also helped me in matters referring to that County. I need not add that the General Editor of the Northamptonshire Record Society has given the closest attention to this, as to every publication of the Society, and her knowledge and experience have been freely placed at my disposal.

In Appendix A will be found a note on the family and connections of Bishop and Mrs. Duppa a subject on which there has been much inaccuracy. In this Appendix my obligations to Miss Margaret Toynbee are heavy. She had quite independently interested herself in Duppa's family and in *Notes and Queries* (September 2nd, 1950 and September 15th, 1951), has published notes on the lives and connections of Duppa's sister, Mrs. Kilvert, and his niece, Lady Salter. She has, however, not only from her store of previous knowledge but by diligent research cleared up for me many points, on which I was more than doubtful.

She has since added to my obligations to her by reading through the typescript, checking the numerous references and suggesting several additions to the notes. In particular, she solved the problem of the lady painter and her husband, who lived at Petersham, and whose identity was obscure (Letter xv, Note 2a). She also discovered that the letters begin in 1650, and not 1649, a mistake into which I was led by the wrong dating in the Dictionary of National Biography of Sir William Boswell's death.

Finally, since not every reader troubles with Appendices, I must emphasise that these family connections of Bishop Duppa explain his intense loyalty to the Stuarts. Not only had he himself been tutor to the Prince of Wales, and one of the most favoured spiritual advisers of Charles I, but his family had been intimately connected with the Royal Family for more than a generation. His father and his elder brother had been Royal Brewers; one of his sisters had been "dresser" to Princess Elizabeth, and she had attempted to assist the Duke of York to escape his gaolers; another of his sisters had married Charles I's Sergeant at Arms; one of his nieces had risked her life to help Charles II after Worcester, while another had married the Royal Carver, and sheltered his brother bishop, Henry King. It was, therefore, no academic attachment to the principle of monarchy, but a personal and family tie that bound Duppa to the Royal House.

Those who require more than this in the way of genealogy, and family history, must be referred to Appendix A.

There are eleven letters the dating of which remains uncertain, as they contain few clues. I include these in Appendix B, with some notes on them. They are not of an interest equal to the rest of the correspondence, on the whole, but that of March 15th (after 1653) which might belong to 1658, is a very good example of the Bishop's style.

I cannot conclude this note without expressing my gratitude to various persons, and would like first to mention the late Sir Edward Parry, first editor of Dorothy Osborne's letters, who gave me encouragement to begin the work. Others who encouraged me then were my cousin, the late Revd. Henry Isham Longden, the late Alistair Taylor, and Sir Keith Feiling.

I must also thank Mr. T. F. Lindsay who made the original transcription of the MSS. —no easy task in the case of Sir Justinian's jottings.

Professor Jocelyn Toynbee has revised and checked the Greek quotations, and with her sister, Miss Margaret Toynbee, has identified several others, both Latin and Greek. In the elucidation and identification of quotations I also owe much to Mr. Alan Ker of Wellington College (now, 1953, Fellow of Trinity College, Cambridge) and to Mr. Colin Haycraft of the Queen's College, Oxford. Mr. J. M. Wylie and the Revd. E. Sutcliffe S. J. are among others who have helped me in this particular matter.

I have tried in the notes to express in every case indebtedness for suggestions and corrections. Miss Anne Whiteman, Miss Elizabeth Walsh, the late Lady Verney were all of assistance ; the Marchioness of Exeter, the Earl Spencer and Major F. H. T. Jervoise are thanked for help in connection with various points affecting their families, and I must not omit in my acknowledgments the many incumbents whose accuracy and willingness to answer enquiries prove that the claims of learning are still admitted by the successors of the Church of Duppa and Laud. The present occupants of Duppa's old Sees, the Bishops of Winchester, Salisbury and Chichester have also given every help. The Revd. J. A. Humphries, Vicar of Gazeley cum Dalham, has allowed me to inspect the unpublished registers of Dalham.

My obligations, over a long period of years, to numerous scholars and correspondents will be found expressed in the footnotes to this book. I trust that they will accept my assurance that this work, which was interrupted by seven years' army service and other difficulties, would never have been completed at all but for their assistance. If I have omitted the names of any who have helped, I hope they will pardon me and take this as an expression of my gratitude.

The Gothic Room,
Lamport Hall.
November, 1954.

GYLES ISHAM

BRIAN DUPPA

Brian Duppa was born at Lewisham, Kent, on March 10th, 1588/9. He was baptised in the parish church of St. Mary on March 18th. It has been suggested that he was christened Brian after Bryan Annesley of Lee, a Lewisham landowner, and a friend and legatee of Sir John Hawkins, the famous Elizabethan sailor[1].

Bryan Annesley was a Gentleman-Pensioner to Queen Elizabeth for thirty-two years, as his monument at Lee Old Church shows. An interesting suggestion has been made by Mr. G. M. Young in an essay "Shakespeare and the Termers"[2] that Bryan Annesley may have suggested the plot of King Lear to Shakespeare. He had three daughters, of whom the youngest bore the suggestive name of Cordell. One of the other daughters tried to get possession of her father's property by getting him certified as insane, but she was frustrated by her sister Cordell, who appealed to Secretary Cecil. She it was who erected her father's monument at Lee. Some years after his death in 1604, she married the step-father of Shakespeare's patron, Lord Southampton. This was Sir William Hervey, whose first wife was Mary, widow of the 3rd Earl of Southampton. His second marriage took place at St. Giles', Cripplegate on February 5th, 1607/8, where the *Registers* describe her as "the Lady Cordelia Ansley"; this fact, not mentioned by Mr. Young, strongly supports his suggestion that she and her father were the prototypes of Shakespeare's characters.

Brian's parents, Jeffrey Duppa and Lucrece Marshall, had been married at Lewisham on December 4th, 1580. Brian was the second son. Jeffrey Duppa, who was purveyor of the Buttery to Queen Elizabeth, and brewer to King James, was apparently of Herefordshire origin, since Brian in his will (dated February 1661/2) directed that provision should be made for the almshouses in Pembridge, Herefordshire "as an addition to the charity begun by my father." But he settled at Lewisham, where three of his sons and four of his daughters were baptised[3]. In Appendix A will be found notes on Brian Duppa's parents, and his brothers and sisters and their relations. Here it will be sufficient to remark that Duppa's family were intimately connected with the Court, as Royal servants, and that they were also bound up with the Navy, in one capacity or another.

Brian was sent to Westminster School as a King's scholar, "where he was instructed in Hebrew by Dean Lancelot Andrews"[4]. This

---

[1] Edward Hasted, *History of Kent* corrected and enlarged . . ., ed. Henry Drake, Part I, *The Hundred of Blackheath* (1886) p.252 and p.247.

[2] G. M. Young, *To-day and Yesterday*, (1948); *Notes and Queries*, April, 1954.

[3] Extracts from the Registers of St. Mary's, Lewisham, made by Lysons in preparing his work on the *Environs of London*: British Museum, Add. MSS. 9456, f. 352. (The Registers were subsequently destroyed by fire). *Westminster Abbey Registers*, ed. J. L. Chester, p.156, which refutes the statement in the article on Duppa in D.N.B. that Jeffrey was Vicar of Lewisham. *Miscellanea Genealogica et Heraldica*, 4th Series, Vol. II (1905–7), pp. 40–3 and 54–6.

[4] See his epitaph in Westminster Abbey. John Dart, *History and Antiquities of Westminster* (1742), Vol. II, p.10.

was a decisive influence in his life. In one of his letters to Sir Justinian Isham he mentions "that excellent man, Bishop Andrewes" and says "if any man hath been so happy as to write like him, I should be glad to see but a shadow of him" (Letter XCIX). At Westminster, he had "the greatest dignity which the school could afford put upon Him, to be the *Pædonomus at Christmas, Lord of his Fellow-Scholars*"[5].

From Westminster, he went to Christ Church, Oxford, whence he matriculated on July 9th, 1605, aged 16. He took his M.A. in 1614, having become a fellow of All Souls two years earlier[6]. There is a bust of him in the Library at All Souls done by Henry Cheere in the 18th century.

According to Wood, Duppa then "travelled beyond the seas"; journeys which find an echo in these Letters, where he marvels at Hobbes' *Leviathan* "as much as I did at a literall whale, which it was once my hap to see upon the coasts of Spain." This is the only allusion to his foreign travels in the Letters, but it is probable that he went to France as well, since his interest in the French Church is marked.

But he was back in Oxford in 1619, when he was Proctor, "unanimously approved in the execution of that office; being not only a most Excellent Scholar, but a Man of a very *Genteel Personage and Behaviour*"[7]. In 1625 he was made D.D., and Chaplain to the Prince Palatine. In 1613 his father had supplied the Princess Palatine at Heidelberg with 20 "tuns of beer", charging 72*s* "a tun" for the better sort, and 60*s* for the second sort, sent in wine casks costing £14[8]. The father's beer may have, by its merits, attracted the attention of the Prince to the brewer's son. He then became Chaplain to the 4th Earl of Dorset, like Duppa a Christ Church man, and (though at this time a leader of the Popular Party) a friend of the Duke of Buckingham, and eventually one of the Commissioners appointed to try his murderer[9]. It was Dorset who, according to Wood, recommended Duppa to Buckingham for the vacant Deanery of Christ Church, an appointment taken up in 1629. Wood's statement is confirmed by no less an authority than William Laud, who at his trial said that the "Earl of Dorset got my Lord Duke of Buckingham to prefer him (i.e. Corbet to a bishopric) to make way for Dr. Duppa his deserving Chaplain into *Christ Church*"[10].

Three years previously, on November 23rd, 1626, he had been married in London at St. Dionis, Backchurch Street, to Jane,

---

[5] Henry [King] L. Bp. of Chichester, *A Sermon Preached at the Funeral of . . .Bryan, Lord Bp. of Winchester* etc. (1662), p.34.

[6] Corpus Christi College, Oxford, MS. 307, f.22, consulted by kind permission of the President and Fellows. Anthony Wood, *Athenae Oxonienses*, Vol. I (1721), p.269.

[7] John Walker, *Sufferings of the Clergy* (1714), p.62.

[8] Pell Records, *Issues of the Exchequer during the reign of James I*, ed. Frederick Devon (1836), Appendix, p.313.

[9] D.N.B.; C. R. Cammell, *The Great Duke of Buckingham* (1939).

[10] *The History of the Troubles and Tryal . . . of William Laud* &c., (1695), Cap. XXIX, p.366. For this reference I am indebted to Mr. H. R. Trevor-Roper.

daughter of Nicholas Killingtree of Longham, Norfolk[11]. Though his wife was older than Duppa, and they had no children, it was an extremely happy marriage, as these Letters bear frequent witness.

In 1625/6 Duppa had become vicar of the ancient Norman church of Westham near Pevensey in Sussex, and he continued to hold this living together with his Deanery till 1638[12]. Duppa evidently loved this magnificent church, for in his will, he gave twenty pounds to the poor of the parish, and a further twenty pounds "to provide Communion plate for that parish if they want it otherwise I give that twenty also to the poore of the parish." No doubt he provided a curate, and resided there in the vacations, for he became thenceforward intimately associated with Chichester diocese (see Appendix A). He was also Vicar of Hailsham (1625) and Withyham (1627), both in Sussex, and both being in the gift of Lord Dorset.

He was installed Dean of Christ Church on November 28th, 1629, and, it is said by some, in the exercise of this office much impressed Bishop Laud to whom, in due course, he owed further preferment[13]. In 1632 he became Vice-Chancellor, an office which he exercised "with great moderation and prudence[14]."

In 1634 he was made Chancellor of the diocese of Salisbury (June 7th), just after he became a Prebendary of the Cathedral (May 21st)[15].

On King Charles I's visit to Oxford in 1636, Duppa entertained him at Christ Church (Aug. 29th-31st), presenting before him a tragicomedy by William Strode called "Passions Calmed or the Settling of the Floating Island." This was "elaborately staged with mechanical bellows and music by Henry Lawes; and it conveyed an appropriate moral lesson, representing the evil consequences of rebellion. . . A parody of Prynne was introduced in the character of Malevolo, a play-hating puritan." The performance, however seems to have been a disappointment, and Lord Carnarvon said "it was the worst that ever he saw, but one that he saw at Cambridge"[16].

Whatever impression this drama made on the King, Duppa himself must have made a favourable one, for in 1638 Charles accepted Laud's suggestion to make Duppa tutor to the Prince of Wales, then eight years old, raising him at the same time to the episcopal bench, as Bishop of Chichester (June 17th)[17]. While Dean of Christ Church, Duppa had made changes in the interior of the Cathedral, which survived till 1856, when Gilbert Scott set about a mediaeval reconstruction.

As was usual with Bishops of Chichester at that time, Duppa also

---

[11] D.N.B., but see App. A for full details of this marriage.
[12] Revd. H. Hopley, *Guide to Westham Church* (first issued 1905).
[13] Revd. H. L. Thompson, *History of Christ Church* (1900).
[14] Wood.
[15] J. L. Chester, *Westminster Abbey Registers.*
[16] H. R. Trevor-Roper, *Archbishop Laud* (1940). See also Thompson, *op. cit.* and Wood's *Annals* where the " mechanical devices " are fully described.
[17] Thompson, *op. cit.*

held the rich living of Petworth in Sussex[18], but he resigned the living of Westham.

In the same year he edited *Jonsonus Virbius*, a collection of verses by various hands in praise of the poet Ben Jonson. Many of the leading wits of the day contributed, including Falkland and Waller, and many are known to have been intimate friends of Duppa, Henry King, Jasper Mayne and Robert Waring. "The designation "Jonsonus Virbius" is equivalent to "Jonson revived"; the latter word being derived from the relation in Ovid's *Metamorphoses*, of the death of Hippolytus"[19a]. According to Aubrey[19b], the name was suggested by Lord Falkland.

Duppa made no changes in Chichester Cathedral (as he had done at Oxford) but did not forget it in his will. No doubt he was mainly occupied in tutoring Prince Charles. The Prince was not his only pupil, as George and Francis Villiers, sons of his old patron, the 1st Duke of Buckingham, were also committed to his charge, and "the actual education of the boys rested more with Brian Duppa . . . than with the nominal trustees"[20].

On December 14th, 1641, Duppa was translated to the more important See of Salisbury, and, in the same year, while the King was in Scotland, "the Parliament ordered Prince Charles . . and his tutor, Bishop Duppa, to reside" at Richmond Palace[21]. This old Tudor Palace, which was mostly destroyed after the Civil War, was largely abandoned by Charles I, but Richmond became a favourite resort of the nobility in his reign, and derived importance from the Prince's residence. It was there, in 1636, that Prince Charles had entertained his father and mother with a masque (nominally under his direction), shortly after they had left the entertainment given them at Oxford by Laud and Duppa[22]. Duppa always retained a great affection for Richmond: it was chosen by him as a place of retirement during the suppression of the Episcopate, and remained his "cheif Palace" when he became Bishop of Winchester, and it was here that he died.

King Charles evidently had a great regard for Duppa since he directed his son to follow his mother in all things save religion, in which he was to trust entirely "to the care of . . the Bishop of Salisbury"[23].

On the outbreak of the Civil War in 1642, Duppa retired to Oxford "to wait on his Majesty, and left not the former till his last days"[24]. He was most generous in contributing money to the Royal Exchequer during the war. *A Narrative* by John Ashburn-

---

18 Walker.
19a Lowndes, *The Bibliographer's Manual* (1864). See also Letter VII, Note 7.
19b MS. Aubrey, 6. f. 95 (Bodl.) See Appendix C.
20 Winifred, Lady Burghclere, *George Villiers, Second Duke of Buckingham* (1903).
21 E. Beresford Chancellor, *The History and Antiquities of Richmond* (1894).
22 *Ibid.*
23 Clarendon, *History of the Rebellion*, Book IX, §74, Letter of Charles I, August 5th, 1645.
24 Wood.

ham[25] records many payments made by him for the King's cause between April 1642 and October 1643. These total £850. None of the other Bishops occur in these accounts except the "Bishopp of Bath and Wells", who gave £200, and the "Bishopp of Hereford", who gave £500.

After the failure of the negotiations at Uxbridge in February, 1645, Duppa accompanied Prince Charles to the West in March, and remained with him till the disasters of that year compelled the Prince to leave England the following year[26]. Meanwhile, the King's cause suffered further reverses, and Charles sought refuge with the Scots at Newcastle. The Scots demanded the Covenant as the price of their support, which Charles was naturally unwilling to grant. But on September 30th, 1646, the King wrote from Newcastle to Juxon to seek advice on the question of the permissibility of granting the establishment of Presbyterianism for a limited period. In a postscript, he added: "I give leave to take assistance of the Bishop of Salisbury [Duppa] and Doctor Sheldon, or either of them, and let me have your answer with all convenient speed"[27]. When the Scots had handed their prisoner over to the English Parliament, and the King was confined in the Tudor Palace of Holdenby in Northamptonshire, he petitioned his gaolers to allow him the attendance of some of his chaplains "whose opinions as clergymen I esteem and reverence, not only for the exercise of my conscience, but also even for clearing my judgement concerning the present differences in religion". Juxon and Duppa were the first names in the list of twelve clerics submitted by Charles. On March 6th he repeated the request with greater urgency but it was denied him[28]. He was only to be allowed to consult clerics who had taken the Covenant. Finally, when the King had been seized by the Army, escaped from Hampton Court, and was kept prisoner in the Isle of Wight, he asked for the assistance of eight divines, again naming Juxon and Duppa first, to advise him in the abortive Treaty negotiations with the Parliament. This was granted, and Duppa went to the King at Newport.

Here Charles "made use of his pious conversation during his imprisonment"[29]. On October 25th, 1648 he preached before the King, during the Treaty of Newport discussions, a sermon "The Soules Solioquie: And A Conference with Conscience", on the text, Ps. 42, 5: "Why art thou cast downe, O my soule, and why art thou disquieted within me?" This was printed the same year[30].

Walker[31] says "whilst he thus waited upon his *Majesty*, he was

---

[25] Vol. II (1830), Appendix.

[26] Clarendon, Books VIII–X; John Drinkwater, *Mr. Charles, King of England* (1926).

[27] Sir Charles Petrie, *The Letters Speeches and Proclamations of King Charles I* (1935), pp.208–9. The reply signed by Juxon and Duppa is dated from Fulham, October 14th, 1646. *Clarendon State Papers*, Vol. II, p.267.

[28] *Journals* of the House of Lords, Vol. IX, pp.26, 69 and 80.

[29] Walker.

[30] There is a copy in the Bodleian Library. It is also listed among the works of Bishop Duppa in Corpus Christi College, Oxford, MS. 307, f.22.

[31] *Sufferings of the Clergy*, p. 62.

intrusted by him with Matters of the greatest Moment and Concern; particularly with supplying the *vacant bishopricks*: and was continud in the *Same Trust* under King *Charles* II during the *Usurpation*." As there is ample proof of the truth of the second half of this statement, it may well be that Walker was correct in attributing Duppa's interest in the matter to King Charles I's directions.

Gauden's text of the Εἰκὼν Βασιλική was brought to the King at this time, and (according to Mrs. Gauden's account) "His Majesty having had some of these Essays read to him by Bishop Duppa, did exceedingly approve of them"; she further says it was Duppa who suggested "that the world should take it to be your Majesty's."[32] Mrs. Gauden, of course, is doubtful evidence on which to convict Duppa of a pious fraud.

It was no doubt at Newport that the King gave him his Bible, printed at Cambridge by Daniel in 1638, which, in 1652, Duppa gave to "Amicorum Optimo et inter priscos nominando", Sir Justinian Isham, who left it "to the heirs of his house successively." This Bible is now at Lamport in the possession of the writer.

Juxon, alone of the Bishops, attended the King to the scaffold, and Duppa, "stripped of his large revenues" retired, with his wife, Jane, to a small house at Richmond.

It was at Richmond in the days just after the death of the King that Duppa became a friend of Justinian Isham. It is possible that they had met at Oxford during the Civil War, but their intimacy clearly dated from the later period. Duppa counted it "a blessing from heaven, that in my meanest condition I have lighted on a freind, whom I should have took a pride to have made choice of when I was at my best" (Letter II, June 18th, 1650). In 1649 Justinian was staying at "the Park", that is, Petersham (Old) Lodge, with the dramatist Lodowick Carlile, a courtier, and his wife, the painter, Joan. He was engaged in business relating to his composition for delinquency, and endeavouring to get his fine reduced. It is clear from these Letters that the Carliles were common friends of Justinian and the Bishop, and their house was "a place", as Duppa says, "something the more beloved by me, because from thence I had my first enioyments of your freindship." (Letter XCVII, January 12th, 1658). The two men were possessed of, at least, one common relative, who may have been the means of their meeting. The mention of "our cousin Lewyn", who makes frequent appearance in these Letters (see especially Letters XXII, XLVII and notes), shows the connection, fully explained in Appendix A.

At any rate, Justinian proved himself a good friend in the days of the Commonwealth, and bought the house at Richmond in which Duppa and his wife lived (Letter X). With the suppression not only of the Episcopate, but of the Book of Common Prayer, and the loss of all its revenues, the outlook for the Church of England was very black. Juxon, Bishop of London, who from 1636 to 1641 held the

[32] Francis F. Madan, *A New Bibliography of the Eikon Basilike* (1950) App. 1, paras 2 and 7, and note 29. I am indebted to Mr. H. R. Trevor-Roper for this reference.

office of Lord High Treasurer, was the senior Bishop at liberty, but he "retired to his Manor of Little Compton in Gloucestershire . . . where he spent several years in a retired and devout condition, and now and then for healths sake rode a hunting with some of the neighbouring and loyal gentry." Duppa, accordingly, took charge of the trust given him by King Charles to maintain the Church of England.

In 1653, he seems to have summoned a meeting at Richmond of the leading Bishops and clergy to consider the problems of the use of the Prayer Book, then under legal ban. This, so far as is known, was the only meeting of Anglicans of a semi-official nature under the Commonwealth[33]. Dr. Henchman (afterwards Bishop of Salisbury and London), Dr. Sheldon (afterwards Bishop of London and Archbishop of Canterbury), Dr. Warner (Bishop of Rochester) and Dr. Hammond were among those who attended. The meeting evidently took place between mid-June and mid-August. The issue lay between those who held (like Dr. Sanderson) that the clergy might keep their cures and "prudentially manage the duty they owe to the public worship enjoined", and those who severely maintained that nothing in the Prayer Book could be omitted[34]. Duppa appears himself to have inclined to the former opinion, but "no pronouncement was ever issued by the Bishops regulating the use of the Prayer Book"[35]. From this point, the Anglican Bishops, largely from fear, made little attempt to exercise their pastoral authority. "Only Brian Duppa of Salisbury, living in the environs of the capital, remained closely in touch with ecclesiastical affairs, and was frequently consulted by the leading clergy"[36].

Both in 1655 and in 1659, Duppa had a leading part in the schemes set in motion by Chancellor Hyde from the Continent to replenish the fast diminishing Episcopate. The Chancellor noted him for his zeal and earnestness[37]. Sheldon was the man most trusted both by Hyde and Duppa, and to him Duppa confided his opinion that Hyde, from "the distance of place that is between us", did not appreciate the difficulties of the Bishops' position, when he expressed his amazement "that so little care is taken of our great business;" had he been nearer "he might pity some of us, and there should be no place for wonder left"[38].

Although, in his letters to Sir Justinian, there is no mention of these negotiations, and indeed it would have been dangerous to allude to them in correspondence which might have been subject

[33] For this information I am indebted to the Revd. Dr. Robert S. Bosher of the General Theological Seminary, New York, and Christ's College, Cambridge, who has put me in touch with much MS. material from the Harleian MSS. at the B.M., and the Tanner MSS. at the Bodleian Library, which I have since examined. He has subsequently developed this subject in his *Making of the Restoration Settlement*.

[34] Bosher, *op. cit.*, p.18 quoting a letter of Duppa to Sheldon, March 21st, 1652/3 in Tanner MSS. 53, f.230.

[35] *Ibid.* p.22.

[36] *Ibid.* p.27.

[37] John Stoughton, *Ecclesiastical History of England*, Vol. II, Chap. 1.

[38] November 16th (1659?): Tanner MSS. 51, f. 159b.

to governmental scrutiny, Duppa was clearly in touch with the remaining orthodox clergy, and also disregarded the law in exercising his episcopal office. He quite clearly used the Prayer Book services, administered the rite of confirmation, married according to Anglican usage, and visited sick beds and death beds. Moreover the fact that his sister Margaret Kilvert had been employed in the Royal household, with which so many of his relations were connected, and that he himself was thought to have an influence over Charles II, would render him suspect to the Republican governments. These Letters indeed provide evidence of his association with many active Royalists such as Philip Stanhope, 2nd Earl of Chesterfield, and Lord Bruce. Both these names occur in John Mordaunt's *Letter-Book*, recently published, which gives much information on Royalist plots[39].

Duppa's name occurs in this book when, after the failure of the Royalist rising of 1659, Mordaunt records: "The Duke of B.... (Buckingham, Duppa's old pupil), got it then, then Dr. D. . . . ." This is the episode vividly related in Letter CXII, when Duppa's library was searched, his papers scattered, and the Republican soldiers scanned with particular attention a letter from Sir Justinian, and "an other letter that exercised the inquisitors was a letter written three years past by my Lord Bruce, who consulted with me . . . . whether the soules of freinds departed ioyn'd to their bodies at the Resurrection, should ether know one the other, or have any mutuall complacence, in seeing the relations which they own'd on Earth" (September 20th, 1659).

In 1656 when Anthony Hinton was examined by the Government, he said that Dr. Hammond's code name was Westenbergh, and not Reeves, and that Duppa went under the name of his old master Andrewes[40]. There is no evidence that Duppa's efforts were directed to other than ecclesiastical ends, but the last thing that the Republican Governments wanted was the restitution of a "Prelatical" Church, of which the corollary was certainly a monarchical Stuart State.

Dr. Richard Allestree, who appears in Mordaunt's letters as "Mr. Alin", and was employed on negotiations between the Court at Brussels and the King's friends in England in 1659 and in the early part of 1660, stated, some time after the Restoration: "In May 1659 I being at Brussells received from the King Charles the 2nd a paper, wherein were these names, Dr. Sheldon, Dr. Hammond, Dr. Lucy, Dr. Ferne, Dr. Walton, with one other, which I have forgot, in cypher, which I was commanded, when I came into England, whether I was then going to decypher, and carry, from him to the bishop then of Salisbury, Dr. Duppa, with a message to this purpose, that he did desire him as his tutor, and require him as his subject, all pretenses whatsoever layed aside, without delay to cause the

[39] *The Letter-Book of John, Viscount Mordaunt 1658-1660*, ed. Mary Coate, Camden Society, Third Series, Vol. LXIX (1945).

[40] Rawlinson MSS. A 42, f. 329. The date is September 12th, 1656. Thurloe, *State Papers*, Vol. V, p. 407.

bishops then alive to meet together, and consecrate the above named persons bishops, to secure the continuation of the order in the Church of England. The dioceses they were to be consecrated to were also named in the same paper. The paper and message I did deliver to the bishop of Salisbury, Dr Barwick, afterwards dean of S. Paul's going with me to him at Richmond[41]."

The searching of Duppa's house in August 1659 seems to have convinced the Bishops that any attempt for them to meet and hold a regular consecration would cause them to join the Bishop of Ely in confinement in the Tower, where they would be unable to achieve anything, and despite this solemn charge from the King, nothing was done. It is, perhaps, unfair to blame these men, mostly of advanced years, if they were too timid to act, and Duppa as the most prominent, was most under hostile observation.

After the failure of the Royalist rising in 1659, Duppa, like other Royalists, seems to have been surprised by the turn of events in early 1660. When General Monk marched south, and entered London in February, his intentions were unknown. On February 27th, Duppa could write to Sir Justinian: "Parlaments and Armies, changes and revolutions fill the heads of other men, and we like Archimedes are drawing lines, while Syracuse is taking. But, alass, what is left for us to do?" (Letter CXVII).

But a month later, there came a change, and Duppa writes (March 27th, Letter CXVIII): "if the voice of the people be an oracle to be hearkned after, it never spake lowder, nor better", and Sir Justinian, in his reply to Duppa's letter of April 23rd, wrote: "Mee thinks I see your Lordship welcoming your King with teares of joy, and even ready with old Simeon to say *nunc dimittis*, &c. But God I hope will yet reserve you to be a maine instrument of good to this afflicted Church and State."

This proved true, and despite his age and infirmities, Duppa played almost as important a part in what has been called the second Restoration, that of the Church of England, as he had played in securing its continuance in the days of the Commonwealth. As Feiling observes[42]: "at the Restoration, the Church's leaders formed a real galaxy of force and learning, well fitted to stamp on a whole generation of laymen their own immovable and massive principles." Of the names given by Feiling, many are mentioned in Duppa's letters to Sir Justinian:—Seth Ward, Sheldon, Henchman, Thorndike, Sanderson, Jeremy Taylor and Juxon.

The King, however, owed his restoration more to the City of London and the Presbyterians than to the Anglicans and Royalists. This would not have been the case had the rising of 1659 succeeded, and Duppa was filled with apprehension after the King's return with

---

[41] H. C. Coxe, *Catalogue of Oxford College MSS.*, Vol. II: MSS. Collegii Vigorniensis, liv, p. 15.

[42] Keith Feiling, *A History of the Tory Party* 1640–1714 (1924), p. 126.

so questionable a backing. He wrote to Sheldon (August 11th, 1660)[43]: "You are the only person about his Majesty, that I have confidence in, and I persuade myself that as none hath his ear more, so none is likely to prevail in his heart more, and there was never more need of it, for all the professed enemies of our church look upon this as the critical time to use their dernier resort to shake his Majesty's constancy."

Indeed, the restoration of the Church service seemed strange after so long an interval, even to someone so naturally Anglican as Pepys, who, in his diary, records how he went with Admiral Montagu, now Earl of Sandwich, to Whitehall Chapel, on Sunday, July 29th, 1660, "where I heard a cold sermon of the Bishop of Salisbury's (Duppa's), and the ceremonies do not please me, they do so overdo them."[44]

Duppa had just been appointed Lord Almoner (July 7th), and in August he was translated to the See of Winchester (Letter CXIII, August 27th). On September 24th the solemnities of his translation were performed "to the great joy of many Lords and Gentlemen, as well as the reverend clergy, who have all a deep sense and memory of the prudence and piety of that eminent Prelate, to whom the whole nation owes a lasting tribute, not only for his great example of virtue and godliness, but for those excellent seeds and principles so happily laid in the youth of our Sovereign Lord the King, when he was Prince of Wales and under his Lordship's tuition"[45].

On Sunday morning, October 28th, 1660, Duppa presided, and, under mandate from Juxon, now Archbishop of Canterbury, was chief consecrator at Westminster Abbey at the first post-Restoration consecration of bishops[46].

In his letters to Sir Justinian, the new Bishop of Winchester gives a hint of some of the troubles that faced him. He kept his house at Richmond "which I look upon as my cheif palace," as his four official residences were "for the most part so demolished, that I have not the fourth part of one left to shelter me" (Letter CXXIII). Further "the king . . . having commanded, that not onely old tenancy should be regarded, but that new purchasers should be satisfyd, hath so tied up our hands" that he could not dispose of the Church property as he thought fit. The Church was suffering, not for the first time, from the King's desire to strengthen his position politically[47]. Nevertheless, the Bishop found himself in the possession of ample funds. During his tenure of the See of Winchester, which he held but a year and a half, he is reported to have received in fines as much as £50,000. Out of this large amount he remitted £30,000

---

[43] Tanner MSS. 49, f. 17. These letters in the Tanner MSS. are not in Duppa's hand, but later copies.

[44] Pepys' *Diary*, ed. H. B. Wheatley.

[45] *Mercurius Publicus*, 1660, No. 40, p. 625.

[46] *Ibid.*, No. 44, p. 693.

[47] I owe this suggestion to Miss Anne Whiteman, who cites *Documents relating to the history of the Cathedral Church of Winchester in the seventeenth century*, ed. W. R. W. Stephens and F. T. Madge (Hampshire Record Society (1897)), esp. pp. 115, 116.

to his tenants, and expended £16,000 in acts of charity[48].

There are no letters to Sir Justinian after 1660, and Duppa himself did not long survive.

On February 4th, 1661/2 he made his will "knowing how short my dayes must now necessarily bee in respect of my infirmities and because I am now arrived at the age of seventy two years." He commended his soul to Almighty God ("I die in the faith of his Catholique Church") and after making provision for his wife, nephew and other relatives, he gave large sums to the cathedrals and learned societies with which he had been associated. Nor did he forget the poor of the parish of Lewisham where he was born, or Westham, where he had been for a short time vicar; he gave £50 each "unto those commanders of his late Majesty's Army . . to be chosen by my executors . . . as have been ever faithful and loyal, but are not yet provided for"[49]. In a codicil added on March 26th, 1662, he left £300 "towards the repaire of S. Paul's Church."

In his last years he built almshouses for ten poor women at Richmond, on the Hill, which he endowed "for the maintenance of the poore people" placed there. Over the door of the hospital, he caused to be placed this inscription: "That a poor bishop vowd this house, but a great and wealthy one built it"[50]. On March 26th, 1662, at Richmond he died. King Charles visited him on his death bed, and "craved his blessing on his bended knees by his bedside." So in the words of his epitaph in Westminster Abbey, where he is buried, "folded in the arms of his Royal pupil, he breathed forth his pious soul."

Mercurius Publicus recorded[51]: "He died as he had lived, honoured and beloved by all that knew him, a Person of so clear and eminent candour, that he hath not left the least spot upon his Life or Function maugre the busy sedition of those brethren who have blackened the very surplice, and made our Liturgy profane"[52].

---

[48] Stoughton, *op. cit.*, Vol. II, Chap. 2.

[49] Copy of Will in P.C.C. Laud 73, Somerset House; contemporary copy at Lamport.

[50] Wood. Duppa's Almshouses were originally erected on Richmond Hill. But becoming " decayed by age, their site was sold to James Ewing, who undertook their rebuilding on their present site." This is near Michel's Almshouses, on the same side as the R.C. Church, in a place called the Vineyard. This evacuation took place in 1852. The inscription over the gateway is as follows:

"DEO ET CAROLO
VOTIVA TABULA

I will pay the vows which I made to God in my trouble." Manning and Bray, *History and Antiquities of Surrey*, Vol. I (1804) give the original inscription as: "In memoriam auspicatissimi reditus CAROLI secundi ad suos, hoc Ptochotrophium, ad honorem Dei et levamen Pauperum, extrui curavit B.D.E. *Winton* Regi ab Eleemosynis, Ao Dom. 1661." This inscription is now on a tablet over the inner entrance. The Almshouses are still (1952) occupied. (E. Beresford Chancellor, *History and Antiquites of Richmond*, and information from Geoffrey Courtney Esq. of Richmond, Surrey).

[51] *Mercurius Publicus*, 1662, No. 13, p.199. See Appendix C below.

[52] He left £500 to Salisbury Cathedral for an organ; £200 to Chichester Cathedral; £500 to the Dean and Chapter of Christ Church; £200 to Winchester Cathedral; £200 to the Warden and Fellows of All Souls College; to the poor of Westham £20; to the poor of Lewisham " where I was borne " £40; to the poor of Greenwich £40. For his numerous legacies to relations see Appendix A.

His grave is in the north aisle of Westminster Abbey near the north ambulatory gates, inscribed "Hic Jacet Brianus Winton"[53]. His nearby monument is now nearly hidden by the massive memorial to Wolfe. His widow, in her will, left £200 to her executors to erect this monument[54], which is signed by Balthasar Burman, son of the better known Thomas Burman, master mason of St. Martin-in-the-Fields, who died in 1674.

Duppa's will was proved on May 16th, 1662. His wife, Sir John Adler, and Dr. Richard Chaworth were the executors; Sir Justinian Isham, Dr. Gage and ffrancis Phelips of the Inner Temple, the overseers.

The original portrait "drawn by Master Wright" (John Michael Wright, 1625–1700), was left by Mrs. Duppa in her will to Gilbert Sheldon, Archbishop of Canterbury. This was painted between 1660 and his death, as it shows him as Prelate of the Garter, a dignity traditionally belonging to the Bishops of Winchester by right of their office. The original cannot be traced, but there is an 18th century copy by Hugh Howard in the hall of Christ Church, Oxford[55]. This picture formed the basis of the engraving by R. White prefixed to Duppa's *Holy Rules and Helps to Devotion* printed in London in 1675, after Duppa's death, with a preface by Benjamin Parry, afterwards Bishop of Ossory[56]. Mrs. Duppa also left "my late husband's picture in little with Rubies" to "the Lady Cholmoly," but she does not mention the artist, and the miniature itself does not seem to have survived.

In addition to the sermon preached before King Charles I at Newport, printed in 1648, and *Holy Rules and Helps to Devotion both in Prayer and Practice*, a MS. at Corpus Christi College, Oxford, lists the following works by Duppa:[57]

> Angels Rejoicing for Sinners Repenting
> In Serm by R. R. F. Br. D now B. Sal. London 1648.
>
> A guide for the Penitent: or a Modell drawn up for the helpe of a Devout Soule wounded with Sin. London 1660.
>
> The Life of Archbishop Spotiswood
> Printed before his Hist. of the Church of Scotl. London 1654[58].

His old friend Henry King, Bishop of Chichester, who, in the days of the suppression, had found a refuge with Duppa's niece Lady Salter at Iver, preached his funeral sermon at Westminster Abbey, and confessed that it was difficult for him to speak of one whom

---

[53] Dart, *op. cit.*

[54] Will of Jane Duppa, dated October 15th, 1664: proved November 9th, 1665. Katharine A. Esdaile *English Church Monuments* (1946), pp. 49, 50.

[55] Mrs. Reginald Lane Poole, *Catalogue of Oxford Portraits*, Vol. III (1925), p. 27. A 19th century copy of the Christ Church portrait is in the Bishop's Palace at Winchester, and there is another version at Salisbury.

[56] There is a copy in the Bodleian. See also Lowndes.

[57] Corpus Christi College, Oxford, MS. 307, f. 22.

[58] John Spottiswoode's *History of the Church of Scotland* was published in 1655.

he knew so long, and so well, but, after praising his charity and learning, gave him this character in words which were echoed by the historian Eachard[59]: "He was every way Qualified, both in the comeliness of His person, and the Gracefulness of his Deportment, and the Excellency of His Parts: all which Capacities rendered Him worthy the service of a Court, and every way *fit to stand before Princes. Prov.* 22 29."[60].

It is traditionally supposed that Duppa was responsible for the "Form of prayer with Fasting to be used yearly upon the Thirtieth of January, being the Day of the Martyrdom of the Blessed King Charles the First" which was included in the Book of Common Prayer until the middle of the nineteenth century[61]. Some support is given to this tradition by these Letters, as I have pointed out in the notes. But this service is necessarily somewhat partisan, and a better guide to the devotional temper of his mind is given in *His Holy Rules and Helps to Devotion* written "in the time of his sequestration". The prayers of his composing in this book are in the great liturgical tradition, and this brief notice of his life cannot better be concluded than by quoting one of them.

"O Heavenly Father, who hearest the prayers of all that seek Thee, purifie the intention of my Soul in all the prayers I make to Thee; that I may neither seek nor desire anything, but in relation to Thee, through Jesus Christ, Amen."

---

59 Lawrence Eachard, *History of England*, Vol. III (1718), p. 91.

60 *A Sermon preached at the Funeral of . . . Bryan Lord Bp. of Winchester*, p. 36. See Note 5 above.

61 E.g. The Book of Common Prayer, London; printed by John Baskett and the Assigns of Thomas Newcombe and Henry Hills deceased 1713.

JUSTINIAN ISHAM

Justinian Isham was born at Lamport, according to his father's notes, "upon a Sunday being the 20th of January, 1610 [by our reckoning 1611] about seven o'clock of the evening, and was baptized the same day fortnight being the third of February." His father was Sir John Isham, knight and afterwards Baronet of Lamport, Northamptonshire.

Sir John's grandfather, another John, had with his brother Robert joined in the purchase of the Manor and Advowson of Lamport in 1560 from Sir William Cecil, afterwards Queen Elizabeth's Lord High Treasurer Burleigh, who had recently acquired them from John de Vere, Earl of Oxford : this John Isham was the fourth son of Euseby Isham of Pytchley who died in 1546. The Isham family had held lands since the thirteenth century in Pytchley, where a younger branch of the family had moved from Isham (only two miles away), where they had held lands since before the Conquest.[1]

John Isham, who bought Lamport, a younger son of a large family, was a citizen and mercer of London. His father, who had twenty children, had left him only £5 in his will, but he had prospered exceedingly, and became not only thrice Warden of the Mercers Company, but Governor of the English Merchant Adventurers and a Freeman of the City of London. On his retirement to his estate at Lamport, he built himself a house there in 1567, and devoted himself to "plantinge, buildinge, making of pooles, including of groundes and all other workes of good husbandry as though he had been brought up to them from his infancy." He was, his son tells us, "a wise man, although altogether unlearned, writing and reading Inglish only excepted." He died in 1595, aged 70, and was succeeded by his son Thomas, who though blind from the age of "a dussen or fourteen years," was evidently a great reader, and a collector of rare books. He also wrote the history of his family, and several works which have survived in MS. In 1867, in a lumber room at Lamport were discovered "a small collection of the choicest Elizabethan books. Many of them were unique and were not previously known to be in existence, while the majority were known only in single copies elsewhere"[2]. These books were sold in 1894, and divided between the British Museum and the Britwell Court Library. The twenty-four volumes acquired by the British Museum

[1] See the article on Sir Justinian Isham in the D.N.B. and the printed sources there quoted on the Isham family. More recently, Oswald Barron's *Northamptonshire Families* (V.C.H. (1906)) provides a detailed genealogical account of the family and the *Visitation of Northamptonshire* 1681 (ed. H. I. Longden, Harl. Soc. Vol. 87 (1935)) contains a full pedigree from John Isham of Lamport. The writer's "Historical and Literary Associations of Lamport" in Vol. I, No. 1 of *Northamptonshire Past and Present* published by the Northants Record Society in 1948, gives an account of the Isham Family with special reference to Sir Justinian Isham. References from contemporary records and letters in this account are taken, unless otherwise stated, from the Isham MSS. deposited on loan in the Northamptonshire Record Office.

[2] *The Times*, August 15th, 1894.

Sir Justinian Isham, 2nd Bart.

From the miniature by Samuel Cooper (signed 'S.C.' and dated 1653) in the Lamport Hall Collection.

Lamport Hall (showing John Webb's front) in 1720

By Peter Tillemans (died 1734).

From a drawing in the British Museum, reproduced by permission of the Trustees.

To face page xxxii

RICHMOND FROM THE HILL

From the original picture by John Wootton in the possession of the Honble. Mrs. Basil Ionides, and reproduced by her permission and by courtesy of *Country Life*.

Bishop Duppa's Almshouses are shown on the right of the road, below the Roebuck Inn, which is the large building in the foreground.

To face page xxxiii

were described by Mr. Robert Edmund Graves, assistant keeper of printed books, as "the most important additions in English literature made for many years." The books acquired from Lamport by the Britwell Court Library were dispersed at the sale of that library in 1919, and fetched over £50,000, much more than ten times the price which the whole collection realised in 1894.

Their subsequent history is testimony to the acumen of Thomas Isham, who acquired the books. The blind squire's son, John, who succeeded in 1605, was also something of a scholar, and read Italian.

It is not surprising if, with such a father and grandfather, Justinian had literary tastes. Moreover his maternal grandfather was William Lewyn, a Judge of the Prerogative Court of Canterbury, and described on his daughter's tombstone as "learned William Lewyn." He was a friend of Gabriel Harvey, and public orator of Cambridge University[3].

Great care was bestowed upon Justinian's education. He was first taken in hand by the curate at Lamport, Mr. Bunning; next transferred to the care of Mr. Clerke, at Uppingham School, then quite a new foundation. On April 18th, 1627, he was entered a Fellow-Commoner of Christ's College, Cambridge, a college of which his great-great uncle Robert Isham had been a benefactor[4]. His tutor was the Revd. Joseph Mede (or Mead), a distinguished scholar and newsletter writer. His tutor became a friend, and went to stay at Lamport, where he found the hospitality rather overwhelming. He was pressed to prolong his visit, and, planning to depart early one morning, described how "Sir John came down in his night shirt" to dissuade him "but in vain"[5].

While Justinian was at Cambridge, Sir John was created a Baronet by King Charles I on May 30th, 1627. One of his fellow students at Christ's, was John Milton. In one of the letters to Bishop Duppa, Justinian mentions Milton, but only to reprobate his views on divorce.

Christ's College and its Fellows at this time have been the subject of close study owing to Milton's residence, and Professor David Masson in his *Life* of Milton says of Joseph Mede, "apart from his casual relation to Milton as one of the senior Fellows of Christ's College, he was a remarkable man;" he further describes him (quoting one of Mede's biographers) "as an acute logician, an

[3] William Lewyn died April 14th, 1598. There is a monument to him, his wife, four sons, and seven daughters, with an effigy, in Otterden Church, Kent. See account of him in D.N.B.

[4] John Peile, *Biographical Register of Christ's College*, Vol. I (1910). See also the writer's "The Connection of the Isham Family with Christ's College" in the *Christ's College Magazine* (1927).

[5] For Revd. Joseph Mede see D.N.B. under Mead. Mede's correspondence with Sir Martin Stuteville, who married Susan, sister of Sir John Isham, is contained in Harleian MSS. 389 and 390 at the British Museum. It is extensively quoted in *The Court and Times of Charles I*, ed. R. F. Williams (1848). There are several letters from Mede to Justinian at Lamport. That he did not forget his old tutor is shown by a reference to him in one of these Letters (Letter xv, Note 6).

accurate philosopher, a skilful mathematician, an excellent anatomist (being usually sent for when they had any anatomy in Caius College), a great philosopher, a master of many languages, and a good proficient in the studies of history and chronology;" adding that he was withal "a very benevolent man, with a kind word for all the young scholars, and even for the dandy fellow-commoners, whom he called 'University-tulips.' "[6]

There is no doubt that contact with such a man was a strong formative influence in Justinian's character. Mede took immediately to his young pupil, and described him in a letter to Sir Martin Stuteville (May 5th, 1627) as "a sober discreet and understanding gentleman"[7]. On May 19th of the same year he said: "I confess I love the gentleman upon this short experience with some degree more than a tutor's affection."

Ecclesiastically, Mede seems to have been a moderate. His pupils were called "Medians" because they "kept the medium" between the pupils of Mr. Power, a High-churchman, whose followers were "thought too loose like their tutor," and those of Mr. Chappel (Milton's tutor) "thought too precise called Puritans"[8].

Justinian resided at Christ's till Michaelmas 1628. His study was elaborately "dressed" for him with hangings "fine matts, a canopie and curtains." He wrote to his father (April 25th, 1627): "I am compelled to write that I may obtain diverse things which I want, which are, a peece of plate to have in my chamber, a table cloth or 2, and a pillow-beare. That plate which is in the butteries is very little, and, therefore, cannot be borrowed, the plate also which should be given to the College must by every comm[oner] be given in money, which is five pound 10 groates. My tutor is a very honest man, and carefull of his pupills, he hath made me acquainted with the best governed gentlemen." The books Justinian bought, though not remarkable at that date, are of interest. He bought for 16*s*. Alsted's works, Xenophon, Gellius, Eustachius, Schyblerus, and Digges' *Pantometria*. This last work was a "Geometrical Practise" dedicated to Sir Nicholas Bacon, and published in 1571, and is noteworthy as foreshadowing those scientific interests which formed such a part of his mind.

Justinian, on going down from Cambridge (the Fellow-Commoners usually stayed only a year), went to the Inns of Court, where he was admitted to the Middle Temple on October 11th, 1628. Robert Tanfielde, his father's lawyer, wrote on October 27th to Sir John: "Your sonne is well both for health and order, who is allready a good proficient in the law." While in London, Justinian seems to have taken a great interest in the political life of the time. On March 5th, 1629 he wrote to his uncle Paul D'Ewes, one of the six Clerks in Chancery, who had married recently his aunt Lady Denton, and was

[6] D. Masson, *Life of Milton*, Vol. I (new and revised edn. (1881)), pp. 124 and 127.
[7] These and subsequent quotations from the Mede–Stuteville correspondence are in Harl. MSS. 390.
[8] John Peile, *Christ's College* (1900), p. 138.

the father by a previous marriage of Sir Simonds D'Ewes, the antiquary. In this letter[9], he describes the scene in which the Speaker of the House of Commons was forcibly held down in his chair, while the Remonstrance was passed.

> "On Monday last Mr. Speaker was appointed by the King to signifie to the Lower house that the Parliament was adiourned untill the 10th day of this month. But as the Speaker began to deliver his message (the gentlemen presently foreseing what he was to say) commanded him to be silent: whereupon as he was about to go out of the House they plucked him back by force and held him in his chaire. So locking the doore to themselves they lay'd the key upon the table, which donn, after divers speeches by sundry men spoken, with a general voice they proclaimed that none should give tunnage or poundage, and also that they were traitors to the King and State who either favoured Arminianism or Popery, as Bishop Lawd sayd one, as my lo[rd] Treasurer (Weston) sayd another, everyone particularising whom hee thought fitt."

Not all Justinian's diversions in London were so serious, however. His old tutor, Joseph Mede, wrote to him on January 16th, 1633: "You tell me of the Queenes Pastorall at Somerset House, but what say your courtiers and Innes of Court gallants to Mr. Prinnes' book against not only acting, but beholding such enterludes? I think you were never so pepper'd in your lives. And see the luck of it: it must be published even just the next day after the Qu[een's] Pastorall." The juxtaposition of the Queen's Pastoral and the publication of *Histrio-mastix, The Players Scourge; or, Actors Tragoedie* was not so lucky, however, for William Prynne, as on this account he was sentenced "to pay a fine to the King of £5,000, to be degraded from his profession of the law, and to lose his ears in the pillory."[10]

Later that year, Justinian had "a license to pass beyond the seas",[11] and seems to have gone to Holland. In a small Bible (1625) which was at Lamport in 1880, but which cannot now be traced, was this note: "This was the only booke I carried in my pocket when I travelled beyond the seas the 22nd yeare of my age and many years after Just. Isham." On his return to England in 1634, he was married on November 10th at All Saints, Tottenham, to Jane, daughter of Sir John Garrard 1st Bart. of Lamer, Herts. Four daughters were born of this marriage, but on March 3rd, 1639, his wife died after giving birth to a prematurely-born son, John, who lived only 13 days. There is a curious monument on the north side of the chancel[12] at Lamport to Mrs. Jane Isham, where three boy angels support the inscriptions "Religiosa Deo, Casta Marito, Liberis Chara". There is also a small monument to the infant son with some verses by Justinian:

---

[9] Harl. MSS. 383, No. 82. It is printed in modernised spelling in *The Court and Times of Charles the First.*

[10] Lowndes

[11] July 14th, 1633: "license granted to allow Justinian Isham to pass beyond the seas." (Records of the Exchequer cited in *The Genealogist*, New Series, Vol. xxv, p. 261).

[12] See the writer's *All Saints Church, Lamport* (1950).

"I saw the world too soone and soone I died,
But had I longer lived to have espied
A world of mischiefe in this world contain'd
I might have lost that which I now have gain'd."

The deaths of his first wife and son were followed by a "burning sweating feaver", which, as he told the Parliamentary Commissioners after the Civil War left him "never very healthy," but he seems both during his marriage and after to have devoted himself mainly to scholarly pursuits.

There is, still, in the Lamport Library a first edition of Bacon's *Instauratio Magna* on to the flyleaf of which Justinian has copied the inscription on the tomb at St. Albans. Justinian appears to have written an 'Epitome' of this work which has not survived. On July 23rd, 1629, William Rawley, Bacon's chaplain and biographer, wrote to him that he had "perused diligently your observations or rather Abridgement of the Lo[rd] St. Albans greatest work, his *Instauratio Magna*: and perceyve you have not onely saluted, some of the extreme coasts, but have made an exact and industrious perambulation through all the parts of that work. Wherein I cannot but admire your genius, that among the men of our nation, your self is the second, or third man, that I know of who hath addicted himself or profitted by those studies." These are high words of praise, but Rawley's opinion of his ability is further shown by his urging Justinian "for the benefitt of our age and the honour of the deceased, to undertake some titles of the Natural History: wherin I would recommend unto you that designed title, in his L[ordshi]p's [Bacon's] *Historia Ventorum of the Sympathy and Antipathy of things* for an Assay, in the compiling thereof to follow his L[ordshi]p's way in those 200 titles extant in Latin which would be a work worthy of your judgement and embracement."

Bacon, indeed, was the inspiration of the scientific movement in the 17th century, and the real father of the Royal Society. It was natural that Justinian should become friends with other Baconians, and he formed a friendship with two very interesting men: Samuel Hartlib and John Comenius.[13] Hartlib, German-Polish on his father's side and English on his mother's, who had settled permanently in England in 1628 at the age of thirty, won the consideration of men as diverse as Milton, who dedicated his *Tractate of Education* to him; John Evelyn, who called him "master of innumerable curiosities;" and Seth Ward, who noted his "great and unwearied zeale for learning."[14] As was his manner, in his letters to Justinian, he gave news of the Thirty Years War in Germany: "God doth show Himselfe abroad beyond all expectations discovering the Austrian

[13] G. H. Turnbull, *Samuel Hartlib. A sketch of his life and his relations to J. A. Comenius* (1920); H. Dircks, *A Biographical Memoir of Samuel Hartlib* (1865); R. H. Syfret, "The Origins of the Royal Society", in *Notes and Records of the Royal Society of London*, Vol. v, No. 2 (April 1948).

[14] Seth Ward's letter is in Add. MSS. 6271 of March 15th, 1662. See also Evelyn's *Diary*, September 27th, 1655.

weakness, and giving inferior Princes hope to cast off the yoake. For doutless the pride and power of that house is the great if not the only reason of the power and spreading of the Gospel." But Hartlib's designs were not confined to the spreading of accurate news. He aimed at the reformation of education on Baconian principles, at remedying the "errors, defects and inconvenience of our English husbandry;" at the union of all Protestant Churches; and at the studying and application of science to all branches of life. It is clear from his correspondence with Justinian that Joseph Mede had been a friend of Hartlib, no doubt at Cambridge where Hartlib had been in his youth, and possibly Mede was the means of introducing the two men. Mede, in his old age, was offered a chaplaincy by Archbishop Laud, which he declined: "May I have revealed myself not to be desirous of any preferment, which should transplant me from the University" (March 14th, 1638). He died in 1638, and Hartlib speaks of him as "Mr. Mede of worthy memory" in a letter dated August 15th, 1639.

It was Hartlib's design to bring to England J. A. Comenius, the great Czech educationist, whose work "Praecognitorum Librum III" (now known as *Pansophiae Christianae Liber. III*)[15]- he lent to Justinian, and on June 30th, 1639 he wrote from Duke's Place, "By the last post I get some extraordinarie matters from Lesna which put mee upon the utmost endeavours of love and solicitude for the principal inhabitant thereof. I see now plainly that if the good and worthy man (I meane stil Mr. Comenius) were provided with a competency of his subsistence but for one year, he should neede no further assistance upon the same groundes from any mortal man whatsoever."

Comenius did in fact come to England in 1641, encouraged by Hartlib and his friends to think that Parliament was on the point of establishing a commission to put in practice some of his "pansophical schemes", including the establishment of a "Universal College"; to found a universal language leading to the adoption of one true religion; and universal peace.

Although prepared to welcome Comenius, and even to contribute to his support in England, Justinian warned Hartlib that the times were hardly propitious for "pansophical designs": "these tymes of distraction", he wrote on August 5th, 1639, "(like troubled water) will hardly receive the image of it now so well as they otherwise might."[16] However, when Comenius did arrive in 1641, Justinian wrote to Hartlib[17] assuring him of support both immediately and yearly as long as Comenius stayed in the country, both on his own account,

[15] This Latin work was not published till 1951. See John Amos Comenius *Two Pansophical Works*, ed. G. H. Turnbull (1951); (text in Latin, introduction in Czech and English).

[16] The quotations from Justinian's letters to Hartlib are taken from G. H. Turnbull's *Hartlib, Dury and Comenius* (1947).

[17] For a full discussion of Hartlib's part in the activities of the group who founded the Royal Society see a recent article by G. H. Turnbull in *Notes and Records of the Royal Society of London*, Vol. x, No. 2 (April, 1953.).

and on behalf of Sir Christopher Hatton of Kirby. He also approached Dr. Williams, the learned Bishop of Lincoln, who, when Rector of Walgrave, had been a friend of his father[18], on Comenius' behalf. In his letter to Comenius, Justinian (October 9th, 1641) apologised for the "barbarisms and peradventure false constructions" in his Latin, for it was unusual for "Englishmen of my sort (to our shame be it spoken) to write in Latin." On December 1st, 1641, Comenius acknowledged a gift of £10 from Justinian, in a letter full of compliments, and on December 13th Justinian wrote that England would prove a fruitful soil for Comenius' endeavours if the State were "once better settled;" he promised however to recall Comenius to the mind of "his Lordship [Williams] now preferred to higher dignities," and therefore "more capable of conferring some good things upon Mr. Comenius." But Williams, although he had recently been released from the Tower, where Laud's hostility had confined him, and become Archbishop of York, enjoyed only a brief period of favour with the Parliament. He counselled the King to sacrifice Strafford, but Pym and his associates were now determined to get rid of the Bishops altogether, and neither Williams nor Pym (who had also seemed interested in Comenius' ideas) had leisure or inclination for "Universal Colleges" in Chelsea. Comenius withdrew to France where he was more successful with Richelieu, but the Cardinal died before he could be of much assistance.

However, the scientific side of the "pansophical movement" alone bore fruit, and Justinian himself forms a link between the earlier Baconian disciples, Hartlib, Comenius, and Huebner (all of whom he knew), and men like Boyle and Seth Ward, who lived to found the Royal Society after the Restoration.

More space has been devoted to this subject than would be proper in a short memoir of this kind, were it not the intention to show the learned background of Justinian and his friend Bishop Duppa. Lord Bruce, one of Hartlib's associates, was a friend of Duppa, Seth Ward of both Duppa and Justinian, and it is small wonder that the two friends in their letters discussed Grotius, Descartes, Pascal: indeed their reasons for doing so are the same that gave scientific studies their stimulus after the Civil War: learning, and particularly scientific learning, was a relief from the endless wordy and bloody conflict into which religion and politics had led them.

In the years before the outbreak of the Civil War, Justinian appears to have continued in some way in the practice of the law, for he was solicitor to the Earl of Essex, and during the war, the propriety of the Lord General's papers remaining in such "malignant" hands was discussed.[19]

[18] For the relation of Bishop Williams and Sir John Isham see the writer's article, "The Affair of Grafton Underwood Feast." (*Northamptonshire Past and Present*, Vol. I, No. 4).

[19] *Calendar of the Proceedings of the Committee for Compounding*, ed. M. A. E. Green, Part I, p. 24, August 19th, 1645. "The treasurers to consider the Earl of Essex's papers remaining with Mr. Isum."

In 1637 his father bought for him an estate of just under one thousand acres at Shangton in Leicestershire (about fourteen miles from Lamport) which remained the property of the Ishams until 1919. Sir John, his father, is said to have "borne great sway" in his native county and to have been esteemed "an able and upright magistrate" in King Charles' reign.[20] His wife had died in 1625, and Justinian and his wife during their short married life, and Justinian and his daughters later, made Lamport their headquarters.

But this life of scholarship, the law, and the county was ended when the war broke out in 1642. Justinian betook himself to the King's Court at Oxford where, on May 20th, 1644, he made a will "in perfect health, yet amidst the calamaties of these civill wars which threaten the ruins of this Church and State, I cannot but consider my owne dissolution as alwayes at hand, which yet is in thy hands, O most merciful Father." In another place he speaks of himself as "being now at Oxford driven from my children, friends and home, for the preservation of a good conscience towards God, my King, and Country."

He left all his property to his four young daughters Jane, Elizabeth, Judith and Susanna, and among charitable bequests £10 a year to the parson of Shangton on condition that twice a year he or his successors should preach a sermon "in the defense and explanation of our Liturgie, and read the common Praiers fully and constantly on the Lords Dayes and on such other dayes as is ordered by the Church of England." These strong Anglican opinions are the background of the letters that passed between Justinian and the Bishop. In this draft will, he also says: "My bookes, especially those marked by myselfe in their margent, and also my papers and notes (although now in no order), I yet desire may be preserved by my nearest friends, by which they may perceive my inclinations, who having now no liberties to come by them, either to correct or bring them into forme, am yet glad to remember they have more weakness than wickedness in them."[21]

It is easier to discover what happened to the ageing Sir John Isham, who remained at Lamport during the war, than it is to trace exactly what happened to Justinian. There is at Lamport a letter under the Royal sign manual demanding £500 of Sir John "for the defence of Our Person, the Protestant Religion, and the Lawes of the Land." The gentry of Northamptonshire were fairly evenly divided between the King and the Parliament. Spencers, Comptons, Ishams and Wakes were for the King, Drydens, Knightleys, Yelvertons and

---

[20] Wotton's *Baronetage*.

[21] A MS. book of poems, a few poems on odd sheets of paper, numerous small "lives" of clasical heroes, various memoranda on sacred history, and some scientific notes in Justinian's handwriting have survived. But they are mainly later in date than the period of intense scholarly activity 1634-1642. It is possible that the others perished in the Civil War.

Montagus[22] for the Parliament. Indeed, allegiance often depended on some accident. In Colonel Hutchinson's *Memoirs*, there is a passage describing how the Squire of Kelmarsh (Mr. Hanbury), having "made plate and horses ready to go in to the king, that had now set up his standard at Nottingham," was persuaded by the Puritan Hutchinson "to carry those aids . . . to my Lord General Essex, who was then at Northampton."[23]

The presence of Essex at Northampton—a strong Roundhead town—indeed overawed the Royalist gentry, and men like Sir John (whatever their connections) were forced to contribute to the support of the Army and to endure, as Sir John complained, "frequent quarterings of Parliamentary tr[oo]ps, my house standing on two great rodes."[24] The Revd. William Noke, the Rector, who was a distant connection of the family, was driven out as a "Malignant minister,"[25] and a Puritan intruded into the living, Sir John himself being denounced to the Parliament by the parishioners as a man "who is and hath become an enemy to the cause defended by Parliament."[26] He was also accused of sending men and horses to Holt House in Leicestershire, when it was a Royalist garrison.[27] Although Sir John had attained an immunity for his goods and house signed by Sir Edward Nicholls, Richard Samwell, John Crew and Edward Hardy, addressed to "all Captains, officers and soldiers within the County of Northampton" (May 2nd, 1643), he was not free from molestation. Letters passed (unsigned) between Justinian and his sister Elizabeth at Lamport, in one of which he says: "I have lately heard by divers how some forces broke into your house, and chambers in the night, which, whatsoever they did there, was more barbarous and savadge in regard of the affright yourself and little children might be put to at that season, then if in the day tyme they had come and turn'd you all out of doors."[28]

These wartime letters of Justinian bear only the date of the month, and caution is continually urged: "I should thinke if the high chamber doore (as ye have heard mee speake of) were made in the roofe of the closet that has the black doore, that your selfe [presumably Elizabeth] or him whom you are with [Sir John] may lie there more securely, at least from rogues and robbers. There is little hope of releiving you as yet from hence [Oxford] and therefore neglect nothing lawful for your securities."[29]

Owing to changes made in the house since that day, it is not possible to guess if this secret chamber was ever made, but this

[22] But not Lord Montagu of Boughton, who, as Lord Lieutenant, executed the King's Commission of Array, and was rewarded by the Parliament with life-long imprisonment (*The Montagu Musters Book*. Northants Record Society, Vol. VII (1935)).
[23] *Memoirs of Colonel Hutchinson* (1906), pp. 123-4.
[24] *Northamptonshire Past and Present*, Vol. I, No. 1 (1948), p. 22.
[25] *All Saints Church, Lamport*, p. 16.
[26] *Ibid.*
[27] *Calendar of the Proceedings of the Committee for the Advance of Money*, ed. M. A. E. Green, Part III, p. 1314.
[28] I.C. 3273.
[29] I.C. 3274.

glimpse of the hazards of a Cavalier house in Roundhead country is as authentic as any thrill contrived by the author of *Waverley*; in one letter Justinian anxiously enquires "I hope my bookes are safe."

When indeed the King's Army was near enough to Lamport to promise relief, it was to suffer defeat at Naseby, only six miles away. There is still at Lamport a blood-stained buff coat of one of Rupert's troopers, and the tradition is that its owner was hidden in an apple-loft after the battle: a pretty romance that there is no means of disproving.

The end of the Civil War found Justinian not surprisingly classed as a delinquent. Cavaliers were forced to "compound" for their estates, the alternative to which was confiscation. Justinian on September 18th, 1646 "compounded" for his delinquency. He argued before the Parliamentary Commissioners that, although in the King's quarters, he had never borne arms, and that his whole estate at Shangton was valued at £600 a year. The plundering of his writings moreover had delayed his composition.[30] On December 6th his fine was fixed at 1/10 of the value of Shangton, £1,100. His assessment had already been respited on the grounds that he had been solicitor to the Lord General (Essex), and employed in his service.[31] Subsequent petitions, however, failed to reduce the sum fixed in 1646, despite Justinian's plea of "charges, debts, and other incumbrances on his estate." It was while engaged in arguments with the Committee for Compounding, during which time he was lodging with his friends the Carliles at Petersham, that Justinian became intimate with Bishop Duppa. But on March 18th, 1650, his fine was confirmed. Two days later, Justinian was obliged to leave London in accordance with an Act passed on February 26th whereby all Papists, soldiers of fortune, and delinquents were forbidden to come within twenty miles of the capital. It was then that the present correspondence began, and the first surviving letter is dated May 28th, 1650.[32] He was, moreover, all through the Commonwealth regarded as a suspect, and was imprisoned in 1655 and 1658—indeed, whenever there was a scare that a Royalist rising was imminent. There does not seem proof in the Lamport papers that he was, in fact, engaged in any conspiracy, but he made no secret of his Royalist and Church of England opinions.

For the years of the Commonwealth, the best evidence for his life is supplied by the Duppa letters, and it is not proposed to do more than sketch the main happenings of these years. He succeeded to the Baronetcy on his father's death (July 8th, 1651). Although he had suffered (as Wotton's *Baronetage* puts it) "severely in person and estate", he was still regarded as a rich man, and was able to devote

[30] *Calendar of the Proceedings of the Committee for Compounding*, Part II, p. 1494.

[31] *Calendar of the Proceedings of the Committee for the Advance of Money*, Part I, p. 485.

[32] For a detailed analysis of the circumstances of the beginning of the correspondence see Introduction to 1650. For the Act of February 26th, 1650, see Gardiner, Vol. I, p. 247.

himself not only to improvement of his estate, but to building.

He built first a new chancel for Lamport Church as recorded in one of his draft replies to Duppa (1652). Then, after his marriage, he added a new front to the old home at Lamport, employing the most accomplished architect of the day, John Webb, the favourite pupil of Inigo Jones, and one who had married a kinswoman of Charles I's Surveyor. Webb's letters and plans have survived, and are in fact of great interest. They throw light "not only on the progress of the work, but on the ways of an architect of that time, on his means of communication (largely through the carrier), and on the chances of his being able to combine visits of inspection with visits to other work within a reasonable distance."[33] The letters show, moreover, that Webb not only designed the house, and the rooms, but gave advice on the purchase of pictures, actually introducing a dealer, one Maurice Wase, "whose paintings and prices the enclosed note will show you." But Justinian sometimes preferred his own views to Webb's, and insisted on a Frenchman, Pierre Benier, executing the still existing fireplace, in preference to Webb's desire to employ Joshua Marshall.

Webb's remark that most of the gentlemen of England had some knowledge of the theory and practice of architecture is certainly borne out by Sir Justinian, who supervised the masons himself in Webb's absence, and from his prison at St. James's in 1655 sent detailed instructions to the contractor.

But even more important to him than his building, was the search for a second wife, who would be capable of producing an heir. This quest for a wife may be traced in the Duppa Letters. Oddly enough, he is mainly remembered today as the unsuccessful suitor of Dorothy Osborne, who laughed at his learning, and christened him in her letters to Temple "Sir Soloman", and "the Emperour." It is perhaps not surprising that a widower of 42, in indifferent health, and with four unmarried daughters, made little appeal to a young woman of 26, who was deeply in love with someone else. But even Dorothy, who knew him very slightly admitted to Temple: "You tolde mee once that of all my Servants you liked him the best " and when he married elsewhere she said: : "The spitefull man meerly to vexe mee has gon and Marred my Country Woman, my Lord Lee's daughter."

This lady, Vere Leigh, whom he married in 1653, bore him a large family of sons and daughters and seems to have been happy enough in the "Vyle house hee has in Northampton shyre" (as Dorothy called Lamport).

The Restoration of 1660, however, put an end to Sir Justinian's fines and imprisonments, and launched him, as a man of fifty, on a new career as a "Parliament man." The Cavalier Parliament of 1661 was a different Chamber from that of 1629 which he had seen as a youth; and no man could have been more loyal than the new Member for Northamptonshire. But to Cavaliers of the old school,

[33] J. A. Gotch, *The Old Halls and Manor Houses of Northamptonshire* (1936).

the Restoration was a disappointment. As he wrote to his father-in-law, Lord Leigh (1669): "you see in general what a wretched return hath been made for (God's mercie), that wee are fallen into so dissolute and licentious an age that every man dreads to think what his children may thereafter be exposed to."

The education of his own children—he had two girls and six boys by his second wife—was indeed one of his principal cares. His eldest son, Thomas, was naturally his chief preoccupation, and he promised him £6 a year to keep a diary in Latin. "Nothing can come amiss for you to turn into Latin, even your talk in the nursery." This diary was translated by the Revd. Robert Isham, and privately printed, with introduction and notes, by Walter Rye in 1875. "In its way", wrote the late Lord Ponsonby,[34] "it is a unique diary, and the matter chosen by the boy is both interesting and amusing." There are, naturally, constant entries about "catching rabbits, netting partridges, trapping martens and fishing, and also about gardening and the planting of trees." But the news of the great world is not forgotten, and the Polish victory over the Turks is chronicled on the same day (November 23rd, 1672) as this item: "Sharper of Scaldwell found a hare which we hunted and killed after breakfast." Sir Justinian taught the boys Euclid, and when in London, on his parliamentary duties, never failed to send books for his children, and enquiries after their welfare. On one occasion he wrote: "I take Tom's letter very wel with the account he gives me. I can yet heare of no cooke fitt for you, but shall endeavour it, or what els you desire. I have got 3 Homers for Tom and the rest with much adoe; I hope they will deserve them." More unusual, perhaps, was the great interest taken in his daughters' education. We learn from her brother's *Diary* that Mary Isham was an accomplished Latinist, and on January 18th, 1670, she wrote to her brother: "We continue to read and conster our French chapter every night." Her sister Vere, we learn from a monument at Lamport, was "learned beyond her sex and years in mathematics and algebra."

It is satisfactory to think that Sir Justinian himself did not give up his scholarly interests. On November 7th, 1673, Henry Oldenburg, the Secretary, wrote to inform him that, on the proposition of Dr. Walter Needham, he had been unanimously elected a member of the Royal Society of London. "My Lord Bishop of Salisbury [his old friend, Seth Ward] who was in the chaire this day, giveth you his humble service." When the time came for the elder boys to go to the University, Sir Justinian broke with the long tradition of the family and sent them to Oxford, to Christ Church, where his friend Dr. John Fell was Dean. He told the Dean that he favoured "the antient and severer way of education", advice that, one may be sure, was not disregarded by that strong Tory.

In 1670, he added to the family estates by buying from Lord Mandeville, the son of the Earl of Manchester, the original Montagu

[34] Arthur Ponsonby, *More English Diaries* (1927).

home in Northamptonshire, the Manor House and estate of Hanging Houghton, which adjoins Lamport.

His health, however, did not improve, and at times he was too ill to go to London. On March 2nd, 1675 he died of a sharp fit of the stone at Oxford, where he had gone to place his second son, Justinian, at Christ Church.

His son Thomas inherited his father's artistic tastes, and in his travels in Italy, acquired books, pictures, and marbles, now among the household gods at Lamport. But he was far more bent on pleasure than his father, and after much dissipation, he sought to redeem his embarrassed fortunes by marriage to the daughter of a City merchant, Abraham Vanden Bende, but the marriage never took place, as he died of smallpox on the eve of his wedding. His brother Justinian was much more the son of his father, upholding in fourteen Parliaments, either for the town or county of Northampton, the High Anglican and Tory traditions of his house. He is the direct ancestor of the present family.

The scholarly tastes of the first Justinian, and his name, have been inherited by many of the family. The fifth Baronet, a friend of John Bridges, the county historian, was specially interested in the county's antiquities; the sixth Baronet was Vice-President of Magdalen College, Oxford, and an eminent lawyer; two of the family were heads of Oxford colleges in the 18th century; the eighth Baronet commanded the Northamptonshire Militia during the Napoleonic wars, and the tenth Baronet was a pioneer of rock-gardening, vegetarianism, and spiritualism. But it is safe to say that none of the Ishams reached the comparative eminence of Bishop Duppa's old friend, and none of them left such a deep imprint on Lamport.

By his will, Sir Justinian left a small farm at Brixworth, the income of which still provides "The Isham Charity" with funds to enable the sons of poor parents in the "two ancient townships of Lamport and Hanging Houghton" to be apprenticed to useful trades. Webb's "High Roome" is still the principal apartment in Lamport Hall, many of Sir Justinian's books are still in the Library, and the pictured faces of his two soverigns, Charles I and Charles II, are still in the "High Roome." His own portraits by Lely and Gaspars are still on the walls, and Samuel Cooper's exquisite miniature still forms the best likeness of this learned, unusual Cavalier. Although, not surprisingly, he won neither the hand nor the esteem of Dorothy Osborne, he had a gift for friendship. Men as diverse as Samuel Hartlib, Brian Duppa, Ralph Verney, Seth Ward and Thomas Browne were all his friends, and in printing the record of his most intimate friendship, it may be felt that the best of the man has been preserved.[35]

[35] Justinian was buried in Lamport Church in the vault under the Isham Chapel, which he built. In 1700, Sir Justinian, his son, got William Stanton to design the beautiful mural monument to his memory, which is to-day (1950) unfortunately nearly invisible owing to the organ placed in front of it.

1650

Introductory Note

"It is never possible for men of the sword to rear the temple of recovered freedom"—Gardiner.

On April 9th, 1649, Justinian's cousin John Stuteville wrote to Sir Simonds D'Ewes, who had begun the war as a supporter of the Parliament: "The punishments which have been inflicted on us already, shew apparently our sinnes and sickness to be epidemicall. Have we not suffer'd in every part? I can not say the head is sicke: but (alas) quite cut off, and in the roome thereof a prodigious Hydra sprung up. I am sure our heart languisheth. Our free Parliaments (which have formerly beene the very heart and vitals of the Kingdome) are now driven away, and confined to a very few, within the walls of the House of Commons, and those over awed by the sword . . . Truly, Sir, I looke upon the souldier, but as the instruments and executioners, I look upon God as the chiefe agent, who hath a great controversy with us; and if wee doe not, all sorts of us, as we have sinned, endeavour to prevent him by our praeparation to meete him, by true and unfained repentance, *Actum est de Anglia.*" (Harl. MSS. 374, No. 282).

The mood of our correspondents is less defeatist, and indeed, the year 1650, in which the correspondence begins, was not without hopes for the Royalists.

In Letter II, Justinian speaks of the "sadd calamatie for which the very Saints cry out *Usque quo, Domine*", the only allusion in these letters to the King's death. In August 1649, Cromwell went to Ireland, and his successful campaign there, extended well into 1650.

In his absence, the Commonwealth had much to contend with. The danger of Charles II returning, and renewing the war, unfettered by the principles of his father, became a reality when on May 2nd, he concluded a treaty with the Covenanters, and in June he landed in Scotland, to be greeted at Aberdeen with the sight of Montrose's arm over the gateway. The Commonwealth in 1649 had defeated the Levellers, and had begun to defeat the King's cause in Ireland. But this threat from Scotland was far more serious, with Cromwell and much of the army still away, and the Parliament resorted to two panic measures; first, the Engagement, which bound all men to promise allegiance to the Commonwealth, without King or House of Lords, and which indeed was taken by many Cavaliers with the intention of breaking it as opportunity offered, but which men like Fairfax refused to take; next, the severe provision exiling from London all delinquents and persons disaffected to the Commonwealth, and requiring them to remain at their homes.

It was this last enactment that had a direct bearing on the opening of the correspondence. Justinian Isham, as we have seen, had been in London or at Petersham in 1649, dealing with the matter of his composition for delinquency. The House of Commons on January 5th 1648/9 had ordered all delinquents and Papists to leave the City of London and its Liberties, and to withdraw a distance of ten miles, except such persons as Francis Allen and Samuel Moyer licensed to remain "to prosecute their compositions" (*Journals of the House of Commons*, Vol. VI, p. 111). Such a licence for Justinian, signed by Allen and Moyer and dated January 25th, 1648/9, still exists (I.L. 3467). He must therefore have been in London at the time of the King's execution. The confirmation of his fine, fixed originally in 1646, was on March 18th, 1650. On February 26th, 1650, an Act was passed ordering all delinquents and Papists to leave the London area, to take effect from March 20th, 1650. Justinian thus had to leave his friends at Richmond, and return to Lamport. It was then that the exchange of letters began. Justinian's first letter miscarried, and the surviving letters begin with the Bishop's of May 28th.

Justinian evidently addressed his letters originally, for security reasons, to Mrs. Duppa, but as he says in his draft reply to the Bishop's first letter, the fact that the letters were addressed on the outside to a lady and inside to a gentleman might arouse suspicion, and he seems to have dropped any superscription till the next year, when Duppa suggested they should be written to his wife (Letter XV, April 8th, 1651). The fact that both correspondents felt the need for caution from the first has an important bearing on the correspondence.

Common friends such as Thomas Aldridge, Mr. Michel, Richard Chaworth are all discussed, and mentioned by name. The anxiety of Justinian's Richmond friends for his return is constantly stressed. Literary matters are discussed in this initial year, as they are throughout the correspondence. The whereabouts of the papers of Sir William Boswell, the King's agent at The Hague; the founding of an Academy by Sir Balthazar Gerbier; publication of new works by Archbishop Ussher, and the Dutch Rabbi, Menasseh Ben Israel, are all mentioned.

At Lamport, Justinian's father, Sir John, still lived, but without influence in the county, where, before the war, he had been a person of importance. In November, Lamport was searched for arms (Letter IX, December 4th, 1650, Reply).

Justinian, himself, already classed as a delinquent, demurred at taking the Engagement, and in April drafted a letter to "Mr. Scott" seeking to "obtain a license by you or your procurement for my free passing to them [his children], and to London if you think convenient where I shall come to give you thanks for so noble a favor, and what account of my selfe as you please to desire. Sir, to deale cleareły with you I should not have bin so troublesome upon such an occasion had I bin thoroughly satisfied in the engagement, which as yet I have not subscribed, but assure you as I am Xian [Christian] and a gentleman of my faire and inoffensive carriage, having never yet bin a man of armes but continueing a studious life and indeed never very healthy since a greate feaver a while after you had bin visited with yours and a long ague after it." It may seem surprising that Justinian should approach such a man as Thomas Scott at all, since he was both regicide and Republican, but Scott was also a Cambridge man and it is clear that the two men had once been friendly.

Justinian alludes to "our former acquaintance, when I lived at Mr. Colman's in Churchyard Allie; and the knowledge then of your candour and ingenuity with our mutuall expressions of fair quarter to each other however our judgements differed." Whatever his record, Scott was the right person for such an application, since in 1649 he had been appointed to "manage the business of intelligence both at home and abroad for the State" (C.S.P. Dom. 1649–50, p. 221), which gave him "an important influence both in foreign and domestic policy" (D.N.B.). He does not appear to have done anything for Justinian. He was an uncompromising Republican, and an opponent of Cromwell. At the Restoration he was tried, condemned and executed. Justinian's letter to him is drafted on the back of a letter from Ann, Lady Montagu (by birth an Isham of Barby) of April 23rd, 1650 (I.C. 279).

During this year, the Bishop was troubled by the problem of his house. He lived in a modest house at the foot of Richmond Hill. In the 18th Century, a fine house known as 5 Hill Street was built in the place of Duppa's "cottage", although parts of the old house may have been incorporated in the new. 5 Hill Street was then converted into a cinema, the staircase and cellars remaining intact. This cinema to-day (1952) is the Gaumont.

But, in 1650, Duppa was worried about the immediate rather than the distant future of his house. His landlord was "in the mind to sell" (Letter III), but asking more than the Bishop's straitened means could supply. Justinian, however, himself acquired the house towards the end of the year, for at a Court Baron, held for the Manor of Richmond, on December 27th, 1650, the house was conveyed to "Justinian Isham of Com' Northton Esq. his heirs, and assigns for ever." The Bishop was thus secured in his residence for the remainder of his years of sequestration, and even after the Restoration, it continued to be his home, and it was here that he died.

The year 1650, which, at its beginning, had seemed bright with hope, closed darkly. Charles' acceptance of the Covenant, Cromwell's victory at Dunbar (September), and the death of Charles' brother-in-law, William II of Orange, which meant a republican Government in Holland, were all bitter disappointments to the English Cavaliers.

Small wonder if our correspondents sought solace in the pages of Seneca and Plutarch.

Letter I

[May 28th.]

Sir, I write to you now, not because I receaved your last letter, but because I did not receave it. For though you did your part in point of freindship to write to me; yet a drunken water-man (who is onely so sober now as to confess he lost it) fail'd in his care in the delivery of it. And it is well that the freindship founded on those termes which hath been the basis on which ours is built is not any way the more perishable by any such failing as this; no more then a building wer likely to fall because som one tie or pegge of it miscarried. I confess, how ever, it is a loss to me; for though a merchant may be so rich as patiently to endure the newes of one shipwrackt vessell, yet when he begins to fancy to himself, that somthing might possibly be in that one vessell, which because he knowes not what it was he knowes not how to sett a valew on; I find my self in that merchant's condition, and though I am secure of your freindship, yet *Comato aeque ac calvo ingratum est comam velli,*[1] for I valew it so much, that I would not willingly loose an hair of it. Whether this paper may not run the same fate, and perish before it come to your hands I know not, and therefore I say the less; adding onely that which cannot be left out, that I am your very true freind, and servant.

Br: Sar:

Yesterday I receaved a visit (for your sake) from your old freind Mr. Aldridge[2], and his kindness is not onely in that, for I have besides receaved severall books from him. I pray putt it upon your score, and thank him for it. Richm: May 28

[Endorsed reply of Sir Justinian]

The miscarriage rather then the loss of my letter mentioned in your Lordship's last shall not make mee willingly miscarry in omitting any part of freindship which your Lordship shall so account. The most of that letter as I remember was in the relating of some men's opinions and books lately come forth so that I know not any thing in it, farther then that the in side and superscription appear of different genders, that may occasion suspicion where ere it falle. But by the failing of it I faile not to find the account your Lordship is pleased to make of me. *Magnum hoc ego duco quod placui tibi, qui turpi secernis honestum.*[3]

Letter II

[June 18th.]

Sir, I began to doubt whether my third letter came to your hands, or no, for it was trusted with a waterman, who (as I found afterwards) had dealt with a stronger kind of liquor, and could not give me any good

[1] *Comato aeque ac calvo,* etc. "It is just as unpleasant for a person with much hair as for a man with little to have it pulled out." Adapted from Seneca, *Dial.* IX, 8, 3.

[2] " Mr. Aldridge." Thomas Aldridge (or Aldrich), son and heir of John Aldridge of Norfolk, was Fellow Commoner of Christ's College, Cambridge, Easter 1625, and was admitted Lincoln's Inn 1627. He gave £10 to the New Building at Christ's (1637–40). Several times mentioned in these letters. He lived at Richmond. (Venn, *Alumni Cantabrigienses*; A. H. Lloyd, "The Benefactors to Fellows' Building," *Christ's College Magazine*, Vol. xxxviii, No. 119, Michaelmas Term, 1929; Isham Correspondence).

[3] *Magnum hoc ego,* etc. "I consider this important that it pleased you, who can distinguish well between what is honourable and dishonourable." Horace, *Sat.* i, 6, 62-3.

account, what was become of it. But the last that I receaved from you dated the tenth of June (for at this distance we must do as merchants do, and punctually return the date) putts me in some assurance that there was no miscarriage. I confess I did not much fear into what hands the letter came, for unless freindship be treason, there was no danger in it. And howsoever my own low fortunes may make me desperat, yet my love to you will temper me so farr, that I shall write nothing that may bring praeiudice to yours.

The Hill, and prospect[1] that you speak of I have lately visited, and have by the magick of a strong fancy enioy'd your company there as if you had been present; for freindship wer but a brutish thing if there could be no use made of it but onely when we enioy'd the obiect. And I must needs say that your last letter is so full of kind expressions, that had you given me no other occasion, that alone had been charm enough to lay absence asleep, and to make me think I had you with me. I will not look for any constellation for it, or say *Nescio quod me tibi temperat astrum*[2], for I look higher, and count it a blessing from heaven, that in my meanest condition I have lighted on a freind, whom I should have took a pride to have made choice of when I was at my best.

And for the account you are pleas'd to give me of the composure and quiet of your mind, (which is the onely antidot against the poison of these times) I am so much pleased to hear of it, that I shall in mine own particular be much the quieter for it. The anchor that we both hold by must be the same, not fasten'd in the sand, (for that many times comes home again, and deceaves the seaman) but cast within the vail, where (we have St. Paul's word for it) it is sure, and stedfast. Sir, I wish you the happiness (either the same, or greater) which I wish to my own soul, and whensoever I may contribute any thing toward it, be sure you have no where a more affectionat freind then

Your poor, and humble servant
B.S.

June 18

My nephew Chaworth[3] saith he will write his own thankes to you for your care of his health. The box which you speak of or what ever else

[1] "The Hill, and prospect." Richmond.

[2] *Nescio quod*, etc. "Some star or other moulds me to your measure". Persius, *Sat.* v., 51: *nescio quod certe est quod me tibi temperat astrum.*

[3] "My nephew Chaworth." Richard Chaworth (1598–1672), who is often mentioned in this correspondence, the son of John Chaworth of Wiverton, Notts, by Jane Vincent of Bernacke (Barnack) Northants, was baptised at Epperstone, Notts, on October 3rd, 1598 (information from the present Rector, the Revd. N. M. M. Turner: Foster, *Alumni Oxonienses*, gives his age at matriculation in 1621 as 18, which must be wrong). His elder brother George was created Viscount Chaworth, and one of his sisters married Sir Edward Leech, Master in Chancery, the father of Dorothy Long, also often mentioned in this correspondence (*Visitation of Nottinghamshire* 1614). He matriculated from Christ Church, Oxford, in October, 1621, and was B.A. 1622, M.A. 1625, D.C.L. 1640. He was Chancellor of the diocese of London 1637–63, and of Chichester 1660, Vicar General 1663. He was M.P. for Midhurst in 1640. The Chaworths were Royalists, and Lord Chaworth is several times mentioned as such in the *Memoirs of Colonel Hutchinson*. Dr. Chaworth himself, was evidently confidentially employed by Charles I, during the war, in raising money for the Royalist Armies. Among the accounts of "monies as have been received and paid for your Mats service and by your appointment by Jo. Ashburnham since the 1st of April, 1642 to the 26th of October, 1643" is this entry: "To Dr. Chaworth, etc., that went to Cambridge 0109.00.0." There are other references to this journey to Cambridge, e.g., "to Mr. Poolie for three journies to Cambridge." These journeys were perhaps to collect college plate, etc.,

is yours, I shall be as diligent to praeserve as any thing of mine own. But I do not yet fear rifeling, and I hope my condition is so well known, that none will come to rob an hospitall. Your freinds hereabouts ar well, and my wife is so much your servant, that she would take it very ill, at my hands, if I should not give her a place in the rear.

[ENDORSED REPLY OF SIR JUSTINIAN]

Since our letters have so farr passage I shall continue scribbling, and with the date of mine shall signifie that of yours last receaved. But if freindship be made treason, then in plaine termes I had rather be hang'd for it, then condemn'd for the contrarie. Most evenings I walke abroad, and suppose your Lordship upon the Hill, beholding the selfe same setting sun as I do heere, and that as our sight at this distance meets in the same object, so may our minds even at that very instant, in begging blessings upon us from a better light that never setts; and fortiefying our selves against the powers of a blacker darkness. This I beleeve farr more efficacious then the two needles (so much spoke of) being touched by the same magnett and sett upon round trenchers in the midst of an alphabet. I cannot but beleeve, a diviner touch upon our spiritts. Nor could I ever since our first acquaintance but think your Lordship the very person propos'd by Ecclesiasticus: *Cum viro sancto assiduus esto, quemcumque cognoveris observantem timorem Dei, cujus anima est secundum animam tuam: et qui cum titubaveris in tenebris, condolebit tibi.*[4] Your Lordship has many wayes instructed mee where to cast anchor amidst these stormy tymes: had not your letter shewed it, I find your very seale[5] a sermon upon that text; but how wel [will] they answer? yet as the mathematicians say *Proportio in tribus minimum terminis consistit*[6], so am I to mention the third and best terme, as your seale answers to your letter so your letter to your life. And this I am sure is beyond all the proportions that ever Euclide taught, the Golden Rule is but dross unto it, or all whatever gold

which afterwards got the colleges into trouble. Again "John Browne servant to John Ashburnham Esq." deposed that between November 1642, and October 26th, 1643 he received "from Dr. Chaworth and Doctor Jansen" the enormous sum of £10,667 14*s* 03*d*. (*A Narrative by John Ashburnham*, Vol. II, (1830), Appendix, p. xxxvii). On December 18th, 1663, Richard Chaworth was knighted. He died at Richmond and was buried there on November 16th, 1672. His first wife was Mary Croft, niece of Bishop Duppa, who was buried in the choir of Christ Church, Oxford, November 25th, 1645. His second wife (to whom there is a monument in Richmond Church) was Lady Sophia Bertie, fourth daughter of Robert, Earl of Lindsey, who was buried at Richmond on January 1st, 1689/90. He was the executor of his uncle (Duppa's) will in 1662. For the family connections of Bishop Duppa and his wife see App. A. (Foster; G. E. C., *Complete Peerage*; Wood MS. F. 4, f. 79).

[4] *Cum viro sancto*, etc. Ecclesiasticus Cap. XXXVII vv. 15 and 16 (Vulgate). A.V. v. 12 which translates: "But be continually with a godly man, whom thou knowest to keep the commandments of the Lord, whose mind is according to thy mind and will sorrow with thee if thou shalt miscarry."

[5] "Your very seale". The Bishop's seal has a figure of our Lord imposed on an anchor. According to Izaak Walton (*Life of Dr. John Donne*) this seal was one of several made to the design of Dr. Donne, and sent to "Dr. Duppa, Bishop of Salisbury" and other "friends and benefactors" including Sir Henry Wotton, Dr. Henry King, and Dr. Hall. The design, where the picture of Christ Crucified is nailed "not to a cross, but to an anchor (the emblem of hope)", Donne caused to be "drawn in little" and "engraved very small in Heliotropian stones, and set in gold"; they were sent to "many of his dearest friends to be used as seals, or rings, and kept as memorials of him and of his affection to them."

[6] *Proportio*, etc. "A Proportion consists in at least three terms", e.g., as A is to B so B is to C. The three terms are A B and C.

it selfe can command. Your fortunes, my Lord, (you mention) in respect of your selfe I am sure must needs be low; you ever look't above them, by casting anchor upward, quite contrarie to the way of the world. *O curvae in terras animae*[7]. But that which I know lies so heavie upon your Lordship's spiritt, and all good men's, is the sadd calamitie for which the very Saints cry out *Usque quo, Domine*[8].

I can say no more. In such cases you have the best cordialls by you, in you, and know how to submitt unto His will *Qui quaecumque voluit, fecit*[9]. But yet as wel-meaning weomen will be praescribing to those they wish health better things sometymes then they can either make or make use of themselves, I shall only say to your Lordship what you have oftener read *Miserere animae tuae placens Deo, et contine: congrega cor tuum in sanctitate ejus, et tristitiam longe repelle a te*[10].

My Lord I crave both your pardon and your blessing.

Your Lordship's most humble.

Letter III

[July 10th.]

Sir, I have no fault to find with you, but that you ar too kind to me, and sett a valew upon me, which when I take my own scales in hand, there ar so many granes wanting, that I must necessarily think, that either you take me without weighing, or give me an allowance more then ordinary out of your own goodness to make it up. But how ever it is, I had rather you should be deceaved in me, then by me, who have no other end of loving you but for your self, though the streightness of my fortune might otherwise render my freindship suspected.

The Hill that you speak of I do not so often visit as when you wer with me, nor with so much contentment, for though the landskip be good, yet the nearer prospect of a freind is infinitely better. Besides, it is but the setting sun that I see there, whereas the rising sun would bring more comfort with it, but I fear, I am too old to rise early enough to see it.

Though I have some inward comforts of my own (for I may call that mine own which my God gives me), yet I am none of those creatures *Quae rore suo victitant* that live upon their own moisture, and therefore forbear not your counsell to me as a thing superfluous for I have not onely need of it, but as comming from you I have som more then ordinary delight in it. The blessed spirits in heaven have an essentiall happiness, but the schoolmen say, there is an accidentall beatitude besides, that addes to it: and though I were fuller of comforts then I am, yet I should still have room for those that I receave from you.

---

[7] *O curvae*, etc. "O souls bent down to the ground." Persius, *Sat.* II, 61. The original has *in terris*.

[8] *Usque quo, Domine.* Ps. XII v. 1. *Usquequo, Domine, oblivisceris me in finem* (Vulgate). "How long, will thou forget me, O Lord, for ever" (Common Prayer Book, Psalm XIII). The allusion is, of course, to the killing of King Charles I.

[9] *Qui quaecumque*, etc. "Who doth whatever He will."

[10] *Miserere animae*, etc. Ecclesiasticus Cap. XXXV. 24 (Vulgate). A.V. v. 23 which translates: "Love thine own soul, and comfort thy heart, remove sorrow far from thee: for sorrow hath killed many, and there is no profit therein."

That which you read in the diurnalls concerning Sir William Bosvile[1] is very tru, for he died the 12th of April last, a person whose death I should have more lamented had he lived in times that had been worthy of him. But as we ar, and as we ar likely to be, happy is he that hath his exit first, while there ar som few good men left to give their *plaudite*. His lady is a freind of mine, of long continuance, and wer she and her papers here in England, I might possibly praevail with her in the disposing of them.

There ar many bookes com out of late, of which onely the titles com to me, for I see few of them, but onely such as som freind or other casually brings. Among the rest there is one of that learned Jew Menasseh Ben Israel[2] dedicated to them who have now the authority over us, and given me by a Parlament man who understood it so little, that he told me it was the book of a converted Jew, but when I red it I found the Jew had a designe rather to convert them. There is an other treatise[3] (which I

---

[1] "Sir William Bosvile." Sir William Boswell, a Suffolk man, was B.A. from Jesus College, Cambridge, 1603/4, M.A. 1607, Fellow of Jesus 1606–29. He was secretary to Lord Herbert of Cherbury, when he was Ambassador in Paris in 1620; apparently, secretary to Bishop Williams, when Keeper of the Great Seal; and secretary to Sir Dudley Carleton, Ambassador to The Hague, 1625. He succeeded Carleton as Ambassador there in 1633 (when he was knighted) and where he continued his predecessor's policy in supporting Prince Maurice and the "Gomarists" against the "Remonstrants", who were advocates of Arminian doctrine. On the outbreak of the Civil War, he tried not unsuccessfully to keep Holland neutral, despite the efforts of Walter Strickland, Cromwell's envoy, and the natural propensities of the States General. He was a scholar and man of letters. He was friendly with the Revd. Joseph Mede, Sir Justinian's tutor at Cambridge, and introduced his writings to the Continent. He possessed most of the "written bookes" of Dr. John Dee, the astrologer (see Note 11 and Letter CV, Note 3). Some diplomatic correspondence now in the MSS. at Lamport may possibly have belonged to him, in his capacity as secretary to Carleton. (I.C. 5038–5098). The D.N.B. gives the date of his death as 1649. This led me to misdate the earlier letters. But that he died in 1650 is proved by a letter in the Clarendon State Papers, dated May 12th, 1650, where the writer, Richard Watson, says "Sir William Boswell is dead" and speculates on the choice of a successor (*Calendar of Clarendon State Papers*, Vol. II, p. 58).
His wife, whom Duppa evidently knew, was Margaret, daughter and eventually heir of Sir Ralph Bosville of Brabourne, Sevenoaks. (Will proved 1682). She founded scholarships at Jesus College, Cambridge. Brabourne (or Bradbourne) is not far from Lewisham, and Duppa may have known the Bosvilles in his youth.
(D.N.B.; Venn; D.N.B. article on Mead (Mede); B. Dew Roberts, *Mitre and Musket* (1938). His correspondence is in B.M. Add. MSS. 6394 and 6395).

[2] "Menasseh Ben Israel." Menasseh (or Manasseh) Ben Israel (1604–57). This "somewhat dreamy Amsterdam Rabbi and physician" (*Clarke Papers*, Vol. II, p. 172, note a) took on himself the cause of Judaism in England. He petitioned the Long Parliament "for the return of the Jews into England" (January 5th, 1649). He was eventually successful with Cromwell, and a synagogue was established in London. His *History of the Jews whilst in England* was published in London in 1656, and several other of his works were published here. The book referred to by Duppa is *The Hope of Israel by Menasseh Ben Israel, Dedicated by the Author to the High Court of Parliament of England, and to the Councell of State.* It was published on July 4th, 1650. (See Lucien Wolf, *Menasseh Ben Israel's Mission to Oliver Cromwell* (1901); D.N.B.; Gardiner, *History of the Commonwealth and Protectorate*, Vol. IV, p. 12.)

[3] "There is an other treatise . . ." This is : *The History of the Rites, Customs and Manner of Life of the Present Jews throughout the World.* Written in Italian by Leo (sic) Modena. Translated into English by Edmund Chilmead 1650. Published April 21st, 1650. For Edmund Chilmead (1610–54) see D.N.B., Foster, Wood, *Ath. Ox.* (ed. Bliss, III, 350–1), and Walker. He was chaplain of Christ Church, 1641, and being a Royalist was ejected in 1648 and came to London in great necessity.

onely have seen the title of) of the rites and customes of the present Jewes written in Italian, but translated into English by a person, whom I know so well that I conceave the book may be worth the sending for. While I was writing this, in comes your freind Mr. Aldridge (who is so much mine for your sake that I desire you to thank him for it) with a little treatise but with the huge title of *Anthroposophiatheomagica*[4]. I was affraid at first it might be som coniuring book, but after I had red a leaf or two (for I have yet red no more) I found the deepest point of magick will be to coniure out the sense of it. It will be no newes to tell you that the Primate's *Chronoligy*[5] is now published, but the book it self is yet newes to me, for neither can I rise to the purchase of it, nor is he so freindly as to send me one. But I will weary you no longer; onely let me som times hear from you, for a letter of yours sweetens my thoughts for a week after.

My landlord[6] is still in the mind to sell, and I, to fitt my self for a bargain with him, have sold my hangings, and my little lease in Northfolk, but he keeps his rate so high, that there is no reaching him, and therefore what will becom of the house I know not. But this I can assure you that he that is in it for the present prayes daily for you, and is

Your very tru, and humble servant,

B.S.

Richm: July 10

[ENDORSED REPLY OF SIR JUSTINIAN]

M[y] L[ord] I thanke you for taking so well that libertie of use with you, and peradventure therefore the more with you, because I would take less to my selfe, being oblig'd to a stricter observance of my owne ana even when you have it from mee, I have often begun the verse: *Paratus sum*, but when I shall come to *et non sum turbatus*, God knowes. And yet I know the first not perfect without the latter.

[4] "A little treatise with the huge title." "*Anthroposophia Theomagica on the Nature of Man and his state after death*, of Eugenius Philalethes and *Anima Magica Abscondita; on the Universal Spirit of Man* by the same: fine portraits of Cornelius Agrippa 2 vols 12 mo in one 1650" (Lamport Library Catalogue), ed. C. Edmonds, 1880). Thomas Vaughan, the author, was born at Newton near Brecknock in 1621, and was twin brother of Henry Vaughan, the Silurist. He was educated at Oxford, and became a noted chemist, and admirer of Cornelius Agrippa. The publication of this work involved him in an acrimonious controversy with Dr. Henry More. He died in 1666 "as it were suddenly, when he was operating strong mercury, some of which by chance getting up into his nose killed him." (Wood, *Ath. Ox*; D.N.B.; Lowndes).

[5] "Primate's *Chronoligy*." The first part of James Ussher's *Annales Veteris et Novi Testamenti* was published in 1650 (folio). The author (1581–1656), appointed Archbishop of Armagh in 1625, was of a Puritan temper, but considered a great scholar. *The Annals of the World* (1658) by Ussher belonged to Sir Justinian. It was translated by Fuller from the Latin. Ussher was Primate of Ireland, the Primate of all England (Laud) having been executed, and the Primate of England (Williams) having deserted the King, was living in obscurity in Wales, where he remained till his death.

[6] "My landlord". This was "Peter Richard, Junior, of London, Merchant" who on December 27th, 1650 surrendered the "Messe or tenement late or now belonging as they now are in the tenure of Brian Duppa S.T.D. and late Bishop of Sarum" to Justinian Isham.
(Extracted from Court Rolls of the Manor of Richmond (originals in P.R.O.) in Richmond Public Library, communicated by Miss Courlander of Richmond to the Revd. R. S. Mills, Vicar of Petersham, through whose kindness they are here quoted).

The fault you find with mee is indeed of such a nature that you cannot absolve mee of it, for that I shall not be brought to confess it. 'Tis not I my Lord that sett a valew upon you, nor the royall stamp it selfe so much as your owne intrinsic virtue which is truly your intrinsic valew. Yours at this time came somewhat late to mee after the date, it coming to Mr. Mansell[7] I believe immediately after the carrier going out of towne, which is alwaies on Thursday morning. I heard lately also from Mr. Aldrich of your welbeings. But what blust'ring booke had he gott to encounter your Lordship with? The new Academy[8] I suppose this hott weather is melted to nothing, but certainly had hee entered into it with that title, he had blowne them all up. The booke he only shew'd me before I came out of towne. The author, a Welsh-man, and of Oxford, peradventure knowne to your Lordship, but has dranke so deeply of Agrippa that I doubt the braine some what turn'd.

Certainly if any thing in the world can moove a man's muscles it is this serious canting; I undertake not to understande the depth of their art, but I dare say their delivery of it is very fantasticall and I believe deceitful. Menasseh Ben Israel should have don well to have remembred of a law amongst the Jewes mentioned by Josephus. Let no man spoile any strange temple, nor take that which is dedicated to any God. But he may sooner be term'd Christian then they Jewes in that point. A little before my leaving the towne I mett with a booke newly translated out of French stil'd, *The Characters of the Passions*, writt by Sieur de la Chambre.[9] Peradventure your Lordship may have formerly seene it, 'tis not that of the Lord Monmouth's translation[10], but a tract I think much beyond it, or indeed what I have mett with in that kind, it being but the beginning of a much greater designe therein mentioned.

I wish the papers that Sir Wil. B. left of Englishmen's especially as Bacon's and Dee's[11] etc. might be still preserved in English hands, peradven-

---

[7] "Mr. Mansell." On September 26th, 1650 from St. James's Park, Robert Mansell states that he has sent Mr. Isham's letter on to Petersham, and since received a letter which he encloses. His wife "and Besse" present their service, and "would bee very glad to taste of your Northamptonshire bacon" (I.C. 289a). There is a draft reply by Justinian on the back of this letter obviously intended for Bishop Duppa. "Now for both men and books together your Lordship's course of life besides your innate and acquired abilities hath sett you higher to discover more then most of the knowing men of this nation." He concludes: "For ought I know to the contrary [I am] bound to another ha' year's absence from your parts and what then as our Maisters please, etc." See Letter XIII, which may well be an answer to this draft.

[8] "The new Academy." This was presumably the foundation of Sir Balthazar Gerbier fully described in the notes to Letter IV. The "blust'ring booke" is Thomas Vaughan's *Anthroposophia Theomagica*.

[9] "*The Characters of the Passions*". *The Characters of the Passions, Written in French by the Sieur de la Chambre . . . Translated into English* was published in London March 23rd, 1650. (*Catalogue of Thomason Tracts*). Marin Cureau de la Chambre (1594?–1675) was a physician.

[10] "The Lord Monmouth's translation". *The use of the Passions, Written in French by J. F. Senault, and put into English by Henry Earle of Monmouth* (1649). Senault was a French hagiographer (1601–72).

[11] "Dee." Dr. John Dee (1527–1608), mathematician and astrologer, was one of the celebrated figures of the sixteenth century. In an unpublished letter at Lamport (I.C. 272) Arthur Dee (1579–1651), his son, an alchemist, writing to Thomas Aldridge on December 15th, 1649, from Norwich, says: "Sir Wylliam Boswell the K agent at the Hage is possest of most of his written books, whom I have sollicited for many yeares, but to no purpose." (D.N.B. and Lamport MSS.) See Letter CV, Note 3, and Letter CVIII, Note 3.

ture Sir John Dingly[12] may assist your Lordship in it.

My Lord you are now planted by the water side, neither is it (they say) good removing of old ones. I wish your continuance where you are (unless etc.), and doubt not but so you may either as it is, or to b[u]y upon such termes as another will give; which if you be not ready for, it shall be made ready for you, or what ever els may pleasure you that is in the power of

Yours.

Letter IV

[August 7th.]

Sir, Though my letters come slow, yet I am glad they come sure, not that there is any danger in them either to the receaver or the writer (for unless it be criminall to be able to write, and read, I shall otherwise take care to keep my self innocent, and you too) but that I am desirous, that once a month at least, you should hear you have a servant living to pray for you, though unprofitable for all other uses.

The mushroom Academy which you mention, was onely in request (as it seems) when it was new sprung up, for since you gave us som of the first scenes of it, I can hear no newes of it at all, so that I verily beleive it is sunk at White Fryers, but whether it may not rise again (as the Spanish Queen did) in som other place I can not tell. For as long as Sir Balthasar[1]

---

[12] "Sir John Dingly." Considerable confusion has been caused by the fact that there were two Sir John Dingleys alive at this time, and both connected with Richmond.

(*a*) Sir John Dingley of Woolverton, Isle of Wight, who married Jane Hammond, sister of Lady Temple, the mother of Sir William Temple, and sister of Dr. Henry Hammond. He was a zealous Parliamentarian, and there is nothing to show that he was specially interested in literature, or had had any connection with Holland.

(*b*) Sir John Dingley, Secretary to Elizabeth, Queen of Bohemia. He was born at Boston, Lincs. 1593. He matriculated as a pensioner from Christ's College, Cambridge, in July 1606 (Peile, I, 258, and Venn, who, however, confuses him with the other Sir John Dingley). He contributed £20 to the New Buildings at Christ's 1639–42. He was tutor to Prince Frederick Henry, the eldest brother of the Elector Charles Louis, Prince Rupert and Prince Maurice. After Frederick Henry's death in 1629, he became Secretary to the Prince's mother, Queen Elizabeth of Bohemia, and was intimately connected with diplomatic circles in England and Holland, where he spent much time. He was knighted after 1637, and before 1649, in which year he is mentioned in the Clarendon State Papers as being in Holland. He was presumably back in England by July, 1650, and would have been the obvious person to ask about Boswell's papers. He lived at Richmond, where he died, and was buried December 24th, 1671. There is a brass plate to his memory on the west wall of Richmond Church. In his will (P.C.C. 3 Eure) proved January 26th, 1671/2, he mentions certain named books in Spanish, Latin, Italian and French, which he left to a cousin.

("A list of Monumental Brasses in Surrey" compiled by Mill Stephenson, *Surrey Archaeological Collections*, Vol. XXXII (1919), pp. 76–7; M. A. E. Green, *Elizabeth, Queen of Bohemia*, new ed, p. 402).

Miss Margaret Toynbee has recently cleared up the whole question of the two Sir John Dingleys in *Notes and Queries*, Vol. 198 Nos. 10 and 11, 1953.

[1] "Sir Balthasar" and "The mushroom Academy." Sir Balthazar Gerbier, was a Zealander (1591?–1667), who served the Duke of Buckingham as a painter, and King Charles I as a diplomatist. He dealt largely in pictures when King Charles' collection was sold. In 1652, he was employed by Cromwell to treat with Holland. (Gardiner, Vol. II, p. 188). What is known of Gerbier's character justifies Duppa's remarks. His "Academy" is an interesting subject. Horace Walpole says that it "was imitated from one established by Charles I, in the eleventh year of his reign,

is sure, that the maior part of men are fooles, he cannot despair of keeping the chair and having disciples.

If Mr. Aldridge hath mett with you, you can want no other intelligence, either concerning the publick, or the personall affaires of your freinds. Since that time much noise there is abroad, but we in these parts ar still in the same quietness you left us, and like the hooded hauk *in spe, et silentio.*

I hear little of bookes, for I have not seen my book-freinds of late. The Primate's *Chronology* is too dear for me, and yet, I confess, I have a great mind to see it, because he told me himself, that if ever he did any thing satisfactory that was it. Nor have the new *Characters of the Passions* com to my veiw, but I have heard of them under another name, as being written not by De la Chambres, but Des Cartes[2].

I keep my self so close an anachoret, and make so few visits, that I am not likely suddainly to meet with Sir John Dingly, but when I do, I shall confer with him, what probability there may be of recovering those papers, though at the present little can be don in it, there being troubles now as well on that side of the sea, as this.

I am still in the same feares of having my house bought over my head, though I have for the praevention of it, fitted my self as well as I could by selling my hangings, and calling in help from som freinds, but the demands ar so high (no less then 280*l*) that I begin to lay aside the thought of it, and leave all to that Providence which hath hetherto disposed of me. I thank you for your very kind offer of assistance to me, and though at this time I make no use of it, I shall keep it as a reserve being mindfull of the advice that Bacon gave to Essex[3], that cordiall waters wer not to be taken but in cases of greatest necessity.

Sir, I am,

Your very tru freind, and servant

Br: S.

Aug: 7

[Endorsed reply of Sir Justinian]

I humbly thank you for that you are still pleas'd to favor mee with your letters, 'tis much more then the words in them however excellent that they bring. They represent your selfe unto mee. And as Plutarch tells us how Democritus writt that wee should pray we might see happie images in

and called Museum Minervae . . . None but who could approve themselves gentlemen were to be admitted to education there, where they were to be instructed in arts and sciences, foreign languages, mathematics, painting and architecture . . ." (Walpole, *Anecdotes of Painting*, ed. Wornum (1888), Vol, I, p. 276). Gerbier, who had fled to France as a former agent of Charles I, returned to England in March 1649 for the purpose of opening an Academy for education on Baconian principles. He apparently opened two Academies, one in Bethnal Green on September 1st, 1649, and the other in Whitefriars for foreign languages. (See G. H. Turnbull, *Hartlib, Dury and Comenius* and H. B. Wheatley's edition of the *Diary of Samuel Pepys*, Vol. III (1893), p. 147, n.1 (note to May 28th, 1663)). For the Bethnal Green Academy there is ample contemporary record. Wheatley mentions the Whitefriars Academy but gives no authority for his statement. This allusion of Duppa's at least gives it substance, but it does not seem to have lasted long.

[2] "Des Cartes". Duppa appears to have confused De La Chambre's book, mentioned above, with *The Passions of the Soule, by René Descartes. Translated out of the French*, published in London May 24th, 1650.

[3] "The advice that Bacon gave to Essex." Bacon was treated by Essex with great generosity, but he was said to be largely responsible for the Earl's conviction and death in 1601. (D.N.B.)

the aire, that good ones and proper to our nature may rather come to us then ill ones and unlucky, presupposing (though falsely) there are good and bad images flying in the aire, which give a good or ill impression unto men inclining them to vice or vertue. But how he himselfe by reading the stories of the most noble, vertuous, and best given men of former tymes did teach himselfe to shake off all lewd conditions, if perchance the comparing and conversation of those with whom he was, did acquaint him with some unhappie or ungracious touch. I may confess (however unlike I live or unable to follow) the images of the best and bravest persons of former ages are often before mee, and I no sooner see your letters but cry out *Antiqua virtute, homo ac fide.* Me thinks I see you, I have you, I talke with you, I walke with you, and mervaile not that faith can remove mountains, when every fancie brings your Hill hither to mee, where I take many a turn with you, sitt downe with you, looke about, conferr freely upon what's next without affectation, concurr without any manner of flattery, and take a kinde of pleasure even to condole with you. With your letter I had the same day Mr. Os[4], by whom I was very joyfull to heare of your so welbeing as to goe where he left you. The Pri[mate][5] is now in these parts with the L[ady] P[eterborough][6]. He preaches every weeke and hath great resort unto him. Mr. Stephens[7] was lately with me.

---

[4] "Mr. Os." This is presumably Mr. John Osbeston, an old servant of Justinian's, for whom see Letter LXXXVI, March 24th, 1657.

[5] "The Primate." This is, of course, Ussher.

[6] "Lady Peterborough." Henry Mordaunt, 2nd Earl of Peterborough, was a Royalist. His wife was a daughter of Barnabas O'Brien, Earl of Thomond. He was forced to compound in 1646, and again in 1649 for his part in the rising of 1647, and he lived at Drayton, Northants, quietly during the Commonwealth, in order to pay his debts. But it was the 2nd Earl's mother, "a lady of very haughty spirit", and a daughter of Lord Howard of Effingham, who was the special patroness of Archbishop Ussher, and it was in her house at Reigate that he died in 1656. Her husband, the 1st Earl, had joined the Parliamentary side in the Civil War, owing to his wife's influence, which perhaps explains why she was able to entertain Ussher at Drayton; "great resort" was permitted to this house, the owner of which was particularly obnoxious to the Government (D.N.B. and N. V. Stopford Sackville, *Drayton House* (privately printed 1939)).

[7] "Mr. Stephens." This is Jeremiah Stephens (1591–1665), whom we shall meet frequently in these letters. In Letter XVII he is called by Duppa "my cosin." His father, the Revd. Walter Stephens, is described by Foster as "of Herefordshire", which probably explains the connection with the Duppas, since Jeffrey Duppa founded almshouses at Pembridge (see App. A). Walter Stephens matriculated from Gloucester Hall, Oxford on January 10th, 1574/5, and was M.A. 1580. He married Alice, daughter of Thomas Browne of Shrewsbury, and Jeremy was the eldest of five sons. (*Visitation of London* 1634, Harl. Soc., Vol. XVII). As neither Jeremy's father nor mother provides the clue to the relationship with Duppa, it is possible that Walter Stephens' mother was a Duppa, and that she may have been an aunt of Jeffrey Duppa. Walter was Vicar of Bishop's Castle, Salop, till his death in 1629. Jeremy Stephens' baptism is recorded in the parish registers there on October 17th, 1591. (Information from the present Vicar, the Revd. A. Maryon Watson). Jeremy Stephens, like his father, was an Oxford man (B.N.C., matriculated June 19th, 1610). He married on April 9th, 1635 at Campton, Beds., Mary, daughter of the Revd. William Goldsmith, Rector of Campton. He was Chaplain at All Souls, Rector of Quinton 1622 and of Wootton, Northants 1626 and Prebendary of Lincoln 1639. He quarrelled with his parishioners, and "many of them, aged and poor, trudged to London to petition against his oppression." The Committee of Sequestration replaced him at Wootton before 1647 by the popular Puritan divine Daniel Rogers. The northern wing of the Rectory was erected by him, and bears a tablet inscribed DEO: ECCL:IE:STEPHENS:POS: 1630 (*V.C.H., Northants*, IV, p. 296). Walker, who made great use of his notes on the persecution of the Northamptonshire clergy, says that he was "plunder'd,

Mr. Leech[8] visited me as he went into Darbyshire and hope to see him as he returns. Thus kept from the sight of your Lordship myselfe, I rejoyce to see any that either has lately or may shortly see you.

Letter V

[August 28th.]

Sir, I know you ar no worshipper of images; or, if you wer, you need not look into the aire for them, or seek for them any where but in your self, where you may find a theater of God's making, a soul not onely free from the vices of the time, but full of all good impressions. As I do not flatter you, so I know I cannot corrupt you with saying so, and therefore have no other designe, but to turn you from all other images to your own, and like Antipheron in Aristotle, when you would look upon a good copy, to sett your selfe before you. As for my own particular who really think my self very happy in your freindship, I shall desire you not to love, but to valew, me less, for otherwise you will keep me in a continuall fear of being found too light, and to need more granes then your charity, (though it be very great to me), can reasonably allow me.

I wrott you word in my last that I had confined my self like an anachoret within my own walls, but this being not under the religion of a vow, I was the very next day drawn out by the importunity of freinds as far as Fulham; and it was well that I was not out of the compass of my circle, for the evill spirits wer abroad that day, and seeking whom they should devour, seas'd upon som guilty of my faults, loyalty, and religion. But, I thank God, having considered all things, I have sett up my rest, and whether I escape, or suffer, I hope I shall keep that evenness of mind, as to be aequally affected to either, for though I am no such stoick, as to have no affections left, yet I shall strive to be so much a Christian, as neither to please nor displease my self too much with whatsoever shall

imprisoned, barbarously used and silenced." In 1660 he was restored to his Rectory at Wootton where he died on January 9th, 1664/5. There is a tablet in the chancel of the Church at Wootton with a long Latin inscription to his memory. He was the friend and coadjutor of Sir Henry Spelman, the antiquary, and author of the *Concilia*. He was a learned man, and edited St. Gregory *De Cura Pastorali* (1629), and works by Cyprian and Spelman. Selden interceded for him, when he was in trouble with the Parliamentary authorities. He was one of the numerous "loyal and orthodox" clergy assisted by Justinian, during the Commonwealth. (Walker, D.N.B., and Foster).

[8] "Mr. Leech." James Long (see Letter v, Note 3) married Dorothy, daughter of Sir Edward Leech, Master in Chancery, whose wife Jane was sister of Richard Chaworth (see Letter ii, Note 3). *The Visitation of Cheshire* 1613 (Harl. Soc., Vol. lix) gives Edward Leech's father as "Robart Leiche Doctor of the Civell Lawes and Chancelor of Chester." They belonged to a cadet branch of the Leeches of Carden, Cheshire, themselves a branch of an ancient family who held Chatsworth from the time of Edward III till that of Edward VI, when Francis Leech sold the estate to the Cavendishes. In an early 19th-century pedigree at Chatsworth (for which I am indebted to Mr. Francis Thompson, the Librarian at Chatsworth) it is recorded that "A detachment of Dragoons from the Parliamentary Garrison at Nantwich on June 12th, 1643 plundered Carden Holland and made prisoner its owner John Leeche Esq." Sir Edward Leech had three brothers, Thomas, Robert and William. He settled at Shipley, Derbyshire, after he was knighted in 1621 (Foss, *Judges of England*, Vol. vi, 1603-1660, pp. 9, 215 and 403). His family continued at Shipley till their heiress married into the Miller family. The allusion here (Mr. Leech) is to the brother of Dorothy Long, for we know that in 1650 he visited Justinian at Lamport. On the back of a letter of September 1650, Justinian drafted a reply to a letter of Mrs. Long, dated September 5th, 1650 (see Letter v): "I humbly thank you for your brother's courtesie in coming to see mee." (I.C. 289).

happen. Those few words, "Thy will be don," settle the soul more then the loadstone can possibly operate upon the needle, which still varies, and hath the motion of trepidation; but he that resignes himself into God's hands heartilly and without praevarication, is not touchd with the loadstone; but is that very mountain of loadstone which (Gilbert[1] saith) is under the Northpole, and cannot be removed.

Your last letters had the hap to be brought to me that day wherein I was honor'd with a visit from the lady of Ham[2] who is not onely inquisitive after you, but desires you should know it; for though the Coronell[3] rides, and hunts with her husband[4], she can distinguish so well, as to think that your company might be of more advantage to him. Whether you will take any notice of this to her self (which I think you will not) or convey any complement by me (who am engaged to repay the visit) I shall leave to you to think of. The person who mett me at Fulham told me that your father had sent for him, and that he was then travelling towards you, but I, though I had then the letter in my pocket, chose rather to send it by the carrier, as finding that so sure a way, that I was unwilling to change it.

---

1 "Gilbert." William Gilbert (1540–1603), physician to Queen Elizabeth, in his work *De Magnete, Magneticisque Corporibus* (1600), declared the earth to be a magnet. (D.N.B.).

2 "The lady of Ham." This is Elizabeth Murray (*c.*1628–98), who is known to history as the Countess of Dysart, a title to which she succeeded on the death abroad of her father, William, 1st Earl of Dysart, *c.* 1654. She married Sir Lionel Tollemache in 1647 (?), and lived at Ham House, Petersham, which, in its present form, is really a monument to her times and taste. She seems rather a strange visitor for the Bishop, but she attracted very diverse types, and, as Burnet records, "Cromwell was certainly fond of her." She was obviously a friend of Justinian's, and the friendship continued many years. (D.N.B., G.E.C., *Complete Peerage*, *Ham House*, *A Guide* (1951).) See also Letter LXVII A, Note 1.

3 "The Coronell." This is James Long (1617–92), only son of Sir Walter Long of Draycot Cerne, Wilts, by his first marriage with Lady Anne Ley, daughter of the 1st. Earl of Marlborough. He was a nephew of Sir Robert Long, 1st. Bart, and succeeded to his uncle's property and baronetcy in 1673. He served with the King's army during the war, and by 1644 was a Colonel of horse in Sir Francis Doddington's brigade. In March 1645 he was taken prisoner with nearly 400 men near Bath, in circumstances which, according to Clarendon, reflected discredit on him. He was exchanged, and in August 1645 took Chippenham for the King. On May 4th, 1649, he paid a fine of £714 for his estates and obtained a pardon. He was fond of hawking, and Aubrey says that shortly after his release, while hawking on Hounslow Heath, he met Cromwell, who took a liking to him. He was a friend of Aubrey who noted he was "for insects exceedingly curious and searching long since in naturall things." He was obviously the kind of person to interest Justinian, though the Bishop speaks of him with some reserve. His wife Dorothy, daughter of Sir Edward Leech, whom Aubrey describes as "a most elegant beauty and wit", was a very frequent correspondent of Justinian's. (Aubrey, *Brief Lives*, Wotton's *Baronetage*, J. E. Nightingale, *The Church Plate of the County of Wilts* (1891), and information from the late Alistair Taylor, the historian of the Jacobites). See Letter LXXI, Note 3 and (for the Leeches) Letter IV, Note 8.

4 "Her husband." This is Sir Lionel Tollemache, 3rd Bart. of Helmingham, Suffolk, a gentleman of good family, about whom history has little to say. He stayed at Lamport with Sir Justinian in 1657. See Letter LXVII A, Note 1.
There is an amusing letter at Lamport from Mrs. Long (I.C.288) dated September 5th, 1650, describing to Justinian the society of these friends at Richmond. "I have neighbours" she writes "which will not let me be solitary". She gives an amusing sketch of a lady, who from what is known of her may well be Lady Dysart. "She is grown a great student, reads Dr. Donne and Sir W. Rawley, to which she uses (my sweet Ovid) as a key, is perfect in her Amor – works exquesetly in gumworke, hath entered her selfe head of the second form in our Academy, knokes me down with my owne weapon, making the word Valentine odious to heare it, so fulsomely it is pronounced by her."

I am glad the Primat hath found a good old lady to support him; our Savior, and His Apostles wer ministred to by women, and Pythagoras hath given that sex this character τῆς εὐσεβείας οἰκειότατον ἔστι τὸ γένος τῶν γυναικῶν[5], I will not despair therefore but som of them may grow old, and good enough to consider me. But I want nothing as long as I have your freindship, which I persuade my self you will continu by this entercourse of letters, till writing and reading be once again counted treason; and then we must leave, but I never, to be

Your very tru freind, and servant
B.S.

Richm: Aug: 28.

Your freinds with me, and about me, ar your faithfull servants.

[ENDORSED REPLY OF SIR JUSTINIAN]

To be taken off from beholding other images and looke more into my selfe I beleeve may much concerne mee, but instead of your Lordship's getting me a copy from thence, I had rather, and indeed you had more obliged me, to have told mee freely what I should then have blotted out. I know that such castigations are not so pleasing to the tast of many (however sound and wholesome). But very much even with them I find it is according to the hand that applies truly. I have often (though secretly) bemoaned the condition of most men, together with my owne, to think how much better use wee may sometymes make of our enemies, by their upbraiding of us, then of our best freinds so over tender of admonishing; and yet that commonly is first caus'd from the tenderness of the patient who will not be touch'd. In the mean tyme how do we loose tyme and our selves, for not daring to be true, first to our selves, and then to one another; I have now seene so much of the world that like him who, when he hath gon a great way, looks back, considers how he hath hastened, where gon about, where amiss, and from that very looking behind learnt afterward to looke better before him; some wayes being so rugged, and others (through too much smoothness) as slippery, make the jorney dangerous. To looke therefore upon them who are gon so long before, may wel be for our direction, nor yet for knowing the way only, but indeed our selves, which we can scarce measure but by comparison with others; so that we had need goe sometymes abroad that coming out of a fresher aire we may judge the better of our owne close roome (otherwise we find how our very senses in such like cases are easily abus'd). Nor mervaile therfore that C. Gracchus[6] a passionat man (whilst speaking to the people) had his freind behinde him with a flute to regulate his voice, since most men are so farr from regulating them selves, as they seldome so much as know their owne errours, nor sometymes their very advantages which by another's direction they might better improve. If your Lordship now find me too blame for writing thus freely to you, 'twill be as great an errour in you to conceale it from mee. Since your Lordship has pleas'd to vouchsafe me your letters, I pray pardon me for telling you wherein they may be of most benefitt to me, wel knowing my imperfections of a far

[5] τῆς εὐσεβείας etc. "Women are most prone to piety." Pythagoras' works exist only in fragments.

[6] "C. Gracchus." The Gracchi, Tiberius and Caius, "rendered themselves famous for their eloquence, sedition, and an obstinate attachment to the interests of the populace, which at last proved fatal to them" (J. Lempriere, *A Classical Dictionary*, (1788)).

higher straine then that Spanish gentleman's, who having bin at a Bishop's table, and after his great entertainement there, upon the way back, was freindly told by the Bishop of his undecent manner of eating, tooke that, (as wel he might) farr better then all the meat he had given him.

But however this subject may be more proper for discourse then letter because of miscarriage, yet where that cannot be, certainely very much (as using a 3[r]d person) may handsomly and more deliberatly be convay'd in paper. When and in what manner your Lordship will please so farr to befreind mee, I leave to you, but for the thing it selfe, I shall earnestly begg it much rather from your Lordship then any other person that I know.

Your Lordship hath now mett with a tyme to be exercised in, and as God's judg[ments] are unsearchable and His wayes past finding out, so there is now nothing left, being not able to comprehend them, then, as 'tis sayd of the Philosopher, absolutely to resigne and throw our selves into that gulph and there to be swallowed up in it.

Letter VI

[September 24th]

Sir, You have sett me a very hard task, and therefore if I should ask longer day for it, it wer not unreasonable. But being of the same mind as I was, when I wrott last that the best, and the noblest act of the soul is that which is reflexive, I shall continu my former advice rather to seek your self within your self, then in any thing without you. You know what your pocket book saith, that a man's own mind will tell him more then seven watchmen that stand upon a tower; which though it may be tru somtimes in the way of praesaging events to com, yet the sense will best hold, and more universally, if we apply it thus, that seven watchmen, (take them in what language you will speculatores, or ἐπίσκοποι[1]) let their sight be never so sharp, and their diligence never so great, cannot discover farther into me then skin deep. My outward actions (which ar in most men personated) may fall under the survey, but that which is within (and onely is my self) is still invisible. This truth being laid, what a blind work do you invite me to. For though I can without flattery tell you (*cuius causas procul habeo*[2]) that I have not known a temper of more aequable harmony then yours, of more piety towards God, more temperance towards your self, and more freindship toward them whom you have made happy in owning them, yet when I have said all this, unless you your self can upon a nearer enquiry say so too, I have said nothing. For who knowes the thoughts of man, but the spirit of man that is within him. But this I will promise you, that wherein you shall so fail that I shall take notice of it, I shall not spare you, for there is no tru freindship, that knowes not when and where to be severe. In the mean time, the best corrective for what is past, and the best praeservative against all evill to com, is a daily inquisition upon your self: *Anima mea quid didicisti hodie ? cui vitio obstitisti? qua parte melior es* ? ar quaestions of so much use, that St. Paul might have own'd them, as well as Seneca[3]. The issu of this is, that unless you will help me to somthing that I may find fault with,

---

[1] ἐπίσκοποι. Some play is intended on the word ἐπίσκοποι which also means bishops.

[2] "Whose cause is not mine to plead."

[3] *Anima mea*, etc. "My soul, what hast thou learnt to-day? What temptation hast thou resisted?" Duppa appears to have been acting as Justinian's spiritual director, in much the same way as Jeremy Taylor did to Evelyn (see his *Diary* under date March 18th, 1655).

I must return πάντα καλῶς[4]. The patient must do so much for his phisitian, he must say where the pain lies, or else the dosis must be given at random. But since the Jesuits themselves have been denied the priviledge of receaving confession by letters, I shall by no meanes press it, but stay the time till we may be so happy as to communicate our thoughts at a nearer distance, and with more advantage. Howsoever, as long as we ar thus separated, continu to me the comfort of your letters, which I never receave without joy, nor read without being the better for them. If I have not answered your expectation in this return, condemne me not for it, for without Galilaeo's glasses[5] I cannot see spots in the moon, at least, not such as you enquire after. Your freinds in the vicinage long for your company, which I believe you find by som of their letters. My part is to pray for you, which shall not be neglected by

Your very tru freind and humble servant

S.

Sept: 24

Your letters dated the 10th cam to me the 20th.

[ENDORSED REPLY OF SIR JUSTINIAN]

I cannot but agree with you that a man's best witness is alwaies within him, as to the maine points of apparent vertue and vice, but humors and dispositions, habits, etc, the seeds of both, are often I think better observ'd by an other then a man's selfe, and best by a man's selfe when comparing with others. Not being yet so humorous, as 'tis sayd of D. Overall[5a], who sending for a physitian, and asked by him how he did, told the phisitian he sent for him to know that; who therefore presently left him, and in that as much as with another humor peradventure transported himselfe. Certainly the mind's physick as well the body's is best to be applied according to the generally accepted discoverys. 'Tis pittie that Verulam's discourse[6] *De Agricultura Animi* (as he terms it and accounts it deficient) is it selfe so short. But there (as he useth) I think he hath devided the art aright; and according to that of the buq. The knowledge of the naturall constitution; the disease, and the cure. To goe about the last without looking upon the first he conceives is as 'twere to make a garment without taking measure. A blind business indeed as your Lordship sayes. He therefore layes his foundation in the first of all, which is in the characters of dispositions. Wherein I believe a stander by may sometymes see better then a gamester. What I have collect-ed in this kind and how better furnished by your Lordship, you

---

[4] πάντα καλῶς. "All well." This phrase (in Latin and Greek) commonly occurs in connection with the returns made in episcopal or archidiaconal visitations.

[5] "Galilaeo's glasses." Galileo (1564–1642), the Italian astronomer, "succeeded in producing a telescope of threefold magnifying power", which he subsequently improved. His *Letters on the Solar Spots*, printed at Rome in 1613, was the beginning of his dispute with the ecclesiastical authorities (*Encycl. Brit.*).

[5a] "D. Overall." Dr. John Overall (1560–1619) was a Fellow of Trinity College, Cambridge, who in 1596 became Regius Professor of Theology. He was subsequently Dean of St. Paul's, Bishop of Coventry and Lichfield, and Bishop of Norwich. He was a noted scholar to whom the Authorised Version of the Bible owed much (D.N.B.). According to Fuller, he was "one of the most profound School-Divines of the *English Nation*." (T. Fuller, *The Worthies of England* (Suffolk), (1672)).

[6] "Verulam's discourse." Justinian had early been a disciple of Bacon: see Introductory Memoir.

remember. But as Plutarch writes *vita P. Aemilii*[7] [blank, *sic*.]. So doubtless the best use a man can make of such is to come home to one's selfe, nor can there be any subject more proper for a man's discourse with his freind or any culture so profitable as that of the mind which will need continuall dressing. And yet how it may be meliorated and improved, and what is to be digg'd out of it, will much depend upon observation of the manner of the soyle, what it can bare, and then what fittest. But such choice books as treate of men and their manners I find are not so easie to be understood without a more then ordinary knowledge of men first, so that we understand not men I think so well by bookes, as such bookes by the knowledge first of men. The very subject of this knowledge V. complaines we have only some few flowers but not gather'd into an art.

Surely for a man to looke into the best writers of men's lives what they have bin, then into the choicest romances what they may probably be found to bee, and examine all upon the good and sound principles of what men ought to bee, this may afford something towards such a knowledge. I have I confess, for want of other company, of late entertained my selfe with books that have much of company with Plutarch's *Lives*, the *Arcadians*, and Aristotle's *Ethicks*, as comparing many things in them. Where I find such variety if I may so call it of postures of the minde in the first, such beautifull colors in the second, lay'd upon such like and other shapes: and in the last such excellent proportion'd lines out of which both the others seeme to be rais'd: that from a due observation and laying them together, alle sculpture, drawing and painting of outward figures, however in their kinde excellent, seemes to me to afford a very meane delight in comparison of it, and I am sure nothing so usefull.

But as for the first I know none to whom I would more willingly confess, so in the latter I had rather be discovered to my selfe by your Lordship then any one person living.

Fidelia vulnera . . .
like Mrs. Car Pictures[8] [rest indicipherable].

Letter VII

[October 22nd]

Sir, I persuade my self that you ar not of that Roman's mind who said: *Dic aliquid ut duo simus*[1]; for either that sowr man had nothing of freindship in him; or if he had it was such as the contrary elements have which maintain their freindship by opposition. And therefore if I do not *reciprocare serram*, I know I shall not offend you, though I cannot satisfy you.

---

[7] "Vita P. Aemilii". Justinian has left a blank after "Aemilii" to fill in the quotation, but has not done so on the draft reply. He probably (after looking it up) added it. Lucius Aemilius Paulus (Macedonicus) was son of Lucius Aemilius Paulus (consul 216 B.C.), who fell at Cannae.

[8] "Mrs. Car Pictures". There are some nearly indicipherable words at the side of the page in the draft reply; first a Latin quotation, which begins clearly enough *Fidelia vulnera*, and may be a recollection of Proverbs XXVII, v. 6, although the Vulgate Version varies,. A.V. translates "Faithful are the wounds of a friend: but the kisses of an enemy are deceitful." Then follows a very rough passage in English which begins "like Mrs. Car Pictures." This probably was a development of the argument about the "beautifull colors." Mrs. Car = Mrs. Carlile, for whom see Letter XV, Note 3.

[1] *Dic aliquid ut duo simus*. "Say something in order that we may be two", i.e. differ. Their views usually so agreed that they were in effect one person. See also Letter LV, Note 1. Adapted from Seneca, *De Ira*, III, 8, 6.

And the truth is, I am not yet satisfied my self, what my business in this particular is, no more then the phisitian you speak of, was. For as a phisitian, setting aside som fallacious symptomes, which deceave him oft'ner then instruct him, knowes no more of his patient then he will give him leave, so a freind, though he may have som advantages, which an occasionall phisitian (being sent for onely upon som present exigence) hath not, yet all the symptoms which he judgeth by may be fallacious too. For who knowes the spirit of man, but the spirit of man that is within him? the nearest freind that is, can be but a looker on, the looker in must be my freind himself. For whereas *Totus mundus agit histrioniam*, there must needs be a great difference between that which passeth in the tiring house, and that which is acted on the stage.

Had the tract you speak of been extant, I beleive the author would have had my thoughts, that the best culture had been that which is reflexive; for to ask abroad who or what I am, is to lock up my own dores, and to enquire of my neighbor what is don at home.

But would you know what I think of you? I shall deal clearly: I think you in the first place a person religious towards God, without which foundation laid, all the superstructions, and accessories, of mathematicks, or any other part of philosophy, ar but such buildings as children make with cards, and blow them down again upon a fancy; for whatsoever the πάρεργον may be, the ἔργον,[2] the business is in this life to fitt our selves for a better. Whatsoever leads not thether, is but like the wand'rings of a traveller, who leaves the roade, and in stead of arriving to his iourney's end, is picking flowrs in som by-meadow, and is benighted before he thinkes of it. I think you besides noble, just, temperat, a man that dares be honest in ill times; that you are a good son to an aged father, a good father to your young children, a good freind to those that you will own, not onely in proffers and words, but really a freind. But then whether you be so, or no, you must ask your self, and the tru verdict must com from within. And besides, though the return from thence may be *Omnia bene*, (for there is no man, that hath not a flatterer within him) I cannot pronounce you ἀναμάρτητον[3]; for the inquisition you make must be severe; Plutarch, and Seneca, and Epictetus ar but as rush-candles, dimme lights to see by; the Scripture is our sunshine, and it is best seeing our selves by daylight. I do not press this to take you off from those innocent and (to som purposes) usefull recreations; but I am affraid of your mathematicks, that the delight you have in them may not swallow you up too much. Do but secure me of this, and I will trust you with all your schemes, and figures. I know you have now your lines sett you, and your five miles circle must contain you, till our state magicians sett you free, and therefore I shall not tempt you farther, then to keep where you ar[4]. For freindship is a magnetick that workes at distance, and as long as you afford me my wonted share in that I shall not complain of absence. I have with this letter sent you a *quelque chose*, not because it is weighty, but because it is not weighty and will not load the carrier.

---

[2] πάρεργον and ἔργον. The incidental result and the real object.

[3] ἀναμάρτητον. Innocent.

[4] The Act of Restraint became operative on October 20th, just before this letter was written. It was a renewal of the Act of February 26th, 1650, ordering delinquents and others to leave London by March 20th. By a further provision of this act of renewal, they were to report themselves in their place of residence so that they might be confined within a radius of five miles (Gardiner, I, p. 247).

Sir, let me be rememb'red in your prayers, and I will promise you, you shall have a part (if not oft'ner, at least) in my morning and evening sacrafice: which is the best and onely way left me to express my self,

Your very tru freind, and servant.

Octob: 22.

[ENDORSED REPLY OF SIR JUSTINIAN]

Since you have by expressing your thoughts of me, civilly shew'd me what I ought to be, I shall endeavour to make your words good. And humbly thanke you for still directing me to the maine. From other studies, I hope no great danger will arise, being no otherwise acquainted with them then for recreation and exercise. The mathematicks I have considered but as an instrumentall learning without which I cannot perfectly apprehend (to leave deeper speculations) not so much as that admirable C. of Aristo's *De Justitia*. But indeed finding my selfe naturally too sanguine to be of a peircing witt (however well I alwaies meant), some edge I have thought to putt to it by those arts which yet I know too much dwelt on may rather abate then sharpen. Having lived thus long I find my selfe to have seene little more then meere outsides and pleasant paintings, and never to have judged off or indeed so much as looked on those bare and true lines out of which they are raised. Sight, hearing and other senses pleas'd, but why? how? or from what proportions, I would willingly now know a little, provided it may be on easie terms, though sure to come short even of understanding what others have left. Des Cartes[5] (I beleive your Lordship heares) is lately dead in Swethland. Certainly a man that knew very much, and directed it to a good end, the benefitt of mankind. His discourse upon the passions (besides that of de la Chambre) I have lately seene in English. I returne your Lordship many thanks for the modell of *Gondibert*[6], the designe certainly both pleasant and usefull. Much of imagery I find even in its description, yet hope it is not (as buildings etc. seeme often), more pleasantly painted then in its selfe. It puts me in mind of the epick poem to which Ben Johnson[7] was encouraged by your Lordship. Though this hath already

[5] "Des Cartes." René Descartes (1596–1650), the French philosopher, was invited to Sweden ("Swethland") by Queen Christina in 1649. Upon his arrival it was arranged that he should instruct the Queen in his philosophy three times a week at five in the morning, "but the severity of the northern winter and these unusually early hours were too much for Descartes. He became ill on February 1st, 1650, and died ten days afterwards." (*Encycl. Brit.*). For his *History of the Passions of the Soul* published May 24th, 1650, and Duppa's confusion of this work with De la Chambre's *Characters of the Passions* see Letter IV, Note 2.

[6] *Gondibert*. Thomas Hobbes wrote from Chatsworth to Edward Howard, October 24th, 1668: "My judgement in poetry hath you know been once already censured by very good wits for commending Gondibert." (App. to III Report Hist. MSS. Comm. (1872), p. 291). Sir William Davenant's poem *Gondibert* was published in 1651 with a dedication to Hobbes. "This poem, on its appearance, was attacked by the wits of the day, to which the author replied" (Lowndes). "modell of *Gondibert*". This is *A Discourse upon Gondibert an Heroick Poem written by Sir William D'Avenant With an Answer to it by Mr. Hobbs. A Paris Chez Matthieu Guillemot* 1650 containing *The Author's Preface to his much honoured friend Mr. Hobbs from the Louvre in Paris, January 2nd,* 1650 and *The Answer of Mr. Hobbs to Sir William D'Avenant's Preface before Gondibert, January 10th,* 1650. Duppa discusses the "moddell" in Letter VIII.

[7] "Ben Johnson." It was Duppa who, in 1638, edited *Jonsonus Virbius*, a collection of verses by various hands in praise of Ben Jonson. There is an account of *Jonsonus Virbius* in the Oxford *Ben Jonson*, Vol. XI (1952) pages 428–9. The text is printed there pp. 429–81.

Justinian's reference to a work of Jonson, which was planned but never carried

come to moe maturity, yet such prizes have commonly the fate of great buildings, to be left imperfect with a foothing. And when all is finished they are but high lanthorns for light in respect of the true sunshine.

To give your Lordship better testimonie how I rank the duties of this life, and with all briefly my opinion of romance, I am so bold (if not vaine) to send a copy of a letter I writt not very long since to my eldest daughter, men usually advising their children to what they are very well perswaded of themselves. I pray correct what I have erred in it.

St. Augustine himselfe I find was a great gazer on those lights for a tyme, but afterward (in that golden C.10, and 7th book of his *Confessions*) he discovered another kind of light.

Now good God at what a glorious light indeed doth this Father heere point at. He that aimes at it had not need to wonder but even forgett what is behind and endeavor himselfe unto that which is before, following hard towards the marke, etc. Phill. 3, 14[8].

And now, my Lord, I hartily thank you for your remembrances of mee in your praiers, and your esteeme of mine, joyntly begging that we may (Phi. 2, 15).[9]

LETTER VIII

[NOVEMBER 13th]

Sir, As your best discourser is within you, so your best teacher is he, *Qui cathedram in caelo habet*, which made David say, I will hearken what God will say within me. Whether Pythagoras heard the musick of the sphaeres, I know not, for we can onely have a single wittness for it, and that is himself; but every man may experimentally find that unless the tumults of his passion and the noise of worldly things hinder him, he cannot but hear the Voice, which in all the passages and accidents of his life shall still cry lowd enough, "This is the way." And truly, Sir, either I am extremely deceaved in you, or I must think that however you may please yourself with recreations on the by, (and those such as ar of a finer nature, and least to do with sensuality) yet your main end, is to hearken religiously to this Voice; and your consulting with me is onely hearkening after the eccho of that which hath been first pronounced within you. I do not deny but that the best of us may have need of outward helpes; for when Plato thought our knowledge to be reminiscence, he implied withall, that the soul had need to have the seeds stirr'd up by outward objects, or else the images in it, would ly like small sparkes raked up in ashes. And if in this kind I may be of any advantage to you in that which concernes your better part, I shall assure you, *Non deerit tibi qui verum dicat*[1], which many times great Princes want.

out, is explained in the opening statement of Drummond's "Conversations", when Jonson visited William Drummond in 1618; "he had ane intention to perfect ane Epick Poeme intitled Heerologia of the Worthies of his Countrey . . . all in Cuplets." (Oxford, *Ben Jonson*, Vol. I, p. 132). This information was kindly supplied to me by Dr. Percy Simpson. Duppa was Proctor when Jonson received his honorary degree at Oxford.

[8] "I press toward the mark for the prize of the high calling of God in Christ Jesus" (A.V.).

[9] "That ye may be blameless and harmless, the sons of God, without rebuke, in the midst of a crooked and perverse nation, among whom ye shine as lights in the world."

[1] *Non deerit tibi*, etc. "There shall not be wanting to you one to tell you the truth."

Of the two Frenchmen whom you mention, the one I have not seen, the other, Des Cartes[2], I have; and though I think I know more by him, then I do by the great speculator Hobbs[3], yet when I call my self to an account, I find, I do but think so: and when I go about to tame and reduce a disordered passion (which is the onely lesson I look after) I reap but little use of it.

What *Gondebert*[4] himself may prove, I know not, but this praeface speaks him very big, especially being lined with the suffrage of his mathematicall freind, so great a distinguisher of dimensions. It seemes they have divided the two parts of logick between them, invention, and judgement. The poet carries away the one, and the mathematician the other, as it wer by a mutuall bargain resolved to commend one the other, and to act over again that passage in Horace: *Discedo Alcaeus puncto illius*[5], *&c.*

I cann no way as yet encourage you to break your circle[6], for though I see many do, yet they ar such who, having little to loose, dare venture their empty barkes in all weathers. What the πάγχρηστον mony may do, whether it may secure you, or no, I know not, but (if you would have my advice) your best way is to ride out your penance, unless som extraordinary occasion drive you to buy out a dispensation. Your lodging here will not be so fitt for you as it was, for the hangings ar gon, and the house it self is upon sale. I should be very much troubled to seek a new plantation, but my landlord's demands ar so high that I cannot com up to them, though I am willing to strein for it. But why should I trouble you with my domestichezza's as the Italian termes them? I shall pass through them as well as I can, and which way so ever I am disposed of whether heer, or else where, *Seu fors ita iusserit exul*[7], I shall still carry along with me the memory of that freindship, which you have afforded me, and remain most affectionatly yours,

BR : SAR:

Novem: 13

Your freinds heer putt in their demand to have their service presented to you.

For the continuance of your charity to your young Dromo God will requite you.

[ENDORSED REPLY OF SIR JUSTINIAN : FRAGMENTARY]

I must acknowledge your favors still multipli'd upon me for your best advise concerning the best part. All advantages are little enough since the earthly tabernacle . . .

I find your lordship's expression to ride out my penance, is to ride within my circle, which I believe I shall, notwithstanding divers of our Cavaleer Lords and others have not stuck to engage themselves beyond it[8] . . . [Rest of page torn out.]

---

[2] "Des Cartes." See Letter VII, Note 5.
[3] "Hobbs." See Letter XV, Note 4.
[4] *Gondebert*. See Letter VII, Note 6.
[5] *Discedo Alcaeus*, etc. "By his vote I am regarded as an Alcaeus." Horace, *Epist.* II, 2, 99. Horace is here speaking of the way in which poets scratch each other's backs.
[6] "Break your circle." The Act of Restraint again; see Letter VII, Note 4.
[7] *Seu fors ita*, etc. "Or as an exile if chance so ordains." Horace, *Sat.* II, 1, 59.
[8] "Engage themselves beyond it." An allusion to the fact that some Cavaliers took the Engagement (see Letter XIII, Note 1) to recognise the Commonwealth without King or House of Lords.

All the Ch.[9] ought to accord to the Roman Ch. in regard of a more powerable Principalitie **Ante Nicaenum Concilium non magno respectu Romae habebatur.* Aeneas Sylvius. *Quae sententia parti non vera est Bello.* Irenaeus communicated with the Asian Churches notwithstanding Pope Victor denounced excommunication against them.
*[Suggested reconstruction: "*Ante Nicaeanum concilium non magno respectu Roma habebatur . . . quae sententia non vera est.*"]

LETTER IX

[DECEMBER 4th]

Sir, That which I mention'd in my last letters concerning my self, was with no designe at all to make you raise any spirits under ground; for neither did I beleive you had the skill, nor could I conceave the *Inferi* wer here. But I find (and I am very much pleas'd with it) that you have so much freindship towards me, that in cases of extremity (which my present condition may probably cast me into) you ar not onely ready *monere superos* to remember me in your prayers, but to look downward too, and to seek out helpes for me, where no body else could find them. As for this particular; before the receipt of your last, I had made shift to praepare such a summe, as might well have served for the purchase of so poor a cottage, but my landlord (otherwise an ingenuous man) being a merchand, and not likely *ab arte sua discedere*, keepes still to his rate of 250*l*, (which is by the 50*l* more then I think any way it is worth) though he gives me very fair words and professeth he will by no meanes putt me to any inconvenience. Upon these termes we yet stand, but what will be the issu of it (if another offer him ten pounds more) I can easily coniecture.[1] How ever for the present, let your ἀπόκρυφα be still ἀκίνητα, and be rais'd up by no hand but your own. Upon a false fear that we had, your two boxes wer convei'd to the honest fisherman's by the water side where they yet remain. I conceave there is nothing in them of danger, but because I knew not, whether there was or no, I disposed of them. For mathematicall schemes may in these times be interpreted plots, and figures of designe[2].

Sir, I seriously thank you, for your expression of so much kindness to me; and however my condition cast me on the receaving side, and render me incapable of acting any thing, or making my returnes, I have an heart full of affection for you, and want nothing but the ability, and the occasion to express my self how really I am

Your most affectionat freind,

B.S.

Decem: 4.

---

[9] "All the Ch." etc. This is a very incomplete draft of what Justinian was going to write. He seems to be alluding to the opinion of the 15th-century scholar Aeneas Sylvius Piccolomini (afterwards Pope Pius II), and the Latin may be reconstructed: *Ante Nicaeanum concilium non magno respectu Roma habebatur . . . quae sententia non vera est.* "Before the Council of Nicaea, Rome was not held in great respect . . . which information is not true." The historical position of the See of Rome much interested Justinian, and he discussed it in letters to his friend Dr. Herbert Thorndike, mentioned later in these Letters. For the suggested reconstruction of the Latin, I am indebted to Professor E. F. Jacob, of All Souls College, Oxford.

[1] Duppa's solution of the problem of his house is found in the next letter.

[2] These two boxes, presumably containing MSS. by Justinian, had been left with Dr. Chaworth or Duppa, when Justinian hurriedly left Petersham in March, 1650. (See Letter II).

[ENDORSED REPLY OF SIR JUSTINIAN]

M[y] L[ord], I know your candor sans designe, but the truth is I cannot so well cleare my selfe who had really a designe when I felt those matters behind me, to express my selfe in that kind upon the next occasion that might require it. And though you ar not now pleas'd to accept my offer, yet your being pleas'd with the offer tells me that I have not offended in it. Your Lordship's care even of what might be misinterpreted, puts me in minde how a Pope[3] was not many ages since accounted a conjurer meerely for having some geometricall diagrams found in his study after his decease. If ignorance alone in these tymes caus'd such a suspicion, I know malice now being joyn'd to it may produce worse effects. The house where I now am as divers others in these parts have bin lately searched as for arms, but under color of it some I am sure have had their very shirts taken from them[4].

LETTER X

[DECEMBER 18th]

Sir, Since I wrott last (which I hope you have receaved) I have in my own defence, and to praevent a continuall fear of being eiected, come at last to an accomplishment of the contract for the house which hath been so long in agitation. And though I have made no use of your mony I have ventured without your consent to make use of your name, and to cause the surrender to be made to you. But because the possession is to be given in the court, where you are not likely at this time to appear in person, I have sent you inclosed a Letter of Attorney to be signed and seal'd by you, and to be returned by the next return of the carrier, the Court day being the Friday after Christmas day. There is a blank left, where I desire you would insert the name of Mr. John Michel[1] of Richmond

[3] "A Pope." This is probably Sylvester II, Gerbert d'Aurillac, Pope from 999 to 1003, "to his contemporaries a marvel of science and learning, in later legend the magician who, at the price of his own soul, purchased preferment from the Enemy and by him was at last carried off in the body." (Bryce, *Holy Roman Empire*, new edn. (1922), p. 143). Possibly John XXI (1276–77) "often referred to as a magician by ignorant chroniclers" (*Encycl. Brit.*) is meant.

[4] Lamport was still "suspect", and remained so during the Commonwealth. On May 28th, 1649, Lord Fitzwilliam had written to Sir John to say that Milton was threatened by "souldiers who (as I heare) under pretence of seeking for Levellers do committ several insolynces" (I.C. 266). But that was just after the failure of the Levellers' rising, and the capture and subsequent death of their leader William Thompson near Wellingborough. In December, 1650, the Government was more fearful of a Cavalier rising.

[1] "Mr. John Michel." In 1658 a Committee was appointed "to take a viewe of New Parke and the deere there," at Richmond by the Common Council of the City of London. "John Michell" was appointed "Clerke to the said Comitee on 8th November, 1658" and paid "13 *li* 6*s* 8*d*" "for his Attendance and entringe theire bills and Warrants for Two yeares ended at Christmas 1658." He was presumably a Richmond attorney, and may well be identical with the man whom Duppa mentions several times. It would be tempting to identify him with the Mr. Michel who, like Duppa himself, founded Almshouses in Richmond, and died in 1696 in his 84th year, but his name was Humphrey not John. Humphrey had a nephew John, who added to his uncle's endowment, and completed the houses, but he would be too late in date for Duppa's attorney. (Sir T. J. Nelson, *Richmond Park. Extracts, from the Records of Parliament and the Corporation of London* (1883), pp. 33 and 34; E. Beresford Chancellor, *The History and Antiquities of Richmond* (1894)). The Richmond registers record the birth of John Michell "son of John Michell and Bennett his wife" on August 24th, 1660, and the burial of two men called John Michell on April 13th, 1675, and August 27th, 1697. For the surrender of the house at Richmond, see Letter III, Note 6.

as your attorney to receave the seisure according to the custom of the Court.

Sir, the house is now your own, and you may make what use of it you please. I shall but keep it for you, till the times will give you leave to take your possession in person, when you will find not onely the house, but them that ar in it very much yours. As this letter is written in hast, so it requires as hasty a return of the inclosed instrument, which may yet com time enough by the next carrier, if his return be (as I think it is) upon Christmas day.

From your most affectionat freind, and humble servant

BR: S.

Dec: 18.

1651

This year saw the Commonwealth at bay. Gardiner estimates that the Government's expenditure must have been three times that of Charles I in 1625 – nearly two and three-quarter millions. Taxation had to be supplemented by sales of Crown and Church property and seventy Royalist estates were confiscated. Charles, after the campaign about Stirling, slipped into England at the head of a Scottish army to meet defeat, and narrowly escape capture after the Battle of Worcester (September 3rd). Cromwell, now at the peak of his fortunes, returned to England on September 13th, was thanked by Parliament, and became an unwelcome neighbour of Bishop Duppa at Hampton Court. Duppa calls him (Letter XXII) "the Topanta of these times." It is the only direct allusion to Cromwell in these letters.

It will be recalled that Justinian in 1650 was petitioning Scott to be allowed to visit his daughters in Suffolk, where they spent most of the troubled years of war with their great-aunt, Lady Denton, and their cousin, John Stuteville.

On February 12th (Letter XIII) the Bishop was hoping that Justinian might return to his lodgings in St. James's Park, but by March 25th (Letter XIV) he had abandoned this hope, owing to the renewal of the Act of February 26th, 1650, which was passed on March 19th, 1651, and which extended the "period of penance" till November 1st, 1651 (*Acts and Ordinances of the Interregnum* (ed. Firth and Rait, vol. III, p. lxxxiv). Justinian, therefore, continued at Lamport, occupied by the increasing infirmity of his father, who was, moreover, being "questioned by malicious men to be sequestered anew" for his part in the first Civil War.

The death of Sir John in July, however, removed both these anxieties, and Justinian then succeeded to the baronetcy. Thenceforward till 1653, the choice of a suitable wife becomes a main preoccupation.

The political tension of the year is reflected in Duppa's suggestion (Letters XV and XVIII) that letters should be addressed to his wife, but "so we censure not the State, opinions and books may be left free to us."

There are several new books referred to this year, Bishop Montagu's translation of the *Epistles of Photius*, a work by Dr. Hammond in defence of the Church, and (most important of all) Hobbes' *Leviathan*, "a monster", says Duppa, of which "Affrick hath not seen a greater". The publication of the *Leviathan* brought Hobbes back to England, and there are several subsequent allusions to him in these letters.

Letter XI

[January 8th]

Jan: 8.

Sir, The businesse which hath so long (I will not say troubled, but) entangled me, is now at an end. The matter of sale is concluded, the mony paid, the title in you, and the possession given in Court to your attorney[1]. The remainder of the business is the paying of the fine, which is not yet don, because we cannot meet with a receaver of it. Many intrigues we have had about it, which to me (who am no ordinary purchaser, this being the first, and the last which I am capable of) have been wearisom at least, and like the climbing up on a sandy hill, where the foot setts forward, and backward both at once, for so the traversing of this poor business hath proved to me. And when I have don all, it is not a place gott to live, but to dy in; which I might expect in better times, but in these wish for. As for the declaring of any trust, which you mention in your letters, I see no need of it, for I do with the same confidence deposit it with you, as they were wont to do their treasure in their temples, and think my self as safe. It is not so among the ἀδύνατα,[2] but possibly we may once more meet together, and then this nothing may be farther debated. It is enough for the present, that you have lent me your name, which in passing the fine, had likely to have been costlier to me, then you ar aware of. Your freinds here, wish you the happiness of a new year, which we ar not likely to enioy much of our selves. And so with my daily prayers for you, I rest as you shall ever find me,

Your tru freind, and humble servant,

B.S.

[Endorsed reply of Sir Justinian]

The difficulties you have struggled with in your late purchase give you now at length a tast of the world's entanglements, that you may the better value the quiet hitherto enjoyed. And now you have bought, I see you so consider the σχῆμα of the world as not to seeme possessing, but as if gott from the stage you have only pay'd for a box to sitt in; and if to dy in as your Lordship sayes, yet *subsilire in astra ex hoc angulo licet.* Butt whether the times be so bad as to make your wish seeme good, pardon me if with Seneca *Plus momenti apud me habent, qui ad mortem veniunt sine odio vitae. et admittunt illam, non attrahunt*[3]. It is not impossible but with old Simeon you may say your *Nunc Dimittis* upon a better occasion, and that after you have seene the Pers[4]. My mention of declaring a trust was only in case I might dy suddenly. I hope ere long, if not reorder'd to the contrary, to visit you (and as often as I can) from London; but for any stay, my dayly occasions will not permitt, and therefore desire no alteration at all in the chamber as for mee. Since the py is so

---

[1] See Letter x, Note 1 for the attorney, and Letter iii, Note 6 for the proceedings of the Court.

[2] ἀδύνατα="impossibilities."

[3] The two quotations:

(*a*) *Subsilire in astra*, etc. "From this corner of the world one may be transported to the stars." Seneca, *Epist.* xxxi, 11. The correct wording is: "*Subsilire in caelum ex angulo licet.*"

(*b*) *Plus momenti*, etc. "Those people, who approach the time of their death without any hatred of life and take it for granted are higher in my estimation." Seneca, *Epist.* xxx, 15.

[4] "the Pers[on]." King Charles II.

wel approved on, my girles shall be apprentices to the old cook rather then the art shall dy with him, or you faile of it. Your Lordship's complaint of the cold weather tells mee these two caps of hare . . ., which I now send, will not come unseasonably to you.

Letter XII

[January 22nd]
Jan: 22

Sir, If the rest of the year be answerable to the leading day, I shall not want the kindness of my freinds this year, for you have begun it with such a present[1] as might have been rather a bribe to som potentate of the times, then a gift of love and charity (for there is a mixture of both in it) to a man upon the lees, and dregs of fortune, as I am. But you do like your self, and have more pleasure in the courting of the affliction of your freinds, then in the larding of the prosperity of others. I do not know whether I may be thought to exceed or no, in my expressions, but the very plain truth is the py is so excellently good, that it might pose the rhetoritians that have wrote περὶ ὑψοῦς[2] to find figures suitable to it. But to say no more, it is the best we ever did eat (for I speak more iudgements then my own) and your pastry man, though he hath not so many languages as Mr. Boncle, hath so good an hand, and judgement in seasoning that had he lived in the old times, neither Plutarch, nor Athenoeus[3] would have forgotten him. And since my rememb'ring him can conduce little, I must leave him to your rewarding of him, and wish he may live to do you service long. And having said this, you may thank the cold weather, that I trouble you with no longer a letter, or more panegyricks of the py, which will be best commended by eating, and therein we shall not fail. Sir, I am

Your very thankfull, and humble servant,
Br: S.

Letter XIII

[February 12th]

Sir, Whether this letter may find you in St. James his Park, (as som reports make probable) or whether it must travail with the Northamptonshire carrier, the argument of it must not vary; for you will aequally be distant from me wheresoever you are, if it be where letters may reach you. The freindship will be the same, and the degrees of that ar not to be measured by the scale of miles. However, touching the report, I have no

[1] The question of the house at Richmond was finally settled by Justinian buying it for the Bishop. In his will, dated February 4th, 1661/2, of which there is a contemporary copy at Lamport, Duppa left "My House at Richmond purchased in Sir Justinian Isham's name I do give it to my wife during her life, and after to Dr. Chaworth [his nephew] and after his death to Sir Charles Cleaver's lady and her heires." Lady Cleaver (Briana Salter) was his great-niece (See App. A).

[2] περὶ ὑψοῦς. This is the title of the treatise "Of the sublime" which used to be ascribed to Longinus.

[3] "Athenoeus." Athenaeus of Naucratis in Egypt was a Greek rhetorician and grammarian who flourished about the end of the 2nd century and beginning of the 3rd century A.D. He was the author of *Deipnosophistae*, a storehouse of miscellaneous information, chiefly on matters concerned with the table. (*Encycl. Brit.*)

easiness of belief that you will anticipate the period of your penance[1] unless some exigence of your affairs require it, and the state will give you leave to make a broken sentence of it; for otherwise you runne a hazard, and though many empty pockets walk safely here, yet you ar looked upon as having such a purse, as may invite a robber, especially such as act with priviledge *sub magno latrocinio*[2]. I do not suggest this to keep you longer from these parts then your own safety requires, for I have not yet learnt to be so much an enemy to my self as to use meanes to debarr my self from the company I am so much pleas'd with. But I confess I am more pleas'd to see you have so much master'd your self, as to run through this year of mortification with so much quietness, and acquiescence of mind, that I do not remember that any of your letters (I speak onely of those to me) are guilty of so much as one complaint, or grone for it. And to deal ingenuously with you, all circumstances consider'd, I beleive you will tell me when we meet that this hath been a year of triall to you, and however the forced obedience to a command (that must not be dallied with) may lessen the merit of the work, I am very prone to attribute much to you, in that you have without strugling, or labouring for a bought dispensation, subdued your self so farr, as to bear hansomly, what you could not avoid. I find by your last letters, that upon your return, London must be your centre, and the motions therefore that you make towards us, excentricall onely and upon the by. Nor will I any way quarrel with you upon it, for the pleasing your self, and your intending that which most concernes you shall abundantly satisfy me where ever you ar.

Onely there will be som kind of morall convenience, and fittness in it, that being now my landlord you should not prove alltogether a stranger to me least it be over hastily discovered, that I have onely acted a scene in this business, and made use of the name of a person, that will not own me. There is still a chamber here, that will be the better for your beeing in it, and when your more busy affairs will afford you a breathing time, I do not know where you can breath better aire, or with a freind who more highly valews you then

Your most humble servant,
BR: SAR:

Richm:
Feb: 12.

LETTER XIV

[March 25th]

Sir, Since I wrott last to you (which is above a month past) I have not receav'd any return from you. And to say the truth, I did the less expect it because I have been all this time in expectation of somthing better (the enioying of your company), thinking it possible there might have been

[1] "Period of your penance." The Act of February 26th, 1650 had been renewed and extended by the Act of October 20th, but Duppa is hoping that the year of restraint will soon end, and that Justinian would be able to return to his lodgings near St. James's Park, which were kept by Henry Cogan, translator, of whom we shall hear more.

[2] *Sub magno latrocinio.* This is an allusion to the phrase in St. Augustine's *De Civitate Dei* Book IV § 4, where he says "Justice being taken away, what are kingdoms, but great robberies? (*nisi magna latrocinia*)". (Trans. Dods (1871), Vol. I, p. 139). (For this suggestion I am indebted to Sir George Clark).

som small time indulged for honest men to have seen one the other. But it seemes, our Governors think us not humbled enough to be capable of such a favor, and therefore they double their stripes, and renue their punishments, as usurers do their bonds from six monthes to six monthes[1]. But as this hath for the present blasted my hopes of seeing you, so it hath revived my desires of hearing from you, which if you shall please to satisfy, you may give very much content to him, who hath little else of that kind left him, but your freindship. I write the less, because your long silence leaves me in doubt where this letter may find you. I am still quiet in your cottage, and never enioy'd my self more, or the world less. And so having sent this paper rather as a spy (to bring me som intelligence back) then as a letter, I hasten it the more for a dispatch, and remain not alltogether out of hope but that I may once again hear from you, and be own'd by you as

Your very humble servant
BR: S.

Richm: March 25.

[ENDORSED REPLY OF SIR JUSTINIAN]

Not many houres after your Lordship's was writt I beleive that mine instead of my selfe came to kiss your hands. I now find that to faile of a man's expectation is to the minde as that motion of missing a step, or loose-ing (as we say) a man's arme, to the body. Had not the restraint bin reserv'd till the last day I should not have made that account with my self as I did at least to have visited your Lordship, but now they have gott in to the sadle they will have us so managed as to stop at an instant. I confess my selfe somewhat discompos'd and should have thought Seneca and Epictetus a couple of dunces had they mist of what I aim'd at, without regret. I love not to show passion but cannot now forbare troubling my freinds in sending out a little rather then with keeping it all in, to trouble my selfe to much. The content your Lordship is pleas'd to take in hearing sometimes from me is that which must now preserve me. Heere I find variety of cares coming in troopes upon me. My father[2] though very infirme and at this instant questioned by malicious men to be sequestred anew. My children growne to woemen, and my selfe now finding a perfector demonstration by those lines coming into my face, then all that mathemeticians could ever yet show. Their yeares call for h[us-bands] as they for por[tions], my selfe though yet single yet in a manner necessitated to marrie. Now whether I am not to encounter with . . . I pray judge.

---

[1] On March 19th, 1651, an Act confirming and continuing the Act of February 26th, 1650 was passed. This was to continue the exclusion of delinquents, etc., from the capital till November 1st, 1651.

[2] "My father." Sir John Isham, 1st Bart, had succeeded his father at Lamport at the age of twenty-three in 1605. He was thus, by 17th century standards, an old man at 68. His known attachment to the King had already meant many fines and indignities. Abraham Cornish of Nottingham prosecuted Sir John Isham and William Cooper of Pytchley for help which they had given to Holt House, when it was a Royalist garrison. The Nevill family of Holt, Leicestershire, had suffered already severely for their attachment to the Royal cause. Only Sir John's death in July saved him from these new proceedings. (*Calendar of the Proceedings of the Committee for Compounding*, Pt. I, p. 486 and *Calendar of the Committee for Advance of Money*, Pt. III, p. 1314; for the Nevills, Henry, and his two sons, and their part in the Civil War see Nichols, *History and Antiquities of the County of Leicester* (1798), Vol. II, Pt. II, p. 276).

May your Lordship still enjoy your self; I am confident so much the more by how much less the world . . . I must be an actor in it, and very likely to be often out . . . Your Lordship may do me a favor sometimes to prompt . . .

Letter XV

[April 8th]

Sir, I was flattered with a kind of waking dream of mine own, that the twentieth of March might have been an Epocha, from whence we might have computed the return of our freinds. But I am now taught that we are still under the Hegira of Mahomet, and must continue to reckon from their flight, not from their return[1]. It is well, in the mean time, that we ar, first, rational creatures, and can therefore reflect so much the more vigorously upon obiects absent; and next, that by being good Christians, and placing our affections (according to that rule) on things that we do not see, we may learn from thence, to continue love to our freinds, though the iniquity of the times keepes us asunder.

The motion of the Commissary[2] renew'd arouses a great zeal of doing service to the person whom he recommends to you for your choice. And in this, I confess, I cannot blame him for having a desire to make his freind happy. For had I either freind, or daughter that I thought worthy of you, I should fall into the same error that he doth; and pursue you as eagerly; for though it must be your part to chuse, there is still left a

---

[1] See Letter xiv., Note 1.

[2] "The Commissary." This is Thomas Jay "of Middls Esq in thes unhappy warrs his Maties Comissary Generall for Pvisions for all his Armye of Horse" as he is described on his wife's monumental brass in Richmond Church. (A. Cecil Piper, *History of Richmond Parish Church* (1947)). On March 5th, 1650/1 Thomas Jay wrote from Thornton, Middlesex, about a possible bride for Justinian "a widdow" and "an old English Christian" (I.C. 275). This is the first of possible brides mentioned for Justinian, with which subject many subsequent letters are concerned. On the back of Thomas Jay's letter, Justinian has written the draft of a reply which shows the effect of the new Act of March 19th, and further explains why he did not visit Richmond as expected (Letter xiv).
"Sir. You did rightly apprehend the occasion of my not coming as yet towards Richmond and I am sure ere this are acquainted with a new Act which now puts off my intentions of being there this month. And when I shall can give no assurance. I acknowledge myselfe much disadvantaged by being first torne away and now kept from so good a man so good a friend as you there know [i.e. Duppa] (but must be content to converse at distance). I doubted not at first your being very well satisfied in what you pleased to recommend to me. But now you have sent me a picture wherein I see the advantage your pen has over any pencill whatsoever having made all that which it can express but a faire curtaine which you have doubly drawne and given a view of a far fairer prospect with in. And truly as painters shew a lively image of their owne spiritt by drawing but the outward features of others so is yours expressed to me in a compleater draught. Sir your wishes so good and so well sett forth challenge my best thanks to you and indeed those are all I can send in answer to you. The jealousy of the present tyme and my Father's being very infirme makes my condition so uncertaine that I shall not propose anything that may prejudice another through their neglecting of better opportunities but shall be ever ready to embrace any wherein I may express my selfe as I am your affec. ser. J.I." Not unnaturally after this letter, nothing more is heard of Thomas Jay's eligible widow "in heygth decently exalted above the usual size" whose "members, that are for publique view are answerable ministers to the graces of an alluring beauty."

Duppa's connection with Thomas Jay dated back to the Civil War, for in John Ashburnham's accounts of money received for the King 1642–3 is this entry:
"From the Bishopp of Sarum for Mr. Jay . . . 0050.00.00"
(*A Narrative by John Ashburnham*, Vol. ii, Appendix, p.x).

liberty of proposing, and till the choice be made, there is no iniury done to give you a longer feild to chuse in.

Your reprobate boy is come back to his untoward father, and his end will be instead of the good education which he might have had with you to learn his vices.

I fear your letters somtimes have a stopp, because they come without superscription; the commerce that we have is so innocent, that we need not fear to own one the other. You may, if you please, direct them to my wife, as a person whose name will not so probably tempt the opening.

But that I beleive you have intelligence of all sorts, I should venture on the particular of books, which I somtimes hear of, but selldom have the sight of, unless som very good freind supplies me. I will not say, that I want you in this particular, for that wer to imply, that I want you in nothing else, but my lesson must be to know how to want, who have formerly had the happiness to know how to abound.

This morning hath drawn me out of my winter retreat and I have gon upon the strength of it to visit our freinds at the foot of the Hill,[3] where

---

[3] "Our freinds at the foot of the Hill." This is the Carlile family of Petersham, with whom Justinian stayed when in the Richmond area 1649–50. They occur many times in the Letters, although they are nowhere mentioned by name except in Letter VI endorsed reply, see Note 8 and Letter LXXII, see Note 1. They are often referred to as "my neighbors of the Park," and their identification provided one of the major problems of the Letters. I was at first inclined to think that Lady Dysart of Ham was intended, but the mention of a daughter of marriageable age in 1658 made this impossible. The final identification was due to Miss Margaret Toynbee.

The task was made the more difficult, because although the Dictionary of National Biography contained short notices of both Lodowick Carlile and his wife Joan, it was not appreciated that the two were husband and wife; possibly because the spelling adopted for Lodowick was that used in his published plays, "Carlell", and Joan was described as "Anne"—a mistake dating back to the 18th century. As both husband and wife are minor personalities of some importance to Stuart drama and painting, the subject is fully treated in an article in *The Burlington Magazine* (1954). A summary will suffice. Lodowick Carlile (or Carlell), whose father was Master Huntsman to James VI, and accompanied the King to England in a similar capacity, became "Gentleman of the Bows" to King Charles I, and Groom of the Privy Chamber to Queen Henrietta Maria. His first play, *The Deserving Favorite* (1629), was dedicated to William Murray and Thomas Cary, the former of whom was the father of Lady Dysart of Ham House. Several of his plays were performed at Court, and in the Prologue to the second part of the *Passionate Lovers* (1638), he alludes to *his* passion for hunting. He became "keeper of the deer", at Richmond, and was assigned Petersham (Old) Lodge as a residence. This stood just inside the Park opposite what is now the Dysart Arms. It was known as "Mr. Cole's house", and was rebuilt on a grander scale by Lawrence Hyde, Earl of Rochester, in the last years of the 17th century. This house was burnt in 1721, and a third house on the same site, built by the Earl of Harrington in 1733–34, was pulled down in 1834. He married, in 1626, Joan Palmer, the daughter of William Palmer, paymaster of the staff of St. James's Park, a position he probably held through his nephew Sir Thomas Overbury. She was a painter of some repute in her day, who appears in several works of reference as "Anne or Anna Carlile." During and after the Civil War, the Carliles continued to live at Petersham, and appear to have had various Cavaliers as lodgers. In the *Knyvett Letters* (ed. B. Schofield, Norfolk Record Society, Vol. xx, 1949), Thomas Knyvett describes to his wife how he sojourned at the Carliles' "country house." "Thay will furnish with all necessaryes but linning" (Letter 48, May 18th, 1642). Thomas Knyvett was sequestered in May 1644, but stayed at Petersham to try to get his case reviewed, and in letters about that time, expressed his gratitude to the Carliles "for truly, out of my owne home and barr'd of thy companye, better I cannot wish mye self." While at Petersham, he met and was entertained by the Murrays at Ham House. Justinian Isham also lodged there in 1649, when engaged on his "composition" dispute. There is a curious picture at Lamport of a gaily-dressed company at a

I find earnest inquiries after you, for though there is now an alteration in the company, yet there is still an aire of the same freindship left, and they that possibly do not know you, love you for their sakes that do.

But as my intention was not to have wander'd so farr when I began my walk, so neither did I think to have used so many wordes, when I began this letter. I am secure in the mean time that you will think nothing too much that proceedes from so hearty affection, as must allwaies be due to you from,

Your tru freind, and humble servant
BR: SAR:

Apr: 8.

If I somtimes omitt the remembrances of your freinds, it is not their fault, nor mine, who persuade my self, you cannot possibly imagin, that you ar forgotten here.

[ENDORSED REPLY OF SIR JUSTINIAN]

We see those things which have bin folded up for a long tyme gather a crest and ly flatter then at first; some such thing I fancie to my selfe after my continuance here, but upon thoughts of returne to your Lordship, I found my selfe as 'twere open'd anew and unfolded, but now it seems 'twas only to be shaked and lay'd up again.

I think our booke intelligence may be very inoffensive and shall much desire to know what passes in the Republic of Letters, especially from your Lordship, so great a judge in it. Mr. Hobbes[4] now stands high and much look'd on, both in Latin and English. Somewhat (I know not what, but only heare) he hath lately put foıth. That *de Cive* and *de Homine* I think may serve for men to chew upon a while. His aime to demonstrate the nature of man and of human actions as distinctly as the mathematicians have don that of quantity in geometricall figures is the highest reach of man's witt. I find he diggs very deepe (as he had need) to lay his foundation; however he fares among philosophers, the divines and civilians being sure to question his superstructure for their severall faculties. Mr. Selden's booke[5] lately come forth I have only

Staghunt, which was probably painted by Mrs. Carlile, and represents her and her husband and family, with Justinian Isham.

As these Letters reveal, other lodgers in the Commonwealth period were Lucy, Lady Carlisle, the 2nd Earl of Chesterfield, and Gilbert Sheldon. In 1654, the Carliles removed to London, in order to give Mrs. Carlile greater opportunities for painting, but they returned to Petersham in 1656, and at the Restoration, Lodowick was granted an annuity of £200 by Charles II (which seems to have been irregularly paid), and confirmed in his old offices, including that of "Gentleman of the Bowes in ordinary to His Majesty." His son James became "serjeant of the hounds of his R.H. the Duke of York". Lodowick died in London, and his will, made on July 26th, 1675 was proved September 25th, 1675. His wife survived him. Her will, in which she mentions several of her pictures, including the "Princesse in white Sattin," was made on December 3rd, 1677 (with codicil December 31st 1678) and proved August 17th, 1681. She was buried at Petersham February 27th, 1678/9, beside her husband.

[4] "Mr. Hobbes." Thomas Hobbes of Malmesbury, the philosopher (1588–1679). Like Duppa, he had a hand in Charles II's education. His *Humane Nature* and *De Corpore Politico* were published in 1650, and his *De Cive* in English in 1651. His works are frequently discussed in this correspondence: see especially July 14th and 30th, 1651; August 1st, 1654; January 24th, 1655.

[5] "Mr. Selden's booke." John Selden (1584–1654), according to Milton "the chief of learned men, now living in this kingdom," is also several times discussed in these letters: see especially Letter LX. In 1650, he passed through the press the first part of his *De Synedriis et Praefecturis Juridicis Veterum Ebraeorum.* This must be the work here alluded to by Justinian.

heard of and how little he allows now to excommunication. What amongst these late philosophies and the Erastian and Socinian opinions too much in request, I doubt the Church is likely to be stript by learned hands which seemes sadder to mee then all her sufferings from the rabble. Mr. Stephens[6] hath desired me to convey a letter and some papers to your Lordship which till now I could not so conveniently send; his head is still working and now upon an argument, as Mr. Mede[7] would say.

LETTER XVI

[APRIL 15th]

Sir, I perceave it is not so hard to hitt letters, as to hitt faces[1] after a meal, for I had no sooner look'd toward you in my last letters, but within an hour after (as it happen'd before on the last return) I found by yours that you look'd again toward me. I have read formerly among the school men, that the conversation the angels have, is in such a spiritual way, as mutually to be don by thoughts, and their language to be nothing else, but an inward act of their will, by which they open themselves one to the other. It wer well, as the times are, that we had the like, not onely, that innocent commerce may possibly be dangerous but that we might order our returnes as we would our selves, and upon all emergencies have them either sooner or later as we stand in need of them. But we that have gross bodies of flesh, must trust to the carriers' packets, and communicat our thoughts as we can, since we cannot as we would.

You have given me so high an example of your patience in passing your last year of restraint, that I reckon you no longer among the proficients, but among the perfect, and such a one as could have restored out of your own principles a Seneca, and an Epictetus though they had been lost; for though you make use of their names[2], I know your anchor is cast within the vail, and though worldly thinges may shake you, yet it is with so slight a trepidation that discompose you they cannot, no more then bodies, which moving about their centers, still keep the same place. As for your three great enemies, since there is no likelyhood of absolutely routing them, the next consideration in point of prudence is how to deal with them so that they may not rout you. The first you mention is the cares of the world, which, though they choak many a soul, I am secure, that yours is not likely to be hurt by them; the next is your being necessitated to marry, to which if you had given the name of convenience, I should have better have understood it; but I know you ar no stoick, and having your αὐτεξούσιον about you, I am persuaded you ar in no such pressing necessities but that you can take time enough to make a good choice; but concerning the last of the three, I confess I know no other fence you have but either discretion to avoid, or patience to endure, and when no other remedy will serve for redeeming of vexation to have in readiness a morsell for Cerberus, rather then to part with all.

---

6 "Mr. Stephens." For Jeremiah Stephens see Letter IV, Note 7.

7 "Mr. Mede." Joseph Mede (or Mead) (1586–1638) was Justinian's old tutor at Cambridge. For the relations between the two men see the Introductory Memoir of Justinian. Mede was apparently a kinsman of Bishop Duppa.

1 "Hitt faces". Cf. Ben Jonson in the first folio (1623) of Shakespeare "O, could he but have drawne his wit As well in brasse, as he hath hit his face." See also Letter XXXIV, Note 1.

2 "Their names." In his reply to the Bishop's letter of March 25th, Justinian has mentioned Seneca and Epictetus. It is to this letter that the Bishop now replies.

I hear of a book (but I onely hear of it) of animadversions, and observations upon Sir W. Raleigh's *History of the World*[3], and imagin it may be that, which you long ago told me was undertaken by Virgilius Evangelizans, but (as I remember) under the nature of an epitome. I beleive, if it be his, he hath praesented you with one, and therefore I desire you would let me know your judgement of it; for though I have no mony to buy, I still labour under a curiosity of inquiring. Sir, you have my daily prayers, and I still am

Your most humble servant,
BR: SAR:

Richm: Apr: 15.

LETTER XVII

[MAY 7th]

Sir, I would not have you be so partiall to me as to take this for a letter, but rather as an accquittance and an acknowledgement that I have receaved yours. The truth is, I am not certain whether this paper will com time enough to be convei'd by the carrier, for I find, if I do not write on the Tuesday, that commonly they come not to your hands till the week after, and this last Tuesday upon occasion proved a busy day to me, and I am not very clear now; but being unwilling to break, I have chose rather to make a return of few wordes, then none.

I can give you little account of the books you mention, being *de lodice paranda sollicitus*[1]; for instead of buying bookes, I am now selling some. Your old friend Mr. Aldridge[2] hath been so kind to me as to send me the *Logick* you mention[2a], (and interpreting it to be done for your sake, I must lay it upon your score to thank him for it) but the book lay so little a time in my hands that I onely had a superficiall view of it, yet so farr as to perceave that he hath little new, but new termes, and in this hath rather imitated the fancyes of my Lord Bacon, then his judgement in that which

[3] In 1650, Alexander Ross, who in 1634 had published *Virgilius Evangelizans*, published an abbreviation of Sir Walter Raleigh's *History of the World* (*The marrow of Historie first set out at large by Sir W. Raleigh, and now abreviated by A.R.* 12 mo.) and in 1653, *Some Animadversions and Observations upon Sir W. Raleigh's Historie of the World*. He therefore wrote both an epitome and observations on Raleigh's book. The *Animadversions and Observations* was not published till 1653, but it will be noticed that the Bishop has only "heard" of the book, and it must have been in preparation. Possibly Dr. Henchman, who was in touch with the Bramshill household, had informed the Bishop. The Revd. Alexander Ross (1591–1654), described by Wood as "a busy various and voluminous writer" (*Ath. Ox.*, Vol. I (1721), p. 439), was a Scotsman, chaplain in ordinary to King Charles I, Rector of All Saints, Southampton, and Vicar of Carisbrooke, Isle of Wight, in two of which capacities he must have been well known to Duppa. He was ejected from his preferments by the Puritans and went to live at Bramshill, Hants, with his patron, Andrew Henley, son of Sir Robert Henley, Master of the King's Bench. Here he died February 24th, 1654 and was buried at Eversley, where he has a monument, with a Latin epitaph of his own composition. Eversley was to have another (and more famous) literary figure associated with the Church in the 19th century—Charles Kingsley. In Letter XXVII, we are to meet him again in other than a literary capacity. (Walker, *V.C.H. Hants.*, Vol IV).

[1] *De lodice*, etc. "Worried about the purchase of a blanket", i.e. poor as a church-mouse. Juvenal, *Sat.* VII, 66. The original has *attonitae* (*mentis*) not *sollicitus*.

[2] "Mr. Aldridge." See Letter I, Note 2.

[2a] "The logick you mention." This is, perhaps, Robert Fage, *A Compendium of Logick and Rhetorick in the English Tongue . . . with Plain Directions for the more easie understanding and practice of the same.* London (1651).

is more substantiall; but Mr. Morris[3] (who payes me his weekly visit) had the book from me, and therefore I will pronounce nothing peremptorily till I have farther weigh'd it.

If my cosin Stephens[4] com in your way, I pray thank him in my behalf, both for his letter, and his papers; I know his intentions ar very good, but I am so ignorant my self, that I can iudge little of the vialls in the Revelation. And though I had allwaies an haesitancy, and coldness that way, I have of late contracted a greater habit of it, by finding the strange confidence that severall men have, in their different, and contrary expositions. And one accident in particular hath much confirmed me in my ἐποχή. The story is this. There was lately with me a person of very good learning, and with all of a most humble, and modest carriage, who brought me a treatise of his concerning Antichrist, desiring me that I would deal clearly with him, and upon the perusall give my judgement of it. I so farr startled at the argument, as to let him know I was a very unfitt judge of it, having a kind of praeiudice against all former attempts that had been made that way. But this would not serve the turn; read it I must. But being resolved to deal ingenuously, I told him plainely that though he had drawn something very like Antichrist, and had made a shift to fitt all proper texts of Scripture to it, yet I was no way convinced, that it was any other then a cloud in the sky, which som strong fancy might take to be a lyon, and others of as strong an imagination think to be a calf. And therefore advised him, (since he had fix'd upon a person now in being for his Antichrist)[5] he would lett this treatise of his sleep by him for a year, or two, by which time something might happen, that might either undeceave him, or confirm him farther. Upon my mentioning a year, or two, he replied with some trouble in his countenance: "But what if the world shall not last so long, shall not I now *liberare animam*, and point out the Antichrist? and last so long (saith he) I am confident it will not." I had not much to say to the contrary but it might be so, for every body might see that the world was now drawn low, and in the dreggs, little being now left, but the tartar of it, or (as the chimists speak) the *terra damnata*. But withall I told him, that it was a secret which God had seal'd up, when that day, and year should be, and this being not reveal'd to Christ Himself as man, I could not look that any flesh and bloud besides should be made acquainted with it. Upon this we parted, leaving one the other unsatisfied. And thus farr hath this impertinent story drawn me on, which I would not conceal from you; for though the generall day of judgement, may be of a date farther off then either the old Broughtons, or the new

---

[3] "Mr. Morris." William Morris (or Morice) (1602–76) was an M.P. excluded in Pride's Purge, who was knighted at the Restoration. He was High Sheriff of Devonshire in 1651, and is therefore unlikely to be the person here mentioned. (D.N.B.) "Mr. Morris" is mentioned again on February 8th, 1658. He may or may not be identical with this man. See Letter XCVIII and Note 5.

[4] "My cosin Stephens". For Jeremiah Stephens see Letter IV, Note 7. We learn from this letter that he was a kinsman of Bishop Duppa.

[5] "Antichrist" and "a person now in being". Possibly the allusion is to Cromwell, who in May 1650 returned to England after breaking the back of Irish resistance, and in September defeated the Scots at Dunbar. Though "the crowning mercy" of Worcester was still in the future, Cromwell's position was such that he alone might have been selected by this "person of very good learning", whom it is not possible to identify, as Antichrist.

Sedgewicks[6] have placed it; yet our praeparation to receave that day with joy cannot be too soon made, not knowing how soon every man's particular day of judgement may call him away. Had not this story com in my way, you had at this time receaved fewer wordes from me, but *currente rota urceus exivit in amphoram*[7].

Sir, I am,

Your most tru friend and beadsman to pray for you.

BR: S.

Richm: May 7.

[ENDORSED REPLY OF SIR JUSTINIAN]

Your knowledge of the world and men as wel as books will not suffer you so easily I see to assent unto cell-bred opinions. The troth is if a man do but consider the globe of the world with its many and vast nations to which we seeme so small a spot, 'twould make one very cautious how they applied the mysteries of the Revelation unto this angle, but for a man to point out a particular person in it for an AntiCh[rist] I think is to make him selfe to be pointed at indeed. Many such we have had who once thoroughly possesst with some few notions have made the Scripture chime strangely to their fancies. This your Lordship can best observe whose converse having bin so much abroad hath made as cleare a discovery to you of such *idola specus*, as your knowledge in books doth of the *idola fori.*[8]

LETTER XVIII

[JUNE 17th]

Sir, If I can but preserve the main (for letters ar but things upon the by) I shall have little to complain of. For I have a strong persuasion, that though all the letters had been lost (which have mutually past between us) the freindship had been the same, and being a morall, and immateriall fire, might have lasted, though the fewell of letters had been intercepted. And yet I am so much in love with yours, that though I am sure of the substance, I must count it a kind of loss to loose the shadowes of it. The best is, our commerce is innocent, and whosoever lights upon our letters, must strangely torture them, before they will cry guilty; so we censure not the State, opinions and books may be left free to us, for *Nulli gravis est percussus Achilles.*[1] As for the disagreeing of the superscription of the letter from the person designed within, there can be the less danger, because we have so much authority on our side as to justify it before any Committee, that really we ar but one, and ar never likely to take the advantage of Milton's book, or be divorced for want of complacence.[2].

[6] "Old Broughtons, and new Sedgewicks." Hugh Broughton (1549–1612), a rabbinical scholar, published in 1596 *A Concent of Scripture* in which he attempted to settle the biblical chronology. William Sedgwick (1610?–69?), puritan divine and mystic, of Pembroke College, Oxford, was chief preacher at Ely 1644–60; after the Restoration, he conformed (D.N.B.).

[7] *Currente rota*, etc. "When the wheel turns, the jar comes out as a pitcher." Horace, *Ars. Poet.*, 21-2. The metaphor is drawn from a potter, who starts making a wine jar, which turns out to be in fact a pitcher: *Amphora coepit institui: currente rota cur urceus exit.*

[8] *Idola specus* and *idola fori.* These are two leading sources of error described in Bacon's *Novum Organum.*

[1] *Nulli gravis est*, etc. "Nobody minds if Achilles gets a whack." Juvenal, *Sat.* I, 163.

[2] "Milton's book." John Milton's *Judgement of Martin Bucer on Divorce* was published in 1644.

I am troubled for you in the behalf of your Anchises[3], but it is som satisfaction both to you, and those that love you, that you ar upon the place, and present with him to provide that nothing be wanting to him, especially in that which may concern his better part; wherein your piety may be of the greatest advantage to him. And for that part of it which you have committed to me, I shall not fail in my prayers for him. But *firmandus est animus in omnem eventum*, and he that is full of dayes, and hath lived formerly in so much happyness, and reputation in his country, doth not so properly dy, as go out of this life *tamquam satur e convivio.* It is tru the times have afforded him a sowr banquet to close it up; but yet there may be an advantage in that too to strengthen him for his end; for what good patriot can be loth to dy, *cum patriam ipsam ante se mortuam viderit.* I did not intend to have troubled you in looking on this other side of the paper; but I find I have no such command of my self, as to end when I would, for the truth is, I would not end; but as night, (when we wer present), was only wont to part us, so, as long as I am waking, I still think I have somthing more to say. And truly so I have, but I remember your Horace hath a piece of a character which I would fain own, *dicenda, tacendaque, callet.*[4]. And therefore I say no more, but that which I must never unsay, that I am,

Your very tru freind, and humble servant,
B.S.

June: 17.

Sir, I do not well remember, whether in my last I desired you, when my cosin Stephens[5] cam in you way, to thank him for his letter to me, with Parker's copy, and the animadversions upon it. I confess my ignorance, that I am very unable to judge either of the whole matter, or of the distributed particulars, the vialls, and seals, and trumpets. But I beseech you, thank him in my behalf, and let him know that I understand his kindness though not his argument, and shall find a time by letter to himself to signify as much to him.

[ENDORSED REPLY OF SIR JUSTINIAN]

I no sooner mett with that expression your Lordship pleas'd to give our freindship, a morall fire, but I was willing also to think that our knowledge (at least) of such a freindship might be immortall. 'Tis true, as our letters, so we ourselves who write them continue but for a tyme, and yet uncertain how little a tyme that is, but most sure it cannot be very long; my selfe though the younger finde nothing, no, not amongst all the geometricall lines, more perfectly demonstrated then by those lately come into my face. So that were there no warrs, no casualtie, no vexation, yet nature in silent and soft motions formes her course, and *obrepit* (for the most part) *non int* [*ellecta*] *senectus.*[6]

[3] "Your Anchises." Anchises was the aged father of Aeneas (Virgil's hero), whom he rescued from the flames of Troy. For Sir John Isham see Letter XIV, Note 2. Sir John, who was High Sheriff of Northants. in 1611–12, was created a baronet in 1627, having been previously knighted by King James in 1608. On June 28th, 1651, Elizabeth Isham (Justinian's daughter) wrote from Suffolk to Justinian: "The Ladys are very glad to heare my grandfather is somewhat amended." *Tanquam satur*, etc. "As a man, when full, leaves a banquet." Adapted from Horace. *Sat.* I, 1, 119.

[4] *Dicenda, tacendaque*, etc. "He is cunning as to what should be said, and what left unsaid." Persius, *Sat.* IV, 5. This is adapted from *dicenda tacendave calles.*

[5] "Cosin Stephens". See Letter IV, Note 7, and Letter XVII, Note 4.

[6] *Obrepit*, etc. "Old age creeps on unnoticed." Juvenal, *Sat.* IX, 129.

LETTER XIX

[JULY 14th]

Sir, I perceave there is the same use of letters among freinds as there was formerly in the invention of fire which (they say) was first kindled by mutuall attrition of som combustible matter; and finding on my own part, that your letters to me warm, and dispose me to many good thoughts, I am the better pleased with the discovery that mine have the same influence upon you, whom in this particular I find to have so much tinder of this kind, that the least spark from me is able to raise an holy flame in you, and I wish that I may ever be able to do so. I have found much of it in your last letters, where you have sent me such a lesson of mortality, that though it be my daily meditation, yet I find my self more then ordinarily improved by it; for you know (in your opticks) that reflex lines work more powerfully then direct emanations. As for the lines, and features of your face, I hope I shall not find much alteration of them when I see you; but a prolepsis in this kind is a good figure, and of the two I had rather see my self in a glass that tells me that I shall be (by making me more old then I am) then the flattering glass that tells me what I have been, when I can find nothing but the ruines of it.

Pythagoras was the first among the heathen that said philosophy was Μελέτη θανάτου[1] implying by this, that that onely could teach us to free ourselves from the encumbrances of the body, to live in it as if we had nothing to do with it, and to learn to dy before we dy. But all this is but water colours compared with that deeper dy which we have from Holy Scriptures; and though the light of nature may do much, yet had not Pythagoras travell'd for it, and by his acquaintance among the Jewes gott the sight of som passages in Salomon, he could hardly have arrived so farr. What manner of persons ought we then to be, that have the light of the sun instead of his rush-candle? And all this is but to encourage you to go on; for it is a freind of yours that hath said it *Egregia res est mortem condiscere*[2], and there is no such charm against the fear of death as to be able to say in earnest *Quotidie morior*.[3]

I am much pleased that you ar so well fitted with the company, and assistances of Mr. Vaughan[4]. You may let him know that his sister in her poor estate hath lived among us with a very good name; I cannot find that

---

[1] Μελέτη θανάτου. "The self habituation to dying". This forms the theme of Plato's *Phaedo* 81A.

[2] *Egregia res*, etc. "It is an excellent thing to learn all about death." Seneca, *Epist*., XXVI, 9.

[3] *Quotidie morior*. "I die daily". St. Paul, Corinthians I, Cap. XV, v. 31 (Vulgate and A.V.).

[4] "Mr. Vaughan." This is Edmund Vaughan, son of Griffin Vaughan, Vicar of Ashtead, Surrey. He matriculated from Corpus Christi College, Oxford, November 9th, 1621 aged 12. Chorister: B.A., 1628, M.A., 1632, B.D., 1640. Rector of Pitsford, Northants., 1640. Sequestered in 1644, he was reinstated at the Restoration. He died in 1670 at Pitsford, where he is buried with a monument which describes him as one *qui pro optimo Rege Carolo Imo plurimum passus est*. (This monument does not seem to have survived a "Restoration" of Pitsford Church, which involved much rebuilding, in 1868.) He seems during his sequestration to have practised as a doctor. On July 17th, 1649 he wrote to Elizabeth Isham (sister of Justinian), prescribing for her a concoction of rhubarb, senna, aniseeds, "liquerish", and a few raisins (I.C. 270). His name occurs frequently in this correspondence, and in 1652 he was employed by Justinian in his marriage negotiations with Dorothy Osborne. (*Letters of Dorothy Osborne*, ed. Moore Smith, p. 210, Revd. H. I. Longden, *Northants and Rutland Clergy*, Vol. XIV (1942), p. 81, Wood, *Ath. Ox*., A. G. Matthews, *Walker Revised* (1948), p. 285).

her nearest friends have much considered her, but God raiseth her up som helpes, and her own industry is not wanting to improve every thing to the advantage of her fatherless children. She is not now in town, but I shall let her know (for it will be som comfort to her) that her brother is inquisitive, and sollicitous for her.

The report you hear of Dr. Hammond's[5] comming to Holmby, is, I believe, without any great foundation, for having receaved letters lately from him (wherein he gives som account of himself) he makes no mention of it. I could wish it might be so for your sake, for he is an excellent person, and though his learning and abilities be great, yet his goodness and sweetness of disposition beares a rate farr above any thing of that kind. He sent me lately a book of his printed (which before I had seen in manuscript) in defence of our Church Government against those giants of the Presbytery Blondel, and Salmasius[6]. The book is worth your sending for, if you have it not allready. But there is an other production of the press, that Affrick hath not seen a greater monster, and that is Mr. Hobbes his *Leviathan*[7]; a title that I wond'red at at first, but when I found how like he was to the Leviathan that Job speakes of, who plai'd, and sported himself in the Deep, I liked his judgement better in the title then in the book, for certainly (Lucian excepted) none ever was more gamesome in religion then he is. And yet as in the man, so there ar strange mixtures in the book; many things said so well that I could embrace him for it, and many things so wildly and unchristianly, that I can scarce have so much charity for him, as to think he was ever Christian. But if you have not yet read him, I would not anticipate you, but rather expect your judgement of him. Sir, I pray for you, and am

Your most affectionat tru freind
BR: S.

Richm: July 14

---

[5] "Dr. Hammond's comming." Henry Hammond (1605–60) was Fellow of Magdalen College, Oxford, 1625, D.D., 1639, Canon of Christ Church, Oxford, and Public Orator, 1645. In 1633 he became Rector of Penshurst, where Dorothy Sidney, afterwards Lady Sunderland, Waller's "Sacharissa," was brought up. His fame as a theologian long survived. When Boswell asked Johnson what commentaries on the Bible to read, he replied: "I would recommend Louth and Patrick on the Old Testament and Hammond on the New" (*Life of Johnson* ed. Birbeck Hill, Vol. III, p.58). Justinian's friend Dean John Fell wrote Hammond's Life. His sister Mary married Sir John Temple, and was the mother of Sir William Temple, who married Dorothy Osborne. (D.N.B., *Letters of Dorothy Osborne* ed. Moore Smith, Julia Cartwright, *Sacharissa* (1893), *Walker Revised*, p.217).

[6] "Blondel". David Blondell (1591–1655), a French Protestant divine. Professor of history at Amsterdam, 1650.
"Salmasius". Claudius Salmasius or Claude Saumaise (1588–1654), a celebrated French classical scholar. Professor at Leyden, 1631. His best remembered work is the *Defensio regia pro Carolo I* (1649) to which Milton rejoined in 1651.
Hammond's book is *Dissertationes quatuor, quibus Episcopatus Jura ex S. Scripturis et primaeva Antiquitate Adstruuntur, Contra sententiam D. Blondelli et aliorum* (1651).

[7] *Leviathan*. *Leviathan, or The Matter, Forme and Power of a Commonwealth, Ecclesiasticall and Civill* by Thomas Hobbes was published with a dedication to Mr. Francis Godolphin dated from Paris April 15–25th, 1651. The publication of what has been called "one of the great books of the world" caused Charles, to whom a copy had been presented by his old mathematical tutor, to banish "from his court that father of atheists, Mr. Hobbes" (G. P. Gooch, *Political Thought from Bacon to Halifax* (1914)). Duppa's reaction to the book is typical of Royalist and ecclesiastical circles. Hobbes left the exiled Court and returned to England, having made his peace with the Commonwealth in 1651. We are to meet him again in this correspondence. See Letter XV, Note 4 and references there given.

LETTER XX

[July 30th]

Sir, It is none of the least of God's blessings to you, that you have with so much piety assisted your father in the last act of his life; for though you could not recompense his former care of you in the lumpe, and the whole passages of your education, yet what you have don in this one particular hath the spirits of all duty in it, and quaestionless God will look upon it so as to give you a full return of it in an over-flowing measure of your children's piety to you. Your comfort is that he died in a full age[1], and in such a time, when they who had enioy'd the faelicity of living under former times, could not think it a punishment to dy, when there ar so few temptations left us to desire to live. But then, when I look upon that part of your letter, where you describe his manner of death (that εὐθανασία which Augustus so much wish'd for) I read in that God's greater favor to you, for though it is tru that stormes and tempests should be wellcom, when they drive the ship into the haven, yet the lookers on that ar any way engaged, have a more chearfull sight of it to see the same thing don by a fair, and a gentle wind, and a death without pangs and grones hath much of the resemblance of it.

Your charity in his behalf ar the right offerings for the dead, and the sacrifice of almes rightly disposed will draw down a greater blessing on your estate, and make it firmer to your posterity then all the cunning of conveyances can do. As for that particular which you have committed to my trust, I shall faithfully dispense it; for though I am not ashamed to tell you, that at this time, a summe so small is more than I can suddainly command, yet I hope within a few dayes I shall be strong enough for it.

I am much pleas'd in your behalf that you have so excellent a lady in your neighborhood[2]. For if her vertues be answerable to the fame that goes of

---

[1] "Died in a full age." Sir John Isham died on 8th July, 1651, aged 68.

[2] "Lady in your neighborhood." This is presumably Dorothy Sidney, who in 1639 married Henry Spencer, 1st Earl of Sunderland. He was killed at the first Battle of Newbury in 1643, when fighting for the King. For seven years after his death, she lived at Penshurst, but on September 24th, 1650, she left Penshurst to live by herself at Althorp, where she remained for the next ten or twelve years, devoting herself to the education of her son, and the management of his estates. She filled in the courtyard at Althorp, and built the magnificent staircase, which survives. She acquired the services of Dr. Thomas Pierce, Fellow of Magdalen College, Oxford, who had been ejected thence by the Parliamentary Commissioners, as tutor to the young Earl. "Lady Sunderland's residence in Northamptonshire was especially memorable for the great kindness she showed to the distressed clergy in the neighbourhood, many of whom found shelter in her hospitable house, when they were ejected from their livings" (Julia Cartwright, *Sacharissa*, p. 126). Dorothy Osborne (Letter 31) cast doubt on the "great acquaintance" Justinian had at Althorp and "what an esteem my Lady had for him." But there is evidence in letters both at Lamport and Althorp that this was no idle boast. One quotation from a letter at Althorp will suffice. It was written about this time as it is addressed to "Mr. Isham."

"Sir, My being very sorry that any occasion confines you to your house is no pretence for the least favour from you because in that my interest is much concerned since by it I lose your company which shall at any time be very welcome to me, and for the civility that I have already received from you and that greater obligation you intended me, I can make you no return but thanks which are neither adorned with good expression nor valuable for coming from me, yet you shall find that I desire what I cannot act the doing your service D. Sunderland. I hope a very great headache is some excuse for a very ill letter."

(I am indebted to the present Lord Spencer for this transcription). There is a copy of one of Van Dyck's portraits of Lady Sunderland at Lamport. This appears to be a head taken from a portrait at Petworth. From its quality, it is by one of Van Dyck's immediate followers or pupils.

her (I do not mean that cheap fame that is blown about by a vulgar breath) she will be able to make converts of your whole five miles circle, or at least have so much goodness in her as to render them inexcusable if they do not study to be like her. If this lady hath not allready made her choice of a fitt person to assist her in her devotions, there ar two men (for whom I dare venture that poor credit which is left me in the world), the one is Mr. Waring[3], who, I believe is free, and hath no present engagement on him; the other Dr. Main[4], both of them as of unblameable life, so of excellent parts, and such as you need not blush to recommend to her.

Of that same *dæmonium hominis* (the dimensions of whose *Leviathan.* it seemes, you have not yet taken) I shall say no more, but leave him for you to wonder at as much as I did at a litterall whale, which it was once my happ to see upon the coasts of Spain[5]. But I dare recommend another book to you in stead of it, new printed, but an old author of above 800 yeares standing, and that is the *Epistles* of that famous Photius[6], whom Baronius[7] is so angry with, for not being able to digest the Pope's universall supremacy; and yet all the rest of the Christian world is so much obliged to, for his *Bibliotheca*, that we had lost the very names of many excellent tracts, if this library of his had not praeserved them. The epistles wer transcribed out of the manuscript copies of our library at Oxford by Bishop Montagu[8], and deposited with Daniel[9], the printer of Cambridge who hath now publish'd them with the Bishop's translations. I confess the book I esteem as a great jewel, and though I could point out to you many particular epistles in it, wherein I am more pleas'd then in the rest,

[3] "Mr. Waring." Robert Waring (1614–58), like Duppa, was educated at Westminster, and Christ Church, Oxford, where he was a student, 1632–48. He bore arms for Charles I in the Oxford garrison, and, after the war, retired to Shropshire under the patronage of Sir William Whitmore. He was elected Professor of ancient history at Oxford in 1647 but was deprived in 1648. (D.N.B., Wood, *Ath. Ox.*, *Walker Revised*).

[4] "Dr. Main." Jasper Mayne (1604–72), was admitted Sizar of Jesus College, Cambridge, 1623, but migrated to Oxford; D.D., 1646. Chaplain to the King and Archdeacon of Chichester, 1660, Canon of Christ Church, 1660–72. He was a dramatic author in earlier life. Apart from plays, he published *Certaine Sermons and Letters of Defence and Resolution to some of the Late Controversies of Our Times* (1653). In his *A Remembrancer of Excellent Men* (1670), Clement Barksdale included an appreciation of Bishop Duppa adapted from Mayne's dedicatory epistle to Duppa prefixed to his sermon preached at the consecration of Herbert Croft as Bishop of Hereford (1662). Duppa, as Dean of Christ Church, was his earliest patron and benefactor. (Foster, D.N.B., *Walker Revised*).

[5] "Coasts of Spain." This is Duppa's only allusion in this correspondence to the period 1612–19 when he "travelled beyond the seas" (Wood, *Ath. Ox.*).

[6] "Photius." Photius (*c.* 820–91), Patriarch of Constantinople, was excommunicated in 879 by Pope John VIII who vetoed the legates' decision to make him Patriarch. This caused a schism between the Greek and Latin Churches. His *Epistolae gr et lat cum notis per Rich Montacutum* was published in 1651 (folio) (Lowndes). See Letter LXX, Note 1.

[7] "Baronius." Caesar Baronius (1538–1607), was made a Cardinal in 1596. His *Annales* is a standard work on Church history. (*Encycl. Brit.*).

[8] "Bishop Montagu." Richard Montagu (1577–1641), Chaplain to King James I, was an Anglican controversialist, who wrote books against both Protestants and Catholics. His answer to Baronius was issued as *Analecta Ecclesiasticarum Exercitationum* in 1622. He was made Bishop of Chichester in 1628, and Bishop of Norwich in 1638. He was a High-churchman, much attacked by the Puritan majority in the House of Commons. (D.N.B., *Encycl. Brit.*).

[9] "Daniel." This is Roger Daniel, Printer to the University of Cambridge, who in 1638 printed the Authorised Version of the Bible containing in Acts Cap. IV, v. 3, a very material error, "ye" for "we". A copy of this Bible which had belonged to King Charles I was presented to Justinian in 1651 by Duppa, who had been given it by the King. It is still at Lamport.

yet I had rather you should read them all; and would send you the book, but that I know it is no hard thing for you to gett it.

For your being a young house-keeper I shall take the less pity of you; first because you have sufficient materialls to work upon, and next if the work be uneasy to you, you cannot want choice of helpers. My business onely is to pray heartily that God may direct you in your choice[10], for as your happiness will consist much in it, so neither can I be unconcerned in it, who have now little happiness left else what I shall see you enjoy. For Sir I am without any designs upon you,

Your most tru freind and humble servant,

BR: S.

July 30

[ENDORSED REPLY OF SIR JUSTINIAN]

M[y] L[ord], Notwithstanding my endeavor to satisfie my selfe and owne conscience in the first place concerning my duty to my father living, and his memory now deceased, it is no small comfort to me to find your Lordship's approbation in what I have don, as it still shall be my request to have your directions in what I ought to doe. My father's funerall for many respects being private in the night, having had no order from him to the contrary, I found my offerings to poor neighbors about me better accepted with them, and more convenient to my selfe then to have invited the greater sort to a small and unfurnis'd house, to have had no canonicall service and the sermon diversly scan'd, and to have exposed both my selfe and company by drawing a concourse, to the pleasure of the soldiers then quartering round about us. I have since bin beholding to my choicest acquaintance and neighbors for their freindly visits, and though my house at present is unfitt for entertainment, yet I am bold to challenge their excuse untill I have first in a manner rebuilt a chancell which I am now very busie upon, that it may be both made and kept (as it ought to be) a house of praier, and the common tomb to our family for three or four defunts already. My building I intend to have substantiall, and grave without pictures or guildings either in windowes or walls, and if the tymes will not afford such to stand, then our generall epitaph must be *caelo tegimur*[11].

---

[10] "Your choice." The choice of a second wife.

[11] *Caelo tegimur.* On a blue marble slab within the Communion rails at Lamport Church is this inscription:

Sr John Isham Knt & Baron[tt]
Only son of Thomas Isham
Esq Married Judith Daughter
Of William Lewin Doctor of
the Civill Law & Judge of the
Praerogative Court Had by Her
One Son Justinian and Two
Daughters Elizabeth & Judith
Lived 68 yeares 11 months
& Died the 8 of July
1651

Among the MSS. at Lamport is a poem in Justinian's handwriting probably intended as an addition to this monument, but never executed, perhaps for the reason here mentioned.

What glory can we take in long descents
Or benefit by high borne blood that rents
It selfe? By painted Pedigrees and mouldy seels
When Vertue only nobleness reveales
What Monarches or inferior Men are made
That must not use the Sexton and his Spade?
Impartiall death nor Mitres spares nor crownes
Frees neither Lord nor Ladye Kts or Clownes.

Letter XXI

[August 19th]

Sir, I have been in doubt whether I should write, or no, or if I did, whether I should use any other forme, then that innocent one of old, *si vales, bene est, ego quidem valeo*[1]. For though my letters have nothing of publick business in them, yet when I write to a freind (especially such a freind as you ar) it is like writing to a wife, and letters of this kind, though never so harmless, ar obiects for no eyes but theirs to whom they ar directed.

But the truth is, this letter is not so much to you as to that good daughter of yours[2], who is allready in possession of so much of her inheritance, as to inherit your goodness while you ar yet living, and consequently so farr to study the art of hospitality, as to exercise it at such a distance that no freindship but yours could have taught her the way to do it, But to com to the upshot of the business, we have here tasted both of the workes of her dairy, and her pastry, and desire you would let her know, that if the first fruits of her huswifery be so good, she need not despair of being an excellent guide to your family, and at last to a family of her own when your care hath guided her to it.

I do not know whether I shall suddainly write to you again; for I do not love my letters should be flyblown before they com to you; for though the commerce between us have no danger in it, yet I hear that seales cannot fence letters from being open'd, and though I do not much dislike there should be many witnesses of my obligations to you, yet I had rather pay them to you in privat, then call in the country to look upon me. But Sir, I am ready to be both in publick, and in privat,

Your most true friend, and humble servant,

Br: S.

August 19

My wife (who presents her humble thankes to you) is much pleas'd with the name of Jane, and begins now to be so much the more confident, that all who bear the name must necessarily be good huswives.

The chancel rebuilt by Sir Justinian has survived to this day, but the embellishments which he refrained from giving it were added by his grandson Sir Edmund, 6th Bart., as a result of a legacy from his brother, the 5th Bart., in 1737. There are many letters at Lamport referring to the execution of an intended depository, designs for which were done by John Webb, the most eminent pupil of Inigo Jones. For some reason, these designs were not carried out, and in 1672 a chapel was added to the chancel on the north side, which has since served as a place for monuments. Under it, the vault was made. Sir John was the last Isham to be buried in the chancel itself, where are also the graves of his father, and grandfather. (See the present writer's *All Saints Church, Lamport* (1950)).

[1] *Si vales, bene est.* "All is well if you are well; I certainly am". A customary valedictory ending to Cicero's letters. See Letter cix, Note 2.

[2] "That good daughter of yours". For Jane Isham, the eldest of Sir Justinian's four daughters by his first wife, see Letter xxii, Note 5. This letter was presumably written while her father was still unmarried to his second wife. It might be 1651, when Sir Justinian had just succeeded. It is addressed to him as Sir Justinian, so it cannot be earlier. Duppa's postscript to his letter of October 15th where allusion is made to the "huswifry" of Jane Isham connects the two letters, and that of October 15th is clearly 1651, from the allusion to Cromwell's new residence at Hampton Court. The letter of January 4th, 1653—which can be certainly dated from the Comet allusion—mentions another example of Miss Jane's culinary art. For Mrs. Duppa see Letter lxxxv, February 7th, 1657, Note.

Letter XXII

[October 15th]

Sir, I make a quicker return to your last letter not because I hasten to be out of your debt (for all the speed I can make will not compass it) but that I may know when I shall ow a greater debt to you, by having your company once more, which I have so long fasted from, that there is reason you should at last give me a good meal.

As my condition is, it is Θεὸς ἀπὸ μηχανῆς[1] that keepes me from sinking under it; for it is not Epictetus, or Seneca, nor the bare reading of the 37th, or the 73rd Psalme (though in their severall kinds they ar all excellent instruments toward it), but it is the work of that great Comforter without whose strange influence upon me I had been ὡς σκεῦος ἀπόλωλος as a broken vessel. But by His Grace I am what I am, and every day take out a new lesson of valewing worldly things at a just rate. I have had formerly my share in them, and have parted with all that concernes my self with as much quiet and content of mind, as ever I enioy'd them. I confess I had besides a pretious state[2], which was too publick to be call'd exclusively my own, but I have lived to see that swept away, and to pay a daily tribute of teares for it. I did not intend at first to draw any of my own melancholy into this letter, much less to say any thing that may fright you from my company. For whatsoever my passions may inwardly work upon me, I dare promise you a chearfull countenance, for your sight and presence is able to clear many of my clouds, and when I cease to look chearfully upon you, it will be time to bid the world farewell.

If you write again before you come (which I do not expect unless som new thunderbolt warn you to keep aloof) give me some notice of the time, and how you mean to dispose of yourself. I believe your lodging in the park[3] will not at this time be so convenient, being so near to the Topanta of these times[4], and so vigilant a watch kept that none but such as ar initiated into the same mysteries should come within that circle. But your lodging here is as you left it, onely that you have now a more legall title to it, for not onely the lodging, but the house is yours, and if you balk it now, it will be thought that I have plai'd the impostor in your name.

Sir, I am now so full of expectation of seeing you that I shall say the less. God increase his blessings upon you, and yours, and recompense the kindness which you have shewn to

Your afflicted, but most affectionat freind,

B.S. October 15th.

My wife and I make it our earnest sute to you that we may not be forgotten to your daughter Jane[5], whose huswifry we have had so bountifull a tast of.

---

[1] Θεὸς ἀπὸ μηχανῆς. This phrase, derived from the appearance of one of the Gods in ancient Greek tragedy, has passed into the English language in its latinised form *Deus ex machina*.

[2] "A pretious state." Duppa's "Bishoprick."

[3] "Lodging in the park" that is, of course, Petersham [Old] Lodge, the residence of Lodowick and Joan Carlile. See Letter xv, Note 3.

[4] "The Topanta of these times." Is Duppa here anticipating Gilbert's "Lord High Everything Else"? After the Battle of Worcester, September 3rd, 1651, Hampton Court was put at Cromwell's disposal as a private residence (Maurice Ashley, *Oliver Cromwell* (1937)).

[5] "Your daughter Jane." By his first wife, Jane, daughter of Sir John Garrard, 1st Bart. of Lamer, Herts., Justinian had four daughters of whom the eldest, Jane, died unmarried on November 29th, 1655, and was buried the next day at Lamport. These "fower daughters" were one of the principal reasons alleged by Dorothy Osborne for her rejection of Justinian's suit (Letter 4, January 15th, 1652/3). Jane kept house for her father after her mother's death.

1652

This year saw the consolidation of the Commonwealth's authority in the three kingdoms. At the same time, difficulties between Army and Parliament intensified, which increased the importance and position of Cromwell. This year also saw the beginning of the Dutch War, a war much disliked by the Army, and even by Cromwell, who deplored the necessity of fighting fellow Protestants and fellow Republicans.

These stirring events find little echo in this correspondence. Indeed this year is the most barren in the whole series of letters.

There is no doubt what Sir Justinian's principal pre-occupation was – his second marriage, and the ill success of his suit with Dorothy Osborne may have led to the destruction of the letters of this year, if, as is more than likely, they discussed this project.

On October 25th, 1651, the Revd. Jeremy Stephens wrote to Sir Justinian after a visit to Bedfordshire, the home of his wife's family: "There is a great accession of fortune happened to Sir Peter Osborne and to some of his children. An aunt died lately, who having no child living hath left him almost a thousand pounds yearely in land. And the Colonel hath lately entered into possession of a Lordship in Yorkshire left him by his uncle the Earle of Danby. For the elder brother, I am told he is not disinherited by his father, as I was formerly told, but only Sir Peter made a feofment of some part of his estate and woods, for payment of money for his composition, and his daughter's portion 4th [£4,000], which is already in their hands as she receiveth the interest yeerly and the principall is ready in the hands of the feoffees [trustees], whensoever she shall marry. There is a great good opinion of your selfe before any other, and though I told my friend that I could promise nothing of your coming yet, I said that this terme, you would give an answer at London . . . only I wish you as much happiness in your choice as your selfe can desire, but of the gentle-woman I heare singular commendations." (I.C.301). The family thus introduced were the Osbornes of Chicksands Priory in Bedfordshire, who, though they are nowhere mentioned by name in the Duppa Correspondence, are clearly named here. Sir Peter Osborne had held Castle Cornet on the Isle of Guernsey for the King with great gallantry till in 1646 he retired to St. Malo, where his youngest daughter, Dorothy, joined him in 1648. On her way she had stopped in the Isle of Wight where she had met and fallen in love with young William Temple. It is more than likely that she had become known to Bishop Duppa, then at Newport in attendance on the King. In 1649 Sir Peter and his daughter returned to England, where he was heavily fined for his loyalty. They lived at Chicksands, and at the end of 1652 Dorothy took up her old acquaintance with Temple, and wrote the love letters that have become justly famous.

On January 8th, 1652/3 (Letter 3) she wrote telling Temple how "some friends that had observed a gravity in my face, which might become an elderly man's wife . . . and a Mother in Law, proposed a Widower to mee, that had fower daughters, all old enough to be my sisters: But hee had a great Estate, was as fine a Gentleman as ever England bred, and the very Patterne of Wisdom. I that know how much I wanted it, thought this the safest place for mee to ingage in, and was mightily pleased to think I had mett with one at last with witt enough for himself and mee too." It is clear that Dorothy Osborne is now speaking of the time (the end of 1651) when "there was a great good opinion" of Sir Justinian at Chicksands. When she met him, however, the favourable impression was dispelled: "'twas the vainest, Impertinent, self conceated, Learned, Coxcombe, that ever yet I saw." It was not perhaps surprising that Sir Justinian, aged 42 and a widower, "never very healthy since a great feaver", made little appeal to a girl of 26, whose heart was already engaged elsewhere. From the tone of her letters it is clear she knew him only slightly, and she admitted (Letter 25) that Temple once said: "Of all my Servants you liked him [Justinian] the best."

After Jeremy Stephens' first mention of the idea of the marriage, events moved swiftly. On May 8th, 1652, Henry Osborne (the Colonel) set down in his diary: "Mr. Vaughan [Edmund Vaughan, Rector of Pitsford] sent to Mrs. Goldsmith* [Dorothy's duenna] for a plaine answer." About this time the Osborne family were negotiating with her cousin Sir Thomas Osborne (afterwards the famous Earl of Danby), but on May 17th, 1652, Henry Osborne wrote: "Sir I. Isham came to town and came to my sister." Mr. Gibson, Vicar of Haynes, near Chicksands, was commissioned to write a formal letter to Sir Justinian on June 23rd. But when Henry Osborne called on Sir Justinian in London on July 4th, the baronet informed him he "had entertained a new treaty."

The failure of the marriage negotiations is amply explained in a letter of the Revd. Seth Ward, dated June 28th, 1652. Ward was a learned man, Savilian Professor of Astronomy at Oxford, and was evidently a friend both of the Ishams and the Osbornes, and he wrote at length to justify himself in the abortive marriage negotiations. He is possibly the "great friend at Oxford" to whom Sir Justinian wrote, according to Dorothy Osborne, "a long and learned character of mee," which would serve Temple "to laugh at this seven year" (Letter 6, January 29th, 1652/3).

---

*William Goldsmith, was Rector of Campton, Beds., in which parish Chicksands lies. His daughter Mary married on April 9th, 1635 "Jeremie Stephens of Wooton" which explains why Stephens was so well able to inform on conditions in the Osborne family. (Parish Registers of Campton, Beds.; for William Goldsmith, see Venn). William Goldsmith also had a son Daniel, who was the husband of the Mrs. Goldsmith whom Moore Smith describes as "Dorothy's Duenna." This Daniel succeeded his brother-in-law Jeremy Stephens in the Rectory at Wootton.

LETTER TO SIR JUSTINIAN ISHAM FROM SETH WARD (I.C. 314)

" For the Honourable Sir Justinian Isham, Baronet, with speed. Leave this with Mr. Hicks next door to the " Red Lion" in Drury Lane."

"Honourable Sir,

It hath been from the knowledge I have of your goodness that I have ever taken to myself a liberty of speaking freely to you, and upon all occasions to discover my apprehensions without jealousy of offence. Upon this foundation I shall humbly presume to make a brief reply to the intimations of your letter. First then, for what concerns myselfe I shall only repeat what I have formerly said, that (by the L. or the C.) no word was ever spoken to me of joynture before my comeing over to you from thence, nor anything discovering any expectation of £800, neither had I any the lest [least] order to mention anything of that nature to you so that I could not *plainly tell* you anything concerning it.

Againe I must repeat that at my returne from you I never mentioned nor ever thought of any addition to sh: [Shangton], neither upon my utmost recollection can I imagine from whence such an expectation should be raised unlesse from the generall intimations of your respect to her (which I did really beleive to be great) and from my confidence that if you came to converse freely together it would be a match. If you had been pleased to be present at my first discourses (at London) with the L. or C. you might then have been as wel satisfied in that particular as my selfe, and I should not have feared to have then obtained that of your justice for which I must now engage your noblenesse and charity.

In the meanetime it doth appeare that there was such an expectation and therefore (all things now considered) it is no marvaile it was mentioned.

As for the terrible apprehensions of Mr. G., I doe assure you Sir they were never any of mine. I have often at Lond: discoursed to you my conceit upon the standing upon that to what end it was and I doe not see any cause to change my mind. I doe not deny but that I thinke a concession in that small difference might be much desired, and I have a great assurance that there was no intention to breake upon that score, and that the cheife satisfaction desired was in other things more conduceing to the happiness of life.

As for the complement to mee that all the desire of the L. was that I might be satisfied, I confesse my selfe to have bene so mannerly as to beleive all of it, I know very wel that your satisfaction was more desired, but to say so was perhaps too much liable to interpretation. The consent of the L. to Mr. G's beleife of closeing elsewhere I can wel enough understand how it may proceed from a civility and readinesse to pardon things done upon mistake. There can be no such assurance of the forgivenesse of an error as to make one beleive it was not an error. This interpretation may possibly appeare a little strained but there are deeds to be alledged against words. For if that would have bene done if this had bene knowen, why was it not done when the L. knew it from yourselfe, and with the disadvantage too of apprehending (though erroneously) a tergiversation in you?

You see, Sir, it was not in vaine that in the beginning I made an apology for liberty of speech, my pardon wil be the easier if I be considered as a clearer of mistakes *not on one side onely*, the effect of which endeavour wil somewhat appeare by the enclosed which I lately received from the Col: and send it nakedly to you without any comment or application. I shall onely say that I am still much assured that you have it in your power to render two noble persons as happy as any couple in the world, and that you may do soe is the desire and wish of your

S.W.

Oxford, June 28th, 1652

I humbly desire to heare from you for the receipt of the enclosed with as much speed as you shall thinke fitting."

SIR JUSTINIAN'S DRAFT REPLY.

"Sir, I had yours yesterday dated June 28th and in it the enclosed of June 18th. Your former letter (with that in it much differing from these bearing date but June 17th). Now what strange planet judge you hath governed this affair but in this last enclosed the mention of these very words from the C. to you. I suppose you have heard from Mr. G. how out of his good intentions he was the cause of that great mistake between us concerning the joint[ure], which as my sister told me did so surprise her, she not in the least manner expecting any such thing, that she knew not in what manner to take it, and could not understand it in any other sense but that Sir P. had a mind to break off the treaty and chose that way to do it. Here am I absolutely to seek what the meaning should be, unless the " L " assuring herself of a promise from me to make an addition, should think I retracted it. That letter Mr. G. should have shown her and so sought to fly off. Now, Sir, I call God to witness I never sent a plainer and more direct message in my life then by you who carried not only my offer for joint[ure] but the very particular of it without any syllable from me of any such thing as addition ever intended, but indeed told you the contrary as I well remember in a blunt expression that if there was any affection for me the offers and estate were enough, if not too much. Thus plainly did I deal with you however gross the mistake came to be afterward. But now Sir ever since the receipt of your former letter with Mr. Gn's in it, when I found the " L " looked no further than your satisfaction and her consent to Mr. Gn's belief of closing elsewhere, it would have inclined me to entertain another treaty elsewhere with what success God knowes, but never shall I show plainer dealing and a truer affection than really I had for yours."

It will be observed that Sir Justinian in his reply to Seth Ward makes use of almost the same expression ("entertain another treaty") that he used to Henry Osborne (the C or " the Colonel "). " Mr. G " is of course Mr. Gibson.

It is clear that negotiations had gone very much farther than Dorothy Osborne's letters to Temple (written some months later) would lead one to suppose. The cause of the breaking off on the Osborne side seems to have been the jointure, rather than dislike.

Sir Justinian himself was emotionally engaged, a fact usually irrelevant in 17th century marriage negotiations, and by no means apparent in the other " addresses " which he paid. There is one very significant point. Dorothy Osborne (Letter 4, January 15th, 1652/3) says that Sir Justinian gave his daughters " such precepts as they say My Lord of Dorchester gives his wife, and keep's them soe much Prisoners to a Vile house he has in Northampton shyre." It is extremely unlikely that Dorothy had ever visited the " vile house " at Lamport, but she may well have known that it was an Elizabethan house, and neither she nor Sir Justinian could have been expected to like anything so "irregular". At all events on May 12th, 1652, David Papillon, who was a Huguenot, sent Sir Justinian, no doubt at his request, plans for a new house at Lamport to cost about £1,500. He tried to dissuade him from adding a new block to the old mansion *si fort repugnant aux reigles de l'art* (I.C. 312), (the plan eventually adopted, as will be seen, after Sir Justinian's marriage). It is just possible that Dorothy herself may have had a hand in these plans, and that by bestowing on the old house an unflattering epithet, she was an unconscious element in its eventual improvement. It was not, however, Papillon who carried out the changes, but John Webb, who seems to have been less unwilling to add *un nouveau corps de logis à votre vielle maison.*

On his rejection by Dorothy, Justinian seems to have tried to engage himself in several other places, before renewing his suit to her, as related by her in Letter 25 (June 11th, 1653). But this event belongs properly to the next year and must be dealt with there.

Dorothy herself seems to have heard, after the breaking off of the negotiations in June 1652, that Sir Justinian was to be married to "a daughter of my Lord of Coleraines". There is no support for this statement in the letters at Lamport, although we hear much in 1653 of his negotiations in another quarter – with the daughter of Sir John Gayer, Lord Mayor of London : see Letter XXVIIA, February 15th, 1652/3 of this correspondence. But this affair also belongs properly to the next year.

Letter XXIII

[January 20th.]

Sir, It is not amiss that your own country in these times agrees so well with you ; but how ever the ayre may be agreeable to your health or not, I assure you my prayers shall never faile you; which I promise you with the more confidence, because I know no act of freindship, which an act of state cannot take from me but onely that. I can yet shutt my self up into my closet and when I have pray'd for him whom they have proscribed, and for his freinds whom they now persecute[1], I have both charity, and leasure enough to pray for them too that God may turn their hearts. As for your own particular (in whose happiness I am much concerned) I am so much the better satisfied, that as nothing can corrupt you, so nothing can discompose you. You may possibly want company, but as long as you ar present to your self, you have that which will abundantly supply it. And without quaestion we ar never in the way to be truly happy, till we know how to be alone. I do not vent this to entice you to an hermitage (unless it be where I may have a cell near you) or to make you love the country longer then you have reason, but to suggest the uses you may make

One indication that this letter belongs to this year is the mention of Hobbes, which connects it with the argument in Letter XIX.

[1] "Him whom they have proscribed" and "his freinds whom they now persecute" refer to Charles II and the Royalists after the battle of Worcester, September 3rd, 1651.

of it, which I persuade my self by this time you ar very perfect in. For though the mathematicks may be your recreation, and Hobbs may say somthing well toward the advancing of that study, yet I know you have severer and diviner thoughts, then he seemes to be acquainted with; and I need not name him to you, *qui nullam eruditionem esse duxit, nisi quae beatae vitae disciplinam iuvaret*[2], much less need I persuade you to believe it, who in your last letters have given such excellent expressions of it.

As for my self I am as you left me, and secure my self the same way as the tortoise doth, by not going out of my shell. Some of your freinds have visited me since you went, Mr. Aldridge in a direct visit, Mr. Banks[3] on the by, being in quest for you, besides my neighbours of the Park[4] who wer lately in a full brigade with me. My intelligence that I had with new books is quite lost, since I lost you, which makes me apply my self more earnestly to the old. I have somthing to do to refrain from enlarging this letter farther, but considering that you will receave in this packet another from your cosin Lowen[5], which may prove voluminous enough for both, I shall stopp heer till I hear farther from you. Your postscript of your letter concerning Leicestershire[6] putts me in some fear,

---

[2] *qui nullam eruditionem esse duxit*, etc. "Who held it be be no learning unless it assisted the discipline of the happy life." Cicero, *De Finibus Bon. et Mal.*, I, xxi, 71.

[3] "Mr. Banks." On May 11th, 1651, "Signor Giovanni Bankes" wrote from "Augusta" (? London) a letter in Italian to Justinian, regretting that circumstances prevented their meeting *tra i bosche ameni e campi Elesée di Richmont*. This erudite gentleman is presumably the "Mr. Banks" here alluded to. In his draft reply to this letter, Justinian alludes to Signor Bankes' travels among "goodly cities" (I.C. 295 and 296). See also Letter LXIX, Note 5.

[4] "My neighbours of the Park", that is, the Carliles of Petersham, and their numerous party; see Letter XV, Note 3 and Letter XXII, Note 4.

[5] "Your cosin Lowen." John Lowen (or Lewyn) was the son of Daniel Lowen of Gerpins, Essex (died 1631), the second cousin of Judith Lewyn, who married Sir John Isham, 1st Bart. He was third cousin of Sir Justinian. His mother was Susan Turke, third daughter of John Turke of Wrotham, Kent, who married Mary Marshall (or Maresall), the sister of Bishop Duppa's mother Lucrece. He was thus a first cousin once removed of Bishop Duppa and so correctly described as "our cousin". He was baptised at St. Olave's, Hart Street, March 25th, 1613. A King's Scholar at Westminster, 1629, he was a ward of King Charles I, matriculated from Christ Church, Oxford, 1633, aged 19, and was then a Student there (B.C.L., 1642). In a petition of 1665 (?) he stated that he had been ejected from Christ Church in 1650 by the rebels, for refusing to subscribe, and giving a public defiance to the National Engagement, tendered in the audit house, Christ Church, by the pretended Commissioners. In this petition, he stated that he was "bred under Brian Duppa, late Bishop of Winchester" (*C.S.P. Dom.* 1665–6, p.150). Wood, (*Fasti*, Vol. II, p. 231) gives the year of his ejection as 1648, the day (August 7th) that he was made D.C.L. He was admitted to Gray's Inn, November 13th, 1635, but not called to the bar till June 29th, 1655: he then lived at Doctors Commons. He was restored to his doctorate at Oxford in 1660, made a J.P. for Essex, and lived at Rainham. In 1664 he was made Principal Registrar to the Bishop of Winchester. He died in 1677/8 and was buried on March 20th, at St. Olave's, Hart Street (*Registers*, Harl. Soc., 1916); (T. E. Watson, *History and Pedigree of the Family of Lewin* (1919), additions, p. 265, Foster (where the residence of his father, Daniel, is given as Northall, Herts), Wood, *Ath. Ox.* and *Fasti*, G. F. R. Barker and A. H. Stenning, *The Record of Old Westminsters*, Vol. II (1928), p. 594, *Visitation of Essex*, 1664–68 ed. J. J. Howard (1888), p.59, T. Wright, *History and Topography of the County of Essex*, Vol. II (1836), p. 517; see also App. A). There are several other references to him in this correspondence, e.g. Letter XL, January 4th, 1654 and Letter LXII, January 9th, 1655. Mrs. Duppa, in her will of 1664, left "Doctor John Lowin the summe of Fortie pounds."

[6] "Leicestershire." Presumably the Bishop is here alluding to the fine which Sir Justinian had already paid on his Leicestershire property, and fears that the same procedure may be applied now that Sir Justinian has succeeded to Lamport, which is in Northamptonshire.

that the place where you are may run the same hasard. For the jealousies of these times know no bounds; as their guilt increaseth, so do their feares. But, I doubt not, there is a providence that watcheth over you for your safety, to which my daily prayers shall commend you, having no other way left to express my self, how much I am,

Your affectionat freind, and faithfull servant
B.S.

Richm: January 20.

My wife, and nephew present their service to you. Your boyes are safe[7].

[ENDORSED REPLY OF SIR JUSTINIAN]

'Tis true, I am heere in a good aire; but I have somewhere read, or somtyme fancied, that good and agreeable conversation is as requisite to the health of the minde as a good aire to that of the bodie. With your Lordship upon the hill I enjoyed both, and as much as is in you doe still partake of both, of your conversation by letter, and of the best aire (I think that can be) your praiers. However your Lordship is shut up I find your charitie boundless. And now my L. since you have pointed me to my seate, I am bound both to praise God for you and pray for you as being,

M[y] L[ord,]Your etc.

But indeed what can I say of your circle whose center is infinite? It joyes mee very much to find your Lordship concern'd in mee, that howe'er I know my selfe to be every way of a very slender and slite constitution, yet supported by your Lordship I may run up to something, and though absent, yet (as hee amongst the ancients being struck down by his enimie, prayed him he would give him his death's wound before, least his freind that lov'd him, seeing a wound on his back, should be ashamed of him) I shall endeavor to be worthy your owning. Nor do I only valew my selfe because of your Lordship's esteeme of mee, but to speak freely because I have alwaies found in my selfe (since our first acquaintance) a very naturall propension to honour and love you. Certainly one of the best signes (I think) that ever was in mee. For my being no more discompos'd, which your Lordship pleases to take notice of, it is now my business that there may be *quies alta et ab alto veniens*,[8] having alwaies admired that saying of this author, *nec quicquam magnum est, nisi quod simul et placidum*.[9] And for coming to this I cannot forgett the same Seneca, *etiam si quis tam bene purgavit animum, ut nihil obturbare eum amplius possit ac fallere, ad innocentiam tamen peccando pervenit*.[10] I confess this church porch of

[7] "Your boyes are safe." This is an allusion to the picture by Vandyck, still at Lamport, of the Infants Christ and St. John. The bill from Mr. Maurice Wase says: "The two boyes of Van Dijk the lowest price will bee 24 pounds." It is alluded to in a letter of John Webb dated May 31st, 1655. The picture was in the Royal Collection, and may have been at Richmond. It is possible that this letter belongs to 1655, i.e. immediately before the purchase of the picture. On the other hand Letter LXIII, which certainly belongs to that year, is dated January 24th.

[8] *Quies alta et ab alto veniens.* "Deep quiet issuing from deep within." This appears to be an adaptation of a passage in Seneca, *Ad Gallionem De Vita Beata*, IV, 4. *Sequatur hilaritas continua et laetitia alta atque ex alto veniens.*

[9] *Nec quicquam magnum est*, etc. "Neither is anything great unless it is also calm." Seneca, *De Ira*, I, 21, 4.

[10] *Etiam si quis tam bene*, etc. "Even if in some way the mind has been so purified that nothing can disturb or deceive it any more, nevertheless it is by error it arrives at innocence." Seneca, *De Clementia*, I, 6, 4. The original contains a *iam* before *purgavit*. This reference has been recognised and verified by Mr. J. M. Wyllie, and the translation is by the Rev. Edmund Sutcliffe, S.J.

moralitie, which by the ***purgavit***, seemes to have a kind of holy-water in it to be used, is much to be prefer'd before the mathematicall steeple which by its order and harmonie can at best but chime us into the temple, endangering those who stay but in the belfrie to be intangled or catcht up by those lines they deale with. But your Lordship's divine directions, much beyond both, bring mee into the very cho[i]re, where I am to partake of higher mysteries, the best of other things but conducing to them.

LETTER XXIVA

[JULY 27th.]

Sir, I was the last week gott beyond Graves end[1], and that was the reason you heard nothing from me, and though it may be you looked not for it, yet I, having gott a habit of writing to you, cannot easily forbear it when I am within distance. But as I remember you sent me word from London, that your occasions would speedily bring you back again; if it prove so, I know you will not deny me the happiness of seeing you; if otherwise, you must look hereafter for longer letters, for they ar not few words that will serve to make my acknowledgment of your continued freindship, and kindness to me, which if I do not sufficiently thank you for, you may be sure that God will – I have no more to say at this time, but that I pray for you and am

Your most affectionat tru freind and humble servant

BR: SAR:

Richm: July 27

[ENDORSED REPLY OF SIR JUSTINIAN]

My Lord, I think it but an equal civility considering how little your Lordship travells to congratulate your returne from beyond Gravesend as another's from a forraine country: but wheresoever you goe I find 'tis not from your selfe nor your freind, not beleeving that your Lordship only return'd to your thoughts of me when you came home but that I travell'd also with you; may I be worthy so faire a memorie and that f . . . bitt . . . your Lp. professed to have gott [three or four indicipherable words] which I hope cannot be accounted any ill one amongst the rest so very excellent.

[1] "Beyond Graves end". Gravesend was the first port on the Thames, and "by a grant of Richard II enjoyed the privilege of conveying passengers to and from London: the vessels depart from Billingsgate every tide at high water on the ringing of a bell, and from Gravesend every flood" (Paterson's *Roads*, 18th edn. (1829)). Thus in the 17th and 18th centuries, the usual mode of travelling to mid-Kent from London was by water to Gravesend, and thence by road.
The most likely place for Duppa to be visiting "beyond Graves end" was Cobham Hall, which is fourteen miles from the port. In Letter LIII (August 15th, 1654) Duppa says that he had been "sollicited to make a summer journey to Cobham" (see Note 6), and it may well be that the present letter records an earlier visit there. The owners of Cobham (the Duke and Duchess of Richmond) would certainly have been well known to him. James, 1st Duke of Richmond and 4th Duke of Lennox (1612–1655) was one of the most faithful of the nobility to King Charles I. He was with the King at Newport in 1648, when Duppa was also in attendance, and he was one of the small company that went to the unceremonious burying of Charles at Windsor in 1649. Thorndike (*q.v.*) was his Chaplain. Moreover, his wife, Mary, whom he married in 1637, was the only daughter of George, 1st Duke of Buckingham, and sister of the 2nd Duke and Lord Francis Villiers, who, as boys, were Duppa's pupils. (See Introduction, "Brian Duppa", Note 20). She may well be the "Lady Duchess", who, in 1658, exhausted Mrs. Duppa's supply of distilled water (Letter C and Note 4), and she appears to have had Margaret Kilvert, the Bishop's sister, in her service in 1657 (see App. A). The Duke and Duchess lived in retirement at Cobham, a house traditionally assigned to Inigo Jones, during the Commonwealth.

I am now for Suffolk[2] and think to be for London about three weeks hence, but whatever my occasions may be there or anywhere els, me thinks I find a deviation in my compass till I point upon Richmond.

[2] "Now for Suffolk". The first Osborne marriage negotiations broke down early in July 1652, when Sir Justinian received Seth Ward's letter of June 28th. He informed Henry Osborne on July 4th in London that he had "entertained a new treaty". He then evidently decided to visit his aunt and daughters in Suffolk. The defeat of Charles and his Scots at Worcester in September 1651 had led to a relaxation of the measures taken against delinquents in 1650, and Sir Justinian was once again free to move about.

1653

The conflict between Army and Parliament came to a head in the spring of this year, and in April Cromwell put an end to the sittings of the Rump with the aid of some forty musketeers. "What shall we do with this bauble? Here take it away." With these words, the Long Parliament and the symbol of their authority were dismissed. Cromwell then became a dictator, and the first of many expedients was tried to fill the vacuum left by the disappearance of King, Lords and Commons: a nominated body of godly persons, which by a narrow majority of twenty, assumed the name of Parliament, without the approval of Cromwell and the Council of State. This body, known to history from the name of one of its members as "Barebone's Parliament", attacked its work in no uncertain spirit.

Although the all important question of Sir Justinian's second marriage still absorbed the attention of our correspondents in this year, these great national events affected their letters. On August 24th, Barebone's Parliament passed an Act declaring "that only marriages before a Justice of the Peace would be recognised by the State" (Gardiner, Vol. II, p. 292). Sir Justinian, who had in the early part of the year been pursuing enquiries for a bride in several directions, finally fixed on Vere, daughter of Thomas, 1st Lord Leigh of Stoneleigh Abbey, Warwickshire, who wrote him an affectionate letter early in August. The marriage was hastily concluded lest, as Bishop Duppa put it, "the Act for Marriage should overtake you, and the Justice of Peace becom your preist." But the nominated Parliament took on graver matters than the Act for civil marriages, and in December, while discussing a motion to deliver up to Cromwell the powers received from him, the Parliament broke up, the Speaker leading forty members to Whitehall to resign their powers, a minority remaining seated, till they, like the Rump, were turned out by the soldiers. Of this "vertigo that hath happened in the head of our Government" Duppa gives an account, which is vivid and conclusive. It was, indeed, "a mock-shew of a Parlament", and it was not only Royalists who asked: "What may be the issue of this onely God knowes." The solution, a new constitution, drawn up by the Army, under which Cromwell became Protector, was seen by Duppa as "a wonder", prepared indeed before the calling of the nominated Parliament, "which . . . was a train laid to make something that follows, the more plausible."

Two great ladies, one of whom had played no small part in history, visit the Bishop at Richmond. Lady Carlisle, the friend of Queen Henrietta Maria, who betrayed the designs of the Court to Pym, and Lady Devonshire, to whom the poet Waller dedicated his *Epistles*, did not suffer the Bishop "to be so much an hermit" (October 19th). The picture of Lady Carlisle, "formerly waited on by all the great persons of the Court," now walking "single and alone to the seat on the top of the Hill," is earnest to the Bishop of her reformation.

But the principal subject of the letters in this year is the second marriage of Sir Justinian, and it is as well to be clear as to the various proposals made. It will be recalled that in 1652, negotiations with Dorothy Osborne had broken down and Sir Justinian had addressed himself elsewhere. Dorothy herself (Letter 3, January 8th, 1652/3) heard he was to marry "a daughter of my Lord of Coleraines." This was Hugh Hare, first Lord Coleraine, whose wife was a Montagu, who lived at Totteridge, Herts. But this rumour finds no confirmation in letters at Lamport. Sir Thomas Pelham, 2nd Bart., wrote from "Haland" (Halland in Laughton, Sussex) that his daughter "god willinge . . . wil be att London on Wednesday or Thursday the first or second of September which is the sole errant of this paper, but to present myself and my wife's service to you" (August 22nd, 1652). Sir Justinian in his draft reply said: "No opportunity hath since been omitted to make myselfe better known to your daughter to whom I have made my addresses and with your leave and hers shall willingly wait on you at Haland about a month hence where I hope to make a further progress."*

Progress, however, there seems to have been none, and early in 1653 we find Sir Justinian paying his addresses in another quarter, and here Bishop Duppa himself takes a hand! He sent Dr. Humphrey Henchman, Chancellor of Salisbury diocese, who had been "very instrumental in forwarding His Majesty King Charles II's escape into France, when he came in disguise to Salisbury" (*Magna Britannia* (1731), Vol. VI, p. 179), to "Bramsell" House, Hants, to make enquiries about one of the daughters of Sir John Gayer, Lord Mayor of London, who had died in 1649; she was sister-in-law to Andrew Henley of Bramshill (as it is usually spelt). Dr. Henchman was charged not to reveal the name of the suitor, but Sir Robert Henley, Andrew's father, "the old fox", seems to have guessed the name. But by March these negotiations were ended, despite the lady's "great portion". Sir Justinian himself declared "so great a fortune and good fame cannot induce me to make my selfe too cheape to the City, or to be any way bound in the interim before I find the least shew of acceptance from them herein."

In June, he made fresh addresses to Dorothy Osborne. "Would you think it, that I have an Ambassador from the Emperour Justinian that comes to renew the Treaty?", wrote Dorothy to Temple on June 11th, 1653 (Letter 25). The passage in which she describes her reception of this proposal is typical of the raillery with which she describes his suit: "in Earnest tis true, and I want your Councell extremely what to doe in it. You told me once that of all my Servants

* Sir Thomas Pelham had a daughter Judith, who married Sir John Monson, son and heir of Sir John Monson, 1st Bart. Their son Henry, afterwards 2nd Bart., was born on September 17th, 1653, so it is probable that their marriage took place about the time her father made his will on January 13th, 1652/3. She appears to have been the only daughter of marriageable age at this time.

you liked him the best, if I could doe soe too there were noe dispute int: well i'le think on't, and if it succeed I will be as good as my word, you shall take your Choice of my fower daughters; am not I beholding to him think you? hee says that hee has made adresses (tis true) in severall places since wee parted, but could not fixe any where, and in his opinion hee see's nobody that would make soe fitt a wife for him as I." She suggests sending him to Temple for his answer: "when hee can bring mee a Certificate under your hand, that you think him a fitt husband for mee, 'tis very likly I may have him, till then I am his humble Servant, and your faithfull freind." By June 18th Dorothy had had a "skirmish" on the subject of the "Emperour and his proposalls", and "all the People that I had ever in my life refused were brought againe upon the Stage, like Richard the 3ds Ghosts, to reproach mee, withall." It is evident that Sir Justinian had informed Bishop Duppa of the renewal of his suit to Dorothy, and that in his letter of June 9th the Bishop was hoping for a favourable issue: "Somthing there is that in relation to you keeps me impatient, that until I can hear from you of that great business, which your happyness of this life, and (in som respects) of the next depends on." But he waits for news of this "in the long walk" at Richmond. We do not know how soon after this second rejection by Dorothy, Sir Justinian approached Vere Leigh, but in his letter of August 3rd, the Bishop speaks of Justinian's letter from Warwickshire, and comments: "You have hetherto in contriving your choice mett with many, and som of them strange diversions, and from whose hand they com, I need not tell you."

On August 4th, 1653, Vere,* wrote to the "truely honoured Sir Justinian Isham", assuring him that his "affectionate endearements [are] become very considerable with your most assured friend," and they were married later in the month (the exact date is not discoverable as the Stoneleigh registers are imperfect). Dorothy in September (Letter 37) adds the comment: "it was not mine it seems to have an Emperour, the spitefull man, meerly to vex mee has gon and Marryd my Country Woman my Lord Lee's daughter." However that may be, the union lasted twenty-two years, there were many children, and they seem to have been very happy. Certainly Sir Justinian's replies are now more cheerful: "I have now brought my wife to my house, and have it full with our freinds about us."

Letter XXIVb

[January 4th.]

Sir, Since the time you wer pleas'd to make my house your home, I never thought that I enioy'd you more then when you wer at your own home. I confess you have been nearer me, and at the same time you have been farther off; for, though your other kindnesses reach me at all distances, yet the kindness of writing was laid aside on both parts; on yours, because you had not onely the business of a prudent man to mannage the estate left you, but that great business of chusing an help like to your self, of the

* I.C. 324

difficulty of which they wer wont to say that *sapere, et amare ne Jovi quidem contigit*[1]: And for my own particular I forbore that I might not interrupt you in that which so highly concernes you. For ether you must make your self very happy in your choice (which shall be my daily prayer for you) or you must resolve to lay up a stock of patience, if it prove otherwise.

Your letters (you may be sure) wer very wellcom to me; but when I mett with those expressions of your over-much love to me (of which you borrowed the metaphor from the starres), I had the curiosity to wish, that the similitude you made, had putt you in mind to have said somthing of that blazing aequivocall starr[2] which lately appear'd, and is now vanish'd. For though I do not take you to be that bold astronomer, who was confident that nothing could be don, or seen in those partes of heaven without his knowledge; yet I beleive, things of this kind pass not without your observing. They say (for I then saw it not) it appear'd first on December the 9th; that the motion of it was from the south east to the northwest, but every day slower then other, and lesser, being toward the disappearing of it, no bigger then a starr of the first magnitude, but much paler, and duller. At somtimes there was a taile, or beames cast from it eastward, but at other times not discernible. I could tell you of the Pleiades, and the Medusa's Head, about which this small comet was discover'd; but considering my ignorance in these things, I shall supersede the saying of any thing more, and stay the time till you shall reveal it farther to me. And as I understand little of the comet it self, so I understand less of the events that ar bespoken to follow it. Onely I see there is a strange coniunction of combustions at this time, which whether kindled from heaven, or from the sinnes of this nation (which threaten us more then any comet can do) are likely to involve us all, if the prayers of good men cannot quench them.

We have receaved your good daughter's great kindness in two collers of brawn, whereof one is the greatest part of our feast this Christmas time, the other is laid up in pickle in expectation that you may possibly eat part of it your self. I wish that (as she doth in this) she may in all things imitate her father's vertues, which will prove a greater portion, then any thing else that can be given with her.

Unless I hear from you, I shall not write the second time, because (as I remember) you sent me word that your return to these parts would be very suddain. Sir, I write long letters to no bodie but to you, partly because I love no body so well, and partly because when it is to you, I cannot do otherwise. And so with a great confidence, that whatsoever I say or do in this kind is as freindly interpreted, I please my self in thinking that I have been all this while in company with you while I have been writing to you, and shutt up the rest of your trouble with the old crambe[3]

---

[1] *Sapere et amare ne Jovi quidem contigit.* Herrick in *Hesperides*, "To Silvia", freely renders this Latin proverb, well known in the seventeenth century, "None is discreet at all times; no *not Jove Himself, at one time, can be wise and love.*" The proverb would appear to derive from Publius Syrus, *Sententiae* A. 22, *Amare et sapere vix Deo conceditur.*

[2] "That blazing aequivocall starr." On December 20th, 1652 a comet appeared which lasted till January 20th, 1653 (*Universal Library or Compleat Summary of Signs containing above* 60 *treatises*, 2nd edn., London; printed for T. Warner at the Black Boy and J. Battly at the Dove, both in Paternoster Row by A. Curzon 1722). Duppa's allusion to "a strange coniuction of combustions" may be an allusion to Blake's defeat in the Battle of the Downs by Van Tromp in November, 1652.

[3] "Crambe." Cabbage: "only *fig.* and usually in reference to *crambe repetita*, cabbage served up again. Juvenal vii, 154" (*Shorter Oxford English Dictionary*, ed. C. T. Onions, 1933).

that cannot be too often repeated, that I am,

Your most tru freind, and most affectionat servant
B. Sar:

Richm: Jan: 4.

Letter XXV

[January 13th.]

Sir, The flouds, and frosts and stormes that we have felt here, hath kept my little cosin from giving me any visit (though invited to it) till yesterday. And then I proceeded punctually according to my directions; I told him that upon som train of thoughts (as the man of Malmesbury calls them) I had consider'd of somthing that might prove happy to two freinds of his, and that there wanted nothing but to make both the parties sensible of it. For that which related to the male I undertook, and desired him (if he thought it wer a thing manageable by him) to undertake the other, at least so farr that we might try the pulses on both sides, whether it wer likely to find any harmony between them. I confess I did not find him very confident that he could do it, and I did like him so much the better; but he hath required time till this day fortnight to bring in his intelligence.

For the present state of things in that family, his coniecture is that the young Lord B[1] is still the person design'd, being young, and hansom, and having (as they say) six thousand pounds per annum; the other Lord is talk'd of, but his person and fortunes being under a cloud, the balance is not likely to weigh down on his side. But the upshot of all is (if his discourse be right) that the old lady (who is the onely Sybill that must give the oracle) is likely for som yeares to deal as that Duke of Burgundy did, who, having no heir but a daughter, made her a property to serve his occasions. I shall say no more for the present, but leave the rest till my fortnight's intelligence be brought in, and by that time possibly your own occasions may bring you into these parts, where this business may be more freely debated of.

We ar very sorry here for the distempers of your daughter, but I beleive she is now in her second climacterick, and alterations at that time ar incident to both sexes. But you putt us in hope that she is past the worst, and may be a guide to your family till you find another. Your hare-py is the best we have tasted yet, and though your pastry man may grow old, his workes ar nere a whit the less lasting, for I hope to keep som of it till I see you again. Your letter dated the 27th of December cam not to my hands till the 8th of January, and whether mine may not stick by the way as long, I know not. I direct them still to the park gate, till I may be better guided. And so with my prayers for you, which is all the service I can do you (and I am persuaded will not be alltogether unprofitable to you), I rest

Your tru freind, and most humble servant
Br: S.

Richm: Jan: 13.

[Endorsed reply of Sir Justinian]

I find you have had the trouble to employ our cosin, but I pray let it not trouble you farther if nothing come of it, for so I have reason to think;

[1] "Lord B" etc. It is impossible to say who these people are from the meagre details given. The "little cosin" is certainly Lowen (Lewyn). From the draft reply it would seem that another bride is being proposed for Sir Justinian. She appears to be daughter of an old lady, who wishes to find a rich husband for her.

though some reason also not alltogether to neglect what might so conveniently bee tryed without exposing my selfe.

My children, I praise God, ar well recover'd, though it still continue a sickly season among many hereabouts. I hope ere long to be for London, but cannot so certainly determine when, as not to stay long when I goe. I have not now so much leasure for books as formerly, but think of St. Jerome, who when he grew old left off his former way of translating, endeavoring then as he sayd to translate *verba in facta*. So now I shall be put upon action and less reading. But as all my undertakings (I am verily persuaded) will be the more prosperous through your Lordship's good wishes and effectuall praier, so shall you never want an acknowledgement of it from,

Your &c.

Letter XXVI

[February 1st.]

Sir,Your kindnesses ar so frequent, and so often repeated, that you hardly give me a breathing time to thank you. But since it is so naturall to you to be bountifull to your freinds (especially to such who by the iniquity of the times ar condemned to those wants as to have nothing left to return), I very much desire you to beleive, that wer the tables turn'd, and you in my condition, and I in yours, I would strugle hard to shew really as much love to you, as you have don to me. In the mean time, it is my daily prayer to continue you in these doubtfull times, in such a condition that you may do good (for all good men hold by a very uncertain tenure), and for my self, I have no feares at all, but that God will ether raise me freinds to support me, for that small remnant of life that is left me, or give me such a measure of patience, as will abundantly serve in stead of it. The best cordials ar those that ar within us, but there is need of those that ar without us too; and in that I find you do not deal as phisitians do, that give them to their patients in spoonfuls upon som great extremities, but in whole, and great vessels which we ar likely to use moderately, and to receave more good by your praeventive cordialls, then we should otherwise do by all their phisick. But there is somthing yet to be said, and it amounts to this, that if you steal again into Northamptonshire,[1] without seeing us here, I shall not half so much valew your very kind present, for, beleive it, your company is farr more acceptable to me then any thing you can give me. And particularly at this time I have somthing to consult with you concerning my self. But let not this over hasten you, but take your own time (as your occasions may give you leave) and whensoever it is, you com to a family that next your own, none can love you more, and I being the head of it have the greatest reason to subscribe my self,

Your very faithfull freind, and servant
Br: Sarum.

Richm: Feb: 1.

---

[1] Sir Justinian is evidently in London engaged in marriage negotiations. The letter is addressed: "For Sir Justinian at Mr. Cogan's House in Charing X." (See Letter xxxv, Note 2). On the back of a letter dated January 9th, 1652/3 (I.C. 308) from Jeremy Stephens, sending "the first tome of our English Councells, and laws" (Spelman's *Concilia*), Sir Justinian has drafted a letter to an unknown lady: "Not yet at London by reason I could no sooner make returne to Mr. Flint. But I begg your excuse if I think long before I goe till I may at least heare of you, not supposing it now necessary that paper be a witness to what either of us are already assur'd of in our selves, or what I hope we beleeve of each other. If I may find from your faire hand you are well that only word will be a sufficient letter to your . . ."

LETTER XXVIIA

[FEBRUARY 15th.]

Sir, Though I know nothing, which I would not do, to be instrumentall to your happyness; yet as your condition now is in relation to the temporary happiness of this world, there is nothing that concernes ether you, or me (for my concernments go along with yours) so much as your second choice in marriage. I know you are wary, and you ought to be so; many overtures have been made to you, and som of them so strangely, that with my purblind eyes I thought I saw the hand of Providence working in them, but I have found how short-sighted we are in things of this nature, which are not discovered till we see the event of them.

Somthing of this kind you committed to my charge, when I saw you last; and it was by way of enquiry; but being to go out of town the same day, and wanting leasure, and opportunity to follow it so farr, as might give me a full light of the whole business which you desired to be satisfied in, I made choice of Dr. Henchman[1] (a very discreet person) without naming you at all (though I confess when I had given the character of you, I found by his lookes that he could give a shrewd guess, who was meant by me) and I did the rather committ it to him because he was to stay in town behind me, and would have the more leasure to give the better account of it. You know, I do not use to make long stories, but in this I must relate particulars that you may the better know what is past.

The way that I took of employing the Doctor in this business, was not by word of mouth, but by letter, wherein (knowing that he was to meet with the old man) I desired him to shew that part of the letter which concern'd you (but still without naming you) and to propose it with all necessary enquiries concerning her person and her estate, and withall to let him see the character that I gave of you (which I could really do, and never fear to be call'd to account for). Before I could have any answer of this, I was gon out of town, but the Doctor being mindfull of his charge, took Richmond in his way to Salisbury, and gave me this account; that the old man having read that part of my letter, which was cheifly a character of you, and the rest a desire of being satisfied in the estate and condition of the young lady; he first answer'd to the latter, and commending her for her modesty, and education, concluded her as a match for a very good man, having to her portion (as he reported it) above ten thousand pounds; but withall advised the Doctor that in his return to the west, he should

[1] "Dr. Henchman." Bishop Duppa has made choice of Dr. Humphrey Henchman (whose letter he encloses) to sound the Henley family regarding the marriage of the sister-in-law of Andrew Henley, without disclosing the name of the party. The mention of Bramshill, Alexander Ross and Mr. Abdy give a sufficient clue to enable the parties to be traced, beyond doubt. Dr. Henchman (1592–1675) was a Canon and Precentor of Salisbury in 1623. Like Sir Justinian, he had been educated at Christ's College, Cambridge, and was elected a Fellow of Clare in 1617. He was a friend and contemporary at Cambridge of Michael Honywood, Fellow of Christ's, and Herbert Thorndike, Fellow of Trinity, and shared with them "a strong attachment to the Church and care for reverence and dignity in its worship" (J. H. Srawley, *Michael Honywood*, Lincoln Minister Pamphlets No. 5, 1950). Equally all three friends suffered deprivation during the Puritan regime. Henchman was deprived of his Rectory of the Isle of Portland during the Civil War, which he spent with the King's army, and he is best remembered for the assistance which he gave to Charles II to escape to the Continent after the Battle of Worcester (*Boscobel Tracts* ed. J. Hughes (1887)). After the Restoration he was rewarded by being made Bishop of Salisbury, in which diocese he succeeded Duppa. He played an important part in the Savoy Conference, and was translated to London in 1663 where he remained Bishop till his death in 1675. (D.N.B., Venn, Walker.).

take Bra[msell][2] in his way where his son was, who probably was able to say more to it. But at the loose of the discourse, saith the old fox, do you think that I know not whom my Lord meanes? or if you do not know I will tell you, that it is Sir Justinian Isham; for I am not ignorant of the freindship and relation that is between them. How he should make this coniecture, I know not, but one of the two it must be, that ether *Prudentia* (as Tully saith) is *quaedam divinatio*, or else Alex: Ross hath been the heyfer that he hath plow'd with.

But there is a second part of the story yet behind which came to my hands this morning from the Doctor after he had been at Bramsell, and that I chose rather to convey to you under his own hand, then to transcribe it.

Upon the whole matter (as the phrase of law is) there is mony enough to be had. But ether I am deceaved in you, or your heart moves not upon that hinge. I would nether have you chuse her onely for her portion, nor to be so hard-hearted to your self as to refuse her for it. My prayer is, that God may direct you in it, for concerning her person (which must make up your happiness) I am in the dark, and have no spectacles of my own that can reach so farr. If you think of proceeding in this way, there will be a kind of necessity of returning speedily to London; for among other advertisements from the old man, one was, that Mr. Abdy (a man I know not, but one, it seemes, trusted with her guardianship) is now very diligent in finding out a match for her. Before you can resolve any thing, you must see the person, and trust your own eyes, which will tell you more then seven watchmen from a tower. And so without any farther enlargements I remain,

Your most tru freind, and humble servant
B.S.

Richm: Feb: 15.

Letter XXVIIb

[Humphrey Henchman to Bishop Duppa]

[February 12th.]

My very good Lord,

I have imparted the business to the young gentleman by reading that part of your letter which concern'd it. He very much magnifies the disposition of his sister in law; he sayth that she is not at all ingaged, that the portion is £10,000, of which £7,500 is ready in a chest, £500 in Ligorne and £1,500 in

[2] "Bramsell." The famous house, Bramshill Park, Hants, was built by Edward, 2nd Lord Zouche who died in 1625, leaving it to his cousin Sir E. Zouche, who soon sold it. In 1640 it was acquired by Sir Robert Henley, Master of the King's Bench. He is the "old fox" referred to, since his son Andrew in 1646/7 married Mary, daughter of Sir John Gayer, Lord Mayor of London, and it is evidently her sister whom Andrew, "the young man not so cunning as the ould", so praised. Sir Robert Henley died in 1655/6, and was buried in the Temple Church, February 29th, 1655/6, worth, it is said, £4,000 per annum. Sir John Gayer, who had been impeached and imprisoned by the Parliament in 1647/8, had died in 1649, which explains why the young lady had a guardian. This guardian was Alderman Robert Abdy of London, who "before 1643" had married Catherine, another daughter of Sir John Gayer. He was made a baronet at the Restoration. There were two other sisters of Mrs. Abdy and Mrs. Henley, Sarah and Elisabeth, "not at all ingaged" at their father's death, and one of these was the proposed bride of Sir Justinian. "The heyfer" "Alex: Ross" is the Revd. Alexander Ross; (see Letter XVI, Note 3.) Andrew Henley was his executor, and found in Ross's books in the Library at Bramshill "about a thousand pounds in gold." (D.N.B., V.C.H. Hants, Vol. IV, G.E.C., *Complete Baronetage*, Wotton's *Baronetage*, Walker, *Sufferings of the Clergy*).

severall lands in England. The estate of the other part in land, did not displease, he doubted not but he could prevayle with his sister to attend much more to the person then to the estate, but the age, the widower, the daughters, all these will be obstacles, especially the daughters, for his age may pass undiscovered, this last he thinks will be such hinderance as he very much doubts will not be removed by his rhetorick or authority with her: yet he will make tryall and use his best skill: and if she is so prudent and vertuous as he describes her, and he will faithfully render the gentleman as your letter reports him, she may very probably throw off that nicety of the daughters, for the enjoying of so gallant a person.

The young man was not so cunning as the ould in the discovery of the person, but made most wide coniectures, in which ignorance I left him, but from hence I collect that Alexander R. hadd not discours'd with him about it. I hope that I have followed your Lordship's directions fully, and if I may be any wayes serviceable to your Lordship or the noble gentleman I will act chearfully and faythfully.

I pray your Lordship's benediction and rest
Your Lordship's most humble and obedient clerk
HUMFR: HENCHMAN.

Sarisbury. Febr. 12.

LETTER XXVIII

[MARCH 29th.]

Sir, I find by your letters, that you ar return'd to your own home again, where if you can make up your contentment (which will be much in your own power) I do not know what greater worldly happiness to wish you. It is your center; and however your occasions may draw you out to som short wand'rings in the circumference, yet your resting place must be there. And when I consider what advantages you have more then others of your quality which live about you, that know not what to do with themselves in a rainy day, I am the more confirm'd, that God hath given it into your power, to be as happy for this world, as you shall think fitt to make your self; and for the happiness of the next life, he hath given you an understanding and a religious heart to weigh the faelicities of both, and so far to praefer the latter, as to place your cheifest care and study how to compass that. Whether marriage may be a help to you in ether, you can best determin in your own brest. But I find, as to this last particular (motion'd by me, but not without commission) you ar cold enough; nor will I blow the fire if so great a portion, and so good a fame cannot work upon you. Besides, we ar likely to have troublesom times, and the single life may be best fitted to go through them. As for the continuance of my respects, and affections to you, you have them so much in your own keeping, that I cannot dispose of them otherwise, till I becom so unworthy, that you grow weary of retaining them. I have nothing to beg of you, but that I may see you when you com into these parts, though it be but (as good angels wer wont) to appear, and vanish.

Sir, I shall pray for you, and yours, which is the onely service I can pay you, for so much freindship as you ar pleasd to shew to

Your very faithfull, and humble servant
BR: SAR:

Richm: March 29.

My wife, and my nephew Chaworth[1], ar your humble servants.

[1] "Nephew Chaworth." For Richard Chaworth, see Letter II, Note 3.

[ENDORSED REPLY OF SIR JUSTINIAN]

However heere at my center, yet my thoughts being there with you, I account that no wand'ring. Next terme[2] I purpose sometime for London and so to attend your Lordship, but to give a rationall account now of my seeming coldness in that you write of, I suppose had the proposall so fully made received an entertainment you might very well have expected to have heard from them ere this, but being unpartiall to my selfe, I may reasonably conjecture that those obstacles mention'd of yeares and children may cause their cessation from any farther enquirie. But truly I find no backwardness in my selfe where I may in likelyhood praevaile, yet so great a fortune and good fame cannot induce me to make my selfe too cheape to the City[3], or to be any way bound in the interim before I find the least shew of acceptance from them herein. I may be in an error, if so I hope to be shortly rectified when I waite upon your Lordship, whose love and freindship I account one of the greatest blessings from heaven upon

Your &c.

My service to Mrs. Duppa, Mrs. March[4] and Dr. Chaworth. I hoped some good occasion might have brought him into these parts ere now, being very desirous yet to see so much of your family heere.

LETTER XXIX

[MAY 16th.]

Sir, You left with me an expectation of seeing you again before your return to your own home[1]; and you added somthing more, that I should not onely see you, but that you would bring your daughters with you, whom I love allready as being yours, but when you have made me acquainted with them, I foresee that I shall ask you leave, that I may love them for them-selves. But I am very sollicitous least I should be unhappily absent when you com, and therefore must needs woo you to let me know, when that day of kindness shall be; not that I intend to make any praeparations for it, (for in my lowest condition I can entertain them that I love extempore, and they that love me will be contented with it). But because being invited forth on Wensday next, I shall carry feares along with me least you should com that day, and both of us be disappointed, I cannot forbear to let you know of it.

Sir, I praescribe no time, but keep your word (which I beleive you never yet broke) and all quarrels will be praevented. I have nothing farther to do, but to pray for you and in all kindes to express my self,

Your most faithfull freind, and humble servant

BR: SAR:

Richm: May 16.

LETTER XXX

[JUNE 9th.]

Sir, Though your letter mentions a suddain return, I cannot forbear writing to you, partly because I do nothing more willingly then write to you (though sparing enough to others) and partly to let you know, that I look

---

[2] "Next terme." The law term: this would have been the Easter Term.

[3] "Too cheape to the City." This is an allusion, of course, to the source of Miss Gayer's wealth.

[4] "Mrs. March." She was the sister of Mrs. Duppa. See App. A and Letter LXIV, February 21st, 1655, Note 1. The name is usually Marsh.

[1] Sir Justinian is still in London.

upon it as a great kindness, to let me know how you disposed of your self, for till I receaved your letter I was in som expectation, that possibly you might have kept this last festivall with us, which we heere did both solemnly, and chearfully enough, *excepto, quod non simul esses*. I was never yet guilty of being a busy-bodye, or over-curious in the concernments of others. But somthing there is that in relation to you keeps me impatient, that untill I can hear from you of that great business, which your happyness of this life, and (in som respects) of the next depends on.[1] But I shall look for nothing of this (for letters ar not fitt conveyances) till I can meet you again in the Long Walk. And so with my daily prayers for God's direction of you, in this, and all thinges else, I rest,

Your very tru freind, and humble servant
BR: S.

Richm: June 9.

LETTER XXXI

[AUGUST 3rd.]

Sir, Your last out of Warwickshire[1] cam safely to my hands, but I forbore to make any return because you mention'd in that letter som probability of your comming into these parts. And, indeed, concerning the great business of your life, which you ar now about, I can more properly serve you with my prayers, then with my letters. You have hetherto in contriving your choice mett with many, and som of them, strange diversions, and from whose hand they com, I need not tell you. The same Providence that formerly hath guided your affaires, watcheth still over you, and as long as you propose to your self noble and religious ends, will never leave you. I shall say the less, because you give me som hopes of seeing you; when if you shall please to open your brest farther, you shall meet with a brest as open to you, both to receave what you shall trust me with, and to communicate my thoughts with you. Your two sweet daughters have so much of you in them, that we cannot despair of being kept in their memories as being very faithfull servants both to you, and them. And for the other two, whom I am yet unknown to, I must needs beleive, they ar of the same strain. God bless them all to you, and guide you in your choice of a person that may prove so kind to them, that you may seem rather to have resumed your former match then to have made a second. Sir, I pray for you, and am (what I cannot vary from) your very tru, and affectionat servant,

BR: SAR:

Richm: Aug: 3.

---

[1] This letter was obviously written in the short period of the resumption of negotiations with Dorothy Osborne. The date is a confirmation of Moore Smith's dating of Letter 25 of Dorothy Osborne, June 11th, 1653, which letter was assigned by Judge Parry to May 10th. For it is in this letter that Dorothy speaks of "an Ambassador from the Emperour Justinian, that comes to renew the Treaty."

[1] "Warwickshire." Sir Justinian has been visiting Stoneleigh Abbey, Warwickshire, the seat of Thomas, 1st Lord Leigh of Stoneleigh. This nobleman owed his elevation to the peerage to the welcome which he gave to King Charles I in 1642, when the citizens of Coventry shut their gates in his face. Sir Justinian's marriage to Vere Leigh took place later in the month at Stoneleigh.

Letter XXXII

[September 7th.]

Sir, I have been expecting all this time, when I should give you the *Para bien*, as the Spaniards call it, and forbore to trouble you with any letters of mine, till I knew in what condition they might find you. When you did me the favor to see you last, you made hast away, least the Act for Marriage should overtake you, and the Justice of Peace becom your preist[1]. Since that time, though I conceaved the business was don, I could not praetend to know any thing of it, till the good man of the Cross-Keyes brought me your letter dated the 27th of the last month, but brought it me so late, that at the same time he deliver'd it to me, hee told me the carrier was gon, and consequently the answer must be deferr'd till the next return.

I have been the more punctuall to give you an account of this, that I might not appear so cold in my affections to you, as to deferr the co-gratulating of you in the greatest business of your life. I have long pray'd that it might prove happy to you, and I have the greater reason to beleive my prayers ar heard, because I beleive you ioyn'd in the same prayers with me, and wer so farr from hastily engaging your self, as if you had expected rather God's direction in it, then your own. How you have been cros'd in other offers, your self best knowes, and how smoothly you have gon on in this, enough to make the old saying creditable, that "Marriages ar made in Heaven." I know not this Lady whom you have made happy in your choice, but I know you so well, that I cannot but beleive all things good of her, because she is your choice. I have but one request to you in this particular, that when you have bestow'd all the affection, that a good husband owes to an excellent wife, you would still reserve a proportion for your poor old freind, who pleaseth him self more with your freindship, then with any outward worldly thing besides. Sir, I pray for you both, and the truth is you ar now so ioyn'd, that none can pray for you separate. The good, or evill that may happen to you must be in common; onely you cannot exclude me from having a share in both, who am very faithfully,

Your most affectionat freind and humble servant
Br: Sar:

Richm: Sept: 7.

I am call'd out upon to make a postscript full of good wishes from my wife, and som other of your servants about me. But upon resuming the reading of your letter, I find I have an other business lies upon me, which now I have no leasure to speak to, but you shall hear of me hereafter.

[Endorsed reply of Sir Justinian]

Your praiers and hartie wel wishes have not bin wanting to me upon all occasions, but now I find them pour'd forth upon this maine action of my life, which cannot be so indifferent but must render me more happie or more miserable then it found me. As God had appointed it so I trust His blessing will goe along with us, but shall not anyway bespeake your Lordship's good opinion of her because my choice. Only leave you in suspension till I may make her known to you, and I believe then occasion a better beliefe of me *in her* selfe for having the freindship of so worthy a

[1] "The Justice of the Peace becom your preist." The Act for civil marriages, passed on August 24th, 1653, was the sole legislative achievement of Barebone's Parliament. (Gardiner, Vol. II, p.293).

person. A treasure certainly in the best tymes, but in these so much the more to be valued by how much they are worse; where 'tis hard even to meet with one without some tokens of the generall contagion. Now, Lord have mercy upon us.

LETTER XXXIII

[SEPTEMBER 21st.]

Sir, Though I do not yet know that you have receaved the letter which I last wrott, and consider withall that in the first year of marriage, there is a great measure of civility to be used in not being troublesom to him, whose business must be (if he mean to make himself happy) to please himself with his own choice, yet I cannot forbear; for freindship is a transcendent that overlookes all relations, and upon the strength of that, I cannot let you alone, but must have somthing to say to you, though it be nether business, nor ceremony, but somthing between both, for they border very near, and in matters of kindness, he that expresseth no ceremony, may signify that he meanes to have no farther business with me.

You wer pleas'd in your last letter to let me know of an encounter that you had with my cosin Lowen, who shew'd you a sermon of mine that he had in writing. Upon which, out of a too much love to me, you grounded a request, that I would make a collection of such sermons of mine as wer within my reach, that they might be copied out for you. And first I must tell you, that they ar in loose papers, and so blotted and blur'd, and inter-lin'd, that I can hardly be mine own interpreter; and next, God hath dealt so well with me, that he never yet left me open to that temptation as to sett a valew ether upon my self, or upon any thing that hath com from me. I do not speak this to excuse my self from complying with any desire of yours, (for I know no person living, whom I had rather trust with any thing that concernes me, even with my failings and imperfections), but onely to let you know that it is no easy thing in this particular to obey you; but if you will give me time (for amanuensis I can have none but my self) I shall make ready somthing for you, that may remain with you in your privat closet, as a testimony of my love to you, though probably of little to my self.

You do not tell me whether you took a copy of that which my cosin shew'd you. If you have not, I shall the easier send it you because it is transcribed allready, and which was in a manner forced from me by a freind of yours, who ether was, or seem'd to be, so affected with it, that nothing could satisfy but the giving of the copy of it, and because it concerned the better part, the soul, I could not be so uncharitable as to deny it. I expect to hear by your next letters, whether you ar return'd to your own family. But wheresoever you ar, you cannot escape my prayers, which watch over you in all places. And so without further molesting you, I am,

Your most faithfull, and humble servant
BR: SAR:

Richm: Sept: 21.

This morning I was unexpectedly visited by my Lord Conway[1], and

[1] "Lord Conway." This is Edward, 2nd Viscount Conway, summoned to Parliament 4 Charles I in his father's barony of Conway. (His father was Secretary of State 1623–1630). He commanded the Royalist Cavalry at Newburn in the Second Bishops' War in 1640, when he was defeated. Clarendon says of him: "he was a voluptuous man in eating and drinking, and of great license in all other excesses, and yet was very acceptable to the strictest and the gravest men of all conditions . . .

Mr. Denham[2], both of them very good company, but the time was short, and they quickly vanish'd.

My wife desires very much to be honor'd by you in the remembrance of her service to your Lady, and if you will do as much for me, you will have don all, that at this present I can require of you.

Letter XXXIV

[October 5th.]

Sir, I find that we ar not yet com in a right track of sending and re-sending letters and answers, but ar rather in som such disorder, as men use to be after a meal, where there is a difficulty of hitting faces[1]. But this may be rectified, if we take our weeks; this mine, and the next yours; for so there will nether be a loss on ether part, nor a coincidence. And for the persecution with which you threaten me, I must needs tell you, that you have given a freindly commerce a most ungentle name. And how ever I am sparing in this particular to others (for I know no one man that hath the trouble of so many letters from me, as your self), yet if you be but half so well pleas'd with this entercourse as I am, we shall both mutually embrace our persecutions of this kind, and by continuing it sweeten all other persecutions, which in these times ether have or may happen to us.

As for the commands which I have receaved from you (for all your requests have the power, though not the lookes of them), I meet with som difficulties in the obeying of them, partly for want of such an amanuensis, as I might trust with som dangerous truths, as ar not to be trusted with every scribe; but cheifly because (though my poor fortunes wer so farr enlarged as to have the advantage of such a one near me) I can fitt nothing for another's transcribing, till I have first transcribed it my self, which, if my infirmities increase upon me (as they have lately begun) I shall hardly bring to pass. And yet nothing of this is to be look'd upon as an excuse, for you have an absolute power over me to dispose of me, or mine as you please. As for my copies reserved of any thing of mine printed, I am the less able to satisfy you because nothing of mine was ever yet printed by my consent, and I must grow much more in love with my self, then as yet I am, when I give way to it for the future.

You tell me that you hope shortly to be in a settled condition at your own home, and ar you not so when you ar where your Lady is? for *Tota domus duo sunt*[2] and you two must now make up the home where ever you pitch.

---

he had always . . . reserv'd so much time for his books and study, that he was well vers'd in all parts of learning . . . He was of a very pleasant and inoffensive conversation" (*History of the Rebellion*, Book II, §83). He died in 1655. He was connected with Bishop Duppa through his sister Helegonway, who married Sir William Smith of Hill Hall, whose second wife was Anne Croft, sister of Mary Croft, 1st wife of Richard Chaworth. These ladies were nieces of Bishop Duppa, the children of his eldest sister Ann, who married Edward Croft of Wigmore (Margaret Toynbee, "Anne, Lady Salter," *Notes and Queries*, September 15th, 1951).

[2] "Mr. Denham." This is (Sir) John Denham (1615–69), poet, Royalist, and, after the Restoration (much to the disgust of John Webb, who expected to be appointed), Surveyor-General of Works. In the *Gramont Memoirs*, he is described as "One of the brightest geniuses England ever produced for witty works" (ed. Vizetelly (1889), Vol. II, p. 18). With these two visitors, no wonder the Bishop found his morning pass quickly!

[1] "Hitting faces." See Letter XVI, Note 1.

[2] *Tota domus duo sunt.* "Two make up the entire household."—Adapted from Ovid, *Fasti*, IV, 543.

However you do well to arme your self with the Apostle's admonition, for the times are likely to be such where the *habentes* in all kinds may have reason enough to praepare themselves to be among the number of the *tanquam non habentes*. But if you shall continu your freindship to me, I shall have nothing to complain of, being very fully satisfied in being own'd by you as,

Your very faithfull freind and humble servant
BR: SAR:

Richm: Octob: 5.

[ENDORSED REPLY OF SIR JUSTINIAN]

I suppose my sending of letters severall wayes and at uncertaine tymes may cause the uncertaine deliverie of them, but now I shall continue to send by Mr. Glanvill at the next dore to the Black Horse in St. Clement's Lane neere Temple Lane, (if your boy bring your Lordship's directly to the carrier Branson[3] at the . . . [Ram] in Smith[field] it will be the less liable to miscarriage). And though I meet not alwaies with your Lordship's letters on the Saturday night after you send them, yet I shall not faile to send once in a fortnight or 3 weeks at utmost, God willing, where ere I shall be. I have now brought my wife to my house, and have it full with our freinds about us, and yet me thinks I am as one that . . .

LETTER XXXV

[OCTOBER 19th.]

Sir, Your letters cam very orderly this last week, and now I begin to think it possible that once in a fortnight, *nisi quid humanitus contigerit*[1], we may mutually hear one from the other: which whether it may be a trouble to you having the cares of a second wedlock upon you I know not, but to me *in re perdita*, who have few cares left, but those which I have made tame, and familiar to me, it will be such a refreshment (for so your old landlord Cogan[2] makes the Chineses speak) as the rain is to a feild of rice.

---

[3] "Branson." He was the Northampton carrier. It would seem that Bishop Duppa wrote his letters on the Monday and that if things went well Sir Justinian received them on the following Saturday. "Dorothy Osborne generally received her letter when the carrier came down from London on Thursday. She then began a letter to be ready for him to take up on Monday." (Moore Smith, *Letters of Dorothy Osborne*, pp. xlix and l).

[1] *Nisi quid humanitus contigerit.* "Unless anything should happen according to the common lot of man,"—adapted from Cicero, I *Phil.*, iv, 10.

[2] "Your old landlord Cogan". Henry Cogan (died 1655), an assiduous translator, published *The Voyages and Adventures of Fernand Pinto, a Purtugal: During his Travels . . . in the Kingdoms of Ethiopia, China . . . Japan.* Done into English by H. C. Gent London (1653). The work is dedicated to William, Earl of Strafford. Duppa had, no doubt, in mind the words addressed, in this work, to Pinto by the King of Bungo (*sic*)—*Thy arrival*, said he unto me, *in this my country is no less pleasing to me, then the rain which falls from Heaven is profitable to our fields that are sowed with rice* (Ch. XLIV, p.175). There are constant references throughout the book to the "Chineses". Another of Cogan's works, a translation from the Italian work of Girolamo Lunadoro (*Relatione della corte di Roma* (1635)) and Fioravante Martinelli's addition to Lunadoro's book (1650), entitled *The Court of Rome* (1654), is dedicated to Sir Justinian Isham. The Epistle dedicatory speaks of Sir Justinian's "vertuous and generous inclination to grace and cherish all that may any way conduce to the advancement of knowledge and good Arts."

There is a letter from Cogan at Lamport, dated May 11th, 1654, (sealed with the coat of arms of Cogan of Somerset—"three aspen leaves" according to Burke's

That you ar now com to your own house, with a well-chosen wife, and all the blessings that belong to it, hath hardly left room for me to wish more to you, but onely that your contentments may grow upon your hands and multiply in all the effects which may make mariage happy. And this I can no way doubt of, when I consider through what variety of accidents Providence hath guided you to this choice, where I wish you may be fix'd, and never be putt to the third trouble.

I am for the present in the midst of two very noble neighbors, my Lady Devonshire[3] at Row-Hampton, and my Lady Carlile[3] at Petersham,

---

General Armory) in which the writer begs the acceptance of the dedication of *The Court of Rome* (I.C. 343); and, on this letter Sir Justinian has drafted a reply expressing thanks for "your kind remembrance of mee who am now meere rustick", and praising Cogan's exercise of his "pen in the enriching both your countries knowledge and language." In this draft, he wishes that he was "taking a turne with you in the Park where I had the happiness of your conversation," an allusion to Cogan's house at Charing X near St. James's Park, where Justinian stayed in 1649, and, at other times, when in London (see Letter XIII, February 12th, 1651 and Note 1 and Letter XXVI, February 1st, 1653). He was named in Inigo Jones' will (dated July 22nd, 1650, proved August 24th, 1652) as one of the two overseers, and also received a legacy of ten pounds. He is described as being of the Parish of St. Martin in the Fields, where Jones himself resided. It was perhaps through Cogan that Justinian became friendly with John Webb. Henry Cogan died in 1655, and was buried in the Church of St. Martin in the Fields on April 3rd (Registers of St. Martin in the Fields). His will, dated October 9th, 1649, was proved on May 14th, 1655. He had pathetically little to leave his son James, and his widow Mirabella. In 1643, the Committee for the Advance of Money had ordered Henry Cogan, Thames St. and Charing X, to be brought up in custody to pay his assessment (*Calendar of Proceedings of the Committee*, I, p. 219). From this brusque summons, and the dedication of his books to people like the Earl of Strafford and Sir Justinian, it is not impossible to deduce Henry Cogan's political position. The fact that several of Duppa's letters are addressed (e.g. February 1st, 1653) to "Mr. Cogan's house near Charing X" shows that Justinian continued to lodge there, when business called him to London.

Another Henry Cogan was alive in 1650, when Jones made his will, and the two men have been confused (e.g. Logan Pearsall Smith, *The Life and Letters of Sir Henry Wotton* (1907) and James Lees-Milne, *The Age of Inigo Jones* (1953)). The other Henry Cogan, who was perhaps the translator's father, died on May 3rd, 1651, but in his administration (P.C.C. January 29th, 1651/2.) is described as "late of the Tower of London." This man was Sir Henry Wotton's servant, and was then granted a reversion (1625) to the office of Controller of the Mint, which office he enjoyed from 1640 (*C.S.P. Dom.* 1638–9, p. 198; *ibid.*, 1639/40, p. 423). The letters of administration of his goods were issued to his creditor, Thomas Knevett.

[3] "My Lady Devonshire at Row-Hampton, and my Lady Carlile at Petersham." Christian, Countess of Devonshire, daughter of Edward Bruce, 1st Lord Kinloss, married at the age of twelve and three months, in 1608, William Cavendish, afterwards 2nd Earl of Devonshire. About 1650, she purchased (as a widow) Roehampton House, Putney. She was a zealous Royalist, and patroness of men of letters. She died in 1675 (G.E.C., *Complete Peerage*). In one of the undated letters (see App. B. No. 4) Duppa mentions his anxiety over the Countess of Devonshire's dangerous illness. When Duppa's house at Richmond was searched in 1659, Lady Devonshire's house was also searched—possibly because they were known to be so friendly (*C.S.P. Dom.* 1659–60, p. 76). Mrs. Duppa in her will mentions "a greate bellyed cuppe" given her by Lady Devonshire. This Mrs. Duppa bequeathed to Sir Richard Chaworth.

Lucy Hay, Countess of Carlisle, daughter of Henry Percy, 9th Earl of Northumberland, married, in 1617, James Hay, afterwards Earl of Carlisle. She was Queen Henrietta Maria's "first choice of a friend amongst the English ladies." An unfortunate choice, since it was she who betrayed Charles I's intention to arrest the five Members of Parliament in 1642 to Pym, "the Ox", whom scandal declared had been her lover, "but it almost certainly accused her of too much generosity". In the latter years of the Civil War, her house was the meeting place of a cabal of aristocratic Presbyterians. On March 15th, 1649, she was arrested, and sent to the Tower, where she remained till March 1652. (Carola Oman, *Henrietta Maria*,

who will not suffer me to be so much an hermit as otherwise I would be. For though I love my own solitude as much as ever any hermit did, yet I am not arrived to that sowrness of melancholy as to say, as that monk did, who was wont to call to them that cam to visit him: "Disturb me not, *ego enim mortuus sum*." You would hardly beleive that this great lady (the latter of the two) formerly waited on by all the great persons of the Court, should now walk single and alone to the seat on top of the Hill, and enioy herself more in this retiredness then in all her former vanities (for the gayeties, and splendors of this world ar no better); and really ether she doth so, or personates it (at least) so to the life, that as yet I know not how to discover where the failing is. How ever I am so well pleas'd with the beleif of it, that I cannot forbear communicating it with you, who have learnt by your own vertues to be taken with examples of this kind.

But I must remember that you tell me, that you ar now in the midst of your freinds that reioice with you, and therefore it wer very unseasonable to trouble you with a longer letter. If I be too long allready, I will not take it unkindly if you putt it in your pocket, and take your times of leasure in the reading of it. And so with my prayers for you, and yours, I rest,

Your very tru freind, and humble servant,
BR: SAR:

Richmond: Oct: 19.

I beseech you present my service where it is due though I do not allwaies mention it, and my wive's to boot.

[ENDORSED REPLY OF SIR JUSTINIAN]

My Lord, As in my letters so in my life mee thinks I am now going into the track, after so long being jolted up and down, and in it though not void of care, yet I hope none such as to make me less at leasure for the correspondency with my freinds. Your Lordship being pleas'd to express mine as acceptable to you as the raine to the rice, I must acknowledge your Lordship's to mee, as the rice it selfe to an hungry appetite both delight and nourishment, far different from the converse to be now had with most, which is ether very insipide or if upon a knack more then ordinary, yet like to those *literae nihil sanantes*[4] mention'd by Seneca. Your noble neighbours I cannot but account very happy in being so neere to a St. Hierome-like hermit, whose austerity of life hath yet so much of pietie and humanity as not to disdaigne thier converse. Often have my thoughts suggested to mee that I know no man living more likely to make eminent persons in love with vertue then your selfe. Not those which come meerely from the schooles or out of the cell, how good and learned soever they be, can so wel worke upon those who have bin conversant in Courts, and really standing high are apt to think the rest of the world beneath them, but when such meet with one bred up to the same civilities as themselves, so knowing in their owne arts, so humane

(1936)). Dorothy Osborne, more critical of her sex, did not accept Bishop Duppa's view of her reformation. "I am a litle scandalised," she wrote to Temple on October 23rd, 1653, "I confesse that she uses that word faithfull, she that never knew how to bee soe in her life." Lady Carlisle died of apoplexy a few months after the Restoration. At the time of this letter, she was staying with the Carliles at Petersham Lodge.

[4] *Literae nihil sanantes*. "Literature that brings no healing." This seems to be a free adaptation of Cicero, *ad Att.*, XIII, 12, 1.

as to allow for custome, tyme, place, &c., and yet to be so severe in letting them know that religion and vertue are not meere pedantick termes, and how ever they are sometymes slovenly urged through the meaness and ignorance of many that make profession of them, and as wittily scoffed at by others who never did profess them; yet upon due consideration all passion, heat and vanity sett aside, *lex Domini immaculata convertens animos*[5], &c. And as those physitians think they come in a lucky tyme when the disease is abating, so I believe those tymes and yeares of riott now gon, with those your Lordship converseth with may make your wholesome exhortations the more prevalent.

And now my Lord you may think by my runing so fast I am gott into the track indeed, but I am not ignorant how some men run fastest when out of the way, For myself I cannot have better encouragement from any when I am in, or better direction when out, then from your Lordship, whose praiers I still beg, etc., etc.

Letter XXXVI

[November 1st.]

Sir, You ar now *hombre casado*, an hous'd man, as the Spaniard calls it, and though before your ent'ring into that condition of life, you wer wont to seek your home where you might conveniently find it, and I accidentally had som happiness by it, by enioying your very good company while you wer in that wand'ring condition, yet looking upon that as upon other worldly happinesses which I have formerly enioy'd, as transient things, such as I had no farther title to at all, then what Providence for a time allowd me, I am now content (but it is but a kind of mixt action (ἑκὼν ἀέκοντί γε θυμῷ[1]) to resign you up wholy to that unknown lady, who hath so much reason to possess you, that I dare not tempt you to wander from your own home, and will not offer to purchase so much faelicity to my self, by that which might be so great a loss to her. And therefore till your necessary occasions drive you from it, keep where you ar, and (as you have ever don) next under God be the maker of your own contentment, which certainly you may easier find within your own walls then if you should hunt for it all the land over. I confess I have so much of self love in me, that I do not say this to you without som reluctancy, for after all my grave admonitions, I shall be glad of an oportunity of seeing you again in these parts; for to see you where you are, I have no reason to hope for. You have many thinges in your last letters wherein your love to me hath so much over-master'd your judgement, as I nether dare own, nor contradict; not own, because upon enquiry into my self I find nothing of it, or contradict, for fear I should tempt you to say it over again. The truth is, ether I do not know my self, or you have not eaten salt enough with me to know me. For if I have any thing in me of being a courtier, it is somthing that I am utterly ignorant of, for while I lived among great persons, I applied my self to few of them, nor can I yet make my address to any as they ar great, but as I think them ether good, or capable to be made so. But in this you mistake me not, to think that all my complaisance is with a designe to make them in love with piety and vertu, and to continue them in the communion of a persecuted Church, which though formerly some of them have varied from, by a motion of trepidation at least, yet

[5] *Lex Domini immaculata convertens animos.* "The law of the Lord is an undefiled law, converting the soul." Psalm 18, v. 8 (Vulgate). Psalm 19, v. 7 (C.P.B.)

[1] ἑκὼν ἀέκοντί, etc. "With an unwilling heart." Homer, *Iliad* 4, 43 etc.

now, I am made to beleive, they look directly towards the right pole.

There is a great alteration likely to be at the Park, not so much by the departure of my Lady Carlile (who cam only till she could praepare lodgings in the Piazza[2]), but of all the rest; for the mistress of the family[3] intends for London, where she meanes to make use of her skill to som more advantage then hetherto she hath don. She is really a very good woman, and excellent in her way, but whether this may be a thriving course for her, I am not able to iudge, but I have great reason to wish it may prove so, and laying aside the reputation of not being mercenary, she may look to the profitable part of it.

If I should tell you that I am earnestly desired to write to you for a discovery of the way of making a Lamport hare-py, it might look very like a design of begging a py rather then the art of making it. But I must ether run the hazard of being suspected, or fail a great-bellied neighbor of mine (Mrs Frazer by name), who hath been very earnest with me to procure it, for in all the new bookes of cookery we cannot find it. You see by this the effects of the freedom which you give me, and ether you must cease to be kind to me, or I shall be likely more and more to make use of it. For the present if you pardon this, you may probably encourage me to offend again. Therefore consider what you do, and at all adventures continu to love him who daily prayes for you,

Your very faithfull, and humble servant
BR: SAR:

Nov: 1: Richm.

My wife is very desirous to know whether your two daughters be with you, and to be remembred to them as a great lover of them.

LETTER XXXVII

[NOVEMBER 16th.]

Sir, I began to give you over this last week, and to frame to my self som reasons that might hinder you from writing; but at the very end of the week, I not onely receaved your letters, but I receaved them *cum incremento*, with an excellent hare-pye, of which I gave a liberall share to the great belly, and the rest of it went among those, whose appetites to it wer as great though their bellies wer not. And thus you see I know how to be liberall *de alieno corio*, and did I not know with whom I had to deal with, I should be iealous of my self, least you should look upon me as one of the friers mendicant, who, if you offer them silver they will not touch it, but if you fill their wallet, they go away chearfully with it. But I have a double obligation laid upon me by this favor, for it is not onely a kindness from you, but from your Lady, who hath so much of your disposition in her, that she could easily part with such a present to satisfy the curiosity of a person so unknown to her, for which we return her our humble thankes, according to that princely phrase (mention'd by your self) which you ar now com to the honor to make use of.

I shall tell you no newes to say that how ever the earthquakes ar about us, and severall families and great ladies ar removed, yet the Hill is where it was, and when the wether will bear it, I stand as steadily upon it as the

[2] "The Piazza." About 1631, Inigo Jones laid out "The Piazza" of Covent Garden, including the Church of St. Paul on the West side. J. A. Gotch, *Inigo Jones* (1928), p. 177.

[3] "The mistress of the family," who is to use her skill, must be Mrs. Joan Carlile, for whom see Letter xv, Note 3.

burthen of old age and public calamities will give me leave, and for those that are personnall, and privat to me, I make it my business not to feel them, or at least not to trouble my freinds with them.

And the truth is you do very prophetically guess at my thoughts when you imagin me there in a brown study (as the phrase goes) and meditating upon the uncertainty and vanity of worldly things; an argument which I am so full of, that I could not keep it from running over, when accidenally in that place I had the conversation with that great lady[1], who having gon through both fortunes was a great example, and a willing hearer of all those uses which I could make of it.

I find the infirmities of age grow so fast upon me, that though I fancy to my self a great measure of contentment, in visiting you under your own roof, yet I dare not promise my self so much happiness, being now every day more and more likely to becom such a plant-animal, that feedes upon the grass about it (as long as it will last) and goes no farther. As for your own particular, you ar at a greater freedom, and have such advantages, that you can as easily bring your self hether, as think your self here.

I am not yet fitted to send you any thing of my own, but I can with more ease, and farr more confidence, send you a book of Dr. Taylor's[2] which cam to me warm from the press, and hath no longer cool'd in my hands, then during the time wherein I reade it over. You will find it to be a discourse occasioned by a conference he had with a Jesuit, against whom he hath argued with so much sharpness as if all his study had been in controversies, and yet hath framed his bookes of devotion so as if he understood nothing of them.

My nephew Chaworth hath been now a week at Draycot,[3] and when he returnes, I shall promise you for him, that he shall give you a full account of his journey. My wife presents her service to your good Lady, and your daughters, and thanks you for all your kindness to her. Though I told her that this was needless (for you would beleive as much though I said nothing), yet nothing would satisfy, till she had brought me to this wrong side of the paper; where it is high time I should take my leave of you, and give you my benediction, for though the Roman Church will not allow it to second marriages, I shall venture to vary from them, and wish

---

1 "That great lady." This is Lady Carlisle; see Letter xxxv, Note 3.

2 "A book of Dr. Taylor's." The work to which the Bishop here refers is Taylor's *Real Presence and Spirituall of Christ in the Blessed Sacrament, proved against the Doctrine of Transubstantiation*, dedicated to John Warner, Bishop of Rochester. The date of this publication is given as 1654, but it was clearly finished in the spring of 1653, and Bishop Duppa may have had an advance copy of the book as he had of the MS., for on April 11th, 1653, Taylor wrote to Gilbert Sheldon, later Bishop of London (Tanner MSS. 52, B.M., cited by Heber, *Life of Jeremy Taylor*, Vol. 1 of his works, (ed. Heber, revised Eden, (London 1854)): "Sir, I have now sent to the presse, but first to my Lord Bishop of Salisbury to be present, a discourse of the Real Presence, occasioned by my conference with a Jesuit in these parts (Wales)." Taylor's *Unum Necessarium*, published in 1654, was introduced with a preface inscribed to Bishops Duppa and Warner, but both these prelates dissented from the doctrine of original sin as therein expressed (Heber, *op. cit.*, p. xlii), and Duppa resented the fact that the book was dedicated to him, when his criticisms had not been taken into account. Taylor, however, speaks of Duppa in a letter to Sheldon as "a wise man and good man", a conclusion which these letters endorse.

3 "Draycot." "My nephew Chaworth" on September 1st, 1653 wrote to Sir Justinian to congratulate him on his marriage, and said 'I'me summon'd to Draycott [Wilts], my neice [Dorothy Long, wife of Colonel Long, see Letter V, Note 3] being ready to lie downe the next week, who wished her service remembered to you in her last letter (which looks like her last will) humbly beggs the religious education of her Jemmy of us" (I.C. 328).

so great a measure of blessings on you, that you may think your widdower's condition but a parenthesis, and your second marriage to be onely a continuation of your first And so, my best of freinds (if you will give me leave to call you so), I shall detain you with no more words, then these, that I am,

Your very sincere freind, and humble servant,
BR: SARUM. Richm: Nov. 16.

LETTER XXXVIII

[DECEMBER 14th.]

Sir, If you did not hear from me the last week you must impute it to the compact that was between us, that I was not to be confident that you wer returned to your home, till I heard from your self that you wer there. But I fear I have not onely miscarried in this, but possibly the waterman did not bring my thankes to you for the kindness I receaved then, and for all the future kindnesses which you have so prae-disposed of, as if you wer resolved that I should ow nothing to any man but your self. I confess I have not been tempted by many, though I have had som professions made to me, which have been warm in the mouth, but cold in the operation. And I have som reverence to my calling, not to make my self cheap at least (whatsoever my necessities ar, or may be), but this I can say (though it may be to your cost) that *nulli libentius debeo*; for ether I am deceaved (and if I be it is a very strong delusion), or you ar that person made up of so much freindship, as I know not where to match you, especially in these times, when I standing upon the lower ground have no way left me to oblige you. But I will say the less, because I will make up the rest in my prayers for you.

By this time, I beleive, that the vertigo that hath happen'd to us in the head of our Government, is made known to you by divers relations[1]. The thing that was don was so far rationally acted as to make good the old rule: *Eius est destruere, cuius est struere*[2]. And the truth is we are now a praepared matter to work upon; and may be ether molded, or unmolded, as the clay is in the hands of children, or as a house of cards, which they may build and blow down again at pleasure. But all this while God keepes his counsells apart, and what he is building we know not. I do not use to write any thing of this nature to you, but my hand being in,

[1] The graphic account of the end of Barebone's Parliament which follows is an unusual, and most interesting, digression into public affairs. When this nominated body met in July, M. de Bordeaux, the French Ambassador, said : "The new Parliament is composed of persons who believe themselves inspired." Their levelling tendencies were disturbing to Cromwell, and on December 12th, 1653, Sir Charles Worsley and Colonel Sydenham proposed that they should "give back their power to the General from whom it came, on the grounds that the majority were aiming at the destruction of the clergy, the law, and the liberty of the individual." Led by the Speaker, some of the members then trooped off to Cromwell, leaving the remaining members to be dispersed by a file of musketeers (M. Ashley, *Oliver Cromwell* (1937), p.191). Praise-God Barebone, or Barebones (1596?–1679), one of the "fagg-end of the company," who has given his name to the Assembly, was one of the members for London.

[2] *Eius est destruere*, etc. "It is the duty of him, whose duty it is to build to destroy also." Although historians have differed as to Cromwell's responsibility for the ejection of Barebone and his associates, and his knowledge of the proposal to resign to him the powers of the Parliament, it was clearly Duppa's opinion that he planned the whole thing. According to the account given by Gardiner (Vol. II, p.327), Colonel Goffe was unable to reply, when the "fagg-end of the company" demanded to see Cromwell's order, disbanding them. Duppa gives a rather different account of the dialogue between the minority of members and the soldiers. He was not, of course, an eye-witness and not unprejudiced. But see next letter.

I cannot forbear one passage; and it was thus. When som officers of the Army emploi'd by the Generall, cam to give a period to this last mock-shew of a Parliament, the greatest part of the zealous men had such a sudden damp cast upon them, that they went away with their eares couchant and scarse a spirit left among the sons of the Spirit, to protest against it. But not to do them iniury, som relicks of men wer left, that ether out of courage or stupidity kept their places, and when I tell you that Barebones was one (with som very few more) you may well think there was but the sceleton left. And yet this would not be suffer'd, for the commanders (and commanders you may be sure they wer that could dissolve Parliaments) ask'd this fagg-end of the company, why they stai'd, and what they did there. The answer was, that they wer seeking of God; to which was very hansomly replied, that if they would seek God, they should seek Him where He was to be found, but they wer sure, that there He was not. What may be the issue of this onely that God knowes, who, having made the world out of that which the Rabbins call *Tohu*, and *Bohu*, may, when he pleaseth, produce order out of all this confusion. But I have shamefully overrun my paper, and must now say no more then that I am,

Your most tru freind and most humble servant,
BR: SARUM. Richm: Dec: 14.

I beseech you present our humble service to your noble Lady, and your very good daughters.

LETTER XXXIX

[DECEMBER 20th.]

Sir, This is a supernumerary letter, for I wrott the last week, and am not patient enough to stay my turn. For every day now unfolds new wonders, which I beleive your diurnalls ar full of; but I must call them wonders rather then miracles, for miracles com immediately from Heaven, but wonders ar contrived, and brought about by darker principles. The grounds of them have been laid long ago, and whatsoever hath been don since, hath been in order to them, but more remarkably the calling of this last (I know not what to call it), which from the beginning of it was a train laid to make somthing that followes, the more plausible.

When I have said thus much, I begin to call my self to an account, how I slipt into this argument, for you and I deal not often in this way. But to correct my self for this excess, I will deny my self the pleasure of writing a longer letter to you, though your last tempts me very much; for I find in it so much of your care for me, as might require very large expressions of thankfulness (at least), when there is nothing else left to return. But because my turn may com about again before it be long, I will not overlay this paper, but remain in very few words,

Your most affectionat freind,
BR: SAR: Richm: Dec: 20.

In the interval between these two letters, Cromwell had accepted the Instrument of Government drawn up by the Army, and become Protector of the Commonwealth of England, Scotland and Ireland.

When Cromwell opened the first Parliament of the Protectorate (September 3rd, 1654), he maintained that he did not know that the Parliament meant to resign the power into his hands, and that he was ignorant of the Instrument of Government. "The gentlemen who undertook to frame this Government did consult divers days together . . . they did consult: but that I was not privy to their councils they know it" (Carlyle, *Cromwell's Letters and Speeches*, Speech III). The Bishop clearly would not believe a word of this disclaimer, for he saw Cromwell's action as a deep-laid scheme "contrived . . . by darker principles." At the end of this letter he calls himself to account, "for you and I deal not often in this way."

1654

The first year of the Protectorate was not an easy one for the two correspondents. But it was, at least, better than the one that followed it, and than the trying domestic worries of 1653.

Cromwell, or ὁ μέγας, as Duppa calls him, was now something after the pattern of a constitutional King, and although he found this position impossible to maintain, and his relations with his Parliaments were as uneasy as James I's, his personal power was now unassailable. Peace after many difficulties was signed with the Dutch, and the position of the exiled King rendered even more precarious.

The Royalist society, in which Duppa and Sir Justinian lived, appeared slightly more hopeful, and the Protector was supposed to be less opposed to the Prayer Book than the "saints" of the nominated Parliament (Letter XLI, Note 3). Sir Justinian's new wife produced a daughter, which event, as Duppa infers, " promised boys hereafter." He lost his sister Elizabeth, who had been the main prop of Lamport during the Civil War, and he commissioned John Webb, the pupil of Inigo Jones, to build him a new classical front as a "nest" for his Lady.

There are two allusions to celebrated literary figures which deserve a mention. Jeremy Taylor writes to thank Sir Justinian for help received, in a letter of graceful prose, (Letter L), and Selden's death at the end of the year shows that there was keen interest among scholars about how he had disposed of his books and MSS. Strongly as Selden was opposed to Duppa in political matters, it is evident that the two men, on learned grounds, were old friends, and it was natural that there should be anxiety over his literary legacy.

Minor literary figures are also frequently mentioned; Sir Robert Filmer, Dr. Hammond, Dr. Henry More, the Platonist, Dr. Robert Flood, John Hall of Richmond, Dr. Seth Ward, and Jeremy Stephens; a "mixed bag" of political theorists, philosophers, antiquaries, theologians and scientists, at one only in their attachment to the royal cause.

Letter XL

[January 4th.]

Sir, I will not willingly loose my turn, and if I do, you may beleive, it is no ordinary accident that hinders me. I was never yet any of your politicall freinds, though when things wer *in vertigine* (and whether the vertigo be yet off I know not), I gave you som such animadversions as wer so obvious, that I knew not how to avoid them. Our affaires at first wer like an eddy at London bridge, where towards an high tide, the waters run in circles as doubtfull whether they should go on, or retire back; and truly the dissolution of the last thing look'd very like it. But the new Declaration[1]

[1] "The new Declaration." The pamphlet, *Declaration concerning the Government of three nations*, recording Cromwell's speech at his installation as Lord Protector on December 16th, was published on December 21st, 1653 (Ranke, *History of England*, Vol. III, p. 116).

(which I beleive by this time is com to your hands) will clear all this. I will make no commentary upon it, but I beleive (besides the horror of som things), you will meet with many contradictions in it, which you who ar not onely of a loyall, but of a rationall, and mathematicall soul, cannot easily digest.

When you have don with my cosin[2], I pray return him to us, for he hath fed us this Christmas, and we ar not well till we have thank'd him for it. As for my obligations to you, I perceave I cannot please you better then with silence, which in other things is easy to me, but not in this.

I have with much adoo gott the two sermons described, the one is my owne, and the other is so much better, that I should not wrong my self to wish it wer my own. But now they ar both yours, I have not so much time as to correct the errata of the scribe, but you ar so intelligent a reader, that it will be no hard task to do it for me. I have somthing else to transmitt to you, which will come by parcels and degrees, though they ar long in comming. You have in the mean time given us occasion to remember you, which is not more faithfully don in any family then in this poor one, whereof the master of it, is

Your very tru freind, and most humble servant,
BR: SAR:

Richm: Jan: 4.

LETTER XLI

[JANUARY 17th.]

Sir, I perceave that what is but doubtfull here, is certain with you in the country, and if I write somthing now like a polititian to you, I would not have you impute it to any deep coniectures of mine, but to your old freind Mr. Aldridge[1], who hath, for your sake, given me a visit this morning, and tells me that it is a measuring cast, whether in this last Treaty the Dutch have outreach'd the new Protector, or he them[2]. There is still praeparation on both sides for a warr, and what the secret close of this may be is not yet known. That which keepes me undisturbed in all events, is, that I can say : *Scio cui credidi*, and upon the strength of that, so wholy resign all that may concern me into God's hands, as to becom one of your mathematicall cubes of which no motion can alter the figure, for still it will be a cube.

I thanke you for the papers you sent me, and so much the more, because I have still expected that som discreet learned person would take it in hand

2 "My cosin." For John Lowen or Lewyn (as he signs himself in a letter to Sir Justinian dated April 6th, 1654), see Letter XXIII, Note 5.

1 "Mr. Aldridge." See Letter I, Note 2.

2 Dutch situation. See Gardiner, Vol. III, p. 63 seq. The Dutch Commissioners left on January 4th. The situation is well summed up in a letter dated January 4th, 1653/4 to Sir Justinian from "G.W." (Sir George Wentworth of Woolley, Yorks, a zealous Royalist, died October 18th, 1660, who seals his letter with the Wentworth crest, a griffin passant, wings elev. argent): "these printed sheetes will make known to you the condition of our late change, yet now we heare the Dutch Ambassadors are for certaine gone and left little or noe hope of a peace between them." Peace was at length signed on April 5th, and Cromwell secured what he hoped would be a "permanent bar to the advancement of the young prince of Orange" to a position where he could further the cause of his uncle, Charles II.

"The new Protector". On his acceptance of the Instrument of Government, Cromwell became Lord Protector and Chief Magistrate, bound to summon a Parliament on September 3rd, 1654, being entrusted with governing when Parliament was not sitting: it was an elective office for life only (Morley, *Cromwell*, p. 372, Gardiner, *Constitutional Documents of the Puritan Revolution*, p. 405).

(for both those qualities must meet to make that work perfect). This which is don by your freind (whosoever he be) as far as it reacheth, is very clear, and plain, and so much the fitter for the end design'd, which is to satisfy the ignorant, who, having good affections, ar now farther arm'd, both to defend themselves, and to instruct others.

I shall desire you to encourage the author of these notes, to go on and complete what he hath begun, not onely in that which is properly the liturgy, but in the rituals which are ioyn'd to it[3].

I do not know whether you have observed it, or no; but if you have, you have seen the margin of my Common Prayer book charged with notes, which, if nothing else of that kind should com forth, I had in my thoughts to leave (among som other little things) as a legacy to you. But these notes ar scatter'd, and undigested, and since there is another hand hath took care of it, I shall be very willing (when you let me know the person) to communicat with him. For he shall have my collections so freely, that I do not so much as desire to have my name rememb'red ether in them, or for them. I shall draw them up when I hear farther from you, and since you have begun to acquaint me with this, which is allready don, I shall desire to see the rest, and though I may add nothing yet possibly he may be no looser by it. I have return'd you them by this next carrier, that no time might be lost.

The progress of our cosin, he acquainted me with before, but for his going to Oxford, and reading six solemn lectures of Monarchy for his degree, I used all the reason I could to dissuade him, for ether it will be interpreted a flattery to him who is now ὁ μέγας, or if he point to the right Person, he may ruin himself, and not profit the cause[4].

I am now com to the limbus, and have no more room left me, then to wish you and yours more happyness then this year is likely to bring forth, and so very constantly rest,

Your most tru freind, and servant,
BR: SAR:

Jan: 17.

LETTER XLII

[FEBRUARY 1st.]

Sir, I perceave by your last letters, that there is somthing of amorousness in freindship, or else I could never have look'd for such kind expressions from you as look back to the very cradle, and first beginnings of it. But the truth is, though the root of freindship be under ground and not allwaies visible to common eyes, yet the leaves and blossoms, and fruit of it, ar not capable of being hidden. And since you ar pleas'd to take delight in the circumstances of time, and place, and persons, I think my self the more concern'd to praeserve the substance by all the duties of freindship that I can possibly pay you.

You know I do not use to tempt you to com into these parts, for I know how to love you, though I do not see you; but we ar now here left very

[3] Sir George Wentworth in his letter of January 4th had said "the newes is very current about the towne that the Protector expresses thus much that the ministrie would discreetly use the Common Prayer. I hear this from persons of good credite." This hope of toleration may have encouraged the Bishop.

[4] "Not profit the cause." ὁ μέγας is Cromwell; "the right Person" is Charles II; John Lowen is the author of these lectures. His degree (of D.C.L.) was rendered back to him after the Restoration, when such speculations would have been more in vogue. He was not lacking in courage. See Letter XXIII, Note 5.

bare of freinds, not onely of som great ladies, but of that very good woman your landlady of the Park[1], who hath now took an house in the Covent Garden, and to raise up som fortune for her self and children, is resolved there to use her skill for somthing more then empty fame. And you know what this signifies, that when your occasions draw you and yours to London, you may know where to have your freinds doubled and to have a counterpart both of your self, and them. I tell you nothing of the times, and if you please, let it be a condition between us, not to do it. You remember who said to his freind: *Satis magnum theatrum sumus tu et ego*[2], and abating the vainglory of saying it, there is really between us somthing that may make it up. But this fair day I am call'd upon for a walk up the Hill, where I find my seat and miss nothing but you. Sir, I pray for you, and yours, and am,

Your most tru freind, and humble servant,
BR: SAR:

Richm : Febr. 1.

LETTER XLIII

[FEBRUARY 14th.]

Sir, When I speak of the removing of neighbors, I speak of it in the literall, popular way; for 'Ακροαματικῶς as the more knowing party use to express them selves, I look upon them as not remov'd; and I am the more apt to fall upon this consideration, because, if I thought otherwise, I should be much troubled that you and I ar at such a distance. The nearest neighbor is he that is the best freind; or else the Samaritan's parable had been lost.

I have receaved the letter, and the papers from my cosin Stephens[1], which I shall at some time or other give him account of, but for the present I am taken off by som other occasions.

The mentioning of the Covent Garden[2], was not in any design of meeting you there, or that you should take any resemblance of me, who desire to be rememb'red by you in the nobler part of you, where the drawing of features and the laying of colours have no influence at all.

And yet I dare not say that I had no design in it, for (though my meaning was that when your occasions brought your Lady and your daughters to these parts, you would so farr encourage the artist (who hath great affections for you) as to take the copies of them, for though you have now the originalls (and my prayer is that you may not loose one of them,) yet evidence of this kind ar of a perishing condition, and somtimes the

---

[1] "Your landlady of the Park." See Letter XXXVI, Note 3. This is Joan Carlile. Covent Garden was the artists' quarter of London until well on in the 18th century. The miniaturist, Samuel Cooper, whose portrait of Sir Justinian faces page XXXII lived in Henrietta Street, Covent Garden. A near neighbour would have been Mary Beale, whose fame as an artist has outlived Joan Carlile's; Mary's son, Bartholomew, was registered at St. Paul's, Covent Garden in 1655/6, when the Beales lived at Hind Court, Fleet Street.

[2] *Satis magnum theatrum, etc.* "You and I are a sufficiently large theatre." In one of the undated letters (see App. B) Bishop Duppa says Seneca wrote this "to his good friend, Lucilius." (I (D) 123). Adapted from *Epist. Morales* I, 7, 11.

[1] "My cosin Stephens." For Jeremiah Stephens see Letter IV, Note 7.

[2] "Covent Garden". It was evidently Bishop Duppa's wish that Sir Justinian and his family should be painted by Joan Carlile. There is an oval portrait of Sir Justinian at Lamport of about this date, but this picture is generally attributed to Lely (R. B. Beckett, *Lely* (1951) p. 48, No. 260.) It once belonged to Mrs. Dorothy Long, who left it in her will to Sir Justinian Isham, 4th Bart.

counterpart may do som service, when the lease is lost, yet after all this long and multipled parenthesis) I shall really confess to you, that I have had a long studied designe of having your picture, and by that hand rather then by any else. Though I have receaved many kindnesses from you, they have hetherto flow'd from you like the purest balsam, without cutting; but this I am not ashamed to begg of you. And so with my prayers for you, and your whole family, I rest,

Your very affectionat freind and faithfull servant,
BR: SAR:

Richm: Feb: 14.

My wife desires to have her humble service praesented to your Lady, which is implied both in her behalf, and mine in all my letters, though not allwaies expressd.

[ENDORSED REPLY OF SIR JUSTINIAN]

Though at this distance yet I find your freindship to me still keeps me your neighbor, truly my thoughts are very much with your Lordship, but in your letters me thinks I both heare and see you. And so in these I have more then your picture, the lively image of your better part; but enough of you I cannot have, and therefore hope not in any way to be denied. Your Lordship's request for a copy where you have so absolute a command of the originall is easily obtain'd. But your requests (give me leave to tell your Lordship) are all of a straine, to oblige the giver to you as much in their performance, as to it.

Yet as men once in a desperat debt care not how much they afterward run out, so little now do I feare the increasing my obligations to your Lordship, having so long since owed you the utmost of

Your &c.

LETTER XLIV

[FEBRUARY 28th.]

Sir, Since I wrott last, our little cosin[1] was with me, who though he doth not deliver him self in your expressions, hath said as much as might have fill'd a score of letters. And really I was never better pleas'd to hear him speak much, for the subiect matter of what he said, was the happyness which you enioy'd in your late choice, a Lady not onely very good in her self, but suitable to your disposition, which certainly is the highest point of blessing which marriage can possibly afford you, especially when I consider that your disposition is, to be religious towards your God, faithful to your freinds, beneficiall to your neigbors, good to all that have any relation to you, that though you know how to make use of that which is call'd the happyness of this life, yet you sett not your heart upon it, but make your self such freinds of it, as may lead you on to an happyness that can have no end, and of which the former scarse deserves to be a shadow of. And since you both ioyn in this harmony of minds, I can look for nothing but growing blessings upon your family. And though the musick of it be at such a distance, that I cannot yet be an ear wittness of it, yet you must give me leave to be pleas'd with the whispers and ecchoes of it. As for the continuance of it, I cannot doubt, for coniugall love built upon religion, is the house built upon the rock, which no stormes of this world can shake. What I can adde to it is onely my

1 "Our little cosin." This is J. Lowen. See Letter XXIII, Note 5, etc.

prayers, which though they pass for little in the scales of this world, yet God hath another balance for them, and there they have more weight. When I had wrott thus farr, and was about to make an end, I was surpris'd by the honest merchant of St. Martin's Lane[2], who cam to dine with me, and very much desires that you will still own him as one that hath a design to serve you, in all that you can command him. I was not unwilling to transmitt thus much to you, for I know no greater design I have then to be instrumentall in making good men love one the other. And so when you have commended us to your excellent Lady, and the rest of the best of your family, I have no other thing to ask of you, but to continue me in their favor, and yours.

Your very tru freind, and humble servant.
[Signature omitted]

Richm: Febr: *ult.*

[Endorsed reply of Sir Justinian]

I find our little cosin hath made a large relation and am glad he hath found cause to deliver what your Lordship is so wel pleas'd to heare. Your Lordship's good beleife of my disposition is an especiall motive to make mee endeavor it may be answerable to it. I praise God I have mett with one that I hope will so suit with mee as not to have many desires very different from mine owne. A quiet and cheerefull life to ourselves is the utmost of our ambition. We are not likely to be very troublesome to our neighbours, nor I hope to our selves. My cheifest imployment at present seems to me as naturall as to the very birds and crowes about mee, to be busy in building my nest[3] against my wife lies downe[4], not with much greater designe then they, raising no proud structure to sett my heart upon it, but such as if these stormy dayes chance to blow away, yet my rest remaines on a city not built with hands. I still crave the continuance of your Lordship's praiers, and am.

Letter XLV

[March 27th.]

Sir, I find that you have mett the lost letter, and I am the better pleas'd, that it hath fal'n into no hands but yours (not that there was any danger in the loss of it) but because no body was concern'd in it but you. I remember that in your hast'ning away to this match, there was not onely love to your choice, but a great observance to the rules of the Church, from whence you desired to have the blessing rather then from your neighbor the Justice of Peace, and I am confident that blessing will follow you. And the truth is, (without flattering you at all, for I cannot possibly love you so ill as to be guilty of it) you ar a person of that temper, as cannot be dis-

[2] "The honest merchant of St. Martin's Lane." This is John Adler, a Turkey merchant, whom Duppa appointed one of the executors of his will ('Sir John Adler of St. Martin's in the Fields, Knight'). He was knighted after the Restoration. On April 5th, 1655 he forwarded a letter from "my Lord Bishop of Salisbury" to Sir Justinian (I.C. 355).

[3] "Building my nest." This is the first allusion to Sir Justinian's new building at Lamport Hall, of which John Webb (1611–72, pupil and kinsman of Inigo Jones) was the architect. For a full description of this work with reproductions of Webb's own drawings see an article by J. A. Gotch in the R.I.B.A. *Journal*, September 24th, 1921; and Arthur Oswald, "Lamport Hall" in *Country Life*, September 26th, October 3rd and October 10th, 1952).

[4] "Against my wife lies downe." On February 13th, 1653/4 Thomas, Lord Leigh wrote to Sir Justinian: "I am upone the like employment that you are, paching of an oulde house, which hou long I may enjoye is uncertayne . . . I shall extremely desire to see how well a great belly becomes my daughter." (I.C. 336).

agreed with, and if freindship makes up all relations, I know none that hath all the arts of it more then you.

That you ar building a nest for your Ladye's lying down is very wellcom newes to me; for though you had a nest for her, before you had the Lady; yet this care of making all the more convenient for her, implies somthing more, that your affection to her is so great, that you do not onely enlarge your heart, but your house for her.

But that which I am most taken with, is, that you ar one of St. Paul's *Tanquam non*, and look upon all these wordly things as if you had them not. For if you should once prize them above their rate, and sett your heart upon them, you might probably tempt God, that with so free a hand hath dispensed these blessings to you, to snatch them away again, as from him, who loves His gifts more passionatly then he loves Him. Onely among all worldly things, the love that you ar to bear to your dear wife, hath a speciall priviledge. *Nec timendum est ut sit nimium, quod esse maximum debet*[1]. There needs nothing on my part to ty the knot faster, for a couple so well suited have their harmony from within, and no stranger is to entermedle in their joyes. All that I have to do, is to say more for you then to you, and being resolved to make up in prayers what I want in words, I shall say no more, but that I am a

Very faithfull freind, and humble servant to you both,
BR: SAR:

Richm: March 27.

My wife must have her share in presenting her service to you both. And that my letter may not miscarry, I have sent it by my cosin Lowen 3 dayes before the time. The free-hearted honest merchant, I have not lately seen, but I can assure you that he is a great lover of you, and therefore when we meet, your remembrance to him shall not be forgotten.

LETTER XLVI

[APRIL 11th.]

Sir, Though our letters may possibly miscarry, yet as long as nothing of freindship on ether side is lost by it, the adventure will not be great, for whether there be a return or no, the merchandise which we trade in cannot suffer by it; and therefore when any thing intervenes that may make writing a trouble to you, I can satisfy my self that even in that silence of yours I can receave an answer from your thoughts, and as the schoolmen say of angels, that their manner of speech is onely an inclination of their will, that other angels should understand them, so I am not unwilling to beleive, but that we should clearly understand one the other, though we should write nothing.

I am troubled in the mean time, for that which afflicts you, the sickness of your onely sister[1], whose health I shall pray for as being yours. There

[1] *Nec timendum est ut sit nimium, quod esse maximum debet.* "One need not feel apprehensive that what ought to be very great may appear excessive." Adapted from Pliney, *Epist.* VIII, 24.

[1] "Your onely sister." This is Elizabeth Isham, born January 28th, 1609: buried at Lamport April 11th, 1654. She was unmarried. Years before, she had been engaged to John Dryden of Canons Ashby, Northants, grandson of Sir Erasmus Dryden. He was anxious to marry her, but Sir Erasmus and Sir John Isham quarrelled over settlements, and he died unmarried on December 4th, 1631. He was a first cousin of the poet. (*Visitation of Northants* 1681 ed. Longden, Harl. Soc., 1935). After this she had lived with her father at Lamport. She was a fervent Royalist, and wrote "meditations" on religious themes. Her younger sister, Judith, had died in 1636.

is nothing in these times ether within us or without us, that may not putt us in mind of our mortality, but the more then ordinary frequency of examples of suddain death, may very well startle, and rowse us up to a daily praeparation for it. The old Countess of Excester [Exeter][2], having outlived her own loyalty, and pleas'd her self that she had so much wisdom of this world, as to enioy her estate, had but an houre's warning both to praepare her self for the repentance of the former, and to quitt the latter.

My Lord Beauchamp[3], the onely blossom left that looked like any thing of tru nobility, is wither'd away, in a time when there was most need of him. And to com nearer to a late desolation in our own neighborhood, we have lost Mrs. Fraser[4], who being great with child, and lodged in London in her midwive's house, that she might be near her remedy, yet could find none, for she unexpectedly died before the midwife could do her office.

I would not have your young Lady hear this part of the catalogue of mortality, for women in her condition ar too apt to kindle their feares, from praecedents of this kind. But not to tire you out, in so melancholy a theme, I shall say no more, but hartily pray that health may be within your dwellings, and so rest in that prayer

Your very sincere freind, and humble servant,
BR: SAR:

Richm: Apr: 11.

[ENDORSED REPLY OF SIR JUSTINIAN]

Since my last to your Lordship which acquainted you with our condition heere, God hath pleased to take my sister to Him after her 15th daye being ill when we hoped a recovery. There have not any since falen sick amongst us. God grant we make a right use of this His visitation, many in these parts as elswhere being suddenly taken. The last of those late examples your Lordship writes off in regard to her many small children, her husband's absence, and the cause of it, calls for commiseration more then ordinary. The sorrows incident to this life being so great and suddaine might in common reason bind us all to be helpfull to each other in what we may, and yet the cheifest misery of all is that men usually receive more mischeife from one another then what otherwise befalls them: The world it selfe being but a Common Place Booke of such examples setts the higher

---

2 "The old Countess of Excester." This is the second wife of William Cecil, 2nd Earl of Exeter. She was Elizabeth, daughter of Sir William Drury of Hawsted, Suffolk. She was born January 4th, 1578/9, and died at Exeter House, February 26th, 1653/4. She was buried at St. James's, Clerkenwell, where there is a monument to her memory. In her will (proved April 12th, 1654) she gave the residue of her goods to her grandson Lord Grey of Groby, "a zealous Republican", one of the most active of the Regicide judges (died 1657). Her house at Newark was sacked in 1643, and her rich furniture pillaged. The fact that she suffered in the Civil War on the King's account, and left her estate mostly to her Republican grandson, explains the Bishop's allusion. (Barron, *Northamptonshire Families* (V.C.H., 1906), and information kindly supplied by the present Marchioness of Exeter).

3 "My Lord Beauchamp." Henry Seymour, son of William Seymour, Marquess of Hertford, was styled Lord Beauchamp 1646–54. He was married in 1648 to Mary Capel, sister of Arthur Capel, 1st Earl of Essex. He died v.p. at "Tilsy", and was buried March 30th, 1654 aged about 28, at Bedwyn Magna. Lely painted him about 1651/2. The portrait (reproduced R. B. Beckett, *Lely*, pl. 30), was formerly at Savernake (Marquess of Ailesbury). His father was Governor of Charles II, as a boy, when Duppa was tutor. (See Letter CXVII, Note 2).

4 "Mrs. Fraser." See Letter XXXVI, where Bishop Duppa solicited a "hare-py" for her.

prise on true freindship: the effects of which I find in your Lordships' praiers for me and mine, for which I humbly thank your Lordship, and am very well pleas'd that the maine subject of our letters (setting all misteries of State and iniquity aside) is likely to be in a right valuation of the things of this world and to prepare us for a better kingdome.

I am uncertaine of my coming to London but . . .

Letter XLVII

[April 17th.]

Sir, When I wrott last, I was in so much hast, as I could then use but very few wordes, nor am I at much liberty now, for the afflicted widow[1] of that noble Lord having made choice to retire her self, for a time, under my roof, all my thoughts are taken up which way I may best comfort her, and I am not out of hope of settling her unquiet mind, before we part.

But somthing there was which I should have said then, had not that sad accident diverted me; and it is a proposall that was made to me by a very noble, and honest gentleman concerning matching his onely son into your family, a young person of a very good outside, hansom, and well fashion'd, and of such parts of civility, and good literature, as cannot but be very acceptable, and agreeable to you. The father is your countryman, and a great lover of you. But when I have said all this, it may be I have begun at the wrong end, and should have told you first what the estate was, which though it ought not to be the principall verbe, yet the whole sentence will be lame without it. And to satisfy you in this, I must tell you that the proposer is Mr. Rich: Spenser[2]; but what the estate is must be left to a scrutiny which I am not capable of looking into. I profess I am much taken with the young gentleman, as with a person who hath not onely very good parts, but a great measure of discretion to govern them. If there may be way given for a more immediat address to be made to you, there will be no farther need of my letters; but if upon consideration of all circumstances, you shall not find it convenient for you, I shall upon your next intimation, praevent you the trouble of a farther prosecution of it. I can say no more for the present, but to beg your pardon for my intermedling in a business of this nature, which my great affection to your family hath engaged me to return rather then any over busy disposition of mine

[1] "The afflicted widow". This is Mary Capel, daughter of Arthur, 1st Lord Capel of Hadham, a Royalist, who was executed in 1649, whose sister Elizabeth had married Sir Justinian's maternal uncle and godfather Sir Justinian Lewyn (1586–1620). This connection with the Lewyns probably explains the interest which the Bishop and Sir Justinian felt in her. She was born in 1630 and married Lord Beauchamp in 1648. She did not remain inconsolable, for on August 17th, 1657 she married again, Henry, Lord Herbert, later 1st Duke of Beaufort. She died in 1715 and was buried at Badminton. (G.E.C., *Complete Peerage*, Monument to Sir Justinian Lewyn in Otterden Church).

[2] "Rich : Spenser." Richard Spencer was the fourth son of Sir Thomas Spencer, 1st Bart. of Yarnton. His nephew Thomas Spencer, son and heir of Sir William Spencer, 2nd Bart., is probably the young man recommended as a suitable husband for one of Sir Justinian's four daughters by his first wife, all then living and unmarried. The Spencers of Yarnton are described as "countrymen" of Sir Justinian, as they "were nearly allied to the Rt. Honble family" of the Spencers of Wormleighton and Althorp, and Earls of Sunderland (Wotton's *Baronetage*). Thomas Spencer eventually married the first cousin of the Misses Isham, Jane Garrard, and succeeded as third Bart. He died in 1685. His daughter Jane married Robert Spencer ("Robin"), younger brother of the 1st Earl of Sunderland, created Viscount Teviot in the peerage of Scotland. (Burke, *Extinct and Dormant Baronetcies*).

own, in which I beleive none can clear me better then your self who know me to be

Your most faithfull servant and sincere freind
BR: SAR:

Richm: Apr: 17.

LETTER XLVIII

[APRIL 25th.]

Sir, The breach made in your family[1], if my prayers may praevail, shall go no farther. But because near, and domestick examples of this kind, ar apt to have a greater influence upon us, and not onely leave a sorrow for what is lost, but a fear of loosing more, you will have need of renewing daily that great lesson of Christianity, of resigning all that is dear to you into His hands, of whom one, though out of the pale of the Church, had knowledge enough to say: *Charior est illi homo quam sibi*[2]. For though you have lost a sister (or rather parted with her for a time), she hath lost nothing by it, but in her virgin condition may be charitably beleived to follow the Lamb wheresoever He goes. If she hath bequeathed any thing to charitable uses, that may extend farther then your own neighborhood, I desire you would trust me with the distributing of som small portion of it in these parts, for there ar som very good men within the compass of my reach, that have need of it, and I shall ether very faithfully dispose of it, or when you com into these parts, be your remembrancer, and direct you where you may do it with your own hands. You see, in the mean time, what a bold thing freindship is, and how ever I might blush in speaking for my self, with what confidence I can plead for others. But ether I know you so well, that you will thank me, for helping you with the occasion of exercising your bounty in this kind, or I shall despair of knowing any with whom I can any way persuade my self to be so free.

I am at this time under a pain, which St. Austin in his book of *Confessions* passionatly complain'd of, and though the philosophers say that *ossa non sentiunt*, I have felt somthing ether within them, or about them (my teeth I mean) that hath by fitts very much tortured me.

I am none of those that use to tempt you to com into these parts, for as long as you afford me your letters, I both see you, and converse with you in every line you write. And yet I am not so cold, and indifferent in my temper toward you, as not to think the sight of you once more would be a great refreshing to me. The mystery of contracting this term[3] is not yet reveal'd, but of the next it is expected that it should bring forth wonders. What use I make of Mr. Street, you will find to your cost, when you com, which I am willing to coniecture, may possibly be the next term, for after that comes the *magnum inane* of the long vacation. But whensoever, or wheresoever it shall be my happyness to meet you, what ever other changes may happen, I shall be found unalterably the same,

Your most affectionat tru freind and humble servant,
BR: SAR:

Richm: Apr: 25.

---

[1] "The breach made in your family." This was caused by Elizabeth Isham's death: see Letter XLVI.

[2] *Charior est illi homo quam sibi.* "Man is clearer to Him than to himself." Juvenal, *Sat.* x, 350. Juvenal has *illis*, i.e. to the Gods. This reference has been identified by Mr. J. M. Wyllie, Editor of *The Oxford Latin Dictionary*. (See also Letter LVII).

[3] "This term". The law term; see Dorothy Osborne's *Letters* for the habit of the country gentry to visit London during the law terms.

LETTER XLIX

[MAY 9th.]

Sir, There must needs be a great deal of goodness in you, who interpret so fairly the proposall that I made to you. But you may beleive me, that I had no other design in it, then, upon praesupposall that every good person dying left somthing to indigent persons (knowing the wants of som very good men), I could not forbear to tempt you that som small part of the charity might be derived hether, for though this be not your native country, yet since you have honor'd it with your abode, I would have your name as pretious here, as where you ar, and the reward will be the same, for the right Samaritan at what distance so ever will have the fame of the good neighbor. My vagrant fellow servants, I fear, can hardly deserve any part of your bounty, for they continu still (it seemes) that stale imposture (which began many yeares past) of shewing names to a farr different end, then to what they were given. But because necessity drives men to unworthy things, I will do them that kindness as to say no more of them.

The letter inclosed comes to you from a person[1], who is heartily thankfull to you, for the bounty you convei'd to him by me. He hath been lately at London with an intention to make use of som books for the perfecting of a very good work which he hath now in hand. But being here, the labors of the pulpit took him off from the care of the press: for he was not suffer'd to be in quiet. Preach he must, both in season and out of season, till at last being wearied out with it, he is retired back to the Golden Grove, and left this letter with me, as a testimony of his great sense of your goodness to him. You see, I am upon all occasions a charitable broker, to keep a commerce between good men; and if I do at any time exceed my limits, I am sure you will pardon me, and I do not trespass upon many more. This is a praeparing week for an holy time; and therefore if I say the less to you, I shall make it up with praying the more for you. That you have overcom your toothach, I am so much the more glad, because I have participated not onely in the same pain, but in the like recovery. As for your comming to Poneropolis[2], I nether love my self so inordinately much, or you so little, as to tempt you to it. I shall patiently stay the time till your occasions bring you hether; for I have so much of platonick love in me, as to love vertu at any distance, or else I could no way deserve to be esteemd by you, as really I am

Your most tru, and most affectionat freind, and servant

BR: SAR:

Richm: May 9.

[ENDORSED REPLY OF SIR JUSTINIAN]

I have your Lordship's with the Doctor's in it, but he being now gon to Golden Grove, I suppose expects no pursuit from me in answer to his

[1] "A person". This is Jeremy Taylor. See Letter XXXVII, Note 2 for Duppa's connection with Taylor. Jeremy Taylor was Rector of Uppingham from 1638 till his sequestration in 1642. He married in 1639 Phoebe Landisdale at Uppingham. Sir Justinian had been educated at the school there, and may have got to know Taylor there, or subsequently when he was chaplain in the King's Army. After the war he retired to Wales ("Golden Grove") under the patronage of the Earl of Carbery, where he kept school. When in London he ministered "to a congregation of Loyalists in great danger" (H. I. Longden, *Northants and Rutland Clergy*, Vol. XIII).

[2] "Poneropolis." This is London; literally "city of wickedness."

thither. A very large thanks[3] return'd me for so small a remembrance might require it, but I respit, till more opportunity offers it selfe. It was well he could undertake such a journey from that place where they affect to have men preach themselves off of their very leggs, yet they themselves stand where they did. My comming to London appeares to me every day less likely, not but that a meere probabilitie of performing any small service to your Lordship may command it, but in the interim humbly thank your Lordship for your converse at this distance, and your prayers which reach to a much greater where at last we hope to meet.

Letter L

[Transcript of letter from Jeremy Taylor to Sir Justinian Isham, May 8th 1654]

Honour'd Sir,

I received by the hands of my Lord Bishop of Sarum a favour which you were pleas'd to communicate to my needes; for the releife and for the kindnesse I am to you a treble debtor, and if it shall please God I shall live to finish what is in my intendment and upon my hands, I will use some meanes to signify that to you also I am indebted for your incouragment. Sir, you have cast your bread upon the waters, and I hope that after a few dayes you shall find it againe, descending upon your head in blessings. Although I have great reason to resent this kindnesse to mee, yet that which does and ought to please mee, is that you have made your name precious in the eyes of good men by your kindnesse and piety to the Church, and in particular to my Lord Bishop of Sarum. He that crownes those graces in us which Himselfe hath given, will promote and crowne those excellent things by which, as by so many remarques of His favour, he hath separated you from the many. Sir, I account my selfe honour'd by your kindnesse and that you were pleas'd to thinke mee worthy of your faire opinion. I doe also really esteeme my selfe advanc'd if you will account mee to be what I am, most heartily and for many reasons,

Honour'd Sir,
Your most obliged freind and affectionate servant,
Jer: Taylor[1].

May 8. 1654.

To the Honour'd, My very Worthy Freind
Sir Justinian Isham Baronet
present these I pray.
[Endorsed:]"8 May 1654 Dr. Jer. Taylor, to Sir Just. Isham". (I.C. 3320).

---

[3] "A very large thanks." Sir Justinian's monument in Lamport Church erected by his son in 1700 records *erga eos qui in eadem causa fuerant, et praesertim in pios et eruditos theologos munificus et liberalis fuit:* "towards those who were in the same (Royal) cause, and especially to the pious and learned clergy he was munificent and liberal." This letter is evidence that this monumental inscription was not in error. (Le Neve, *Monumenta Anglicana*, Vol. II (1718), p. 163).

[1] In the sale of some of the books of the Lamport Library in 1907 (*Valuable Old Books from the Library of a Gentleman in the Country*, Sotheby, Wilkinson and Hodge, June 17th, 1907), a first edition of Taylor's *Discourse of the Liberty of Prophesying* (R. Royston 1647) was sold. It had this inscription "For Sir J. I. Bart, a Member of the House of Commons at Westm'". The price realised was £2 16s. 0d.

LETTER LI

[JUNE 20th.]

Sir, That you ar now returnd to your own home, and in the midst of those olive branches which compass about your table, is not onely a joy to you, but reacheth farther, and concernes me, who look upon the small remnant of the worldly happyness that is left me, as being onely a complication with yours, and therefore putt in for my share even in this too.

But you do well in the midst of these contentments, to cast som of your thoughts upon the frail and transitory condition of them, and considering how soon they may vanish, not to sett your heart upon them, but to exercise that high point of Christianity, as to resign all that is pretious to you into His hands, Who gave it to you upon no other termes, but to make the best use of it, while you enioy'd it, and chearfully to part with it, when the doner shall recall it.

I have begun to distribute that doal of your charity which you committed to my trust, for which many hungry soules do bless your memory allready, and more will do, when I shall have the oportunity to meet with them. I can onely promise you to be faithfull in my stewardship, but the reward must be yours; I was somthing impatient of not hearing from you, but young Booth[1] satisfied my longing, who after his sea-voyage, thought it not out of his way to make a land journey to you. There is much may be said of the times[2], but the wisest way is to say nothing, but what I dare iustify even in the highest Court of Justice, that I am,

Your most sincere freind, and humble servant,
BR: SARUM.

Richm: June 20.

[ENDORSED REPLY OF SIR JUSTINIAN]

My Lord, That you are so concern'd in my comforts is one of the greatest comforts to mee, so that me thinks we seeme like glasses looking upon one another and multiplying on each the common joyes betwixt us.

And that I may know how to want as wel as to abound, all my branches are now pluck'd from me for a tyme by their aunt into Suffolk[3]. My wife also at present with her father in Warwickshire[4]. So that I was never more alone at my owne house then now, and though visited in the day tyme by neighbours and freinds, yet I see 'tis no meane blessing for a

[1] "Young Booth." Perhaps a son of Sir George Booth, a Royalist supporter, who in the revolt of 1659, undertook to hold Chester for the King, but actually failed to do so.

[2] "The times." This is a possible allusion to the plot of John Gerard, Thomas Henshaw and others to assassinate Cromwell, which was discovered in 1654, and which ended in the death of Gerard on July 10th. Henshaw escaped abroad. The plot lacked support from Charles II, but received the encouragement of Prince Rupert (Gardiner, Vol. IV, p. 145 seq).

[3] "Suffolk." Sir Justinian's daughters by his first marriage spent much of their time with their great-aunt, Lady Denton, at Stowlangtoft, Suffolk. She was Elizabeth Isham, sister of Sir John, born in 1578. Her first husband, Sir Anthony Denton of Tonbridge, Kent, died in 1615. She then married Paul D'Ewes Esq. of Stowlangtoft, one of the Six Clerks in Chancery, father by his first wife of the noted antiquary, Sir Simonds D'Ewes (*Autobiography of Sir Simonds D'Ewes*, ed. J. O. Halliwell (1845)). She died on July 25th, 1664, aged 86. She left Sir Justinian a diamond ring, still in the family, and £40 to the poor of Lamport "so long as the name of Isham shall remain here." This sum has been added to the Isham charity, and £5 is distributed still every Christmas to old age pensioners at Lamport.

[4] "Warwickshire." At Stoneleigh Abbey.

man to know how to entertaine him selfe. But I have more then so, your Lordship's frequent and freindly letters which, though I have not the happiness of a personall conversation, doe so often represent you to me that I am very seldome alone and alwaies

Your.

Letter LII

[August 1st.]

Sir, Since we ar now fall'n into the right track again, I hope we shall keep to it, and how ever the subiect matter of our letters may fall to so low an ebbe, as to com at last to that familiar stile of: *Si vales, bene est*, yet even that may find a mutuall wellcom on both sides.

I complaind in my last of a rheum that haunted me, and so persecuted the few teeth that ar left me, that I have been fain to sacrifice one, that I might praeserve the rest, but how long I know not, for I am now approaching to that time, when I may very well expect that the grinders may cease, and not onely so, but that all the rest of the symptomes of old age (which Salomon in his *Ecclesiastes* out-bids both poets and painters in his description of) may suddainly happen to me; and my business is to praepare my self for that utmost point of my dissolution, to which all these accidents ar but the fore-runners. In the mean space the conversation I have with you by letters and the kindness which I receave from you sweetens that remnant of my life, which being now *in fundo*, and nothing left but the dregs, might otherwise be bitter to me.

But to return to our bookes; for this is a writing age, and the swordmen having assumed the liberty of acting what they please, the pen-men ar as venturous; but in the point of Government, I know no man speakes more truth then the knight you mention[1], who followes it to the right head, and spring, from whence the great witts have wand'red, and have sought for that in their own fancy, which they might have found in the plain Scripture road, where God having created our first father to be the first monarch of the world, gave him the dominion over all His creatures, and if over all, certainly He did not except his posterity that descended from him, which in the space of above 900 yeares might produce more subiects to him then the Grand Signior[2] hath at this day. And however after his death it cannot be found regist'red who succeeded him in this power, and possibly the number of men was grown too great for any one to govern, yet there is evidence enough that the first born of the severall branches of his descendents was both as King, and as Preist; and from this paternall power, monarchy so unquaestionably flowed, that in the whole Scripture being a record of the passages of very near 4,000 yeares, there is no mention at all to be found of any Government but regal. Not [that] there was no other at that time in the world (for som of the petty states of Greece, and Rome it self was becom popular) but that no other could praetend to any originall at first but monarchy, for in that both Athens, and Rome was founded. As for Mr. Hobbs his Chimaera, that Government had its rise

[1] "The knight you mention." This is Sir Robert Filmer, political writer, who died in 1653. He was the author of several works, of which the most famous, *Patriarcha, or the Natural Power of Kings asserted*, was not published till 1680. But Duppa and Sir Justinian may well have known it in MS. It seems to be the work here described as it "derives all power from paternal authority, and from Adam". (Lowndes) Macaulay summarises "those strange theories which Filmer afterwards formed into a system" in Chapter I of his *History* (ed. Firth, Vol. I, p. 60).

[2] "The Grand Signior." The Sultan of Turkey.

from mutuall hostility; I shall leave it to the witts of Oxford to chastise him for it, who begin now to nibble at his great Leviathan, as you may find in the *Vindiciae Academiarum*[3], the author of which (whosoever he is) makes him self very merry with that freakish old man (for so he ventures to call him). In our Richmond author[4] you will find better grounds laid, though I do not approve all his super-structions. The book will com to you ether by this carrier or the next. By this time, I conceave, your good company is return'd to you, and you may have somthing more to do, then to read long letters; and therefore I say nothing of the meeting of the Spaw[5], which is now the riddle that exerciseth every man's brain, and if it be not like Democritus his world, made up of a casuall concourse of atoms, it may produce somthing to gaze at. But I have don, and shall onely adde, that which cannot be left out, that I am,

Sir,

Your most faithfull freind, and most humble servant,

BR: SAR:

Richm: Aug: 1.

This morning before I seal'd my letter I receaved a piece of venison from your freinds of the Park[6] who being com for a few dayes to ayre themselves here, have sent me word that they will dine with me, where among so many that love you (T. Aldridge[7] particularly being one) you may be sure to be rememb'red.

LETTER LIII

[AUGUST 15th.]

Sir, Though I have had no return since I wrott the last, yet I am unwilling to quitt my week, and will rather imagine that your letter sleepes somwhere by the way, then to take any occasion by it of returning nothing. I

[3] *Vindiciae Academiarum.* Bishop Duppa does not seem to be aware that the *Vindiciae Academiarum*, which was published anonymously in 1654, was the work of Dr. Seth Ward (1617–89), who eventually became Bishop of Salisbury. Sir Justinian, however, was well aware of the author's identity as he wrote a draft reply to Dr. H. Thorndike on a letter dated September 28th, 1654, containing these words: "I hear the late booke entitled *Vindiciae Academiarum* was all or the greater part of our freind Doctor Ward's, I pray send me that, as also his booke *De Cometis*, one of which he gave me at first but I heare 'tis now published with some additions" (I.C. 348). *Vindiciae Academiarum*: *containing some brief animadversions upon Mr. Webster's book stiled the examination of academies*: *together with an appendix concerning what M. Hobbes and M. Dee have published in this argument by H. D.* [Seth Ward] *Prefatory Epistle by N.S.* [John Wilkins, Warden of Wadham, later Bishop of Chester] (Oxford 1654).

[4] "Our Richmond author." John Hall of Richmond published in 1654 *Of Government and Obedience, as they stand dissected and determined by Scripture and Reason in iv books* (Lowndes). There is a copy of this work in the Lamport Library. He died in 1656. See Letter LXX, Note 2.

[5] "The Spaw." This must refer to the celebrated visit of Charles II in July—August 1654 to Spa, where he met his sister, the widowed Princess of Orange, and scandal was given to Protestant opinion by their attending Vespers together. (See Clarendon (who calls Spa "The Spaw"), Gardiner, Green, *Lives of the Princesses of England*, Vol. VI, pp. 212–15, and Eva Scott, *The Travels of the King*, pp. 5–8). Queen Christina of Sweden was expected to come to "the Spaw" but, says Mrs. Green, "after keeping the news-mongers in suspense for several weeks", decided not to do so.

[6] "Your freinds of the Park." The Carlile family.

[7] "T. Aldridge." See Letter I, Note 2.

cannot find your name in the catalogue of the New Patriots[1]. who ar to com up the next month to be the bone-setters to this broken, and dis-located state, and, the truth is, you ar not qualified for it. For it seemes that onely they who have don the hurt, must be trusted with the cure, and therefore the event may easily be guest at. The riddle that I mention'd in my last, growes every day more and more a riddle, and not onely the scoutes, and Mercuries[2] ar at a loss, but they that sitt at the helm, know not what to make of it. But Truth is the daughter of Time, and the mother will at last unriddle the daughter.

When I had wrott thus farr, and was not willing to oppress you with much more, in comes my lazy water-man, with a letter of yours that had lain five dayes at Glanvile's[3]. It was extremely wellcom though it cam late; for having brought me into a road of hearing from you, I am not at ease when I fail of it. I find you have receaved our Richmond author[4], a book so much the more gazed at, as it was less expected, that a man vers'd onely in the ministeriall parts of the oeconomicks, should be able to produce such magisteriall points out of the politicks. I hope, I said nothing to tempt you to beleive that I rank'd him with Hooker; onely I find by his own acknowledgement, that it is a book which he hath long convers'd with, and reading of good authors is like walking in the sun, which will leave a tincture upon us, though unawares of it. Howsoever it is good to sett great examples to our selves though we fall short of them, and som comfort there is left even in our very failings, when it shall be said: *Magnis tamen excidit ausis*[5].

You acquainted me formerly with the dispersion of your company, your daughters into Suffolk, and your Lady into Warwickshire, and I should be now willing to hear that you wer all mett again, for Lamport must be the center, and the best settlement is there. I have been sollicited to make a summer journey to Cobham[6], but my rheumes, and som other infirmities have as yet hind'red me, and the truth is, I am not a guest fitted for any place but my own cottage; where as yet I enioy my self without any great wants, but with a great measure of quietness of mind, that being freed from the affaires of this world, I am at the greater leasure to do the duties of the

---

1 "New Patriots." The House of Commons, first Parliament of the Protectorate, which assembled on September 3rd, 1654 as a result of the elections of July in that year, was mainly Presbyterian, but in the West a few Royalists were elected. By the Instrument of Government "all and every person and persons, who have aided, advised, assisted or abetted in any war against the Parliament, since the first day of January, 1641 . . . shall be disabled and incapable to be elected." This would certainly have excluded Sir Justinian.

2 "Mercuries." The Press. *Mercurius Politicus*, one of the earliest newspapers, was the official publication 1650–60. Mrs. Green, in *Lives of the Princesses of England*, says of the Spa Meeting: "A reunion of potentates was projected there, and agents from England met Charles on his way. Altogether spies and newspapers were kept guessing". This fits in with what Duppa says here about "scoutes and Mercuries" being at a loss.

3 "Glanvile's". Many of Duppa's letters to Sir Justinian are addressed "Leave this with Mr. Glanvile near the Black Horse in St. Clement's Lane." See Letter XXXIV, endorsed reply.

4 "Our Richmond author." For John Hall of Richmond see Letter LII, Note 4. Hooker, of course, is Richard Hooker (1554–1600), most celebrated of Anglican apologists.

5 *Magnis tamen excidit ausis*. "He failed despite great daring." Ovid, *Metamorph.* II, 328. The reference is to Phaethon, who came to grief by flying too near the sun.

6 "To Cobham", that is, to visit the Duke and Duchess of Richmond; see Letter XXIVA and note.

ἓν μὲν ἀναγκαῖον[7] and when I pray for my freinds (which is as often as I pray for my self), you and yours can never be forgotten, by

Your most affectionat tru freind and humble servant,
BR: SAR:

Richm: Aug: 15.

[ENDORSED REPLY OF SIR JUSTINIAN]

It seemes my last, as the rest very dull, lay still till your Lordship's letter, (like your selfe) attractive, brought it to you at the first call, but whereas in it your Lordship puts me in mind of my country, my wife and children, and of our neere freindship, I come lately from reading a peice of Tullie which will make up my letter as to all particulars much better then I could[8].

LETTER LIV

[AUGUST 29th.]

Sir, I know not to what to impute the ling'ring of your letters (for that which I receave but now from you, cam to St. Clement's Lane six dayes ago), but ether to the laziness of my waterman, or to the faeminine inscription; for being directed to a woman, it cannot be thought that there should be any business in the letter, and therefore the times being now more open, and our intercourse so innocent, you may safely change the stile, and direct what you write to the Bishop of Salisbury, and possibly that empty title may bring it the sooner to me. As for that bundle of Duties collected out of that excellent book of Tully (which because we begin with it in our youth, we cast aside in our age, when we have most use of it) I know none that hath more authority to cite them, then he who so religiously makes good all the relations that ar there mention'd. A good patriot, a good husband, and so good a freind, that it may be doubted whether that orator could say more then you could do in that argument. Had I been worth a Tully, I should have search'd for somthing to have paid you in your own coin. But for want of purer mettall, I must in plain English return my thankes, not onely for the kindness which I do receave from you, but for that which I may receave, though I have not yet made use of it. Som company at this time interrupts me, or else I should hardly confine my self on this side of the paper, where I am driven to look for room in the margen to subscribe my self,

Your most sincere freind, and humble servant,
BR: SAR:

Richm: Aug. 29.

[ENDORSED REPLY OF SIR JUSTINIAN]

My Lord, I shall observe your owne directions, and without adding what belongs to you only write: "for the Bishop of S[alisbury]". Your Lordship finds I have not yet liv'd so long or wander'd so farr in novelties, as alltogether to continue what I mett with in my youth, and indeed in the review of those classicall authors I have often thought that though we read them being young, yet 'tis impossible to have any right of them untill we attaine to such yeares or thereabouts as the persons were who writt them, and the more like our education, fortune, and imployment, the

[7] "ἓν μὲν αναγκαῖον." "One thing which is necessary." An echo, possibly, of St. Luke, Cap. x., v. 43.

[8] "A peice of Tullie." There is no indication of the passage in Cicero referred to, but the next letter of the Bishop makes it clear that it was from the *De Officiis*.

better interpreters may we be of their meaning. Some things indeed there are which we read over and pass by with such ease at the first, I question whether ever understood.

I lately mett with a liberall, philosophicall and morall interpretation (or rather coniecture) of the three first chap[ters] of Genesis, writt lately in 8vo by Henry Moore[1], fellow of Xst College, Cambr., who hath shew'd great reading upon his threefold Cabbala as he termes it. How farr in it he hath outgon others or himselfe I should gladly heare from some of judgement. Your Lordship once acquainted me with Dr. Flood's[2] grave conceit he had to himselfe in the meaning of those chapters, but I doubt whether any ever yet writ upon them to give a tolerable satisfaction to reason, and have therefore accounted them as misterious and for our beleife.

LETTER LV

SEPT. 13 RICHM.

Sir, Somthing there is more then ordinary (which I cannot ascribe to any constellation, till I can find better grounds for that kind of astrology then as yet I do, but) somthing there is of an higher nature, that in the shuffling together of so many millions of men, among such strange varieties, singles out here and there a pair that think the same things, like, and dislike, though it be at a distance, and agree naturally without any articles of agreement drawn up between them. And ether we deceave one the other, or possibly we may be a pair of them. For I find so much of my own thoughts in your letters, that you never give me the occasion to dissent from you. Nor will I say, as the froward man in the historian, *Dic aliquid, ut duo simus*[1], for I cannot be weary of thinking the same thinges with you *cui nisi optima placere non possunt*[2]. And the hint that I take of saying this, is that very good observation of yours (wherein I wholy ioyne with you) that they must necessarily be the best interpreters of books, who in their parts, and education, and affections too, ar likest to the authors; which may very well be the reason of that which som of the Fathers say, that he who would make use of David's Psalmes, must be of David's spirit, and have the same affections as he that wrott them. As for the book you mett at Cambridge[3], I can say nothing of it, for I have not seen it, and doubt very much, it being a Cabala, whether I shall understand it when I do see it. For I was so short a time (no longer (as I remember) then one afternoon) a disciple to the great master of that art, Robertus de Fluctibus[4], that I dare not so much as praetend to it: yet if it comes in

[1] "Henry Moore." This is Henry More (1614–87), theologian and Platonist. Fellow of Christ's College, Cambridge (1639), D.D. His *A Modest Enquiry into the Mystery of Iniquity* (1664) is in the Lamport Library. More refused all preferments, choosing to remain a scholar. He was loyal both to the King, and the Church of England. The work here referred to is *Conjectura Cabbalistica . . . or, a Conjectural Essay of interpreting the minde of Moses*," published in 1653. (D.N.B.).

[2] "Dr. Flood." This is Robert Flood or Fludd (1574–1637), Rosicrucian. He was M.D. (1605) from Christ Church, Oxford, where Duppa, who was Dean (1629–38), may have met him (D.N.B.). "Flood was surnamed 'the Searcher' from his many searches into philosophy, medicine, etc. His books written in Latin are many, great and mystical" (Lowndes).

[1] *Dic aliquid, ut duo simus.* "Say something in order that we may be two," i.e. differ. See Letter VII, Note 1.

[2] *Cui nisi optima placere non possunt.* "To him that nothing but the best can satisfy".

[3] "The book you mett at Cambridge." This is Henry More's *Conjectura Cabbalistica*. See Letter LIV, Note 1.

[4] "Robertus de Fluctibus." Robert Flood. See Letter LIV, Note 2.

my way and no body be by to reprove me for so much lost time, I am likely to deal with bookes of that kind, as the dames of Rome upon an other occasion dealt with Martiall who forbore to read him, but it was *coram Brutô, Brute recede legent*[5].

I have sent you with this letter a new book of Dr. Hammond's: *calentem e praeso*[6], which though it may be acceptable to you for the argument's sake, yet will deserve a greater valew from you for the manner of his writing. For I never saw more insolency answer'd with more meekness, which if there wer no other testimony for the truth which he defends, might very well pass (as the civilians speak) for a strong praesumption of it. But one particular among the rest I shall commend to you, and that is a digression in the hundred and thirtieth page concerning Hugo Grotius[7], who was certainly so excellent a man, that unless we give way to an ostracisme after death, his memory must needs be pretious to us. All this while I say nothing to you of the divisions of the Senat[8], but do take up your old freind Tully, and read his familiar Epistles, and you will find the very same scene renew'd; onely the persons varied. But being you are to heare from me so soon again, I shall no longer detein you, then onely to tell you what you know allready, that I am,

Your very faithfull and affectionat freind and servant,
BR: SARUM.

LETTER LVI

[SEPTEMBER 26th.]

Sir, I must not pass you by, though your carrier did, for having receaved though but a few words from you, I have that satisfaction at least, that there may be as much freindship in few words as in many. The Lacedaemonians wer a wise people, and their short letters (if we had a collection of them) might be of more use then Cardinall Bembo[1], or Sadolet's[2] ar. But this which I have said is not because I like your short ones better,

[5] *Coram Bruto, Brute recede, legent.* The full quotation is *erebuit posuitque meum Lucretia librum sed coram Bruto, Brute recede, leget.* "Lucretia blushed and put down my (naughty) book, but only in the presence of Brutus: if you go away, Brutus, she will read it." Martial, *Epigr.*, XI, 16, 9 and 10.

[6] *Calentem e praeso*, "hot from the press." Henry Hammond, D.D., Rector of Penshurst (1633–45), was a theologian, whose fame long survived; Dr. Johnson recommends his commentary on the New Testament. For fuller details see Letter XIX, Note 5. The particular book referred to is *An Answer to the Animadversions* [of J. Owen] *on the dissertations touching Ignatius's Epistles and the Episcopacie in them asserted.* (1654). For John Owen (1616–83) see D.N.B.

[7] "Hugo Grotius." This is Huig de Groot (1583–1645), usually known as Grotius. His fame today rests on his *De Jure Belli et Pacis*. His importance as a jurist has obscured his theological work to which Duppa refers. "A Digression concerning some jealousies spread of Hugo Grotius" occurs on p. 130 et seq. of the work on Ignatius' *Epistles*.

[8] "Divisions of the Senat." On September 3rd, Cromwell opened Parliament in state: divisions instantly appeared, and on September 12th the Protector summoned the members to the Painted Chamber to hear a speech on the Instrument of Government. Morley (*Cromwell*, pp. 391–2) comments: "No Parliament supposing itself clothed with popular authority could have been expected to accept without criticism a ready-made scheme fastened on it by a military junto." Duppa is presumably referring to passages in Cicero about the relations between Caesar, Pompey and the Senate.

[1] "Cardinall Bembo." Cardinal Pietro Bembo (1470–1547) was secretary to Pope Leo X. His works include a *History of Venice*.

[2] "Sadolet". Cardinal Jacopo Sadoleto (1477–1547), was a noted letter-writer. (*Encycl. Brit.*).

but to comfort my self, that by this misadventure I could have no longer. I have been of late under som afflicton by the sickness of my wife, but God hath since blest me with som visible hopes of her recovery, without which I should be but *tanquam umbra volitans* and *ambulare inter Orcum et solem*[3], as Apuleius speaks of an half dead man. I should not speak thus passionately of her, but that I committ it to a bosom that hath the like affections, which I beleive I may hear of when your Lady drawes nearer her time[4]. For the present I shall oppress you no farther, but in few words remain,

Your most affectionat freind and servant,
BR: SAR:

Richm: Sept: 26.

[ENDORSED REPLY OF SIR JUSTINIAN]

My Lord, Your Lordship's great kindness to me hath appear'd in the acceptance of my late few lines, and in yours, your great and just sorrow for your wife's late sickness, but this I hope now abated with good signes of her recovery.

My wife I trust now also gathering strength after her late delivery of a daughter[5], which I praise God for as also for the means he hath given me to provide for her with the rest. But to have recourse to our excellent author:—

> *Animus hominis dives, non arca appellari solet quamvis illa sit plena— etenim ex eo, quantum cuique sat est metiuntur homines divitiarum modum—filiam quis habet: pecunia est opus: duas, majore; plures, etiam majore; si ut aiunt Danai quinquaginta sint filiae: tot dotes, magnam quaerunt pecuniam, quantum enim cuique satis est, ad id accommodatur divitiarum modus. Qui igitur non filias plures, sed innumerabiles cupiditates habet, quae brevi tempore maximas copias exhaurire possint: hunc quomodo ego appellabo divitem, cum ipse egere se sentiat*[6].

Your Lordship's approving my last long quotation now and withall to make good your observation whether I am not in a condition now to be a better interpreter of this passage of the author then I have bin formerly. I am

[3] *Tanquam umbra volitans*, "flitting about like a shadow"; *ambulare inter Orcum et solem*, "to walk about between the underworld and the earth." Adapted from Apuleius, *Metamph.* VIII, 12, 3, who, however, used *errare* for *ambulare*. Duppa is quoting from memory.

[4] "Nearer her time." Sir Justinian had doubtless communicated his expectations of a child to the Bishop.

[5] "Delivery of a daughter." Mary Isham was born at her grandfather's house at Stoneleigh, September 20th, 1654. On St. Matthew's Day (September 21st), 1654, Charles Leigh, Lady Isham's brother, wrote to Sir Justinian: "my sister your Lady is safely brought to bed . . . betweene eleven and twelve last night was deliver'd of a daughter" (I.C. 347).

[6] *Animus hominis dives*, etc. "We do not judge the riches of a man's soul by his coffers: though *they* be full, if I see that you yourself are empty I shall not think you rich: for each man considers the standard of wealth to be what is enough for him. If a man has a daughter he needs money: if he has two he needs more, and the more daughters he has the more money he needs. If, like Danaus in the legend, he has fifty daughters he will need a vast amount of money to provide them all with dowries. Every man, as I said before, puts the standard of wealth at the level of his own needs. What then of the man who, though he have no daughters, has instead countless desires—enough to drain even the largest estate in a short time? How shall I call such a man rich when he himself feels that he is in need?" Cicero, *Parad. Stoic.*, 44, *quod solus sapiens dives*.

now returning to Warwickshire, having stay'd here the rather to meet with and make returne to your Lordship's letter, being,

My Lord,

Your most humble &c.

My service to Mrs. Duppa, whose health I hartily pray for.

Letter LVII

[October 10th.]

Sir, I am not onely pleas'd with your transcribing of Seneca, but I look upon you as one who hath so happily digested him, that I see as much Seneca in your letters, when you do not cite him, as when you do. And abating that hypocrisy which Cardan[1] discovers in him, that he never more intended the gathering of riches, then when he made most shew to the world of despising them, I am very prone to beleive that (without any such absolute metempsichosis as Pythagoras dreamt of) much of that morall soul of his, but meliorated and advanced by grace, is now in you, who in the course of your life not onely write, but act his sentences over, which if we beleive his enemies he did not. But to speak my conceptions of him, I could never beleive, that an heart so fowly tainted with that base and dirty sin of covetousness, could write so divine things as he hath don; and therefore, though I have laid him aside this long time, I shall resume him again, that I may be the better to deal with you at your own weapons.

I am at more ease to write chearfully to you, because it hath pleas'd God to recover my wife, and to give a fair deliverance to yours, who though yet a stranger to me, you must give me leave for your sake to be much concerned in. And never be troubled, that it is not a son, for you have yet day enough before you to make your males and females even. Or if not, I shall not need to send you to Juvenall for counsell, for you ar furnish'd with better light, and clearer principles, to think that best for you which that high Providence orders, *cui charior est homo quam sibi.*[2] I am upon an argument that I should say more of, but nether do you need it nor do my occasions at this time permitt me to say more, then to pray for you, and so rest,

Your most affectionat freind and humble servant,

Br: Sar:

Richm: Octob: 10.

Letter LVIII

[October 24th.]

Sir, You have made so hansom an excuse for me allready, that I need make no other apology for my mistaking your quotation out of Tully, who as he had *versatile ingenium*[1], so his stile was as various; in his orations fluent, and full, in his letters concise, but pure, and apposite to his matter, and in his philosophy without a dress, or affectation, as severe as Seneca though they wer of different parties, the one (as I think) an Academick, the other a Stoick. And therefore meeting with that very good passage in your letter, I might the easier slide into the mistake. But the truth is (not to conceal my defects from you with whom I dare trust my self with

[1] "Cardan" is Girolamo Cardano (often called Cardan) (1501–76), mathematician physician, and astrologer. His *De Consolatione* was translated into English by Thomas Bedingfield in 1573, but the passage about Seneca is not there.

[2] *Cui charior est homo quam sibi.* "To Whom man is clearer than to himself." See Letter xlviii, Note 2.

[1] *Versatile ingenium*, "versatile mind." Livy, xxix, 40; referring to Cato major.

all my errors) I have a memory so crazed, that I may apply to my self in earnest, what Montaigne[2] was wont to say; when, having made use of severall passages in bookes, he confest ingenuously, that if he wer threat'ned with the rack, he could not name the authors he had cited. For I have onely left me, som faint ideas and notions of my former reading; and when I meet with them again, I never examin them as the country-Justices do the wanderers, "From whence ar you? " or "From whom do you com?" But if they look honestly, and speak virtuous things, I entertain them without any farther title, for that which is said by any good man, is like the center in a circle, which every line that is drawn from the same principles, as from the circumference aequally reacheth to. But after all this let me desire you not to leave off your quotations, for if I live much longer, your letters will be my best bookes or at least my best remembrancers of books; for partly for want of those bookes which I would have, but cheifly for want of that vigor of mind and strength of body which enabled me formerly for study, I am likely now (especially this winter time) to gett into the chimny corner, where telling sad stories past, and divining the evils that ar to com, I shall have nothing else left to do but to keep my self to a constant way in my devotions, wherein you, and yours ar sure to be rememb'red, which, having no way else to requite you I shall be the more earnest in, that all your kindness may not be lost upon

Your very unprofitable, but very faithfull servant,
BR: SARUM.

Richm: Octob: 24.

[ENDORSED REPLY OF SIR JUSTINIAN]

My Lord, Your complaint of your want of memory now of such particulars as you have formerly read, to mee seems as if a man should be troubled because after many good meales made, or rather a diet of choise meats, he cannot tell you where every dainty bitt which he eat now lies, whereas indeed he hath so perfectly digested the best of it, that he hath thereby gain'd an excellent and healthy constitution, a thing certainly of farr greater consequence then any particular pleasure of the feast can possibly be.

I remember a passage in St. Hierome[3], who, after many translations of his, growing into yeares, sayd then he would endeavor *transferre verba in facta*.

This your Lordship hath so long don the very best of what you have read, that now you may with delight recall not others' choice sayings so much as your own good actions and thereby even heere gain a double life. *Ampliat aetatis spatium sibi vir bonus, hoc est vivere bis, vita posse priore frui*[4].

And yet to extend your Lordship's farther, your freinds and acquaintance may take pattern by it and your selfe still live even in some of them. Nor shall the corruption of the age prevaile so farr over my poor selfe *quo*

[2] "Montaigne." This is Michel de Montaigne (1533–92), French essayist. Florio's translation of his *Essays* made them very popular in England.

[3] "St. Hierome," St. Jerome.

[4] *Ampliat aetatis spatium sibi vir bonus, hoc est vivere bis, vita posse priore frui.* "A good man enlarges for himself the span of his life: to be able to enjoy one's early life is to live a second life." Martial, *Epigr.*, x, 23, 7 and 8.

minus perseverem laudare vitam, non quam ago, sed quam agendam scio: quo minus virtutem adorem, et ex intervallo ingenti ingrat: sequar[5].

[SECOND ENDORSEMENT OF SIR JUSTINIAN]
[DRAFT LETTER TO MRS. DOROTHY LONG[6]]

S.V. In expectation of the Coll's companie heere as your letter long since put me in some hopes of, I was not hasty to returne to it; and indeed have lately bin very much from home, my wife being in Warwickshire delivered of a daughter, whom I shall educate as well as I can, not knowing but that she may live to overtake Mr. Jemy, as nimble as he is in breeches. And wee all now know how much nimbleness is in fashion, as skipping into a coach box, &c., and yet since the book sayes (my only intelligencer) Blessed be God he is pretty cheerfull and walks up and downe, but I suppose you have lately mett with a letter, printed with I.H.[7] to it, which hath somewhat in it more serious. So long as I heere nothing to the contrary from Richmond I hope your healths at Draycot, but I cannot heere it too much confirm'd nor so well as under your hand and seale to

Your

LETTER LIX

[NOVEMBER 7th.]

Sir, You must ether forgett that you love me so well as you do, or if you will needs remember it, you must do it in a severer way, and not putt such a colour upon my imperfections, as that when I complain of want of memory, to raise somthing upon that complaint, which I dare not own, and to persuade me that I am like a Spanish glove, which having all kind of perfumes in it, do onely forgett where they ly. For really my forgettfulness is more then so; for it is not onely privative, and blotts out many things which I have formerly known (though som faint ideas may be left of them), but it is negative, and I do not know whether I ever remembr'red them or no. And though this may be look'd upon as a huge defect in a person that hath lived so long in the world, and in such a way as I have, yet considering the times that I have lived in and the things that I have seen, I am very much of his mind, who when others wer very busy to find out the art of memory, was as inquisitive after som able master, that might teach him the art of forgetfulness. Onely there ar som things, which it wer a curse to forgett,—my duty to God, my loyalty to my Master, and my love to my freind, and when I fail notably in any of these particulars, I shall be no longer worthy to be own'd by you, as

Your very tru and faithfull freind,
BR: SARUM.

Richm: Nov: 7.

---

[5] *Quo minus perseverem laudare vitam, non quam ago, sed quam agendam scio: quo minus virtutem adorem, et ex intervallo*, etc. "Nothing will prevent me from continuing to extol life—not the life I lead but that which I know I ought to lead—or prevent me from worshipping virtue and from pursuing it slowly and only from a great distance". Seneca, *Dial.* VII, 18, 2. (*ad Gallionem de Vita Beata*).

[6] Second endorsement. This is a draft letter to Mrs. Dorothy Long (afterwards Lady Long), a frequent correspondent. She was a niece of Duppa's nephew, Richard Chaworth. Her husband, Colonel Long, succeeded as 2nd Bart. on the death of his uncle Sir Robert, who was Charles II's secretary during his exile. Their son James ("Jemy") died v.p., and the baronetcy went in succession to the latter's three sons, Robert, Gyles, and James (G.E.C., *Complete Baronetage*). See Letter V, Note 3, and App. A.

[7] For the "letter, printed with I.H. to it" see Letter LIX, Note 1

What you mean by the letter of I.H.[1], unless it be somthing call'd the Admonition, I know not.

LETTER LX

[DECEMBER 5th.]

Sir, Till I receaved your letter, I was in suspense whether I might beleive you wer gon out of London, or no; not that I could think, that the vanities of that place had power to detain you, for you ar arm'd with farr better principles then Ulysses was, who notwithstanding all his wisdom, was fain to be tied to the mast that he might not seem to be enchanted with the Syrens he mett with, but rather that your charity to your freinds, and necessity of business wer the cords that bound you there beyond ether your will, or your expectation. But it seemes now you ar gott free, and have no other impediment but durty wayes to keep you from beeing speedily where you would be; and those being overcom (for I am willing to beleive you ar not lodged there, but rest, my freind, by this time in a cleaner place), you may be the better at leasure to receave my wonted impertinencies, which for want of a better tribute, I am fain to return to you for all your kindness. The death of young Danvers[1] I heard of before, which was so much the more unhappy to me in my particular, because he was to have married a young lady, whose power I could have made use of to have persuaded him to do me right. But that Providence which denies me som helpes which I might expect, doth not fail me in raising som other which I did not look for. And as long as my prayers may be heard for the praeserving of you I shall have no anxiety at all for any worldly thing, for though I have mett with many talkers among my freinds that promise liberally to divide estates with me, but if I had need of them, would hardly be brought to Martial's σῦκα μερίζει[2], and divide a figge with me. I assure my self of your freindship as of a better tenure. But the greater your kindness is the more I am bound to a tenderness not to press you in making use of it, of which I shall have so much care, both for your sake, and for my own as to do nothing that may misbecome,

Your most affectionat tru freind,
BR: SAR:

Decem: 5.

---

[1] "Letter of I.H." I am unable to suggest what this may be. Bishop Duppa was similarly at a loss. The "ever-memorable" John Hales lived for a time with Duppa's niece, Lady Salter, as tutor to her son, after being ejected from Eton. (D.N.B. which, however, wrongly describes Lady Salter as Duppa's sister. She was his niece, the daughter of his sister Ann who married Edward Croft of Wigmore. See App. A.)

[1] "The death of young Danvers." Harry Danvers, son of Sir John Danvers, the regicide, died of smallpox November 19th, 1654, and was buried on his 21st birthday in West Lavington Church. He was first cousin of Dorothy Osborne, who calls him (Letter 10) "a handsome youth, and well natured but such a goose." She hoped he would marry Lady Diana Rich in 1653, but they both died unmarried. Although Lady Diana Rich's father, the Earl of Holland, was a Royalist, who was executed in 1649 for his part in the second Civil War in 1648, her uncle, Robert, 2nd Earl of Warwick, commanded the Navy for the Parliament, and "during the usurpation enjoyed the full confidence of Cromwell." It was presumably from this connection that Duppa hoped that Danvers could be "persuaded to do me right." (Burke, *Dormant and Extinct Peerages*, and *Letters of Dorothy Osborne*, ed. Moore Smith).

[2] Martial, *Epigr.* v, 38, 3.

Yesterday I had the newes of the death of Mr. Selden[2], but what, or how he disposeth of the jewells and treasures which wer lately left him, I nether hear, nor am very inquisitive. For though there hath formerly been a long-continued freindship between us, I look for no share in it. His bookes onely I shall enquire after, as being a treasure which he hath been long gathering, and will be certainly of great valew.

[ENDORSED REPLY OF SIR JUSTINIAN]

At length through the ill weather and worse wayes I find home, and all well I thanke God there, whence I now returne my wive's humble service and thanks with mine to your Lordship for your praier booke and Vergil sent her.

LETTER LXI

[DECEMBER 19th.]

Sir, I have receaved a letter from you of so much freindship, that had you never said any thing of that kind before to me, or should forbear for the future to say anything more, I have comfort enough by me, to praeserve me from being brokenhearted for the streights and necessities of this life. And the great security of it is, that God, who in all the passages of my life hath had a strange Providence over me, hath provided you to assist me that I might have the hansomer exit, and to have so much kindness really offered to me, which is daily given in complement, but expires in the very giving it. Sir, I shall say no more, but desire you to beleive that nothing shall be lost upon me, for your reward will certainly com som way or other, and from Heaven, if not from me.

I am very much pleas'd to hear from you that my little book of devotions was acceptable to your Lady, not onely for my own sake, but hers, for it is a great argument to me of a soule rightly season'd to have a taste and relish in things of this kind, which the greater part of the world under-valew as impertinencies, and spend so much of their time in caring for their body, that they hardly know whether they have a soul, or no. But your example, and the practise of your own life may serve as a continuall guide to your whole family without any farther assistance of mine, then to give my *euge*, and to encourage you to go on in making good all relations, which you ow ether to God, or man.

I cannot yet venture on sending you any thing of certainty concerning the mode of Mr. Selden's leaving the world.[1] Som of the atheisticall party (of which the numbers daily increase), that they might have somthing to excuse themselves, spread very unhansom rumors, as if he slighted all things of religion as a cheat putt upon the world, but after so many

[2] "The death of Mr. Selden." John Selden (1584–1654), described by Milton as "the chief of learned men reputed in this kingdom," made a valuable collection of oriental MSS. His part in the impeachment of Buckingham, and still more, that of Laud, can hardly have endeared him to Duppa. Also his attacks on tithes had rendered him suspect to the clergy. It is interesting, therefore, to find Duppa speaking of the "long-continued freindship" between Selden and himself. For details of his jewels, etc. see Letter LXI.

[1] "Mode of Mr. Selden's leaving the world." Selden's *Table Talk*, in which his Erastianism and anti-ecclesiasticism were fully revealed, was not published till 1689, long after Duppa was dead. Archbishop Ussher preached his funeral sermon, and Wood (*Ath. Ox.*, Vol. I) says: "concerning our author's religion, Sir Math. Hale, one of his executors, pronounced that Selden was a resolved serious Christian, and a great adversary of Hobbes of Malmesbury his errors."

yeares of very near accquaintance (and if I should call it freindship, the mutuall kindness that have past between us might have deserved it), I cannot but be one of the last that shall beleive any such horrid thing of him. The estate, which he hath left, they say, is very great, one small part of it to his poor kindred, with som few legacies to freinds (in which roll my name hath been long ago worn out), but the greatest part is to be divided among four executors[2]: 1. Judge Hales, 2. Jewkes, 3. Heywood his old chamberfellow, and 4. Vaughan. The former too I know nothing of, but by report, and what should oblige him to them I cannot tell, but the other wer of more nearness with him and in the compass of my knowledge may go for honest men. But what ever they ar, they have a fair dividend to be aequally divided among them, unless the judge, or sombody for him, act the lyon's part in the fable, and having devoured the flesh leave the skin to be quarrel'd for. As I hear more, I shall communicate it with you though it be out of our common road to intermedle with third persons, having enough to do to treat one the other. And after this long digression it is time to return to our selves, and to assure you that the less I have of outward advantages to serve you, the more deeply I have it imprinted inwardly to express my self very faithfully,

Your most affectionat freind and most humble servant,

BR: SAR:

Richm: Decem: 19.

---

[2] "Four executors." Selden's will was dated June 11th, 1653, and the executors there named are Edward Heyward of the Inner Temple, John Vaughan of the Inner Temple, Rowland Jewkes of the Inner Temple, and Matthew Hale of Lincoln's Inn (P.C.C., Alchin 253: consulted 1951). He calls these men "his beloved friends." Matthew Hale, Justice of the Court of Common Pleas (1654) whom Duppa seems to distrust, was a friend of Baxter, Selden, and the latitudinarian Bishops. He was head of the Committee appointed in 1651, which sat the next year to "remove the inconsistencies of the existing law." This Committee forwarded the draft of several bills, one of them providing for district registries for wills, deeds, etc. in every county in England. But the dissolution of the Parliament in 1653 prevented these bills from ever becoming law. At the Restoration Hale was knighted, and became Lord Chief Justice of the King's Bench in 1671. He died in 1676. (D.N.B., and F. A. Inderwick, *The Interregnum* (1891) pp.214 and 215).
By a codicil to his will, also dated June 11th, 1653, Selden said: "Concerning my bookes, I give and bequeathe all and every my manuscripts not otherwise hereafter disposed of . . . to my Executors named in my last Will and Testament . . . but desiring them rather to part them among themselves or otherwise dispose of them or the choysest of them for some publique use then put them to any common sale. It may do well in some convenient library publique, or of some college in one of the Universities." They were mostly given to the Bodleian Library, where they remain. Certain books were left separately, e.g. "To the President of the Royal College of Phisitians, my Hippocrates *Aphorismes* in Arabic and such peeces of Galen as I have in Arabic." Various pieces of plate, which are minutely described in the will, went to a variety of noblemen. He died at Friary House, Whitefriars, on November 30th, 1654, and was buried in the Temple Church. (Wood, *Ath. Ox.*, D.N.B.) For a recent full account of Selden's bequest to the Bodleian, and his executors' part in it, see D. M. Barratt, "The Library of John Selden and its Later History", *Bodleian Library Record*, Vol. III, No. 31 (March 1951).

1655

In this year, Cromwell, finding the problem of associating his military despotism with a constitutional Parliament too much even for his statecraft, dissolved his House of Commons, and faced a serious rising of Cavaliers. That it was not so serious as it might have been was due to his foreknowledge of the plot. But thenceforth his rule became more military. England and Wales were divided into eleven districts, ruled by Major Generals, who were charged with exacting from Royalists 10% of their rentals, and depriving them of all their weapons. Strongly Puritan measures were introduced; alehouses closed, plays prohibited, cock-fighting and horse-racing put down with singular vigour. "The experiment", as has been well said, "was too short lived to have any permanent effect on the morality of Englishmen, but lasted long enough to leave behind it an abiding hatred of militarism" (Godfrey Davies, *The Early Stuarts* (1937), p. 178).

The slightly more hopeful tone of the letters in 1654 disappears. As a result of the Royalist rising in March, Cavaliers were "decimated" afresh, and scores of them, including Sir Justinian, arrested and confined at St. James's Palace. Sir Justinian seems to have struck up quite a friendship there with Sir Ralph Verney, of Claydon, who had supported the Parliament in 1642, but refused to take the Covenant. In one of his letters Sir Ralph describes Sir Justinian as "a very discreet person, of a plentifull fortune, and of an antient family." In the notes below are some quotations from these two men's letters, some of which are quoted in the *Verney Memoirs*, and others transcribed by me from the MSS. at Claydon, through the kind permission of Sir Harry Verney, Bart.

While in prison together, Sir Ralph busied himself with finding a husband for one of Sir Justinian's daughters, and on July 12th, 1655, wrote to Lady Gawdy recommending one of them for her son. Sir Ralph and Sir Justinian were distantly connected, for Thomas Isham of Wheatfield (of the Ishams of Pytchley) married a Denton of Hillesden, who was an aunt of Sir Ralph. Thomas Isham had been in arms for the King and was fined £10 as a delinquent, and his wife, well known to readers of the *Verney Memoirs* as "Aunt Isham", shared his Royalist views. To her on August 23rd, 1655 Sir Ralph wrote: "Sir Justinian and my selfe are still in Limbo, and though we are daily promised a generall discharge, yet wee see noe greate hope of it at present. Patience is an excellent vertue and at this time very needful for your . . ."

Trevelyan (*England under the Stuarts*, 3rd edn. 1908, p. 309) has well summed up the situation:– "The poor gentlemen had now very little following, but if ever the day came when Royalism should prove the only road back to civilian and settled government, these men whom Cromwell was filling with hatred of all that he most desired to perpetuate in England, would again be the ruling class in the State. It was because of the treatment meted out . . . to the general body of rural Cavaliers, that Puritanism was allowed no religious or civil status in England at the Restoration."

At the end of the year a fresh blow was struck, which affected both the correspondents, when on November 24th an edict was passed ordering that from January 1st, 1656 no person whose estate had been sequestered, should keep arms in his house, or maintain any ejected clergyman as tutor to his family; further that no ejected or sequestered clergyman should keep any school, public or private; and that no such clergyman should "preach in any public place, or at any private meeting of any persons other than his own family, nor shall administer Baptism, or the Lord's Supper, or marry any persons, or use the Common Prayer Book." This harsh enactment was qualified in favour of such "as have . . . given, a reall testimony of their godliness and good affection to the present Government", to whom "so much tenderness shall be used as may consist with the safety and good of this nation." (From a Declaration "Given at Whitehall this 24th of November", B.M. press mark 669. f. 20, no. 20, cited by Gardiner, Vol. III, p. 335, and Morley, *Cromwell*, p. 408, but here transcribed from the original). That this was disregarded by some, at any rate, of the ejected Anglicans without the enaction of the prescribed penalties, we find proof in Richard Drake's diary. This sequestered Rector of Radwinter, Essex, who was then living at Richmond, records in his diary that on May 27th, 1655 Duppa confirmed his step-daughter, and on June 11th, 1657 he himself (with Bishop Duppa and Richard Chaworth acting as sponsors) baptised his son Roger *me ipso ex ritu Ecclesiae Ang. sacra faciente*; an instance of a direct contravention of the Declaration. (*Walker Revised*, and cf. Richmond *Registers*. Drake's diary is in the Bodleian, MS. Rawl. D.158, from which the Latin quotation is directly taken.)

Moreover, Duppa, who had in 1653 held a semi-official meeting of Anglican clerics at Richmond, in order to consider modifying the Act of Uniformity, to enable Anglicans to continue in their benefices, once again took the lead of the English Bishops in defence of their order. Chancellor Hyde sent Dr. Duncan, former Prebendary of York, to England to consult with Duppa regarding the danger of the failing episcopal succession. Duppa, Wren of Ely, Warner of Rochester were all interviewed, and they "were all very glad to hear that care was taken for the preservation of their order: and were ready to . . . do anything in their power that might further it." (G. B. Tatham, *The Puritans in Power* (1913), p. 247). But this matter, like the conference of 1653, got no further than pious hopes.

For Sir Justinian, this interruption of his life was particularly unwelcome, as he was engaged in building a new block to the Elizabethan house at Lamport, in the classical style, to the designs of his friend John Webb. Webb's plans and letters have survived, and were printed in full by J. A. Gotch in the R.I.B.A. *Journal* for September 24th, 1921. Even in prison, Sir Justinian was kept fully in touch with the progress of the work by the contractor, Thomas Sergenson of Coventry, and on his return playfully wrote to Sir Ralph Verney signing himself "Architrave, Freeze and Cornice." A full account of the architectural history of Lamport by the present writer will will be found in *The Reports and Papers of the Northamptonshire Architectural and Archaeological Society* (1953). The birth of Sir Justinian's daughter Vere, and the death of his daughter Jane, brought joy and sorrow at the end of the year.

Letter LXII

[January 9th.]

Sir, I find that though the religious part of observing this Holy Time is laid aside, yet the eating part is observed by the holiest of the brethren, and the lazy part by carriers, whose restyness rather then their rest hath defrauded me of the letter which I the last week very eagerly look'd for. But it is com at last, and I am fully satisfied by hearing of your health, and those that ar dearest to you. And if you would know, how we have past this time here, I shall first tell you that we have perform'd all the spirituall duties that belong to it, and for the grosser matter of good chear, we have lived upon my cosin Lowen's contribution, who is very kind, if he did not over-season it, with those troublesom errors in conversation, πολυλογία, κ' περιαυτολογία[1]. But really his kindness is very great, and he that will not dispense with somthing in matter of freindship deserves nothing. I should not deliver so much, wer it not to you, who loves him, and knowes him as well as I do.

I may possibly hereafter give you a larger narrative of Mr. Selden,[2] but I have not yet mett with my best intelligencers. If there be any thing else to be enquired after (and I know none of your curiosities ar dangerous) I shall be very ready to obey you, but for the present I have not much more leasure then to say, that I am,

Your very faithfull servant,
Br: Sar:

Richm: Jan: 9.

My little cosin is not to be satisfied without rememb'ring him to you.

Letter LXIII

[January 24th.]

Sir, You have not had many letters of mine dated from London, but I am now upon occasion in the midst of the Poneropolis, onely I find one righteous Lot[1] among them, who not onely entertaines me, but (to please me, and himself the more) wisheth heartily that he had you with him too.

[1] "πολυλογία, καὶ περιαυτολογία" "Talking too much, and repeating himself." The Bishop's remarks about his cousin are borne out by a letter of J. Lowen to Sir Justinian, dated April 6th, 1654, in which elaborate thanks are returned for a Christmas at Lamport. "I am content to confess that, however I have accumulated devotions I have bin guilty of too weake, and too lazy a gratitude." See Letter xxiii, Note 5, and Letter xl.

[2] "Mr. Selden." See Letter lxiii, Note 3.

[1] "One righteous Lot." This is Mr. John Adler. See Letter xliv, Note 2, and Letter xlv for the "honest merchant."

I am but newly com, and am making what hast I can to retire back to my own cell, for I can hardly beleive but that the very aire of this place is apt to corrupt the very prayers that ar made in it. About the latter end of the week I shall with more liberty breath them forth at Richmond both in my own behalf, and yours. The night before I cam hether the third Parliament was broken[2], nor could they expect any hansomer dissolution, who would nether comply fully with their great Master that call'd them, nor had courage to say or do any thing for the publick like wise, or good men.

That which you have heard of Mr. Selden[3], of his receaving the Sacrament humbly and devoutly upon his knees and from the hands of a regular authorised minister of this poor Church of England, is very tru, and possibly the Leviathan himself, when the hook shall be putt into his nostrills may do as much.

The book which you mention of him who hath revived the doctrine of Democritus his *Atomes*[4] hath been long ago read by me, and as much as concernes his life hath been breefly extracted by me. The whole bundle of them may at last com to your hands, which ar now dispersed in severall papers. But there ar visitants that call me away, and will not suffer me to enlarge farther. And therefore I shall make it up with my prayers for you, and so rest,

Your most affectionat freind, and servant,
BR: SAR:
From St. Martin's Lane, Jan: 24.

[ENDORSED REPLY OF SIR JUSTINIAN TO MR. ADLER[5]]

Sir, I give you many thanks for your kind remembrances of me, when the bishop of Salis[bury] was not long since with you, from which place he

[2] "The third Parliament was broken." "Oliver Protector, on Monday morning January 22nd, 1654/5, surprises the Constitutioning Parliament with a message to attend him in the Painted Chamber . . . my Lord Protector from his high place speaks and dissolves" (Carlyle, *Cromwell's Letters and Speeches*, Vol. IV, p. 80).

[3] "Mr. Selden." For his death see Letter LXI, December 19th, 1654, Notes 1 and 2. The Lamport Library contains a 2nd edition of Selden's *Titles of Honour* (1631), and his θέανθρωπος, *or God Made Man* (1661) with a fine portrait of Selden by I. Chantry.

[4] "Democritus his *Atomes*." Probably Robert Burton's *Anatomy of Melancholy* originally published in 1621 as by "Democritus Junior." It was several times reprinted in the author's lifetime with considerable alterations. The 6th edition (1651/2) was stated to be "from a copy corrected with several considerable additions by the author lately deceased." Duppa would have a natural interest in Burton, as a Student of Christ Church, where he died on January 25th and was buried on January 27th, 1639/40. (Wood, *Ath. Ox.*, D.N.B.). Robert Burton's signature appears in *Pauli Jovii Historia Sui Temporis* (1556) according to the Lamport Library Catalogue (1880).

[5] The endorsed reply is clearly to J. Adler. The "neighbour and acquaintance" here recommended to Mr. Adler appears to have been Mr. Gerard, for whom see Letter LXVI, Note 2. On April 5th, 1655, John Adler replied: "The gent. whom you recommended to mee for advice and assistance, hee failed not of the former according to the best of my judgement, and had a very willing and ready profer of the latter." But he seems to have caused some offence to Adler by "goeing out of towne without my knowledge." However "the gent." (a mathematician) had a great interest in Mr. Langham's family, and Mr. Adler thinks they may be able to help him more practically as Adler himself was "altogether unacquainted with that part of India" (I.C. 355): see also Letter LXVI. Mr. Langham was, of course, the Ishams' new neighbour at Walgrave, Alderman John Langham, "a Turkey Merchant", created a baronet on June 7th, 1660, for his support of the Stuarts (Wotton, *Baronetage*).

This letter enclosed one from the Bishop, but it has not survived, unless it is No. 8 of the undated correspondence (see App. B).

enclosed them in a letter to mee. I wish I had any opportunity of returning your freindly courtesies but at present am likely to add more to my obligation by entreating your advice and assistance in what you may to this bearer my neighbour and acquaintance, in case he make a voyage to the East Indies, the occasion of his now going to London to be the better informed of it, and the fittest hand by whom I can at present tender your selfe and Mrs. Adler the thanks and service of

Your

LETTER LXIV

[FEBRUARY 21st.]

Sir, At the last turn, I was so down-right a clinick, that I was forced to make use of a secretary,[1] but by God's blessing I am now not onely gott out of my bed, but am attempting by degrees to creep about my garden. Whether it be the gout, or no, I know not, for it comes so favorably, and so seldom, that I am willing, in a kind of gratitude to give it the fairest words I can, and to call it rather som indisposition, or som occasinall and accidentall humor, which I am the more persuaded to do, because I have been at London at late, and deserve som chastisement for being there. I thank you for your care of me in putting me in mind of the doctor you nominate, but my wife hath been my best phisitian, and by applying pultesses, and a plaster of mithridate hath putt me into a very fair way (I will not say to daunce at a marriage but) to solemnise it so farr as to perform the solemn, and holy part of it in that little parlor of mine, which is now becom a chappel, and where next Sunday I am to ioyn the hands of Franck Marsh, with Dr. Turner the Civilian.[2]

And thus you see, I think my self engaged to accquaint you with our domestichizzies (as the Italians call them) our very domestick concernments, for I have allwaies look'd upon you as on a noble person, and of so diffusive a freindship, that you do not onely terminate it in me, but you have a love to all that relate to me. I hope the marriage will prove happy; for though there ar som disadvantages in the match, yet there is a compensation for them by his great affection to her, and by a liberall

[1] The letter from Mrs. Duppa numbered LXXXV (Feb. 7th) is probably the one Duppa here refers to.

[2] "Franck Marsh" etc. In her will, Mrs. Duppa left her sister, Mrs. Elizabeth Marsh, an annuity which, according to a letter at Lamport (I.C. 581), was £200 a year. It is Elizabeth Marsh's step-daughter Frances (Franck), who is being married here. Frances' father was the Revd. James Marsh, D.D., Archdeacon of Chichester and a Royal Chaplain, who died c.1645. Elizabeth Killingtree was his second wife. She survived till 1680, when she was buried at Richmond (September 24th). The civil marriage of Frances (Franck) Marsh and William Turner took place on Monday, February 19th, and it would appear that Duppa married them on Sunday, February 25th (Quinquagesima). (*Parish Registers of Richmond, Surrey*, ed. J. Challenor C. Smith, Vol. I (1903), p. 149).

The bridegroom, "Dr. Turner the civilian", was William Turner (1604–70), who matriculated from Wadham College, Oxford in 1620. He was D.C.L., 1636, Judge of the P.C.C., M.P. 1659 and 1664, was knighted in the last-named year. According to Wood, he was one of the lawyers consulted by Cromwell, in the case of Dom Pantaleon Sa (Gardiner, III, pp. 79–80). Frances Marsh was the second wife of Dr. Turner, who already had a grown-up family (possibly one of the "disadvantages" of the match mentioned by Duppa). There was also great disparity in age between the bride and groom. (Foster; Wood, *Ath. Ox.*; Copy of Bishop Duppa's will; *Walker Revised*; see also "Bishop Duppa's Wife" in *The Genealogist*, New Series, Vol. IV (1887), pp. 116–18, where the date of the Turner-Marsh wedding, which dates this letter, is correctly given as February 19th, 1654/5). See also App. A.

jointure, of 200*li* p' annum, which she with her small portion could not have expected. I know you ar so charitable, that you cannot but bestow som good wishes on this match, and being so happy in your own choice, bestow som short prayer for a blessing upon this.

You wer pleased to let me know by your last letter, that to praevent my wants, you hav provided somthing in bank for me, which if you shall order to be deliver'd to Mr. Adler in St. Martin's Lane may be safely convei'd to me. I know not well now how to begin to thank you, for you began so early, and have continued so long to find out all the wayes of being kind to me, that unless you took my part, and thought your self requited in the very doing of good, I should despair of making any return to you. Onely my prayers ar my treasury, and out of that there will be a continuall duty paid to Heaven for you by

Your most faithfull, and affectionat freind to serve you,
BR: SAR:

Richm: Febr: 21.

[ENDORSED REPLY OF SIR JUSTINIAN]

My Lord, Your letter comming hither tells me that your Lordship's selfe also now is in a walking condition. I hope the worst being over whilst you walke in your garden, you may meet with the renovation of the spring and your owne health togither.

LETTER LXV

[MARCH 6th.]

Sir, The marriage being over, and all the circumstances of it, which use to trouble families with noise (though this was more quietly, and solemnly carried), I am now at good leasure to return you the thankes for your good wishes, which flowing from a person who makes all obligations good in his own family, may have a greater influence on this new-married pair, who, I hope, though they cannot reach the originall, may copy out your happyness. I am very glad to hear that your good Lady is once more a breeder;[1] and though there may be reason for it, that you both may wish it may prove a son, yet there is farr greater reason to submitt this desire of yours to Him, who knowes what is best for you, and is then readiest to give what we desire when we leave it to Him to dispose of it.

We ar here in these parts in such a calm, and stillness, as seamen observe to be a prognostick of a storm; what tempests ar breeding I know not, but feares, and jealousies ar busy; onely such as I think our selves secured by having nothing, but they among us who have anything to loose look sadly upon it, and yet there is not a wise man among us that can tell us why. But these feares possibly reach not so farr as your parts, or if they do, you ar likely to be the less concerned in them because your piety towards God, and your charity to your friends, will be in stead of a wall of brass to you.

I have not yet sent into St. Martin's Lane, for that which you have directed thether for my use, but I shall by the next give you a better account of it. And so with my hearty prayers for your selfe, and those that ar dearest to you, I rest,

Your most affectionat freind to serve you
BR: SAR:

Richm: March 6.

---

[1] "Your good Lady is once more a breeder". Sir Justinian had one daughter only. A second daughter, Vere, was born on September 30th, 1655. Sir Justinian's arrest on June 9th may be responsible for a break in the correspondence.

Letter LXVI

[March 21st.]

Sir, This month hetherto hath been very full of rumors of warrs[1], every tongue hath been full of them, and every eare hath been open to receave them; but as farr as I see, they vanish as vapors use to do, which about this time of the year, having not virtue enough from the sun to raise them higher, fall suddainly back again to the earth from whence they came. In the mean time, I look upon you, as a person so rationally (and which is better) so religiously composed, that all these outward things have no farther influence upon you, then to make you look upward from whence they ar govern'd, and in your own particular to order your self so, as you may give account of it both to God, and men.

I cannot but expect you should be building at home for at this time you ar building abroad; and that you may not think this a riddle, I am to tell you, that, being enabled by you, I am now building a little wall at the lower end of my garden toward the river, which I do not do for any beauty to my dwelling, but for necessity, having had lately a very shrewd mischance by the sinking of the earth in that place, and my self sinking with it, which I still have a feeling of, but the worst is past. What Mr. Adler hath don, for the conveying of your mathematician[2] to the Indies, I know not, but

---

[1] "Rumors of warrs". Cromwell dissolved Parliament on January 22nd, 1655, after telling the members that their bickerings had caused more trouble during the five months they had sat than had existed for years past. Meanwhile, "the Cavalier Party have been preparing and designing to put this nation in blood again" (Gardiner, Vol. III, p. 249 seq.). The proof of his words was soon forthcoming, for on February 19th, Rochester landed in England to put himself at the head of the Royalist insurgents on Charles' behalf. But the Protector was warned, and had taken action to secure his state. On March 8th, only a few enthusiasts rose in arms in scattered places to face swift dispersal or capture. The sole success was in Wiltshire, where Penruddock captured Salisbury, and proclaimed Charles II. But by the middle of March, Penruddock and his men surrendered. Naturally the success of the rising (and its later failure) in his diocese would have a special interest for Duppa. (See Carlyle, *Cromwell's Letters and Speeches*, Vol. IV, p. 110, for an account of these plots.)

[2] "Mr. Adler" and "your mathematician". See Letter LXIII, Note 5. "Your mathematician" probably was "Mr. Gerard", mentioned in letters now at Althorp between Dorothy, Countess of Sunderland and Sir Justinian Isham. These letters have been kindly transcribed for me by the present Lord Spencer. On September 22nd (year unknown) Lady Sunderland wrote to Sir Justinian regarding a new surveyor to succeed Mr. Barret: "I am informed there is one Mr. Gerard that was once your servant and that he behaved himself so well in your service that he gained a very good opinion from you, and I beseech you do me the favour to let me know first your thoughts of him, and if you believe he will be willing to take that employment." To this letter Sir Justinian drafted a reply: "The person named by your ladyship I have good reason to know who finding him faithful to my Father his old master, entertained him somewhat myself and knowing him very honest was willing as much as I could to enable who I found very capable of whatever I put him upon; a good accountant, a good surveyor of land, of some judgement in the nature of it and used to the drawing of leases and the like, I well know him to be; of his knowledge of the mathematics and his late being at the East Indies I say little because not so pertinent to your Ladyship's purpose." Lady Sunderland, the "Sacharissa" of the poet Waller, dated this letter from Rufford, in Sherwood Forest, where she often was after the marriage in 1656 of her elder daughter, Dorothy, to Sir George Savile, afterwards 1st Marquess of Halifax, "the Trimmer", Lord Privy Seal, and Lord President of the Council under Charles II. It may therefore be assumed that "Mr. Gerard" went to the East Indies in 1655, and some time after 1656 was back in England, and a candidate for the post of Surveyor at Althorp. Lady Sunderland, left a widow by her husband's death at Newbury in 1643, was in charge of affairs at Althorp during her son's minority. Dorothy Osborne (Letter 31) mentions that Sir Justinian "used to brag to mee

I am confident, if he hath receaved your letters, he hath don, or will do, whatsoever is in his power, for his desire is great to serve you.

And for your designe of sending him into those parts, I beleive, you may in time reap very much contentment from it, for he will com among a very ingenious people, and though the merchants who converse with them onely for trade sake, usually com away from thence rather the richer, then the wiser, he may probably return improved in both. I wish I had seen him before he had gon, not that I could have given him instructions for his voyage, but that at least he might have receaved my blessing, which shall follow him howsoever as being emploi'd by you; for whom, and for all that relate to you, there is a daily sacrifice offer'd by

Your very tru, and affectionat freind,
BR: SAR:

Richm: March 21.

[ENDORSED REPLY OF SIR JUSTINIAN]

I find that little stormes at this tyme of the yeare as they are suddaine, so soon allai'd. But for your Lordship's wishes of a faire and prosperous voyage to my mathematician, I give you many thanks, and indeed I had enjoyned his attendance upon your Lordship before his going, but that his stay in London, contrary to his expectation, was very short before his taking ship. Sure I am what different opinions soever he hath left behind him, yet that kind of learning he hath bin most vers'd in, will hold carriage, and be as authentick in the Indies as heere.

LETTER LXVIIA*

[1655?]

Sir, I have sent you here inclosed a letter to your Lady. You have it unseal'd, that you may be the more secure, that there is nothing in it, that may create danger to them. I should be willing if it wer possible to hear from you once a day. I am still of the mind, that your restraint will not be long; but probably, som meanes must be first used. What think you

---

always of a great acquaintance hee had there [Althorp], what an Esteem my Lady had for him, and had the Vanity . . . to talke somtimes as if hee would have had mee beleev'd hee might have had her, and would not." However this may have been, letters both at Althorp and Lamport show Sir Justinian and Lady Sunderland to have been on very friendly terms. (Julia Cartwright, *Sacharissa*, Burke, *Extinct Peerages*, *Letters of Dorothy Osborne*, ed. Moore Smith).

"Mr. Gerard" was apparently appointed. I identify him as the John Garrard who, on August 24th, 1661, wrote from "Allthrope" to Sir Justinian about the price for some land for sale at East Haddon, and advised him "to close . . . as speedily as you can, it is alsoe the advise of my friend to you." (I.C. 521). This is confirmed by Bridges' mention of a plain stone in the chancel floor of Brington Church (no longer visible), inscribed "Here lieth the body of John Garrett, Steward to the Honble Earle of Sunderland. He departed this life the 29th May A.D. 1666." Lord Spencer, who drew my attention to this, points out that he must have been considered a very valuable servant, as he is the only one who is buried in the Chancel of the Church.

* These two undated notes may be taken together. On June 9th, 1655, in the middle of his building at Lamport, Sir Justinian was arrested, and carried up to London to St. James's Palace where, with other Royalist gentlemen, and even some who had taken the Parliament's side like Sir Ralph Verney, he was kept all the summer till he signed an undertaking not to plot against the Protector. On the back of a letter from his bailiff, John Capet, dated August 6th, 1655 (I.C. 362), Sir Justinian wrote a draft complaint: "Having bin brought hither from our own houses by souldiers, and heere imprisoned the space of 2 months to the prejudice of our healthe and certaine detriment of our sèverall families affairs and fortunes."

if I should repair to the good lady in my neighbourhood[1], who was wont to have a great deal of kindness for you? but I shall do nothing without your approbation of it; which I shall expect by the next, and rest very faithfully yours,

B.S.

Tuesday morning when the watermen wer gon so early, that I was fain to send this Mercury on purpose.

After I had wrott this my Cosin Chaworth tell me, that you desired that the letter to your Lady whould go the ordinary way, and therefore I have seal'd it, and directed Morris to carry it to Glanvil's.

Letter LXVIIB

Sir, Before I receaved your letter which cam to me last night when I was going to bed, I gave order to a waterman to bring me som word of your health, though the time of your enlargement[2] must be a secret that no man must dive into. But I hope it will not be long, and having the oportunity of this bearer, who onely wants such an occasion of waiting on you, I make it my request, that when you ar sett free, I may see you here. But what ever your durance may be[3], I persuade my self that you ar not onely armed for it with patience but that according to those excellent rules, which religion hath made familiar to you, you can look chearfully upon all such accidents as these, as long as there is nothing within you to reprove you. I am like one of those freinds whom David complaines of, that stands aloof from you, but my heart and affections ar with you, and my prayers ar daily for you, as being in all conditions,

Your most faithfull freind, and servant,

B.S.

Richm: Saterday 3 in the afternoon.

---

[1] "The good lady in my neighbourhood." This may be Elizabeth Murray, Countess of Dysart, of Ham House, who was supposed to have influence with Cromwell. Bishop Burnet said: "Cromwell was certainly fond of her, and she took care to entertain him in it, till he, finding what was said upon it, broke it off.' Lauderdale, whose mistress and later wife she became, is said to have owed his life to her intercession. It is clear from letters in the Isham correspondence that Sir Justinian knew her: e.g. on May 4th, 1663, Elizabeth Lady L'Estrange, Sir Justinian's daughter, wrote: "I was lately to waite upon the Countess of Diser and Sir Lionel [Tollemache] was here with her this day, she is very pleasant and wishes heartily she could see you" (Canon Augustus Jessopp, "The Wooing and the Married Life of Elizabeth Lady L'Estrange, née Isham", *The Norfolk Antiquarian Miscellany*, Vol. II (1883), and *Ham House A Guide* (1951)). See Letter v, Note 2.

[2] "Time of your enlargement." Sir Ralph Verney wrote in August 1655 (*Verney Memoirs*, Vol. III, p. 243):"Sir Justinian Isham and my selfe sit still, and are willing to see how they [the petitioners to Cromwell] are like to succeed, before wee appeare too pressing upon our new masters; but we have a petition ready, which wee hope may bee received at any time; being we crave nothing in it, but what they ought to grant to every Englishman in our condition, as well as unto him or me." On September 16th, Lady Isham wrote to her husband at St. James's saying that she was trying to "suppresse all sad thoughts as much as I am able . . . in respect of your being kept from me . . . for I am now within three weekes of my time . . .' A daughter, christened Vere, after her mother, was born at Lamport on September 30th, 1655.

[3] "What ever your durance may be." On October 4th, Sir Justinian's order of release was signed by Major General Charles Worsley. He gave security that "he shall not at any time hereafter contrive or comitt any act or things whatsoever prejudiciall to His Highness, or to the present Government as it is now established". (I.C. 367.)

LETTER LXVIII

[DECEMBER 16th.]

Sir, Som afflictions we must look for in this life, and possibly they are in the worst condition (if any such there be) that feel none. But these which you mention are very gentle ones, for your daughter[1] (if my prayers may be heard) may speedily recover, and your wife return, and your self be the better for the breathing out of this distemper, which is so unknown to me, that unless you had given a name to it, I should not have known what to have call'd it.

I make hast to give a return to your last, because we are now drawing near to a solemn time, which will require som praeparations on both sides; for I persuade my self that you remitt nothing of your former piety, which by an antiperistasis of the profaness round about us, cannot but in all good hearts increase a greater fervency. I could heartily wish (if the condition of the times might give you leave) that you fill'd a room among us, but how wide soever the lines of the circumference may be, yet meet they shall in the center. We ar yet suffer'd to offer up the publick prayers and Sacrifice of the Church, though it be under privat roofs, nor do I hear of any for the present ether disturb'd or troubled for doing it[2]. When the persecution goes higher, we must be content to go lower, and to serve our God as the antient Christians did, in dens, and caves, and deserts. For all the world is His chappel, and from what corner of it soever, we lift up our devotions to Him, He is ready to listen to the lowest whispers of them.

I shall not look to hear from you till the holydayes be over, but then do not fail me, for I shall be in som pain, till I hear of the health, of you and yours, which is daily pray'd for by

Your most affectionat freind,
B.S.
Richm: Decem: 16.

---

[1] "Your daughter." On his return to Lamport, Sir Justinian wrote to Sir Ralph Verney, then back at Claydon, two letters, the first on November 10th, 1655, alluding to the illness of his eldest daughter, Jane, "worse I doubt for my troubles." She died on November 29th, 1655, and was buried the day following at Lamport. This letter he signed "Architrave, Freeze and Cornice," alluding to his building at Lamport.

Previously, on November 2nd he had written to the same correspondent inviting him to stay at Lamport "where you may see what the want of my presence hath now necessitated me to in very ill season, my house not yet all covered, nor yet, I assure you so open as you shall ever find the heart of Sir, Your affectionate friend to serve you."

[2] "We are yet suffer'd" etc. On November 24th, Cromwell issued a Declaration against Royalist clergy being employed as chaplains, adding however that "tenderness" was to be used to those who "gave a reall testimony of their godliness" (see Evelyn's *Diary*, December 25th, 1655). The Declaration was not stringently enforced (Gardiner, Vol. III, p. 336). Evelyn's gloomy forebodings: "this was the mournfullest day that in my life I had seen, or the Church of England herself, since the Reformation" were true so far as the public worship only of the Church was concerned.

Being new married, his building completed, but still apparently under surveillance, Sir Justinian turned to the question of marrying the daughters of his first wife. The correspondence of this year is mainly concerned with this subject. Jane Isham, his eldest daughter, had died on November 29th, 1655, which left three to dispose of: Judith and Elizabeth, twins, born in 1636, and Susan, born in 1637. The late Canon Augustus Jessopp in *The Norfolk Antiquarian Miscellany* (Vol. II (1883), pp. 242–84) wrote an account of "The Wooing and the Married Life of Elizabeth, Lady L'Estrange, née Isham" from MSS. at Lamport, which is freely quoted in the notes of this year. He points out that these young ladies had made their home largely in Suffolk, with their great-aunt, known till her death, in 1662, by the name of her first husband, Sir Anthony Denton of Tonbridge, who had died in 1615 aged 53. In 1622, she married Paul D'Ewes of Stowlangtoft, Suffolk, and was thus the step-mother of the formidable Puritan antiquary and diarist Sir Symonds D'Ewes, with whom her relations were anything but smooth. Her home in Suffolk proved a safer refuge for the Isham girls during the Civil War than Lamport could provide, when their father was with the King at Oxford. Lady Denton and her nephew John Stuteville of Dalham were always consulted over any marriage proposal, and they did not hesitate to express their views.

The youngest daughter married first. Susan's marriage to Nicholas Carew of Beddington, Surrey, was preceded by careful enquiries into the young man's character and antecedents, which were undertaken by the Bishop. Even so, after the marriage, the Bishop's vigilance was not relaxed and he sends a report which he had received that "your son Carew is fall'n into the snare of gaming" (Letter LXXVIII). He seems to have lived an unexceptionable life, however, and died in 1688. The great-grand-daughter of Nicholas Carew and Susan Isham, Philippa Gee, married Sir Justinian Isham's grandson, Sir Edmund Isham, 6th Bart., in 1751. (*Visitation of Northants* 1681, ed. Longden).

Elizabeth Isham, "who, if we may judge by the number of her lovers, was a young lady of some personal attractions", as Dr. Jessopp said, was more difficult to suit. Or perhaps it would be truer to say, that, in her case, her father was more difficult to suit. Two suitors appear in these letters. Both, oddly enough, have strong Parliamentarian backgrounds. The first was Henry Wright, son of Cromwell's doctor, and the second Captain Thomas Jervoise of Herriard Park in Hampshire, who had fought well for Fairfax.

The first was suggested by Sir Justinian's fellow prisoner, Sir Ralph Verney, but Lady Denton and John Stuteville wrote a joint letter of protest: "not with standing all these splendours, civilities etc. in the sonne" he was not, in their view "a fitt match for any of Sir Justinian Isham's daughters." His father "had been inquisitive, as to know of what constitution, complexion, etc. your daughters are of, as if hee were to administer physicke to them . . . In these degenerating times the gentry had need to close neerer together, and make a banke and bulwarke against that sea of democracy . . . and to keepe their descents pure . . . from that mungrill breed which would faigne mix with them." (Jan. 12th, 1656. I.C. 353.) As if this were not enough, Dr. Herbert Thorndike, charged to make enquiries as to the religion of the prospective son-in-law, reported unfavourably, though he confessed the doctor's estate was large, "they study to make their sonnes heires of their maners as well of theire estates." The rejected doctor's son, however, married elsewhere, and had the distinction of being raised to the Baronetage both by Cromwell and Charles II!

The next suitor, Captain Jervoise, despite his "rebel" background, seems favourably to have impressed both Sir Justinian and the Bishop, but here again Lady Denton thought him "far off and antient", and he was rejected on the ground that Hampshire was too far from the Suffolk home of the beloved great-aunt.

Public affairs are entirely neglected for match-making in this year's correspondence, and there is less even about books than usual, but there is a glimpse of the philosopher Hobbes at Roehampton inveighing against his enemies "the egregious professors of Oxford."

Letter LXIX

[January 15.]

Sir, That you find any relish of comfort in my dry letters, cannot but proceed from that great kindness which you have toward me, and such as many patients have, who ar more wrought upon by the love they have to their phisitian, then by any virtu of the phisick which is given them. But, the truth is, there is not the least hint given by me, but you can so farr improve by your own reason, that there needs no more then a bare remembrancer that may stirr you up to those better thoughts of your own, which being once rais'd, will do the business more effectually then the letters of all your freinds, though you had a Pliny or a Seneca among them. And these ar times that will putt you to it; calm seas require not either skill, or courage in the pilot, but in such a storm as this, you must call in for all helpes, that ether reason or religion can bring with them. And probably you have don that part allready so well, that your *mala* are *jam victa, iam mansueta*, and your *aerumnae bene collocatae*[1]. Or if this be not allready don, that you are in the way to it, and are subduing by degrees the many unexpected difficulties you have mett with, knowing that the way to Heaven is not allwais strew'd with roses, nor the uninterrupted happyness of this life, any way a concluding argument that we shall thereby be fitted the better for enioying the faelicities of the next.

As for my own particular (since you are pleas'd to think it a concernment to you), I shall onely say, that I am in the same condition as a low shrub

[1] *Mala jam victa*, etc. "Your troubles are already conquered, already tamed, and your distresses are well disposed of." Seneca, *Thyestes*, 425 seq.

is in a tempest, for the windes blow over me, but shake me not. For as yet I am undisturb'd, but not secure, for I see as low shrubs as my self rooted up, which is worse then shaking. It is an expression in one of the Prophets, that God would visit his people with an hired rasor[2], meaning that he would not onely cutt off their superfluities, but shave them to the quick, and you know who sayes what is to be don *cum stricta novacula supra est*[3].

I have nothing else to give you an account of, but of my health, which is not worse then an aged and infirm body may very well expect. Onely my old pain in my stomack continues, which afflicts me dayly toward the close of the evening, but leaves me all the rest of my time free. I eat but once in four and twenty houres, and once in a week I lengthen my fast to thirty, but all this will not do, though I conceave fasting to be better for me in this condition then any phisick can be. And for other helpes, I perceave, that you still take care that I should want nothing, though your own sufferings at this time might very well have excused you from considering mine. But I say no more, for you had rather do good things, then hear of them. There ar dayes of recompense to com, when you may be sure of your reward, and to those I dayly recommend you in my prayers, and as long as this small remnant of my life lasts, shall ever be,

Your most obliged, and faithfull freind to serve you,

BR: SAR:

Jan: 15.

[ENDORSED REPLY OF SIR JUSTINIAN]

Your Lordship's last of the 15th of Jan: was as a medicine to my many maladis untill the latter part of it came to discover your Lordship's one indisposition in your stomack, still afflicting you in the evening. Your spare diet I beleive may bring some ease to you, but an absolute fast to 24 or 30 houres I cannot think any way conducing to your health. But I am sure you cannot want good advise by you; which yet must be grounded upon your owne experience.

I shall now crave your Lordship's enquirie if you be yet altogether a stranger to a young gentleman neere you, to inform your selfe better of him, his family and fortune, as you find fitt opportunity. It is Mr. Carew, Sir Francis Carew's son of Beddington in Surrey[4], commended lately to a servant of yours for one of his daughters. I have often heard commendation of his pleasant seat, but to all els a stranger. Peradventure Mr. Michell or some of your neere neighbours can acquaint your Lordship

[2] "An hired rasor" Isaiah, Cap. VII, v. 20. "In the same day shall the Lord shave with a razor that is hired . . ." A.V.

[3] *Cum stricta novacula*, etc. "When the drawn razor is over our head." Martial, *Epigr.*, XI, 58, 5-6. *Quid si me tonsor, cum stricta novacula supra est, tunc libertatem divitiasque roget?*

[4] "Mr. Carew." Sir Francis Carew was the son of Sir Nicholas Throckmorton of Coughton, Warwickshire, who was adopted as heir by his maternal uncle Sir Francis Carew of Beddington, Surrey, whose name he then took. Sir Francis Carew was buried April 9th, 1649, and was succeeded by his son Nicholas, the young gentleman here referred to.

The Carews of Beddington had been seated there since the reign of Edward III when a "charter of free warren" had been granted them at Beddington, Croydon, and other places. Their magnificent house is figured in Nash's *Mansions of England in the Olden Time* (1869–72), and Royalty had often been entertained there. Sir Justinian's reason for making these enquiries will soon be obvious. (Burke, *Extinct Baronetcies* and *Vicissitudes of Families.*)

farther; the young gent: was not very long since Mr. Tripplett's schollar[5]; not yet of age, he hath bin lately to [illegible] a freind of his neere heere. I perceave nothing as yet but well of him; and should gladly have it confirm'd by your Lordship.

Letter LXX

[January 20th.]

Sir, As long as I have the benefitt of your freindship, I shall have the less need of a library, for though I have not the gross bulk of every author (which I am nether able to compass, nor know how to dispose of so much lumber in such a closet as mine is) yet if you continu the kindness to me in pointing out to me what you find remarkable in those bookes you meet with, I shall praeserve your letters as my best bookes; and as som men (old men especially) ar nourish'd better by broths, and jellies, and the juyce of meates extracted, then by the full substance of them, so I shall find it my case, and please my self better, with your short strictures, and animadversions, then to load my self, and my decay'd memory, with more then I could easily digest.

There is an excellent author, Photius[1], the Patriarch of the Greek Church (to whom, I am sure, you ar no stranger), who in his *Bibliotheca* hath left a pattern for us all, and hath summ'd up in one book, not onely the names, and writings, but his sense, and judgement upon many authors, which else had utterly perish'd. I could heartily wish, there wer found som to imitate him; for besides the praeserving the memory, both of greater, and more especially lesser tracts and treatises (which ar commonly lost like pinns and needles, and never recovered again), there might be great use made of it, both in the exercising of every man's own judgement, and giving an edge to the judgement of others.

But while I am discoursing of bookes to you, the great modern writer, John Hall of Richmond[2], is this day carried to his grave. I confess that of

[5] "Mr. Triplett's schollar." Thomas Triplett, Student of Christ Church, Oxford, was Rector of Whitburn 1631 and Washington 1640. He was Prebendary of Salisbury 1645, but sequestered from his living in 1644 by the County Committee. He retired to Dublin, where, according to Walker, he "taught school": on his return to England, he was a schoolmaster at Hayes, Middlesex, where, no doubt, Nicholas Carew was his pupil. He became resident teacher at the Dutch Embassy in 1656, and was restored to his living of Washington on his petition in 1660. Made Prebendary of Westminster, he died July 18th, 1670. (*Walker Revised.*) When at the Dutch Embassy he had "8 or 10 [pupils] at most" (*Verney Memoirs*, Vol. III, p. 358). In his will (January 21st, 1668/9) he gave to Petersham a sum of money to the annual value of £5 to bind child apprentices. The money was vested in John Banks, perhaps identical with Giovanni Banks (see Letter XXIII, Note 3). (Manning and Bray, *History of Surrey*, Vol. I, p. 445). He also endowed an apprenticeship scheme in the parishes of Whitburn and Washington. (Lewis, *Topographical Dictionary*).

[1] For Photius see Letter XX, Note 6. His most important work, *Bibliotheca*, was ed. by I. Bekker (1824-5).

[2] For John Hall of Richmond, see Letter LII, Note 4. John Hall, also a writer, who accompanied Cromwell to Scotland in 1650, also died in 1656, but in August. He is not the same person as John Hall of Richmond. For the former see D.N.B. The British Museum, in addition to *Of Government and Obedience* (see previous note cited above), has two works by John Hall of Richmond:

(1) *New Propositions from his Excellency Sir Thomas Fairfax, Lieutenant Generall Cromwell, and the Councell of the Army concerning the Kings Majesty . . . with His Majestys Gracious Answer* (*enclosed in a letter* [*by J. Hall*] *from Hampton Court*) *and Desires* printed by Robert Williamson, London 1647.

(2) *The True Cavalier examined by His Principles and found not guilty of Schism or Sedition* printed by Thomas Newcomb, London 1656.

John Hall of Richmond's fame as a writer does not seem to have survived.

these late yeares he hath been a great riddle to me, for having known him long by no other character, then being a good accountant of household and kitchen affaires, he appear'd to me on a suddain as a person of a more then ordinary brain, and one that had studied Hooker[3] so much, that as near as an ape could com to a man (which in many resemblances is very near), he could strangely imitate him. But that which rais'd a greater wonder in me, was, that I could not find that he understood any thing of any language at all but his own, nor had farther consulted with authors of any kind, but such as wer ether born English or made so. Insomuch that he seem'd to me ether by a strong fancy to have woven all out of his own brain, or to be inspired with som enthusiasme that transported him to an ability beyond both his own nature, and his education.

And of such enthusiasmes Merick Casaubon[4] hath given the world a treatise not unworthy the reading. The first book that he published[5] he brought to me in written hand, and with great humility desired me not onely to read it over, but to deal clearly with him wherein he had don amiss. And this freindly office I faithfully perform'd to him, for finding him deeply tainted with the Erastian way, which denies any power at all to the Church but what is derived from the Civil Power, not so much as granting to them the power of order (for as for the outward power of jurisdiction in a coercive way, we lay no claim to it), I so farr contested and debated the business with him, that ether he was convinced by me, or at least in civility would seem to be so. This book being printed (and with som alterations in this particular), he was gazed upon the more earnestly, as comming unexpectedly out of a shade into the sunshine, where, as other men wond'red at him, so certainly he was dazled at him self, and finding more applause abroad then probably he look'd for, he did not stopp here, but conceaving that he had gott credit enough, his next design was to publish somthing that might be of more solid advantage, then

---

[3] For Hooker see Letter LIII, Note 4.

[4] "Merick Casaubon." Meric' Casaubon (1599–1671), was a younger son of Isaac Casaubon, a Huguenot refugee. He was a Student (1614–27) of Christ Church where he no doubt made Duppa's acquaintance. He was made a Prebendary of Canterbury in 1628, and became Vicar of Minster and Monkton in 1634. In 1641 he was deprived of these livings on the complaint of thirty-three parishioners from Minster and four from Monkton, that he was a ritualist, exorbitant for tithes, and neglectful of his cure. In 1647, however, six of his former parishioners, of whom all except one had originally signed the letter of complaint, wrote to Casaubon asking him to "desire his living again." Apparently, the conduct of his Puritan successor, Mr. Culmer, was far worse than the ritualism of Casaubon. Mr. Culmer known as "blew dick", bore "the character of a very turbulent, unquiet and debauched man." Casaubon was not restored, but, according to Wood, "Cromwell seemed so sensible of his worth, that though he could not win him over to his desires, yet he acknowledged a great respect for him" (*Ath. Ox.* Vol. I). Cromwell's good opinion was no passport to Duppa's approval. In a letter written in 1661 to Sheldon, Casaubon claimed that he had "suffered much, though I was earnestly solicited . . . by the late great man (or tyrant rather) to accept of considerable preferments from him, which I constantly refused . . ." In 1660 he was restored to his livings. He died in 1671 and was buried in Westminster Abbey. He wrote many books, including *The Vindication* of his father (1624) dedicated to King James (who took much notice of him), ecclesiastical commentaries, and translations from Marcus Aurelius and Epictetus. The book to which Duppa refers is his *Treatise concerning Enthusiasme, as it is an effect of nature, but is mistaken by many for either Divine Inspiration or Diabolical Possession.* London (1655.) It was published November 11th, 1654. (*Walker Revised*, Tatham, *The Puritans in Power* (1913), D.N.B.). See Letter CV, Note 3.

[5] "The first book that he published." Hall's first substantial work was *Of Government and Obedience* (1654).

popular ayre could bring him. And to this end his teeming brain brought forth two treatises more, wherein he did more particularly apply him self to the present Government, for being discontented, and discarded by his former master, he was resolved to wind up his thread upon a new bottom. But from this time he becam a stranger to me, and I was no more consulted with, and that you may easily perceave by his two pamphlets, if ever they com to your hands. But I have don with him, for he is now going to his grave, where I wish all his faults may be buried with him.

I have not yet mett with the romance, nore have I any sharp appetite at all to enquire after it. As for Hobbs[6] (whose way of ratiocination, you say, he seemes to correct) I have lately mett with him at Roehampton, and brought away with me his *Elements of Philosophy* translated into English, with an addition of six Lectures to the egregious Professors (as in scorn he calls them) of the Mathematicks in the University of Oxford, in answer to what they have obiected to him, and for a corollary he dismisseth them with these egregious titles of "uncivill Ecclesiasticks," "inhumane Divines," "unasinous[7] Collegues," *et quic quid splendidabilis obtulerat.* If you have not the book I shall send it to you when I make the next return. For the present, I shall weary you no longer, but with the continuance of my prayers for you, I shall rest,

Sir, Your most affectionat true freind and faithfull servant,

BR: SARUM.

Richm: Jan: 20.

LETTER LXXI

[FEBRUARY 18th.]

Sir, Before this com to your hands, I beleive you ether have or will receave a querulous letter of mine, wherein you may discover somthing of impatience in me upon the missing of a return which I expected from you. Not that I could think that you had forgott me (who had lately so really rememb'red me) but that I fear'd som cross accident might hinder you, for these times ar likely to bring them fast enough upon us. But your letter dated February the 3d having loiter'd by the way till Febr: the 16th, clear'd me of all my feares, and now I can write with less disturbance to my self, or you[1].

The imployment which you trust me with, concerning the inquiry after the condition, and fortunes of a young gentleman in these parts[2], is in part, allready begun, and shall be faithfully pursued by me. His person I do not know, but his family I have formerly been no stranger to. His estate (if my intelligence deceave me not) cannot be less then 1500 by the year, but out of that there is a jointer to his mother of 600 during life.

---

[6] For Thomas Hobbes see Letter XV, Note 4, and Letter XIX, Note 7. "The egregious Professors" were Seth Ward and John Wilkins, Warden of Wadham. See Letter LII, Note 3.

[7] "Unasinous"—"agreeing in stupidity." The reference to the passage in Hobbes quoted by Bishop Duppa is from the *Six Lessons to the Professors . . . in the University of Oxford* (1656).

[1] This gives a clue to the time that these letters took. The Bishop writes on January 20th and Sir Justinian replies on February 3rd. This letter reaches the Bishop on February 16th, but he considers the transit to have taken much longer than usual.

[2] "A young gentleman in these parts." This, of course, is Nicholas Carew. See Letter LXIX, Note 4.

Bedington, his cheif seat (which my Lord of Warwick[3] rents for the present), is no part of the joynter, but a very pleasant place, at least I thought it so many yeares ago. But though I have begun at the wrong end, according to the mode of the world (for you know who said it long ago, *de moribus ultima fiet quaestio*[4]) I shall come now to the main, the disposition, and inclinations of the person, which must be the cheif ingredient to make marriage happy. And concerning this, of all that I yet hear here is nothing but good; his temper (they say) is very gentle, no roughness, or obstinacy in him, which as it renders him in a capacity of receaving good impressions, so, if he light not into good hands, it may betray him. As he yet standes, I cannot hear that he is any way corrupted, and the onely way to praeserve him so, will be his matching into such a family as yours, where the vices of these times ar strangers.

But this is but the first essay of my enquiry; for by your direction I have praepared a way of searching farther into all particulars. Of which you shall hear by the next.

Concerning the postscript about the Coronell[5], though the report of som unhansom carriage of his, hath been long upon the wing, and hath been spred much to his disadvantage, I cannot (according to my rules of charity) give any admittance to the beleif of it. I do not know what weakness might surprise him, but certainly (what ever it may prove to be), malice hath no share in it. I shall detain you no longer, but having once more given you my hearty thankes for the continuance of your great freindship to me (which seasons all the rest of my sufferings with a great deal of chearfullness), I shall pray for you, and yours, and rest,

Your most affectionat tru freind, and servant

BR: S.

Richm: Shrove Tuesday.

LETTER LXXII

[FEBRUARY 20th.]

Sir, Till we gett into the former road again, the motions of our letters cannot keep the time agreed upon. And therefore to redeem the miscarriage of one letter (which slept at Mr. Carlile's[1] longer then it should have don) we ar fain to double our pace, till we gett into the right way again.

Mine which I wrott last I doubt not, but you have receaved, wherein upon som short enquiry, I gave you an imperfect account of the business recommended to me. But since that time, I have had som fuller assurance, by the diligence and fidelity of that person whom you named to me both of the estate, and the quality of this young gentleman, who now applies

[3] The tenant of Beddington was Robert Rich, 2nd Earl of Warwick (1587–1658), Lord High Admiral of the Parliamentary Fleet, during the Civil War, whose grandson married Cromwell's daughter on November 11th, 1656. Although connected by marriage with Cromwell, he refused to sit in Cromwell's amended House of Lords. He seems to have been an unsatisfactory tenant (see Letter CIV).

[4] *De moribus*, etc. "Investigation concerning character will be the last thing that is done." Juvenal, *Sat.* III, 140. See also Letter LXXV.

[5] "The Coronell." This is Colonel James Long of Draycott, for whom see Letter V, Note 3. The "unhamson carriage" report is perhaps that mentioned by Clarendon (Book IX, § 9). "Sir William Waller and Cromwell, marched together about this time [1645] towards the west and making a cavalcade in Wiltshire, had routed, and taken the whole regiment of horse of colonel Long, the high shrief of the county, by his great defect of courage and conduct."

[1] "Mr. Carlile's." This suggests that some of Sir Justinian's letters may have gone to the Carliles' house at Petersham. See Letter III, Note 7, for confirmation.

himself to you, to be receaved into your family. And first for the estate, I am credibly inform'd that it is above 2,200*li* by the year, out of the which his mother having 700*li* a year for her iointure, the present estate to the heir will annually be 1,500*li*. The debts that wer upon it wer satisfied during his minority, and the estate they say is now perfectly clear. A sister he hath, but married, as I hear, and provided for; but brother he hath none. And for his person, and the goodness, and sweetness of his condition, the return that is made to me is: *Omnes omnia bona dicerè*[2]. If there be any other particular which you would commend to my trust, I can easily find a way to satisfy you.

But having said so much in my former I shall weary you no farther, but shall earnestly sollicite God, to direct you in this choice, that you may have many comforts by it.

From your very faithfull freind, and servant,
BR: SAR:

Richm: Feb: 20.

LETTER LXXIII

[MARCH 18th.]

Sir, I am the better pleas'd to find that your intelligence so farr agrees with mine, that there is nothing more to be look'd after but the conveniency of their dispositions, for without that no marriage is happy. And of this, you having them both with you, ar likeliest to be the fittest judge, and without flattering of you (which I shall never be guilty of), I know not any where a better discerner of spirits, which though it was a miraculous gift in the Apostles' times, and ceas'd with them, yet the morall part of it is still to be found among prudent men, which gave occasion to him that first said that: *Prudentia* was *quaedam divinatio*,[1] especially such a prudence as submitts it self to be guided by an higher influence, which will direct both you and them that love you to make their main and cheif addresses to God, that His blessing may go along in the whole carriage of this business, and that nothing may be in this particular ether begun, continued, or ended without Him.

And that you may be the more confident, that I shall ioyn with you in all your devotions concerning it, you have laid such an obligation upon me, by telling me it may be an occasion of drawing you oft'ner into these parts, that wer there nothing else but this, I shall be deeply engaged by the love that I have to my self (for there may be an honest *philautia*), heartily to pray that there may nothing intervene that may hinder the accomplishing of this which Providence hath so farr brought about.

But all this while I am so much in the dark, that I do not yet know, which of your daughters it is[2] whom you ar now disposing of, when the

[2] *Omnes omnia bona dicere*. "All men begin to say everything good." Terence, *Andria*, I, 1, 69–70. See A. Trollope *Framley Parsonage* Chapter I. Nicholas Carew is the subject of this letter. Sir Justinian gave his daughter Susan a dowry of £4,000. Jessopp says £5,000, but the sum was £4,000: see Release of Sir N. Carew (I.L. 2220).

[1] *Prudentia est quaedam divinatio*, "Foresight is a kind of divination." This is a quotation from memory of words used by Cornelius Nepos, *Att*. 16, 4, of the foresight shown by Cicero in his correspondence with Atticus: *prudentiam quodam modo esse divinationem*.

[2] "Which of your daughters." It was the youngest by his first wife, Susan, born November 29th, 1637.

time is of tying this holy knot, and where the residence shall be, whether they with you where you ar, or you with them at Bedington. Nor doth this flow from a curiosity of knowing more then comes to my share, but rather because I have so great a share in all that is yours, that I cannot quietly be ignorant.

The neighbourhood and acquaintance of Mr. Harvey[3] may be of very good use, for he is a person of great civility, and not any way tainted with the disorders of the time. His pleasures ar very innocent, and such as contribute much to his health, being allwaies in exercise, and no lover of the delights of London. His lady not onely a very good wife, but a very good freind, of which I have many expressions from her. As concerning the doctor[4], he is not so much as known to me by sight; there goes a very good fame of him for his skill as a phisitian, but a Christian (as they say) of one of the new editions; a prudent man in the wayes of this world, and rich enough to settle a very good estate. Whether the young man doth *patrizare*, I know not, but well bred he is, and if the new lights have not led him out of the way, I hear of nothing else he stands in danger of. But this will require good deliberation; and you ar so much the safer, in that you do not use to be praecipitate in that which is of so much concernment.

My cheif business is to pray that God may be call'd to counsell, and then

---

[3] "Mr. Harvey." Presumably a neighbour of Nicholas Carew in Surrey. Daniel Harvey (1631–1672) of Coombe or Combe Park, Surrey, nephew of William Harvey, the physician (see Letter LXXXVIII, Note 3) would seem to be the person intended. His wife was Elizabeth, only daughter of Edward, 2nd Lord Montagu of Boughton, who was a neighbour of the Ishams in Northamptonshire. The fact that Duppa mentions Mr. Harvey's "lady" may well be because she would be of special interest to Sir Justinian. Coombe is (or was) in the parish of Kingston, and in the neighbourhood of Beddington and Richmond. They would be nice neighbours for the young Carews. In 1660 Daniel Harvey was knighted, and appointed Ranger or Keeper of Richmond Park, so he was obviously of Royalist principles. He later became Ambassador to Turkey. (V.C.H. Surrey, III, 502, 536: *Misc. Gen. et Her.* 2nd Series, III, 331).

[4] "As concerning the doctor." This was Laurence Wright, M.D. (1590–1657), of Dagenham, Essex, who was physician-in-ordinary to Cromwell. He had "amassed a large fortune by his extensive practice as a medical man" (Jessopp, *The Wooing and the Married Life of Elizabeth Lady L'Estrange*). His son, Henry Wright, was a suitor of Miss Elizabeth Isham. The Bishop has actually written the words "Dr. Wright," but crossed them out. In April 1656, Sir Ralph Verney wrote from Claydon to recommend Henry Wright's suit. Sir Ralph had met the doctor, who expressed great esteem for Sir Justinian and his family, and what good reports he had had of the "young ladies" . . . "the young man I doe not know, but I heare soe well of him and know soe much of his Father that I can say with confidence very few in England can have greater choyce of greater Fortunes, but money is not the thing hee chiefly aymes at in his sonnes marriage; . . . Sir, if you would be pleased to say your daughter shall have five thousand pounds, I am sure his sonne would soon attend you at Lamport, and if you approve him goe directly into Suffolk", i.e. to their aunt Lady Denton's house. Sir Ralph had evidently heard of the proposed alliance with the Carews, for he added in a P.S.: "Some say Sir . . . Cary of Beddington is a pretender to one of your daughters in Suffolke, if soe and that you intend to proceed with the Doctor, 'twere well he knew it, and to which for many reasons." John Stuteville, however, cousin of Sir Justinian and nephew of Lady Denton took, as we have seen, a different view of the proposed alliance in his letter of January 12th, 1656, quoted in the Introduction to this year. The letter is fully quoted in the *Verney Memoirs* (Vol. III, pp. 197–200). Henry Wright was created a Baronet by Cromwell on April 10th, 1658, presumably in recognition of his father's services. This dignity was, of course, disallowed at the Restoration, but soon after, on June 11th, 1660, King Charles made him a Baronet. "It is not easy to conjecture what service he had rendered to be thus highly favoured" (G.E.C., *Complete Baronetage*). He married in 1658 a daughter of John, 1st Lord Crew of Steene, and died February 5th, 1664, aged 27.

there can be no miscarriage. But I shall detain you no longer, for having said enough to these particulars, I shall add no more, but that I am,

Your most affectionat freind and servant,

B: SA:

March: 18.

LETTER LXXIV

[APRIL 8th.]

Sir, Ever since I receaved your last, I have been under the chastisement of so cruel a cold, that I could not well tell what the issue of it might be; for the violence of it was such, as I could nether sleep in the night time, nor eat in the day. But God hath been pleas'd onely to shake this rod of His over me, for the extremity (which I therefore fear'd because I deserved) is so much abated, that I am now able to give you that account of my self, which before I could not do. But however this storm may be over, yet I am daily to praepare for more, for this craz'd tabernacle of mine cannot stand long, being now past my 67th year[1], and so near my utmost declining point, that every slight accident hath strength to cast me down. But this is not by way of complaint, for I am persuaded, that whensoever that happy hour comes, to dy will be a gain to me.

In the mean time, though the presence somtimes of such a freind as your self would be more then an ordinary cordiall to me, yet I can lay aside the thought of all self concernments, when the advantages of my freind, or of any of his relations ar first to be consider'd of. And therefore I do very much approve of that resolution, which may rather settle you where you are, then bring you nearer to me. As for the enquiry that hath been hetherto made, I observed your order to have it don secretly, insomuch that he whom I emploi'd, did not know in whose behalf he did it. But as he tells me since, he quickly heard that from others, which I conceal'd from him, for no sooner did he begin to sift som persons for intelligence, but they could tell him that unless he did it in relation to your family, the intelligence he look'd for could not concern him. But whether known, or unknown, I hope this business is allready so farr advanced, that this particular need not trouble you. And so longing to hear from you, I daily pray for you and yours, and rest,

Your most affectionat true freind to serve you,

B.S.

Easter Tuesday.

LETTER LXXV

[MAY 1st.]

Sir, I had for a time a little court here, but it is now becom a cottage again, and I begin to revert to my own houres, and to my own quiet, and so much the more contentedly, that before I cam to enioy my own I was bless'd in procuring the contentment of an other, whose passions wer so great, that there was nothing I could say could possibly have allai'd them, had not that great Comforter, the Spirit of God made use of so poor an instrument, to shew His power the more by me.

The proposall that I made to you, I am confident you have so farr excused, as to beleive it proceeded not from any over much business in my own nature (who have learn'd from an antient Father of the Church,

[1] Bishop Duppa was born March 10th, 1588/9. This dates the letter as subsequent to March 1655/6. It will be seen that the Bishop has been continuing his enquiries about Nicholas Carew.

that the interposing in matters of this kind brings very much hazard along with it), but from so great a desire of serving you and your family, that I can hardly moderat my self, but (upon hearing of any thing that may (to my thinking) conduce to the happyness of any part of it), I must propose what I hear, and when I have don that, my περιεργία[1] leads me no farther, but am very well content to leave the rest to you. But to resume the proposall, I am still of the mind, that the young gentleman is qualified above the rate of those of his level, that he is discreet above his yeares, that he is civilly and hansomly bred, that he is vers'd in good letters, and no stranger to the mathematicks, and therefore the fitter to be accquainted with you, but above all that, he is rightly principled in his religion, and therefore the more likely to bring a blessing along with him, to the family he comes to.

But after all this ὕστερον πρότερον[2], (for the method of the world is: *De moribus ultima fiet quaestio*[3]), I can say nothing of the estate at all and possibly these times may have brought it so low, that it might be an argument of great imprudence in you to venture your daughter with a good portion to an estate that cannot answer it. Since I wrott first concerning this particular, I have heard no farther from the parties, and therefore *dictum indictum volo*[4], till they move farther in it, and when they do, I shall wholy give it over to you to consider all circumstances, and to proceed according to the great measure of that prudence which God hath given you. And that he may bless you and yours in all your wayes is the daily prayer of

Your most faithfull freind and humble servant,
BR: SAR:

Richm: May Day.

LETTER LXXVI

[MAY 7th.]

Sir, Though I have not heard from you of late as I expected according to the compact that was between us, yet I must not complain of you, for whatsoever the cause may be, I am so confident of it, that I dare assure my self, that unkindness hath no share in it. But if the newes be tru which we hear, that the marriage is allready solemnized[1], or very suddainly to be so, I can frame so many apologies for you, that you shall need to make none. Onely gratify me so much, as to let me know, how you are, and what you do, and whether this marriage be consummate or no, not for any satisfying of my curiosity, but that I may the better know how, and upon what termes, I may pray for you and yours; which I had rather hear

[1] περιεργία. "Officiousness (or over-exactness)."
[2] ὕστερον πρότερον. A grammatical term = "cart before the horse."
[3] *De moribus* etc. See Letter LXXI, Note 4.
[4] *Dictum indictum volo.* "I wish unsaid what has been said." Adapted from Terence, *Phormio*, V, 8, 57–8. *Nolo volo, volo nolo rursum, cape, cedo; quod dictum, indictum est.*

[1] "The marriage is allready solemnized." The marriage of Nicholas Carew and Susan Isham took place at Lamport on May 4th, 1656. The marriage in church was preceded by a civil ceremony on May 2nd, 1656, performed by Edward Hollis, Mayor of Northampton. This was in accordance with the Act of Parliament passed in 1653 (see Letter XXXII, Note 1. For the marriage, see *Northamptonshire Parish Registers, Marriages*, ed. Phillimore and Longden, Vol. II (1909), pp. 108 and 110). Sir Richard Raynsford on April 18th, 1656, wrote to Sir Justinian sending him a "draught of the articles" of the marriage (I.C. 396). He made the point that Nicholas Carew was not yet of age. Raynsford, who was Recorder of Northampton in 1653, was a Royalist, and became Lord Chief Justice in 1676. He died in 1680. (*Northants Notes and Queries*, Vol. IV (1892), § 584).

immediatly from your self, then by the uncertain reports of others.

I have been lately very ill, and am not yet so perfectly recover'd, but that I may still liken my self to a falling building, supported for a time with som few props, which will at last fail me, and leave me to my own dust. There is nothing that sweet'neth more this bitter remainder of my life, then your freindship to me, which, as I shall never do any thing to forfeit, so I am sure, you will never alter. And so begging of God, that His blessing may continue upon your self, and upon your family, I remain,

Your very faithfull freind, and humble servant,
BR: SAR:

Richm: May 7.

LETTER LXXVII

[JUNE 12th.]

Sir, I am glad to find that you ar at leasure to enquire after the old philosophers, while we in these parts nether can hear, nor speak anything but of new plots, and of strange discoveryes; *et eccquis erit finis*? Had your Aesop lived in these times, he would have been hardly putt to, where to have found beasts enow, to make up his Fables; beares, and lyons, and foxes, and wolves could not reach to it. But because any discourse of this may sound contrary to our articles of agreement, I must say no more. As for Aesop (the time of whose being in the world you have rightly calculated), and Planudes his βιόγραφος[1], I can add nothing to what you allready know, for I have had nether of them by me these many yeares, nor have I so much as a Suidas or a Martinius[2] to consult with. But the passage you mention is so very well worth the looking on, that if I can borrow the book of my neighbor at Istleworth, I shall not be long without it. But for the resurrection of Planudes, there will not be any great feare, for they who have gott what they have from the living, will easily keep it against the dead. The great consternation will be at that other Resurrection (which none of the old philosophers dreamt of, and few of our new Christians think of), when we must com to answere for all that we have don, *et quaenam illa turbatio*[3].

I should have ended with one side of a leaf, but that I cannot hold from giving you som account of what is don in my neighborhood. And first I should say (but that I believe you know it allready) that Mistress Overbury is married to a young Baronet near Norwich[4], whose estate of 2000 *li*

[1] "Aesop" and "Planudes his βιόγραφος." Planudes was a 13th century Byzantine scholar who translated the Latin classics, and wrote a life of Aesop (*Encycl. Brit.*).

[2] "A Suidas or a Martinius." Suidas, a Greek, and Martinius were lexicographers, the former a 10th century Byzantine scholar of some importance.

[3] *Quaenam illa turbatio*. "And what a trouble that will be."

[4] "A young Baronet near Norwich." Sir Thomas Pettus of Rackheath, Norfolk, succeeded as 2nd Baronet November 21st, 1654. He married (according to G.E.C., *Complete Baronetage*) "in or before 1640" Elizabeth, daughter of Walter Overbury of Barton-on-the-Heath, Warwickshire. They had no surviving male children, and at Sir Thomas' death in 1671, his brother succeeded him. The date given for the marriage by G.E.C. must be wrong. She was a niece of the Sir Thomas Overbury whose poisoning in the Tower in 1613 by agents of Lady Essex, was the subject of the *cause célèbre* of James I's reign. The mother of Sir Thomas Pettus was Elizabeth, sister of Thomas Knyvett (see Letter IX, Note 2), a friend and former lodger of the Carliles, who may have brought this bit of gossip back with them to Petersham. Mrs. Carlile was herself a cousin of Elizabeth Overbury through her aunt Mary Palmer, who married Sir Nicholas Overbury (the grandparents of Elizabeth Overbury). The will of Mary, widow of William Palmer (proved May 4th, 1653, P.C.C. Brent 293), mother of Joan Carlile, establishes their relationship to the Palmers of Barton, where Sir Thomas Overbury was born.

by the year (as they reckon it) is balanced to the full by the vertues and discretion of his Lady. Next I must tell you that the Park[5] is inhabited again and a new sett of soiourners com, among whom there is a young Lord (grandchild to the Earl of Chesterfield[6]), with whom I am very much taken, and what takes me, you know;—nether honor, nor riches, but a great measure of all kind of worth, and virtu, that may make him amiable to good men. But this is not all, for on the other side of the water, your fair widow of Northamptonshire[7] hath pitched her dwelling, whom I have once visited not because she is fair, but because ether she deceaves the world, or she is very good.

And if all this cannot draw you to visit these parts again, I have no more to say but to please my self in beleiving, that you have so much of goodness within your own dores that you need seek for no obiects of it abroad. And yet when you have a mind to vary the scaene, you may bring your happiness along with you, and find a freind to boot.

BR: SAR:

June 12.

LETTER LXXVIII

[AUGUST 11th.]

Sir, I did once seriously intend not to trouble you farther in this matrimoniall business, and the rather to abstain from it, because I had mett with a passage in St. Ambrose's *Life*, wherein I found that that excellent man, upon a recollection of the accidents of his life, did very much please himself, that though somtimes importuned, he never interposed himself in making any matches of that kind. And though this doth not so farr work upon me as wholy to take me off from doing good offices and from

[5] "The Park." The Carliles had now returned to Petersham Lodge and were entertaining new lodgers.

[6] "Grandchild to the Earl of Chesterfield." Philip Stanhope, 1st Earl of Chesterfield, a distinguished Royalist, Colonel of Dragoons (1642), died in September 1656. This letter must have been written before the Earl's death, when his grandson, the "young Lord", was known as Lord Stanhope. Incidentally, it also shows that Stanhope, contrary to what has been stated, had returned to England before his grandfather's death.

Philip, Lord Stanhope, who became 2nd Earl of Chesterfield in 1656, was born in 1633, and spent much of his youth travelling. "A long residence in Italy had made him ceremonious in his commerce with men, and jealous in his connection with women" (Anthony Hamilton, *Memoirs of the Count de Gramont*). He was involved in the Royalist rising of 1659, and arrested on September 2nd, but released on security October 5th (C.S.P. Dom. 1659–60, pp. 144 and 240). On January 17th, 1659/60 he killed "Mr. Woollie" (Francis Woolly, or Wolley, son of the Revd. Dr. Woolly) in a duel and fled to France (*Mordaunt Letter-Book*, No. 224, p.166). On this occasion Bishop Duppa wrote to him: "Believe it, my lord, I look upon you as one of those few who are likely to redeem the honour of our languishing and allmost lost nobility, and therefore am the more troubled that this unexpected accident should cast such a cloud upon you . . . I have a hart earnestly set to pray for you, that God may not only pardon this offence of yours, but preserve and sanctifie your excellent spirit . . ." At the Restoration, he returned to play a part in the scandals of Charles II's court, and was reputed to have been Lady Castlemaine's lover before her marriage. He rose against James II in 1688, but refused to take the oaths to William III as king. He died in 1714. (G.E.C., *Complete Peerage*, *Letters of Philip, Second Earl of Chesterfield* (1829)).

[7] "Your fair widow of Northamptonshire." Dorothy, Lady Sunderland, was born at Syon House, and baptized at Isleworth October 5th, 1617. Syon is, of course, on the north side of the river, and she may have been visiting her uncle. But she was no longer a widow, having married Sir Robert Smythe of Boundes in 1652. (Julia Cartwright, *Sacharissa*).

being instrumentall to the happy advancing of such holy contracts, yet it hath made me so wary, that unless it be in relation to your family (whose happyness I do so passionately wish), I have been so abstemious, that very few else can accuse me of it. But the occasion why I now appear again in this particular, is to send you this inclosed, which being wrott to a neighbor of mine, I thought it very fitt that you should have a sight of. I shall not need to say any more of the person[1], having allready given you so full a character of him. Perhaps he is not *à la mode* with his doublet open and his shirt hanging out behind, but certainly he hath that better mode of keeping the estate that is left him, which many of the younger gallants have no skill in.

There is a flying report here (but what truth there is in it I know not) that your son Carew is fall'n into the snare of gaming, and I could not forbear to let you know of it. If it be so, though it be early day with him, yet *principiis obsta*[2]; for it must be seriously thought on, what fitt wayes to use to praevent his farther running out. But *pereat inter nos hoc secretum*[3], and let not me be so much as named for the intelligencer. It had been very happy had he lived ether with you, or at least nearer you, where besides your advice, your excellent example might have had more influence upon him.

You see I cannot fall upon the business of bookes, which I shall reserve till these affaires of greater concernment to you be over. If I have said any thing more then I should, you may the easier pardon it, as proceeding from the faithfull heart of

Your very tru freind, and humble servant,

BR: S.

Richm: Aug: 11.

If you see cause, let me have an answer to this motion made, by the next carrier.

---

[1] "The person." Sir Justinian's daughter Susan having made an advantageous marriage (as John Stuteville put it: "Wee heare but little of the gentleman, he is so young, but his familie and fortunes have reached us, and his rare house and gardens have made a sweet smell in our nostrills"), it remained to dispose of the two remaining daughters. Elizabeth appears to have been a lady of some attractions and to have had many suitors. She was born August 27th, 1636. The unfashionable suitor here described by Bishop Duppa is Thomas Jervoise, born March 16th, 1615, son of Sir Thomas Jervoise of Herriard, co. Southampton. As a cornet he served under Sir Arthur Hazelrigg in the Parliamentary Army, later under Generals Middleton, Waller, Fairfax and Massey. He became a Captain of Horse, and on the final disbanding of his troop, Fairfax wrote that he had "demesned himself with fidelity and courage." His father, Sir Thomas Jervoise, was also a zealous Parliamentarian. It is a little strange that Bishop Duppa should have recommended alliance with such a family to his friend. But Sir Thomas Jervoise's second wife, Frances, was the elder daughter of Thomas Jay of Thornton (see Letter xv, April 8th, 1651, Note 2; M.I. to Frances, Lady Jervoise at Winchfield). Thomas Jay was Commissary of Horse for King Charles, and evidently well known to Bishop Duppa. This connection may have led to the Bishop's proposal. Sir Thomas died October 20th, 1654. As will be seen, the negotiations failed, and Thomas Jervoise married Mary Purefoy on July 30th, 1657. Portraits of him and his wife are still at Herriard Park. He served as High Sheriff of Hampshire in 1667 and died in 1693. The present house at Herriard was built by his son and successor. (Information from Major F. H. Jervoise, Herriard Park, January 16th, 1936: see also *The Ancestor*, Vol. III (October 1902) in which is reproduced a portrait of Captain Thomas Jervoise).

[2] *Principiis obsta.* "Resist temptation when it starts." Ovid, *Remedia Amoris*, 91. Nicholas Carew was not yet of age.

[3] *Pereat inter nos hoc secretum.* "May this secret perish between us." Adapted from Petronius, *Satyricon*, XXI.

[COPY OF DUPPA'S ENCLOSURE ENDORSED ON LETTER LXXVIII BY SIR JUSTINIAN]

Sir, I received your letter of the 15th of July but on Saturday last, and that's the occasion wherefore I returned answer no sooner concerning the contents thereof. Although you seeme to conceive that such a portion as 3000 *li* too little to supply my present occasions (as in truth it is), yet my estate is not so meane but that such a sum with a virtuous gentlewoman wel descended may make mee live happily. And therefore I am resolved to proceed to a treatie if you please to bring it on, and will be readie to waite on you about the same where and when soever you appoint. I thank you for your advice and all your other kindnesses to me. I am at present able to make you no other returne.

THO. JERVOISE.

Herriard, 4th August 1656[4].

LETTER LXXIX

[AUGUST 26th.]

Sir, The continuance of my wife's sickness and the failing of all the meanes which hetherto have been applied to her, doth very much discompose me, and doth not leave my thoughts so free as to say all that I would to you. But that I may not be wanting to you in this particular (wherein I am no farther engaged, then as it may be a concernment to you), I shall onely adde, that since you seem to be satisfied both with the character of his person and the valew of his estate, I beleive that your other obiections upon the by, may best receave their answer from the party himself, who, when you shall give him leave, will be very willing to wait upon you. But in the interim, upon the strictest enquiry I can make, I am assured by very good hands, that there is nothing of his present estate but what very honestly is his, and no way mingled with any uniust accquisition, or unconscionable invasion of other men's rights, which might in time destroy his own. That which remain'd of the Marquess's, is left as portion to his sisters, but he disclaimes all share in it[1].

When you write next, if you admitt him to a conference with you, you will more punctually know whether you may recommend him to your

---

[4] This is a copy of Captain Jervoise's letter to Duppa's neighbour. In a draft letter to Mr. Wright (see Letter LXXIII, Note 4) Sir Justinian had written that he had five daughters to dispose of "though 2 but infants;" but "3000*li* I shall pay downe upon an estate and joynture proportionable if there be a liking." (I.C. 4843).

[1] "Disclaimes all share in it." Bishop Duppa is at pains to remove any impression that Thomas Jervoise was enjoying any sequestered (Royalist) property. Herriard Park was not far from Basing House, the great Royalist fortress during the Civil War, which belonged to the 5th Marquess of Winchester, and which was captured by Cromwell in 1645. This proximity cost Sir Thomas Jervoise £6,000 for "corn, cattle, and other provisions commandeered." His total claim was £15,000. In 1649 Sir Thomas was granted the estates of the Marquess until he should recoup the sum of £9,000. In 1651 an Act of Parliament was passed for the estates to be sold, as "land forfeited for treason." Sir Thomas now seems to have done the Marquess a neighbourly turn "by agreeing to accept a sum of £6,000, remitting £1,000 of the debt, and using his good offices to obtain the repeal of the Act, thus saving the estates from being dispersed." (*The Ancestor*, Vol. III, 1902.) This forbearance is, perhaps, explained by the kinship of Sir Thomas Jervoise's first wife (Capt. Jervoise's mother) with the Powlett family. She was (before her marriage in 1601) Lucy, daughter of Sir Richard Powlett, great grand-daughter of Richard Powlett, the younger brother of the 1st Marquess of Winchester. Bishop Duppa's information about the Jervoise family is very accurate, and no doubt derived from good sources, perhaps Mr. Michel. See Letter LXXXI.

daughter. I pray God direct you, and then nothing can go amiss. And let this suffise, From your most affectionat true freind,

BR: S. Richm: Aug. 26.

LETTER LXXX

[AUGUST 26th.]

Sir, This very morning having dispatched a letter to you and sent it away[1], I receaved a very kind message from your son Carew and your daughter, that they had intention to dine with me; which, though I took for a very great favor (having before nether seen, nor heard from them since their marriage), yet the sickness of my dear wife (without whose presence in such an entertainment I should have been but half my self) made me return my earnest desire that they would deferr their comming till som day in the next week, by which time I might have som hope of her recovery. But I found by their servant that this was their last day of being in these parts, being now for London, and from thence in the beginning of the next week resolved for Northampton shire. The reason why I make this long narrative, is, partly to deplore my self for my ill happe in this particular (for I had a very great desire to see them), and partly, that you who know me better may excuse me to them, if I should be so mistaken as to have my answer misinterpreted, if there should be any failing in the delivery of it by their servant.

Sir, there can be none of yours but ar very pretious to me, and that makes me the more sollicitous to be kept in their favor; and that this may not discourage them upon the next oportunity, I shall desire you to assure them in my behalf, that there is none (next to their nighest relations) who doth more heartily pray for their happyness, or who would more faithfully serve them, then him whom you have so many wayes obliged to be,

Your most affectionat freind, and humble servant,

BR: S. Richm: Aug. 26.

LETTER LXXXI

[SEPTEMBER 24th.]

Sir, I forbore to write to you the last week, because I expected to hear from that party in Hamshire[1] from whom Mr. Michel hath brought me a letter, very full of civility, and thankes for my appearing in this business which he lookes upon as a great happyness, but for nothing more then for that near relation, which he shall have to your self by it; and really I beleive that he is no hypocrite in it. For he is a man plain and open, and without any of those subtle reserves, which in treaties of this kind, use to be the cheif ingredient.

[1] Two letters in one day are unique in this correspondence. This letter explains the reason. In a letter undated except for the month and day (August 20) which must belong to this year, Susan Carew wrote to her father: "I intend to see the bishop of Salsbury before we go into the contry which will be next week to frankon" [*recte*, Francton].(I.C. 4103). Francton, Warw., was the home of Nicholas Carew's sister, Rebecca, and her husband, Thomas Temple, a second cousin once removed of Sir William Temple (Manning and Bray, *History of Surrey*, Vol. II, p. 523).

[1] "That party in Hamshire." Sir Thomas Jervoise had the Lodge in the old Deer Park at Richmond, obtaining possession "about the same time as Sir John Trevor obtained a lease of the Park" (E. Beresford Chancellor, *History and Antiquities of Richmond*). His pocket book shows that he lived at Richmond 1644–5, when he held, under the Parliament, the office of High Steward of the Royal Manor of Richmond and Keeper of the Little Park. (*The Ancestor*). Mr. Michel was, no doubt, the Richmond attorney, for whom see Letter x, Note 1.

I desired Mr. Michel to make a iourney thether, that I might the better be informed by him, what kind of house he kept, and how he managed his affaires; for these domestichezzies (as the Italians call them) discover most of a man, for when we com abroad, the ordinary course is *induere personam*. The return he makes, is, that he keepes a civill, orderly house, without ether excess on the one side, or any unhansom grating on the other extreme, and that the whole family seem'd to him conformable to it. For his comming to wait on you, he desires that he may be permitted to do it, about a fortnight after Michaelmas; but he should take it for a double favor, if you would so order it, that ether one, or both your daughters might be then at home with you. But this he submitts wholy to your dispose, for if that be not convenient, he will be very willing to take a farther iourney to see them.

The great kindness you have shewn in having so deep a sense of the infirmities of my dear wife, obligeth me to give you an account, that for these few dayes lately past, there hath been such an intermission of her former fitts, that I have some hope that she may by degrees gett som consistency of health, which she hath so long wanted; though as yet the disease hangs upon her, and is not so overcom. But there is fear, too, that there may be a relapse. *Sed Deus avertat*. In the midst ether of present or future afflictions, your freindship is the anchor to me, which may keep me from sinking. And therefore for my own sake, I am deeply concern'd heartily to pray that what ever may becom of me, your happyness may continue. I beseech you present my service to your son Carew and his lady, who have my blessing, though it be at a distance, but I trust (if my prayers may be heard) shall prove as effectuall, as if I wer nearer to them. For the present, I have no more to say, but that I remain,

Your most affectionat tru freind and humble servant,

BR: SAR:

Sept: 24.

LETTER LXXXII

[OCTOBER 19th.]

Sir, In my last I complain'd of not hearing from you, but I had no sooner dispatched away the letter, but I receaved yours, which, if it had not slept by the way, might have com to me the week before. That I should so soon again write to you is not upon any new business, but in pursuance of that which hath allready been the argument of so many letters, or rather, to say the plain truth, as a piece of civility to the person who comes along with it, and thinkes (for you must give lovers leave to have their fancies) that his journey cannot be successful without it. I can say no more then I have don ether by concerning his person or his fortunes, or if there be any thing to add, his freind that comes with him (not unknown to you) can abundantly supply it. But your own judgement, who best knowes the dispositions of your daughters, and can more exactly way all circumstances then any stander by can do, will absolutely be your best guide, especially if God directs you in it. For which you have my prayers, that He from whom all happyness in marriage comes, may in this particular as in all others, be propitious to your family.

I have no more to say, but that I am

Your very faithfull freind, and humble servant,

BR: SAR:

Richm: Octob: 19.

Letter LXXXIII

[November 11th.]

Sir, I find both by your letter, and by that which you inclosed, and by other circumstances, that the match proposed is not likely to take effect; and my judgement is, that it should therefore be broke off the sooner, which may be fairly don without disparagement to ether party, having not as yet so much as seen one the other. And I have so farr open'd the way to it, that when this person engaged gave me lately a visit to thank me for my proposall of it, I told him that I conceaved there wer likely to be som difficulties in it, not onely in the disproportion of yeares[1], but in her relations to her aunt[2], with whom she hath lived from her childhood, and cannot willingly part with her, especially in such a distance Hantshire is from Suffolk, and therefore I advised him not to sett his heart farther upon it. But before he consents to this he expects to hear farther from you, ether immediately, or by my hands.

In the mean time, though he hath not seen your daughter, yet he hath seen so much of you, that he is very much taken with you, and thinkes his journey is no way lost, having had the happyness of your conversation, though he unhappily failes in his praetences, which I am persuaded, that nether consideration of portion, nor any other circumstance had so great a share in, as the great valew which he putts upon your own person. But I have done; onely dismiss him fairly (and I know you can do no other) and if you bestow a letter of kindness on him it will not be lost. And so at this time in som hast, I have no more to say but that I am,

Your most affectionatly true freind to serve you,

Br: Sar:

Richm: Nov: 11.

Letter LXXXIV

Richm: Decem: 2.

Sir, Upon the receipt of your last letter (which though wrott before cam not to me till the last week), I sent for my neighbor Mr. Michel, and accquainting him with the contents of it, we both resolved to send a dispatch into Hantshire, that might absolutely sett a period to this business, the first motion of which was absolutely begun by this gentleman's great affections to have been united into your family, without any regard at all to that considerable portion which was to go along with it. And therefore I did the rather propose it, that you would your self have given him so fair an answer as might have left him contented, though not satisfied. But since you thought it fitter to leave it to me, I have in this particular sustain'd your person, and according to that sweetness of your temper which you use

[1] "Disproportion of yeares." Captain Jervoise was 41, Elizabeth and Judith Isham 20.

[2] "Her aunt." Lady Denton. There is an undated letter from her to her nephew Sir Justinian at Lamport, which may well refer to this proposal. "The business you writ of we know not how to answer, the party being afar off and antient, having not had the sight of one another, we know not what dislike may bee of either side, but he or any other of your wishinge shall be wellcum heather." Next year Captain Jervoise found a wife in a more congenial family for one of his principles. Mary Purefoy was the second daughter of George Purefoy, of Wadley, co. Berks, a member of a strongly Parliamentarian family. Sir Justinian's daughters by his first marriage were all devoted to "My Lady Denton, whose love and care hathe been from our infancy and is still largely extended to us" (Letter of Elizabeth Isham to her father. February 6th, I.C. 4320).

towards all men, I have as fairly as I could framed an answer, which, because you must now own, I shall in a few words relate the substance of it. And it was thus. I first let him know that you did rightly sett a valew both upon his person and upon the freindship which he shew'd in making this address to you, for which you return'd him many thanks, and should be ready upon all occasions offer'd you, to express as much. As for the impediments that hind'red your giving him encouragement for the farther prosecution of it, they proceeded not from any thing in relation ether to his person, or to his estate, but meerly from this, that your daughters, having been so long under the education of their aunt, there is a great unwillingness on both sides to part, and especially at so great a distance. And therefore having not yet so much as seen one the other, or any treaty begun, there might be a desisting without any disparagement at all, or any breach of the kindness begun between you. And having given you this account, I shall pinn the basket[1], as the phrase is, and say no more of this. When I write next, I shall turn a new leafe, and say something of an other argument. I am now called upon to an other employment and have onely the leasure to write my self,

Your humble servant to pray for you,
BR: SAR:

[1] "Pinn the basket". According to Wright's *Dialect Dictionary*, a "Pin-Basket" is an East Anglian phrase for the youngest in the family. "Pin" is used in the sense of "finish up", often with "up" after it. The sense here is clear, though it does not seem to be a usual phrase.

1657

A brief allusion to the "great banding here, whether a Monarchy or a Republick shall be the result of their many feirce debates", dismisses the subject which occupies most of our history books – "Cromwell and Crown". Indeed, Cromwell and his relations with his Army and Parliament seem remote from the domestic concerns that occupy our correspondents in this year. There are indeed important references to books of a political nature. It is no surprise that Bishop Duppa does not approve of Harrington's *Commonwealth of Oceana*, and that Matthew Wren's forgotten attack on this book receives praise from Sir Justinian. But more famous books than either are discussed; Pascal's *Provincial Letters* and Izaak Walton's *Compleat Angler*. The contemporary views of these works expressed by these correspondents is striking. Interest in the French Church was considerable among the Anglicans, and Duppa's judgement against the Jesuits is clear and not unexpected.

Bishop Juxon makes a brief appearance (Letter XCIV) and so, for the first time, does Herbert Thorndike, whose name thereafter often occurs, and who is to remain a friend of Sir Justinian till his death. The Letters (LXXXVIII of June 16th *et seq.*) about William Harvey, the discoverer of the circulation of the blood, and other court physicians, Mayerne and Lister, are important, and the fact that Harvey was attended by Bishop Duppa the day before he died, seems nowhere to have been noticed.

From Sir Justinian's point of view, the great event of the year was the birth of his son and heir on March 15th. But the illness of his newly married daughter Susan, who, with her husband, had recently become tenants of Pytchley and near neighbours, cast a gloom over the late autumn.

The spring of the next year was to bring fresh imprisonment, but there is no hint of this at present. There are considerable difficulties in dating the correspondence in this year, and in the notes on Letter XCIII the reader will be able to trace in detail the kind of reasoning I have followed in letters where no obvious clue remains.

The fears of Churchmen regarding the Parliament which Cromwell called to meet in 1658 are shown by a letter addressed to Sheldon by Dr. Jeremy Taylor (December 19th, 1657, Tanner MSS. 52, f.216): "I doe not know whether we shall have cause to fear this Parliament or no: for I suppose we shall be suppressed before the Parliament shall sitt; we are every day threatened, we are fiercely petitioned against by the Presbyterians, we are agitated at the Council Table; only we yet go on and shall till we can goe on no longer. If we be permitted, which is yet *sub judice*, the Common Prayer Book is certainly voted to be suppressed."

LETTER LXXXV†
[FROM MRS. DUPPA]

[FEBRUARY 7th.]

Sir, My Lord is fane to make ues of a badd secretary to make a return for your kinde letter. A great tumor is fallen in to his foot that he kepes his bedd. The next returne we boeth hope, he will be able to wright him self, and then give you many thanks for your many great favors to us boeth. He is loath to think it to be the gout, but I fear it will prove so. I becech you let boeth our sarvices be presented to your self and your vartous Lady, and my best love and respect to your dafters.

Sir,
I ame your humbell sarvant,
JANE DUPPA
The 7th of Feabruary.

LETTER LXXXVI

[MARCH 24th.]

Sir, Som occasions happen'd that made me pass over the last week without burthening your carrier so much as with a letter, but accidentally hearing of that happy newes that God hath lately blessed you with a son[1], I could forbear no longer from congratulating so great an happyness to your family. For God hath heard your prayers and the prayers of your freinds; and howsoever this child comes into the world in these evill times, yet there is so much advantage left, that as long as you are praeserved among the living to be his guardian and his guide, his education will be happy under such a father, and being by your example as well as praecept

† This letter is from Mrs. Duppa and it is probable that it belongs to the year 1655; (see Letter LXIV). She was Jane, daughter of Nicholas Killingtree of Longham, Norfolk (died 1607), by his wife Jane, daughter of William Mallory of Papworth Agnes, Hunts. She was baptised on September 18th, 1586, at Papworth (it is actually just over the border in Cambridgeshire). She was married to Duppa on November 23rd, 1626, at St Dionis Backchurch where the parish registers describe her as "Jane Chillington." Her brother William had the degree of M.A. conferred on him on June 16th, 1643, on the recommendation of Charles I, but he died on August 7th of the same year. Her sister Elizabeth married (as his second wife) the Revd. James Marsh, D.D., Chaplain to Charles I. She outlived her husband though older than him, and died, as the result of a fall in her house at Richmond, in October, 1665. She was buried in Westminster Abbey, October 30th, 1665. In her will (made October 15th, 1664) she left bequests to her own and her husband's relations, and £10 to Sir Justinian Isham to buy himself a ring. "My late husband's picture drawn by Master Wright" she left to Gilbert Sheldon, Archbishop of Canterbury, and a miniature of him to "Ladie Cholmily." A miniature of the King (Charles II) was left to the wife of her husband's old friend, Sir John Adler, and one of the Duke of York to Lady Wheeler. She directed her executors "with all possible speed after my decease [to] erect a Monument of two hundred pounds price for my said husband and myselfe," and devised her burial "in the same grave in Westminster Abbey wher the bodie of my deare Lord and husband lyes."

The marriage of the Duppas was (as these letters bear witness) a very happy one. (J. Challenor Smith, "Bishop Duppa's wife", *The Genealogist*, New Series, Vol. IV (1887), pp. 116–18, D.N.B., I.C. 581 (for her death); see also App. A).

[1] "Lately blessed you with a son." The hoped for heir was born on March 15th, 1656/7, and baptised on March 20th at Lamport, by the name of Thomas. His grandfather, after whom he was called, wrote from Stoneleigh on March 15th, 1656/7: "the welcome news of my daughter's safe deliverie of a sonne founde me on my bed and was receaved by my selfe and severall relations with abundance of joy and comfort returning our thankes to God for soe greate a blessing." Owing to his "troublesome ague," Lord Leigh asks for his son Christopher to stand sponsor in his stead. (I.C. 388).

rightly principled in his duties towards God, he may live to see and act better things, then we ar likely to have the opportunity to do.

And thus farr I had written before I receaved your letter, having had the good newes conveyed to me from your old servant John Osbeston. But finding it confirm'd under your own hand, I can with the more confidence continu my thanksgivings for you. For God hath now not onely bless'd you with a numerous issue of those who in the language of the world pass for the *sequior sexus* (as being of a finer, and consequently of a weaker temper), but besides hath given you a corner stone to caement and strengthen the rest of your family; one that I hope may by your care prove like your self, and having said this, I can wish nothing better. Nor shall I mingle any thing with this, though otherwise full of thoughts which I can lay no where so safe as in your bosom. For the present I shall say nothing that may blast ether your joy, or mine, but rest chearfully in all my relations to you (for nothing can embitter them),

Your most faithfull and most humble servant,
BR: SAR:

March 24.

LETTER LXXXVII

[APRIL (N.D.)]

Sir, Whilest I was expecting this last week a letter from you, I receaved somthing more then words; for which anniversary charity of yours, I have nothing to return but anniversary thankes. But if my prayers may praevail, God shall return you not onely yearly but daily blessings for it. *Sed haec inter Deum, et animam meam transigenda sunt*[1].

I am very much pleas'd to think in what quiet of mind you ar at Lamport, with your good Lady and your olive branches about you, and while there is a great banding here, whether a Monarchy or a Republick shall be the result of their many feirce debates[2], your concernments ar of an other nature, how to serve your God, and to govern those in peace whom God hath given you. And certainly of all governments the paternall, as it is the first (for Adam in his Monarchy was an early instance of it), so it is the best, nether occasioned by the hostility which the Leviathan dreames of, nor yet by any virtu of any free election, which will never be made good, till it be proved that children may have power to chuse who shall be their parents. But the theory of these disputes must be search'd for in the new politicks of *Oceana*[3]; and as for the practick of it at the present, it must be as the sword decides it.

[1] *Sed haec inter Deum*, etc. "But this must be a matter for discussion between God and my soul." Christian Latin?

[2] "Their many feirce debates." On March 31st, 1657, the House of Commons presented the Humble Petition and Advice to Cromwell urging him to assume the title of King with a new Constitution, but by the 18th Article the Petition said that if the Protector did not consent to all the articles, nothing else in it should be deemed of force. Cromwell hesitated, but on May 8th he definitely refused the crown. (C. H. Firth, *Last Days of the Protectorate*, Vol. I, p. 149, et seq.; Ranke, *A History of England*, Vol. III, p. 176 et seq, Carlyle, Speech XIV).

[3] "New politicks of *Oceana*." James Harrington's *Commonwealth of Oceana* was advertised as newly published in *Mercurius Politicus* for October 29th to November 6th, 1656. There is a first edition of this important work in the Lamport Library. "It lacks the magic of style, and has therefore joined the great army of books which are often mentioned and seldom read . . . Hume pronounced "Oceana" the only rational model of a Commonwealth, and Coleridge ranked its author with Thucydides, Machiavelli, and Bacon" (G. P. Gooch, *Political Thought in England from Bacon to Halifax*). On the flyleaf of the Lamport copy, Sir Justinian has well summed up the book: *Tant vaut l'homme, tant vaut sa terre.*

But why should I ether trouble my self, or you with this, who being onely as passengers in the ship, ar to be driven on whether willingly or unwillingly to those rocks and quicksands, (for haven there is none to look for), whither these our marriners shall have a mind to carry us. What the confused proceedings are, and what is likely to be the issue of them, whether the continuance of the old chaos, or a new world of their own making, is out of our road to guess at. May I have but the continuance of God's favor, and your freindship to me, I am concern'd no farther, but shall rest with a great calme in all the stormes that may happen,

Your most affectionat and faithfull
freind and servant,
BR: SAR:

Sir, since I wrott this letter, I found there was a conspiracy in your family of being kind to me, for this morning I receaved a very kind present from Bedington[4]. For which, not thinking my own thankes sufficient, I desire you would add yours.

LETTER LXXXVIII

[JUNE 16th.]

Sir, I have in a manner been lost to my self in this intervall of time, since the agreement was made, that I should not write till your return to your own center, which is the proper place of rest to you. But you have now restored me, and after a long parenthesis the sentence may go on, and the commerce of kindness peice again. *The Universall Character*[1] which you mention, though there will be no great need of it between you and me (who understand one the other at a plainer rate), yet I am very glad to hear of it for the publick interest. The first that ever I mett who mention'd it, was that excellent man who in his *Instauration Magna*[2] would lett nothing escape him. But the truth is I look'd upon it, as you do in your mathematicks upon many conclusions, which in the theory are specious, but when they are reduced to practise do many times fail us. Yet I have so much of the *virtuosi* in me, as to desire to hear from you, both what you think of the thing it self, whether it be feasable or no, and next, what the effects and benefitts may be that may arise from it.

Since I had the happyness to see you, I have been again surprised by my old infirmity, and begin now to doubt whether ever my legs will serve me to walk up the Hill again. But this doth no way dishearten me, for I am hast'ning toward a better prospect then any hill or pinacle in this world can shew me.

In the interim, one of the greatest wordly comforts left me is your freindship, for which, being able to return nothing better, you have the prayers of

Your most affectionat freind,
BR: SARUM.

Richm: June 16.

---

[4] "Bedington." The seat of the Carews in Surrey.

[1] *The Universal Character, by which all Nations may understand one another's Conceptions* . . . by Cave Beck was published in London on April 20th, 1657. Lowndes describes it as "a curious work with a frontispiece containing, as it is supposed, a portrait of the author, under the figure of the European."

[2] *Instauration Magna.* This is an allusion to Bacon's *Instauratio Magna* first published in 1620. A copy of this edition is one of the most interesting books still (1954) in the Library at Lamport. On the flyleaf, Sir Justinian, ever a disciple of Bacon, has copied the curious inscription on Bacon's tomb.

We both desire to be presented to your very good Lady as her humble servants.

[ENDORSED REPLY OF SIR JUSTINIAN]

My Lord, I hope the infirmitie lately ceas'd on your Lordship is but temporary, and being a goutish humor tending to the outward parts may less indanger the vitalls. I heare that Dr. Hervey[3], the physitian, also Sir Mat. Leistor[4], both very learned men and praeservers of others' healths are lately dead. Surely I take the greatest benefitt to be had by their art is rather in the freeing or mitigating of paine then in the prolongation of life, which cannot but be miserable where the organs are decay'd.

Casting my eye the other day on the late treatise call'd *The Compleate Angler*, writt by Iz[aac] Wa[lton][5], I there find (pa: 198) what your Lordship too lately proved, that the spawn of a barbell is, if not poison, yet very dangerous meat and especially in the month of May, and had like to have endangered Gesner's life as he himselfe declares. If your Lordship hath not yet seene it, I shall by the next send you the booke of *The Universall Character*. There is a late English romance in 3 parts calld *Cloria and Narcissus*,[6] writt upon the late actions especially of this nation and these tymes, by the honourable person; whose [name] I would gladly know if your Lordship hath heard of the book and author.

---

[3] "Dr. Hervey." This is William Harvey, the discoverer of the circulation of the blood, who died on June 3rd, 1657, at the house of his brother Eliab Harvey at Roehampton (D'Arcy Power, *William Harvey* (1897), p. 166). This eminent doctor would have been well known to Duppa as he was in charge of Prince Charles and James, Duke of York in the early stages of the Battle of Edgehill (October 23rd, 1642), and during the war was with the King at Oxford, where he was made Warden of Merton (D.N.B.).

[4] "Sir Mat. Leistor." This is Sir Matthew Leister, or Lister (1571?–1656), an M.D. of Basle, and physician to Queen Anne of Denmark and Charles I. He was knighted in 1636. In 1644 he assisted Sir Theodore Mayerne, mentioned in the next letter, in the confinement of Queen Henrietta Maria at Exeter. He died December 14th, 1656 (D.N.B.).

[5] "*The Compleate Angler*." *The Compleat Angler* was first published in 1653, without Izaak Walton's name on the title page although the *Perfect Diurnall* of May 1653 advertized it as by "Iz. Wa." The book was reissued in 1655, much enlarged, "the first edition of the book as we know it" (*The Compleat Angler*, ed. John Buchan (1901)). The Lamport Library contained (1880) a copy of Walton's *Lives* of Donne, Wotton, Hooker and Herbert, 1st edn. 1670, with the MS. inscription "For Dr. Huniwood Dean of Lincoln Iz. Wa. . . . *Ex Dono auctoris*". Dr. Michael Honywood (1597–1681) had been a Fellow of Christ's College, Cambridge, and his receipt in 1640 for £20 contributed by Sir Justinian to the "new buildings" at Christ's was presented by the writer to the College in 1929. During the Protectorate, he lived at Utrecht. This volume was sold at Sotheby's with other volumes from Lamport in 1907.

The passage in *The Compleat Angler* alluded to by Sir Justinian is as follows:—"We agree . . . that the spawn of a Barbel, if it be not poison as he says, yet it is dangerous meat: and especially in the month of May; which is so certain that *Gesner* and *Gasius* declare it had an ill effect upon them, even to the endangering of their lives."

[6] The British Museum has a copy of two parts of *Cloria and Narcissus* published in 1653 and 1654, "printed by S. G. London: sold by Anth. Williamson." A later edition of this work was published in 1661 in London "printed by Ralph Wood." The title of this second edition reads *The Princess Cloria or the Royal Romance . . . containing the story of most part of Europe for many years last past, written by a person of honour.* The title page shows King Charles I in armour with a laurel wreath and various emblems.

LETTER LXXXIX

[JULY 8th.]

Sir, The conversation I have with you by letters is so much contentment to me, that though it cannot cure those infirmityes which age hath brought upon me, yet is so much a pleasure to my mind, that my infirm bodie by copartnership is the better for it. And possibly it doth more then this, for since I heard from you (*post hoc*, I am sure, and whether *propter hoc* or no I cannot determine), my gout hath so farr left me that I have nothing to complain of the relicks of it but onely a tenderness of my feet, which, though without pain, keepes me from renewing of my walk and the prospect of the Hill, which for these 3 months I have not had the sight of.

And because you mention the death of Dr. Harvy, and that the best effect of phisick is the mittigation of pain, I shall so farr agree with you, that the mittigation which you speak of is a high commendation to that art, but certainly the virtu of it goes farther, and reacheth to the prolongation of life. And the person which we now speak of (with whom I was the day before he died) was to me a great example of it, who had no pain to complain of, but being of a dry sear body, he praeserved it so long by the rules of art and diet, that his life went out like a spark, without any violence or noise at all.

There wer a triumvirat of excellent phisitians[1] belonging all to the Court, whom for som yeares last past, I had an ey upon, not onely out of freindship to them, but out of som curiosity. For having observed that they wer all three of a severall course of diet, I watched which of them would fall first, their age there was som difference in but not much. Mayern was the first that fell but maturely enough (for he was above fourscore), whose diet was somthing more then liberall; Lister followed him, who, though not abstemious, yet kept himselfe in more reasonable bounds, and lived to outreach seven yeares beyond the other. Harvey closed it up, who would somtimes fast two dayes together, but at last fell with the rest. And if you should ask, which of these diets might conferr most to longaevity, I should subscribe to that of Lister's. But when all else is said, there is an higher Providence, that lengthens, and contracts our dayes not onely without, but against the rules of art.

As for the romance you mention I have nether seen, nor heard of it, but because you mention it, I shall enquire after it. We ar for the present (by the blessing of God) in a reasonable condition of health, and that you may be so, with those that ar dear to you, is the vote of

Your most affectionat freind, and humble servant,

BR: SARUM.

Richm: July 8.

---

[1] "Triumvirat of excellent phisitians." These were William Harvey, Matthew Lister, and Theodore Mayerne. For the first two see Letter LXXXVIII, Notes 3 and 4. Sir Theodore Turquet de Mayerne (1573–1655) was M.D. Montpellier, 1597. He came to England in 1603 and attended Queen Anne of Denmark. He was knighted in 1624. He saw Queen Henrietta Maria "through nine pregnancies, and never let her miscarry," and in 1649, after the execution of Charles I, he came to the help of his ailing daughter Elizabeth, then aged thirteen and "fallen into great sorrow." Duppa's sister, Margaret Kilvert, was the devoted "dresser" of this Princess, and was there to support her "through the terrible ordeal of 1649." She was removed from the Princess in June 1649, much to the girl's distress. Sir Theodore is said to have borne a close "resemblance in appearance and manner to the popular conception of Father Christmas." (D.N.B.; Carola Oman, *Henrietta Maria*; *Notes and Queries*, September 2nd, 1950).

Duppa, closely associated with the Court, as he and his family were, must have known these doctors intimately.

Before the making up of this letter our cosin Lowen gave me a visit, who, upon discovery of what I was about, desired earnestly that his service might be rememb'red to you.

Letter XC

[July 29th.]

Sir, As I make it my business to forgett the world, so I could be well content, in relation to the generality to be forgotten by it, so that I might still have a reserve of a freind or two left me; and one, at least, I cannot despair of, as long as you ar among the living. I cannot complain of want of company (and possibly should I be condemn'd to a wilderness, it would not be greivous to me), for it is not company that makes the life of a man happy. Visitants I have good store, and though all of them ether praetend, or have kindness for me, yet som of them ar impertinent, som lowd and som overtaedious, and ether I must sitt silent (which is no great pain to me), or according to the Verulamian Rule[1], follow the wildgoose chace of every one that converseth with me. But wherfore all this? onely to let you know, what a deep sense I have of the happyness which I once enioy'd in you; and though I have not the reall obiect of it any longer, yet as they who have heard som excellent musick, have long after the sound of it in their eares, or in their mind at least, which may retain the impression of it longer; so fares it with me, who please my self more, with the thoughts of that agreeable conversation which I once had with you, then with all the new modes of men or manners, which many times against my will, I am made a witness of. But since that man by nature is a creature sociable, I must not be froward, and cry as children do, when they have not all that pleaseth them.

The romance which you mention to be in part historicall (for *Omnis fabula fundatur in historia*) is so unknown, that I meet not any as yet, who confess the sight of it. But possibly it may at last com to my hands, and then you shall know my sense of it. That it hath been a scandall to a Bishop to write a romance, we find in the instance of Heliodore[2], but whether it may be so to read it or no, I must referr it to the new casuists of the Society of the Jesuites. Of whom there is a book lately com forth, called the *Provinciall Letters*[3] that gives a very good account. The book I saw in French, out of which I have took an extract of som of their notable cases, and shall send them to you by the next, if I hear not from you that you have seen them allready.

And now in the close I am to thank you for that counsell to me in the way of regiment of health, to abstain from fruits and salt meates. I was never excessive in ether of them, and am much inclined to beleive, that it is not the quality of these meates but the quantity that is offensive. Not fruit, for it is a cooler of the stomack and allayes the choler; not fish, for it is easiest digested by old age, especially not salt meates for they correct the flegme. And thus you see, there is somthing to be said in excuse of all

---

1 Verulamian, i.e. Baconian.

2 "Heliodore." Heliodorus of Emesa (Homs) in Syria, a third-century Sophist, whose romance *Æthiopica* is the oldest and best of the Greek romances that have come down to us. He has sometimes been confused with a later Bishop of Tricca in Thessaly. (*Encycl. Brit.*)

3 Pascal's *Provincial Letters* were first published in English in 1657 (printed by J.G. for Royston at the Angel in Ivie Lane). But Duppa says that he had seen them in French. They were not finished till March 1657, which (with the allusion to *Cloria and Narcissus*) dates the letter.

our disorders. But in earnest, this advise of yours shall sway more with me then a whole Junto of phisitians. For the words of freindship have farr more powr in them, then the rules of art, especially so coniecturall as that is. Sir, I return you all hearty wishes for the health of you, and yours, and rest,

Your most affectionat tru freind, and servant,
BR: SAR:

Richm: July 29.

[ENDORSED REPLY OF SIR JUSTINIAN]

I have bin long since sensible of the trouble your Lordship is often put to by impertinent visitants, of which number in some respects I might have bin accounted, but that your Lordship's favourable opinion of me and my harty desires to serve you causes some reflection of value upon my selfe from the high esteeme which I am sure your Lordship meritts from all. But I was over greedy of the happiness I once had in your Lordship's conversation, and often tymes in earnest did grudge it many others. I have since sufficiently smarted both for the want of it, and by being oppressed by others very little agreable to mee. Reading lately of the Civilities of China[4] in which they are excessive, I could wish one way they have of freeing themselves were in request amongst us, by writing over their doores that they are retired to their garden house, by which meanes they are excused from the molestation of such visits as would otherwise be made to them.

I have not yet seene any thing of the booke call'd *Provinciall Letters*, but shall readily embrace whatsoever your Lordship pleases to impart to me of it. I have lately met with some *Considerations on Mr. Harrington's Oceana*[5], which I am much taken with, and indeed with the author of them though unknown to mee. Mr. Thorndyke now with me tells mee hee is but a young man and son to Bishop Wren. I know your Lordship cannot long be stranger to the book, a very little one to answer so vast a title.

LETTER XCI

[AUGUST 26th.]

Sir, I was very well pleas'd in reading your last, that I did not find in it any mention of your own want of health or of your family, which I was the more affraid of because the report is so generall, that there is a regnant

[4] "Reading lately of the Civilities of China . . . ." The work Sir Justinian had been reading was *The History of that Great and Renowned Monarchy of China. . . .* Lately written in *Italian* by F. Alvarez Semedo, a *Portughess* . . . Now put into English by a person of Quality . . . London (1655). Part I, Chap. 12 *Of the Courtesies and Civilities of the Chinesses* (p. 61) contains this passage:—"By how much the person is of a greater and graver quality, with so much the more difficulty doth he admit of visits: and some to free themselves, and avoyd the trouble of these *Ceremonies*, write upon a piece of paper in white letters and clap it over their gate, *that they are retired to their garden house*: by which means they are excused from the molestation of these *Civilities*".

[5] *Considerations on Mr. Harrington's Oceana.* Matthew Wren's *Considerations on Mr. Harrington's Commonwealth of Oceana*; *restrained to the first part of the Preliminaries* was published in London in 1657, but without the author's name. His father, also Matthew Wren, was appointed Bishop of Ely in 1638, and his Injunctions as Bishop were particularly disliked by the Puritans. He was imprisoned in the Tower from 1642 to 1660 (D.N.B). Matthew, the son (1629–1672), was Clarendon's secretary after the Restoration, and one of the original council of the Royal Society in 1662. For "Mr. Thorndyke" see Letter XCIV, Note 4.

disease which is scattered through all counties more or less, but more especially at this time in yours. And I am the apter to beleive it may be so, because the good aire of Richmond is no praeservative against it, there being at this time scarse any one house wherein there is not one sick of it. There have been long ago epidemick sins among us, and now God sends epidemick diseases. But the great wonder of it is, that whereas formerly they wer wont to fly from the citty into the country for safety, they now fly from the country into the citty, and Poneropolis is becom the most safe though not the most innocent place. Many families (they say) ar removed thether, and many ar glad of the excuse where they have no cause for it. I have but one in the whole citty whom I can call a freind (and though but one, yet he is a very good one), and he is eaarnest in his inviting me to his house in St. Martin's Lane[1]. But I am so great a lover of my own home, that I know no paradise on earth can tempt me from it, any farther then the serving the necessities of my freinds, and the duties which I ow to the Church may require it of me. As for this disease, though it spread for the time, and hath gott the name of a new disease, yet every autumn produceth the like, and fluxes and putrid feavers ar to be expected, where there is no moderation used in eating of fruits, which ar every where in such plenty, that the poor to fill their belly and the rich to please their tast, are likely to suffer by it. But I hope temperance is the guiding vertu of your family, and health will be the reward of it.

I have sent you a breviat of som cases, which I extracted out of the *Provinciall Letters* in French, and with them a book sent me out of France in the year 1644[2], (and if I am not deceaved the very same which you having once seen, you often enquired after, but I could not then find it), where I find many of the same cases, and som of that prodigious nature that I am in a maze to see that any who profess the Name ether of Christ, or Jesus, dare vent to the world conclusions so destructive of every thing that looks like religion, that nether the Talmud, nor the Alcoran can be charged with the like. That which you mention to be written against that new peremptory statesman[3], who sitts down in his chair, and fancies that he hath all the kingdoms of the earth before him, to be new molded and cast into a form of his own devising, I have not as yet seen, but both for the author's sake, and the argument, I shall enquire after it. I am very glad to find in the clause of your letter that Mr. Thorndike is with you, who, as he is very agreeable to you, in the French phrase so in the esteem of all good men, he is a person of so much knowledge and piety with all, that his company will not onely be a pleasure but a blessing to you. Sir, we ar all here in one unison in prayers and all good wishes for you and yours,

---

[1] "A freind . . . in St. Martin's Lane." This is, of course, John Adler. See Letter XLIV, Note 2.

[2] "A book sent me out of France." In the Lamport Library is a presentation copy to "Brian Bishop of Salisbury from Roan 1644 from Wm. Kingsley" of the book in question: *Requeste, Procès Verbaux et advertissments faits à la diligence du Recteur et par l'ordre de l'Université pour faire condamner une Doctrine pernicieuse et preiudiciable à la Société humaine et particulièrement a la vie des Rois, enseignée au Collége de Clairement par les Jesuites de Paris*: (12 mo Paris 1644.)

The donor, William Kingsley, was Archdeacon of Canterbury 1619–48. He was sequestered in 1644, and died in 1648. He married a niece of Archbishop Abbot and had 16 children (Foster). The book, which is an attack on the Jesuits, was probably sent by Duppa to Sir Justinian to peruse, and has remained in the Library at Lamport ever since. Duppa's manuscript "breviat of cases" is also among the Lamport MSS. See also Letter XC.

[3] "That new peremptory statesman". That is, Harrington.

though onely I am the praecentor, and lead the way, in the professing my self,

Sir, Your most faithfull, and truly devoted freind and servant,
BR: SAR:

Richm: Aug: 26.

LETTER XCII

[SEPTEMBER 9th.]

Sir, I hasten the return of this letter, because there is a bottle of that water[1] to accompany it, which is mention'd by you. And though I ioyn not in conspiracy with those good women who use to over beleive the receipts they have, and because they find virtu in them in som particulars, instantly pronounce them to be catholicon, and good for all things, yet I must give this testimony to truth, drawn from 30 yeares experience, that I know not any thing of this nature that better helps the stomack, and more cleares the heart from melancholy vapors, then this doth. And which is one commendation more, it is so perfectly innocent, that it hath all the vertus of strong water, and yet hath none of the dangers of it. My wife by her charity hath made it so known to her neighbors, that this sickly time they have exhausted her store, or else you might have been sure of a larger proportion. But as long as she is among the living, you shall not want your share, and because the frequent return of her infirmities may make her incapable at last to do this service to you, she intends to send the receipt of it to your Lady, who (if our prayers may praevail) may live many happy yeares with you.

But though at this time in hast, I have somthing more to say, in relation to the little book which you recommended to me. The truth is that upon your mentioning of it, as I was impatient till I gott the sight of it, so I was as much pleas'd upon the reading of it. For though the author be but young[2],yet he shewes by this first essay of his that his extraction is a *familia ingeniorum*. For his witt is clear and sprightly, and doth so smoothly deal with his curl-headed adversary[3], as if he meant rather to combe, and gently disentangle the knotts he hath made then to deal roughly with him, which his pride and insolency used toward Dr. Fern[4] might well have deserved. The reply[5] I as yet hear nothing of, and when I do, I shall not

[1] "A bottle of that water." For the curative water distilled in the Duppa household, see Letter C, and Notes 3a and 4.

[2] "Though the author be but young." This letter follows on that of August 26th where Bishop Duppa says that he is trying to get hold of M. Wren's *Considerations* on Harrington's *Oceana*. This was published in 1657.

[3] "Curl-headed adversary." This is, of course, Harrington. See Letter LXXXVII, Note 3.

[4] "Dr. Fern." The Revd. Henry Ferne, D.D. (1602–62), Fellow of Trinity College, Cambridge, Archdeacon of Leicester, 1641, was sequestered from his living of Medbourne, Leicestershire, but busied himself with controversial work. In 1656 he "dared to censure *Oceana*, a copy having been sent him by Harrington's sister" (D.N.B.). The work was *Pian Piano*: *or intercourse between H.F., D.D. and J. Harrington Esq upon the occasion of the Doctors censure of Oceana*. In 1660 he was restored to his living, and his fellowship at Trinity, where he became Master, which post he resigned for the Bishopric of Chester, which he held for five weeks before his death in 1662. (*Walker Revised*).

[5] "The reply." Harrington's reply to his critics, who included Dr. Hammond, called *Prerogative of Popular Government*, was not published till 1658, so it is not surprising that Duppa had not heard of it. It may be "the reply" which Duppa mentions without enthusiasm in his letter of March 15th, 1658 (see Appendix B, Undated Letters, No. 10).

much long after it. But there is somthing shortly comming forth, which will be worth your seeing. But of this more in the next. And so wishing health and happyness to your whole family, I rest,

Your ever faithfull freind, and servant to pray for you,

BR: SARUM.

Richm: Sept: 9.

LETTER XCIII

[OCTOBER 14th.]

Sir, Though I live at distance from you, yet you ar so near me in my thoughts, that I do not pass a day without you. For ether my love to you, or my fear for you, claimes som of my time, what ever my other imployments may be. This last week I was at London, where visits, and noise, and som business kept me from writing, though not from thinking on that which your last letter deliver'd to me. I was troubled to find you had been aguish, but this is a distemper universall[1], and physitians know what to say to it, though not allwayes what to do; but the fitts of the spleen which you speak of, ar of so subtle a nature, and so quaestionable whether they be the productions of the mind or of the body, that not onely the patient that feeles them, but the physitian himself is posed which way to deal with them. They wer wont to tell me, when I suspected those fitts but could not positively say I had them, that this distemper was lodged in the

---

[1] The dating of this and the subsequent letters presented some difficulties. The reasons for assigning them to the autumn and winter of 1657/8 are:

(a) The "distemper universall". "Both 1657 and 1658 were years of high mortality. In the summer and autumn of 1657 a malignant fever, which men called the "new disease" prevailed throughout the country districts" (Firth, *Last Years of the Protectorate*, II, p. 296). There were public fast days on August 21st and September 30th. The disease abated in mid-winter to break out again in April and again in August 1658, when Cromwell and his daughter were both its victims. See also Letter XCI of August 26th and the "regnant disease".

(b) Susan Carew's illness. See Letter XCV of December 8th, 1657, and Letter XCVII of January 12th, 1657/8. Nicholas Carew and his wife had taken a lease from the Washbournes of Pytchley Hall. On March 18th, 1656/7, J. Stuteville had written to Sir Justinain "wee are glad to heare my cousin Carew hath taken a lease of it [Pytchley] and hope that his entrance may be in order to a taking possession of it for your self." (Pytchley was built in the reign of Queen Elizabeth I by Sir Euseby Isham, nephew of the John Isham who bought Lamport. It was sold by his grandchildren in 1632). Here Mrs. Carew seems to have had a daughter who died. ("I am glad of the good newes in the front of your letter concerning Mrs. Carew". Theo. Greene to Sir Justinian Isham, November 12th, 1657, (I.C. 438).) Dorothy Long wrote on November 28th (I.C. 442): "this epidemicall disease haveing but very lightely assaulted me; a great belly proving an exemption from all other maladies; a benefit I am perfectly sorry your sweet daughter Carew injoys not, for whose recovery and long life she hath my best of wishes, so hath your son and all other your relatives." This agrees perfectly with what the Bishop says in his letters of November 10th and December 8th, which I have assigned to this year. Mrs. Carew was recovered in the summer of 1658, for Elizabeth Isham, writing on June 1st (I.C. 463) from Suffolk where the Carews were visiting, says: "She has quite lost her ague and begins to looke much better than when she came, if you please to let her have the money, you would return it to us when she comes to Pitchly . . ."

(c) In his letter of March 1st, 1657/8 Bishop Duppa alludes to "this taedious agu that hath so long affiicted your beloved daughter", and in the same letter says that he is about to enter his grand "climacterik" i.e. his seventieth year. He was born on March 10th, 1588/9, so this date that I have assigned for these letters would agree well.

(d) The Romance, i.e. *Cloria and Narcissus*, despite his efforts has not yet (December 31st) reached the Bishop. It is first mentioned in Sir Justinian's reply to the Bishop's letter of June 16th (see Letter LXXXVIII, Note 6). This helps to date the letter of December 31st as the last day of 1657.

spleen, as a lyon is in his den; if you stirr him not, he sleepes, but if you rouse him with purgative phisick, he will prove a lyon indeed. But as warmth and good diet, with God's blessing may cure the ague, so cheerfulness and moderate exercise may allay, if not take away the other. But the greatest hazard is in that beloved daughter of yours, whom this untoward ague hath seas'd upon at such an advantage, that she cannot seriously intend the delivery of her self from it, least she should praeiudice the delivery of that which is so dear to her.

But God is ready in all extremities to work wonders for us and certainly if the frequency of it did not abate the wonder, I should look upon it as a greater miracle that a woman should be deliver'd of one child, then that she should be deliver'd from twenty diseases. But He who can do the greater can do the less, and having given you another pledge of his favor to you in affording you a grandchild, can as easily restore the voice of joy and health into your dwellings, and into all of your relations. And so without troubling you farther, you have my prayers for all that concernes you, and my selfe,

Your most affectionat freind and most faithfull servant
BR: SARUM.

Richm: Oct: 14.

LETTER XCIV

[NOVEMBER 10th.]

Sir, The health of you and yours is very pretious to me, not onely for my own sake (though self-love may innocently crave a share in it), but really for your self, whom, since I had the happyness to know, I have look'd upon as a person of the clearest soul, and of unmingled principles both toward God and men. And had you been a stranger, and known to me onely by this character, it would have made you very dear to me. But I am satisfied for the present to heer that in this sickly time, the destroying angel hath not com near your house. That it hath touch'd upon a family so near your heart as your daughter's is, I am troubled with you and for you; but since it is onely an untimely branch that is lost, and the stock remaines entire, your joy may very well countervail your sorrow, for there is time enough for her to bring you many branches more.

As for that which concernes my cosin Stephens[1], in relation to a copy which he desires of Bishop Bancroft's *Life*[2], I am so much a stranger to it, that till this time I never heard of it. But I shall now inquire after it, though my Lord of London[3] be so remote from me, that I shall despair of having

[1] "My cosin Stephens." For Jeremiah Stephens see Letter IV, Note 7.

[2] "Bishop Bancroft's *Life*." The Bishop Bancroft in question is probably the Bishop of London, who became Archbishop of Canterbury under James I, and in his disciplinary measures anticipated Laud, rather than his nephew, the Bishop of Oxford, who was a disciple of Laud, and the builder of Cuddesdon Palace. The D.N.B. lists no contemporary *Life* of either prelate.

[3] "My Lord of London." This is William Juxon (1582–1663), who was a Churchman of much the same type as Duppa. He was specially trusted by Laud, who in his *Diary* (July 10th, 1632) noted: "Dr. Juxon, Dean of Worcester, at my suit sworn Clerk of His Majesty's Closet. That I might have one that I might trust near his majesty." He became Bishop of London in 1633, and in 1636 Lord High Treasurer – again much to Laud's satisfaction. He advised the King to veto Strafford's attainder, but Charles preferred to follow Bishop Williams' advice, to his own ruin. He was highly thought of by Charles, and attended him on the scaffold. During the Commonwealth, he retired to Little Compton near Moreton-in-the-Marsh, and occupied himself in private devotion and hunting. He was made Archbishop of Canterbury at the Restoration, but he was then seventy-eight, and seems

any intelligence from him. What he is about I know not, but this I know of him, that he is a person of great industry, and great affections to the poor Church his Mother. He lives in your neighborhood, and if you please to continu to own him and to encourage him, I shall look upon it as a favor in a great measure don unto my self. What Mr. Thorndike[4] is doing I am likewise a stranger to, but am persuaded that it cannot but be good that is drawn out of the treasury of so good a heart as his. For my own particular I am still under my old discipline, the paines of my stomack, which every evening seaseth upon me and cannot be yet cast out ether by prayer or fasting, much less by phisick. But I did not intend to trouble you with this περιαυτολογία.[5] The chastisement is but gentle, nor do I despair of some ease from it. I am not sorry that you cam not up this term, for I infinitely praeferr your quiet being before any content of my own, who am most faithfully,

Sir,
Your most affectionat tru freind,
BR: SAR:

Richm: Nov. 10.

My wife quarrels with me that she is not named in the letter, and requires that I should do her that right as to present her service to your self, and your very good Lady.

---

to have done little except follow others. He does not appear to have been specially active under the Commonwealth, but he was, as Duppa here remarks, far from the scene of affairs. (D.N.B., William Hutton, *William Laud* (1895), Wood, *Ath. Ox.*, *Walker Revised*).

4 "Mr. Thorndike." Herbert Thorndike (1598–1672), several times mentioned in the later letters, was an Anglican scholar and theologian of some note. He was a Cambridge man (M.A. Trinity College 1620), of Lincolnshire origin, who spent his life at Trinity first as a student, then as a Fellow, and lastly (1640) as lecturer in Hebrew, till 1646, when he was ejected. In 1636, John Williams, Bishop of Lincoln, presented him to the prebend of Layton Ecclesia in Lincoln Minster, vacant by the death of George Herbert. Bishop Williams, who was a friend both of Justinian Isham and his father Sir John, was ever a patron of learned men.

In 1639 Thorndike was presented by the Crown to the Vicarage of Claybrook in Leicestershire, whereupon he resigned his prebend at Lincoln, thereby acting in accordance with his own frequently expressed invectives against pluralities. In 1643 he was a candidate for the Mastership of Sidney Sussex College, Cambridge, but was unsuccessful owing to the intervention of the soldiers, who carried off one of Thorndike's supporters before the election. Seth Ward (q.v.) protested at this and declined to vote at all, as did three other Fellows. This left the way open for the election of the Puritan candidate, Robert Minshull, by a minority of the Fellows (Tatham, *The Puritans in Power*, p. 125 note).

Thorndike lost both his living (Barley, Herts) and his fellowship, in the two following years. He then turned to authorship; in 1650, he published two tracts (dedicated to James, Duke of Richmond and Lennox, whose chaplain he was) on Church Government. During the Interregnum he visited Holland, but returned to England and was often in financial difficulties, till he found steady work on Walton's *Polyglot Bible* to which he contributed the Syriac part. In 1659 he published his most important work *An Epilogue to the Tragedy of the Church of England*, which is discussed in Letter CVIII, Note 5. After the Restoration, he was restored to his living at Barley, and took part in the Savoy Conference and the revision of the Prayer Book in 1661. He was then made a Prebendary of Westminster, but was not further promoted.

There are five of Thorndike's works in the Lamport Library, and he was a fairly frequent correspondent of Sir Justinian, who, in 1668, at his own suggestion, offered him the living at Lamport, which only failing health made him finally decline. (D.N.B., *Walker Revised*, and authorities there cited, especially T. A. Lacey, *Herbert Thorndike* (1929). This last work contains a list of his twelve works published in his lifetime, and seven works published posthumously (1854, 1856) from MSS. in the Chapter Library at Westminster).

5 "περιαυτολογία." "Talking about oneself."

LETTER XCV

[DECEMBER 8th.]

Sir, This return to your last had com sooner to you had I receaved yours according to the date of it, but many times it sticks where you direct it, and many times the watermen deceave me and forgett to call for it. And the truth is, I take the more notice of the date, because it was the anniversary of my happy marriage[1] and therefore a day never to be forgotten by me. For though I have receaved many blessings from God of all sorts, yet among those that have concerned my happyness in this life, none can aequall, or com near, the comforts which I enioy in having had for so many yeares such a bosom freind, who hath so faithfully and so affectionatly gon along with me through all the variations of my life and fortunes. Should I say so much to many of this world, they would not easily beleive the sense which I have of it, for ether they have chosen so ill that they cannot apprehend it, or ar so soon weary of a good choice that they sowr their marriage before they give it leave to ripen into so many yeares as mine has done. But writing to you, whom I have so long observed to make all relations good, I am secure that I can say nothing of this kind concerning my own condition, which you ar not likely experimentally to make good in that happy choice which you have made. You ar very well accquainted with him that said: *Faelices ter et amplius, quos irrupta tenet copula*[2], etc. But I must break of abruptly from this argument or else I shall not know how to make an end.

And now I must have somthing to say concerning that *bonus genius* of your country who cures quartan agues; for there is a young neice of mine[3] who hath long languished under the tyranny of it, and iust with those circumstancies as your daughter Carew is, for being lately brought to bed, the ague (which she had before) still continues with her. If you find that this empirick doth generally cure in this kind, I shall not despise him for being an empirick. For had there been no empiricks we should never have had phisitians. And I am not yet confident that the grace of healing is yet ceas'd. For if it had, I could not possibly imagine how Ned Hale of Flower[4] (who could not by name distinguish one bone from another) should becom so good a bone-setter. If you find reason for it, I shall desire you would so farr praevail with him as to communicate the dosis

---

[1] "The anniversary of my happy marriage." November 23rd. See Letter LXXXV, Note.

[2] *Faelices ter et amplius*, etc. "Thrice happy are they who are united in an unbroken love." Horace, *Odes* I, 13, 17-18.

[3] "A young neice of mine." In her will (1664) Jane Duppa mentions "fower of my husband's neices", but there had been many more. See App. A.

[4] "Ned Hale of Flower." Edward Hale of Flore, near Weedon. A man of this name, described as "gent", appeared as surety in £10 with another, for one Thomas Mills of Dallington, miller, who was bound over to keep the peace, "especially towards James Tymes of the same town labourer," at the Michaelmas sessions, 1630. (*Quarter Sessions Records of the County of Northampton*. Northants Record Society, Vol. I (1924)). Edward Halles of Flower (probably the same man), this time described as yeoman, made a will on July 31st, 1637, which was proved on December 2nd of the same year, leaving the residue of his goods, after various bequests, to be sold for his grandson, Edward Hales, aged 21. In his will he mentions as "friends" who were to be overseers of his will two members of families undoubtedly "gentle", Richard Knightley of Preston Capes, and Thomas Andrew of Harleston. The inventory of his goods taken on October 25th, 1637, showed a total of £820.19.0 (Archdeaconry of Northampton, 2nd Series, G.208; copy taken by the late Revd. H. I. Longden).

There was a well known family of bonesetters at Flore called Freeman (*Verney Memoirs*, Vol. IV, pp. 395 and 396), who flourished in 1687.

which he makes use of, ether in specie, or by way of direction, and I will engage my credit he shall be rewarded for it.

As for my own health, as for the present I have the less to complain of, because for these two praecedent nights, I have, by God's blessing, escaped the pain of my stomack. Whether it may revert or no, I know not, but if it do not, though I have had a phisitian for my freind, yet I must thank an empirick for it. I am absolutely of your mind, that between us all salutations, and ceremonies are implied, and therefore I shall say no more, then what you know allready, that I am most faithfully, Sir,

Your most affectionat freind,

BR: SAR:

Richm: Dec: 8.

LETTER XCVI

[DECEMBER 31st.]

Sir, By this time the cheife of our solemnities is over, and having don my duties of thankfullness toward God, I am now at more leasure to return my thankes to you, whose freindship is so great a support and comfort to me. Though I could never observe any main materiall difference between them, yet there is a faction among the schoolmen, between the nominals and the realls, but in the catalogue of my freinds I evidently find the difference, for som of them ar meerly nominall and aequivocall freinds; their words, and their lookes, and their visits are hugely kind, but he that lookes farther shall find nothing, and therfore that I may not be deceaved by them, I hear them, but beleive them not. But withall there ar som (though few) really kind like your self, whom God will certainly reward, though I cannot.

You putt me somtimes in mind to mention to you what bookes com in my way; but I am so much out of the road, and so incapable of maintaining any commerce with stationers, that wer it not for two freindly factors of mine, the one at Thistleworth, the other at Kingston, I should be as great a stranger to bookes, as you may well guess me to be to the men of these times. And besides all this, the nearer I am to my grave, the more I would willingly wean my self from impertinencies, and reading many books is no better. I confess, I have not yet so far conquer'd my self, but if a book com in my way (where ether the argument or the stile is pleasing) that I can refrain from reading it. And of these there ar so few, and those so well known to you, that to name them might be a loss both of my time, and yours. But the romance[1] which you speak of, I have been very inquisitive after (not so much for the author's sake, as for that character which you give upon the bye), but as yet I cannot compass it, nor dare I seem to be passionatly desirous of it, for if Heliodore lost his Bishoprick for writing a better in that kind then hath ever since been published, I may very probably incurr a censure for reading that which is worse.

But there is an other book com forth of the *Lives of the Philosophers*[2], which I was very greedy after, and the rather because in my younger time I had collected somthing of that kind. Whether this be the same author

---

[1] "The romance." The Bishop is still after *Cloria and Narcissus*. See Letter LXXXVIII, Note 6.

[2] *Lives of the Philosophers*. This is probably Thomas Stanley's *History of Philosophy, containing the Lives, opinions and discoveries of the Philosophers of every sect*; with a portrait of the author by Faithorne, and other engravings. The four volumes published in London between 1655 and 1662 are in the Lamport Library. For Thomas Stanley, the classical scholar (1625–78), see D.N.B.

whom you formerly mention'd to me, I desire to know. But whosoever it is, he is very diligent and exact in his undertakings, as farr, at least, as he hath gon; but he hath left so much unsaid as may require a volume greater then what he hath now sett forth; for first he doth abruptly begin with those that vulgarly have the denomination of sages, whereas the prime philosophers wer Orpheus, Linus, Homer, Hesiod, whose lives and workes deserved a mention. Nor wer these the prime but onely in relation to Greece, for all the learning that ether those poets or philosophers had, cam from the more eastern parts, and moved as the sun doth by degrees from the east unto the west, for before there was ether an Homer, or a Thales there was a Trismegistus, a Zoroaster, and the Sibyls, which he might have don well to have begun with. But this is not all he is deficient in, for he hath as yet consider'd onely the Ionick sect of the philosophers; but the Italick sect he hath omitted, particularly those excellent men, Pythagoras, Democritus, Epicurus, with many others. But probably he reserves them for a second volume; and I wish that the same hand may sett them forth, for his diligence is great, and it will require an exact hand to do it. If he and I may be acquainted, as I am promis'd by a third person that we shall be brought together, I shall (if he be counsailable) point out to him such particulars as may make his work more perfect. But I shall say no more at this time, because being resolved to discourse hereafter of nothing but bookes, I must keep somthing in reserve for the future.

I am very much ioy'd that the voice of health is return'd into your dwelling[3], and my prayer is, that it may continue there. What Christmass I keep you may guess, when I tell you that I have the company of my little cosin, and yours, who having first sent me provision more then enough, brought afterward himself in person, and as yet stayes with me. The best of our discourse is that which concernes you, for though he reckons up many Lords and Ladies of his kindred, yet his judgement is so good that he lookes upon you as the cheif of them. And so with as much love as we can *Coniunctim* or *divisim* present to you, I am both your beadsman to pray for you, and

Your most affectionat freind,
BR: SAR:

Decemb: ultimo

The date of my letter putts me in mind to wish you the happyness of the New Year.

[3] Mrs. Carew, probably, is meant.

1658

This year saw Cromwell's final attempt to work with a Parliament, his most secure period of power, and his death. This last event revived Royalist hopes. Richard Cromwell succeeded to the position of Protector, but never had the confidence of the Army. His attempt at "Constitutional" rule was to fail, but all that episode properly belongs to the next year.

With Cromwell's death, the political interest of the letters increases, but there are important allusions to historical events even before that date. In Letter XCVIII (February 8th), for instance, Duppa alludes to the sudden end of the Two-Chamber Parliament "call'd with so much care, and sifted with so much caution, that I did not think it possible, that there could be any heterogeneous Member among them, that should not comply with the generall ends designed." But by the end of the year (Letter CVII, December 7th), Duppa writes of the forthcoming Parliament of Richard Cromwell: "should I say there would be first an Act of Amnesty past, which should make all persons of all parties aequally eligible, I should say more then I beleive, though not more then is spoken." Thus early, "a free Parliament" was being mooted, which further revived Royalist hopes. It was equally being advocated by constitutional Republicans. "The people, being vexed", wrote Mrs Hutchinson in the *Memoirs* of her husband, "with the pocket parliaments and the major-generals of the counties, who behaved like bashaws, were now all muttering to have a free parliament, after the old manner of elections, without pledging those that were chosen to any terms."

Sir Justinian, indeed, had reason once more to feel the heavy hand of the "bashaws", for at the end of April, he was again arrested and kept under guard at Northampton.

During the winter of 1657–8 Dr Hewett, a former Royal Chaplain, had been plotting a rising against the Protector. Charles II had sent over Ormond from the Continent to report on the possibility of a landing, and had tried to secure Spanish support. But Thurloe, Cromwell's Secretary of State, became aware of what was brewing. Early in March, all Popish recusants, and people who had fought either for Charles I, or his son, were ordered to repair to their homes, and not to remove more than five miles from them.

It was not only the Royalists who were feared by the Government. The publication in 1657 of the tract *Killing noe Murder* defended, in advance, the murder of Cromwell, and the Royalists hoped that the extreme Republicans might do their work for them. Thurloe resolved to strike at both enemies. Early in April, 1658, several of the Fifth Monarchy men were arrested, and a few days later Dr. Hewett, and some of the Royalist plotters*. In the provinces, there

* See Firth, *Last Years of the Protectorate*, Vol. II, for a full and documented account of these plots.

were many arrests. On April 27th 1658, Thurloe wrote to Henry Cromwell, Lord Deputy of Ireland: "We have made sure of the cavaliers, haveinge most of them under strickt guard in the severall countryes, and are resolved never to lett them goe, untill the nation be secured against them; judging it very unreasonable, that wee should be alarmed once every year with invasions and insurrections by them."*

On the very same day on which this letter was written, Sir Ralph Verney wrote to ask how his old friend Sir Justinian was faring under this new Terror, for "in these wretched times a man must be allowed to be a little inquisitive after his friends." To this, Sir Justinian replied that he was at present under guard at Northampton, by the orders of Major-General Butler. "Most of us are visited with extreame colds and many taken with vomiting and purging. I am glad 'tis yet so wel with you, endeavor to keepe your selfe soe." He mentions that Lord Cullen, Lord Camden, Lord Brudenell, Sir Edward Griffin *intra multos alios* were in like case under guard at Northampton.† As Thurloe told Henry Cromwell, the Government decided to proceed against the conspirators by a court of law; on May 12th the court met under the presidency of John Lyle. Theodore Greene, Sir Justinian's lawyer, informed his client of the course of events (May 13th, 1658); "Yesterday the High Justice Court was appointed to sitt but I cannot heare whether the Council mett or noe; some talk of a remove in the business that the Act of Parliament is to impower them to precede according to justice, which the Judges (they talk) have declared to be *secundum legem terrae* which is the Grand and Petty Juries. This bone thus throwen in (yf true) will make that Court to be no other than a Commission of Oyer and Terminer. The report is that diverse gent[lemen] of Sussex and these parts are in hold that had commissions and accepted of them [i.e. in the Royalist Army]; yt will go hard with them. I wish them all a swift deliverance by a fair triall. I heare that most of the West Country gent[lemen] who were imprisoned are dismissed, and sent home to their houses, and 'tis hoped, that now the plott is discovered, and the guilty shall receive their doome, the innocent shalbe no further troubled." (I.C. 459a).‡ However, Sir Justinian was not released till July, and Mrs. Carlile, relying on the fact that Cromwell's Secretary of State had married her cousin, went to intercede for him only to find that Thurloe himself had a "pike" against Sir Justinian (Letter CII, June 30th).

Bishop Duppa, apart from his concern over Sir Justinian, must have had a special anxiety over these plots. Captain Henry Mallory of Preston, Sussex, and later of East Hoathly, Sussex, was first cousin once removed of his wife, Mrs. Duppa, and her eventual

---

* *State Papers of John Thurloe*, ed. Birch, Vol. VII, p.99.

† *Verney Memoirs*, Vol. III, pp.414 and 415. J. Wake, *The Brudenells of Deene*, pp. 155, 156.

‡ See Firth, *Last Years of the Protectorate*, Vol. II, p.71. This letter is an important confirmation of the authorities there cited.

heir, and he was intimately concerned with the plot. He was offered the position of Major in Stapley's regiment, which was to secure Sussex for the King, but on his arrest in April he was induced to give information about John Mordaunt's share in the plot. The night before Mordaunt's trial (June 1st) Mallory escaped, instigated and assisted by Mrs. Mordaunt. He was not recaptured until after the trial, and the prosecution, therefore, failed, with the result that Mordaunt did not share the fate of Dr. Hewett, and Sir Henry Slingsby, who were condemned to death, but lived to take an active part in the plots of 1659*. Henry Mallory was committed to the Tower on June 5th, 1658, "condemned and repreived", and was not released till the Restoration†. Bishop Duppa left him £20 in his will, and Mrs. Duppa made him her residuary legatee, so that their apprehension at his arrests and escape can easily be imagined. But on this subject, not surprisingly, the letters are silent. Richard Chaworth's second wife, Lady Sophia Bertie, was Dr. Hewett's sister-in-law, but it is not known when he married her, though it was probably in 1663 (see Appendix A).

But Sir Justinian had domestic cares in this year, besides his incarceration through the plotting of others. His elder twin daughter, Elizabeth (born August 27th 1636), fell in love with the son of an East Anglian knight, Sir Francis Gardiner, an attachment which caused some pain, as her father did not approve of it. His youngest daughter, Susan Carew, whose ague caused so much concern during the winter, had "quite lost her ague and begins to looke much better" when she visited her great-aunt and sisters in Suffolk in June. (I.C. 463). The death of the Carews' tenant at Beddington in Surrey removed the young people from Pytchley, where they had been near Sir Justinian, and from time to time Bishop Duppa gives news of them.

Also August brought Sir Justinian another son, who was called after his father (Letter CIV), and in reply to a letter of Dorothy Long's, Sir Justinian wrote: "The sickly season is now returned upon us which makes me the more earnest after your healths, mine with my late encrease of a young Justinian I beleive not unwelcome to you . . . I pray pardon this error that I have not bin so ready to acquaint you with misfortunes as with the blessings of your faithfull servant" (I.C. 469).

The sickly season claimed an illustrious victim in Cromwell. Letter CV informs us of another famous man who suffered from the same disease at the same season. But Gilbert Sheldon recovered by the aid of the "Jesuits' powder". If Cromwell had deigned to use a powder (so unhappily named for him) he might perhaps have survived too, and altered the course of history.

---

* See Firth, *op. cit.*, Vol. II, p.78 seq, and the references there given to Thurloe, Vol. VII.

† Thurloe, Vol. VII, p.622.

LETTER XCVII

[JANUARY 12th.]

Sir, Your last dated the 26 of the last month, came not to my hands till after the twelfth day, which made me pass my Christmas over with som more sollicitude then ordinary. For I am of Plinie's mind: *Nihil tam anxium, et tam suspensum, quam de eo quem ardentissime diligis nihilscire.*[1]

I find by your letter, that your quacksalver who began to have a name for curing of quartan agues doth not abate in his credit; and I confess it had been a wonder, that a disease which in so many ages had been accounted *opprobrium medicorum*, should now becom the glory of an empirick. But the truth is, there ar two sorts of mountebanks, the learned, and the unlearned. For though I really honor the learned, and in many cases look upon their remedies praescribed as τῶν θεῶν χεῖρας, yet if there be anything new in a disease (and every thing is new which surpriseth the phisitian) I am every day more and more convinced, that the mountebank and he, make up one lottry, where there ar infinite blanks to one lott, and it is Providence of an higher nature, then our own wisdom, that must guide us in the choice. And that Providence hath so farr praevail'd in the cure of this young neice of mine (for whom I was willing to call to your mountebank for help) that without consulting any more with fallacious and doubtfull oracles, she is for the present perfectly recover'd, and I persuade my self that prayer and patience will operate as much for your beloved daughter[2].

But, now that you give me occasion to speak of my neighbors, I must turn the leaf, and give you an account of them. The truth is, I have not any frequent converse with those you mention, onely som visits have past between us: they live privat and retired, but hansomly and plentifully as to themselves[3]. I was never yet invited to eat with them, which I do not mention as any unkindness in them, but rather as one of the greatest favors they can do me. For I am really of that Bishop of Ipres'[4] mind (from whom the family of the Jansenians derive themselves), who, being ask'd of his freind that mett him whether he was going, his answer was (being invited to a feast) *eo ad agendam poenitentiam.* And though for civility['s] sake, I am somtimes driven to do this penance, yet, as all penance is, it is not without regret to leave my round table, and my one dish, which no splendor of any other table can recompense.

But this is upon the by, and to satisfy you farther, I must revert to the persons you mention. And certainly they ar so farr happy, that their dispositions and tempers in both of them seem to be alike *magis sine vitiis, quam cum virtutibus.*[4a] There wants that vigor in him, that is in his father, and his lady is so good as to be like him in it. There is nothing to

---

[1] *Nihil tam anxium, et tam suspensum* etc. "There is no anxiety equal to knowing nothing about him whom you love most strongly." Much adapted from Pliny, *Epist.* VI, 4, 3.

[2] "Your beloved daughter." Susan Carew.

[3] "They live privat." Sir Justinian had many friends in Richmond, but from the meagre details it is not possible to identify this couple.

[4] "Bishop of Ipres." This is, of course, Cornelius Jansen (1585–1638), appointed Bishop of Ypres two years before his death, and remembered for having in his *Augustinus* laid down the religious principles known as Jansenism. Pope Innocent X condemned some of the propositions in 1653, but it was not till the Bull "Unigenitus", issued in 1713 by Pope Clement XI, that Jansenism was finally suppressed in the Church. (Encycl. Brit.)

[4a] *Magis sine vitiis*, etc. "Not bad, but not good." Adapted from Tacitus, *Hist.*, I, 49, 11.

complain of in ether of them, but had the lady been match'd with a livelier temper, she might have been much improved. My neighbors of the Park[5] (a place somthing the more beloved by me, because from thence I had my first enioyments of your freindship) ar I fear in a declining condition (for painting, and poetry have shutt out of dores providence, and good husbandry), but they carry it out hansomly, and with a good mene, and have of late married their daughter, which I am the more engaged to wish it may be happy to them, because I was made choice of to ioyn their hands, and hearts together. And so you see you have gott (*cicadam alis* as the proberb is) a grasshopper by the wings, for giving me by one quaestion, an oportunity of saying somthing, I have gon farther, but I conceave it will not be displeasing to you, because as it concernes your freinds, so it comes from a freind, who valewes nothing on this side of the seas at such a rate, then to bee esteem'd by you as

Most affectionately yours,

BR: SAR:

Richm: Jan: 12.

LETTER XCVIII

[FEBRUARY 8th.]

Sir, I do not wonder at all that in this wether our letters have nether a free nor a quick passage, for all wayes ar so block'd up with ice, and snow that I can hardly have a return from our neighbor citty, but with such a pause, as letters might have been formerly expected from Barwike, or Saint Michael's Mount. But it seemes there is no hardness of wether that can freese up your kindness and bounty from me, which makes its way to me, without staying for a thaw. I did not expect at the beginning of the frost[1], that it would have out-lasted a Parlament[2], call'd with so much care, and sifted with so much caution, that I did not think it possible, that there could be any heterogeneous Member among them, that should not comply with the generall ends designed. But I see all our thoughts ar vain, and while naturall agents work constantly to the utmost of their activity, great councells ar of a more variable and mutable condition; *sed nos hac a scabie tenemus ungues*[3].

[5] This is the reference, which finally determined the identity of "My neighbors of the Park." Joan Carlile was addicted to painting, and her husband, Lodowick, to poetry (see Letters XXVI, Note 3 and IX, Note 2). Their daughter, whom Duppa here mentions, that he has "of late married" was Penelope, born 1632, who married John Fisher of the Middle Temple. The Petersham Registers contain the entries for the baptism of their three children; Penelope, the eldest, born September 27th, 1650, and baptised the same day, John, born May 1st, baptised May 17th, 1660, and Edmund, born March 29th and baptised April 11th, 1661. Penelope Fisher was dead when her mother Mrs. Carlile made her will in 1677, but her husband, John Fisher, was left "one hundred pounds," and was made one of her executors.

[1] "The frost." When Cromwell went to dissolve the Houses, he was unable to travel by boat, as the river was blocked by ice. The frost, mentioned by Duppa, added point to Cromwell's allusion to the condition of the Army—"a poor unpaid Army: the soldiers going barefoot at this time, in this city, this weather." (Carlyle, Speech XVII). Barwike is Berwick-on-Tweed.

[2] "A Parlament." On January 20th, 1658, Parliament met, for the first time under the Protectorate with a Second Chamber. But the Commons showed themselves bent on constitution-making, and on February 4th the Protector, thinking it "high time that an end be put to your sitting", dissolved Parliament. This sudden dissolution surprised both friends and enemies. (Firth, Vol. II, pp. 16–41).

[3] *Sed nos hac a scabie tenemus ungues.* "But we keep our nails off this sore." Martial, *Epigr.* V, 60, 11.

What Mr. Harrington may do in vindication of himself I am not likely to know, for I was so weary of his *Oceana*[4], that I shall hereafter abstain from every small brook, or rivulet that comes from him, and shall onely be content to hear from others to what advantage of his this contest may be carried on. But certainly had this man those parts which in a pleasing dream he fancieth him self to have, he would be such a monster in learning, as might affright every man from medling with him.

As for Mr. Morris[5], he and I ar both wether-bound from seeing one another, but when we meet I am persuaded, I shall find him no admirer of him, for ether I am deceaved in him, or he is much alter'd from his former principles, and in cool bloud can be content to think as one of us do. I heartily pray that God would restore the voice of health to all your relatives. For the present I bless God that I have nothing to complain of my former paines, but I have discovered a new and a worse enemy, and that is the scorbutis, which hath stole upon me unawares, and what meanes I should use to clear my self of it, I am not yet advised. God keep all evill from you and yours, that I may be the longer happy in you, and be look'd upon by you as

Your most affectionat tru freind to serve you
BR: SAR:

Richm: Feb: 8.

I have sent to Mr. Adler to be the person to receive your kindness for me, for which to return you thankes, is all I have left me.

LETTER XCIX

[FEBRUARY 17th.]

Sir, Your letters of January the 25 I was very sollicitous to return somthing to, though it could be nothing else but the sad apprehension which I had that both of you, whom God in his great goodness had made one flesh, wer now becom more literally so then I could have wish'd, being both of you surprised with the same kind of sickness much about the same time. But it seemes that ether this letter of mine hath miscarried, or else that it lay asleep at Glanvile's, and when it is awake, it may possibly find you out.

But what ever my trouble was at the receipt of the former, your latter of February the 9th, hath very much revived me; for beleive it, though I came earlier into the world then to have the same horoscope with you, yet I am so really involved in all your concernments, as if I wer born a twinn with you, for you can nether greive nor joy, but I shall have a share in it. And now we may be at leasure to mention bookes again. And first that MS. which you hear of, ascribed to that excellent man Bishop Andrewes[1], I am

[4] *Oceana.* For Harrington's *Oceana* see Letter LXXXVII, Note 3. The attack was presumably that by Matthew Wren. See Letter XC, Note 5.

[5] "Mr. Morris." Perhaps William Morice (1602–76), M.P. for Devonshire 1648; he never sat, being excluded by Pride's Purge, but was re-elected in 1654 and 1656; M.P. for Newport, Cornwall, 1658. He was excluded every time, but he sat in the Parliament of 1660, and was from 1660 to 1668 Secretary of State. He was a relative of General Monk. After his retirement, he collected a fine library. His principal preoccupation was theology (D.N.B.). See Letter XVII, Note 3.

[1] "Bishop Andrewes." Lancelot Andrewes (1555–1626) was Dean of Westminster (1601) when Duppa was King's scholar there, and was taught Hebrew by the Dean (*a Lanceloto Andrews, tum Decano, Hebraicim didicit*: Monument to Duppa at Westminster). Archbishop Laud was his literary executor, but it was not till 1647 that some of his prayers were published (and also by Richard Drake in 1648) and only in 1675 did a full edition appear.

confident is suppositious, for all his genuin works wer by the King's express order diligently search'd for, and they that made the search wer no ordinary, perfunctory men. But if any man hath been so happy as to write like him, I should be glad to see but a shadow of him, though the substance be not there. The *Sermons* of Dr. Sanderson[2] wer long ago presented to me from the author; and there are (as I hear) in the press another volume of Mr. Farington's[3], which ar greedily expected, who being barr'd from the pulpit, is fain to betake himself to the press, that he may gett bread for himself and his children. As for those which you plead a promise for[4], they ar a due debt, but I know you ar a gentle creditor, and will patiently stay the time, till I can accquire a greater confidence, then ever I had yet, of publishing that to others, which I never yet liked my self. But of this I shall give you a farther account hereafter. In the interim, I am very much satisfied, that I may turn my prayers into prayers for your recovery, which ar both paid with the same devotion, by

Your most affectionat tru freind and servant,
BR: SARUM.

Richm: Feb: 17.

LETTER C

[MARCH 1st.]*

Sir, He that is old enough to dy is gently treated, when he hath nothing above ordinary diseases to complain of. I am now upon the verge of ent'ring upon my great climacterick, that which David sett so many ages past, and to shew that he did not speak at random, parted with the world, and all the glory of it, at that very time which he sett to others, and so praevented those dregs of life, which have nothing in them but κόπους κ'

[2] "Dr. Sanderson." Robert Sanderson (1587–1663), described as "the foremost casuist of the day" in a recent work (Robert S. Bosher, *The Making of the Restoration Settlement* (1951)), and Bishop of Lincoln in 1660, published twenty sermons in 1656. In 1657 he published a further fourteen sermons. His sermons ran to several editions, and the 7th edition (1681) first contained the *Life* by Izaac Walton. (D.N.B., Lowndes, *Walker Revised*).

[3] "Mr. Farington." Anthony Farindon (1598–1658), was a scholar of Trinity College, Oxford, 1612, and Vicar of Bray, 1634. He was Minister of St. Mary Magdalen, Milk St. 1647–56, when he was silenced by the ordinance of 1655. In 1657 Duppa sent him 40s. through Mr. Adler. Collections of his sermons were published between 1663 and 1674. The first volume was published first in 1657. (D.N.B., *Walker Revised*, Lowndes). Farindon sent his volume of sermons to Bishop Duppa, who, in thanking him, added: "It may seem strange to some of your friends that you should unwarily gratify his [Calvin's] discipline by saying that the government [of Bishops] which we plead and suffer for is not absolutely necessary . . . I can no more deny the absolute necessity of this government than I can call in question the wisdom of God and the love of Christ, who had thus ordered that body of His the Church". (Tanner MSS. 52, f. 207v). Replying, Farindon defended himself from the charge of Calvinism, concluding: "The great Bishop of our soules restore Episcopacy to its former splendor and dignity, that it may shew itselfe againe, and moue uncontroulable to his Glory and the Advancement of learning and religion" (Tanner MSS. 52, f. 211v, July 4th, 1657).

[4] Duppa's sermons were not published in his lifetime. His *Holy Rules or Helps to Devotion both in Prayer and Practice* was published in 1675 with an engraving of the Bishop by R. White.

* It is odd that there should be letters on successive days, but the allusions to the "taedious agu" of Susan Carew and to the Bishop's approaching the entrance into his "great climackterick" (i.e. his seventieth year) suggest strongly that this first letter belongs to this year. The following letter (March 2nd) takes up the theme of the letter of February 17th, and it may be that the second letter was written after the clearing up of the muddle over Dr. Hammond's letter.

πόνους[1]. I have at this time an excellent distill'd water recommended to me by a freind, that hath don great cures in this kind of scorbutis, but this does not satisfy me without the advice of an Aesculapius, and therefore I have committed my self to the care of Dr. Nurse[2], once a neighbor of yours in Leicestershire, and now not onely my phisitian, but my very kind freind. The scorbutis, they say, is a disease, that few of us ar free from in som degree at least, though it light heaviest upon aged persons, who cannot easily undergo the remedies, which next to a good diet, cheifly consists in exercise; and this partly the cold wether, and som other infirmities of mine, barr'd me from, having not had my full walk to the top of the Hill these 4 monthes. This taedious agu that hath so long afflicted your beloved daughter workes in these parts after the same manner, and very few can get free from it. But the approaching spring, as it is a resurrection of plants which seemed to have no life in them, so it may give hope to them who have long strugled with their infirmities, that they may then chearfully hold up their heads again, and I am of your mind that the prayers of good men may much contribute towards it.

I am very glad to hear that your noble Lady is still in the breeding condition[3], so fast that you are likely to have a new supply of olive branches round about your tables. God bless her and you, and all that shall descend from you, that as there hath been an early, so there may be a latter blessing in store for you. My wife ioynes with me in all my prayers for you both, and having lately receaved a present from a freind (out of the East Indies) of quilted sattin to make a night gown, she desires your good Lady to accept of it. Her onely doubt is, that it is not worthy of her because she feares that the colour (which was intended to be a perfect purple) may possibly be faded by lying so long on ship bord, but the use and warmth of it cannot be impaired. I have sent it to Glanvile, who I hope will take such order with the carrier that it may com safe to you.

She is much troubled that, finding by a clause in your letter, that the water she sent you is not likely to bring the year about, she hath been so

---

[1] κόπους και πόνους. "Griefs and troubles."

[2] "Dr. Nurse." Thomas Nurse or Nourse (1599?–1667) matriculated at Lincoln College, Oxford, in 1615 aged 15, as "of co. Leicester, pleb." He was licensed to practise medicine in 1626 by the university. In 1640/1 he was admitted a licentiate of the College of Physicians, and was D.Med., 1641. "He was an eminent physician of his time, and was of great practice in the City of Westminster, especially after his Majesty's restoration" (Wood, *Fasti*, ed. Bliss, Vol. II). He died on June 9th, 1667, and was buried in the east cloisters of Westminster Abbey. (For this information I am indebted to Miss Margaret Toynbee, who cites Foster, J. L. Chester, *Westminster Abbey Registers*, W. R. Munk, *The Roll of the Royal College of Physicians of London*, 2nd edn., Vol. I (1878), pp. 230–1, and *Verney Memoirs*, Vol. IV, p. 62).

In his will (proved June 25th, 1667) Nurse bequeathed lands in Oadby, co. Leic. Further testimony to his Leicestershire connection is found in a MS. poem at Lamport in the handwriting of the Revd. Thomas Pestell, Vicar of Packington (D.N.B.), addressed "To Dr. T. N. Physitian 1629", where the poet concludes . . . "theise daymares vexe me so that like a child emptie and whipt, I goe moaning myself to thee my NURSE; whose brest unfolded, brings me both to food and rest. T.P."

Packington, where the author (Pestell) was Vicar till sequestered in 1646; Oadby, where Nurse had property; and Shangton, which Justinian Isham owned from 1637, are all in Leicestershire.

[3] "Your noble Lady is still in the breeding condition." By this time Sir Justinian had a son and two daughters by his second wife. A second son was born in August 1658.

exhausted by my Lady Duchess[4] that she hath but a very inconsiderable remnant left of it. And that which addes to her trouble is, that the maid whom these many yeares she hath trusted with the distilling of these waters, is lately dead within the walls of my own poor family[5]. But if my Lady wants and cannot with ease supply her self, she resolves to take the whole business into her hands, and at the time of the year send you the first fruites of it. And so with our humble service to you both, and our hearty prayers for you I remain,

Your most affectionat tru freind, and most humble servant,

BR: SARUM.

On St. David's Day.

LETTER CI

[March 2nd.]

Sir, Wer it not, that nothing could discourage me from making my self extremely contented in writing to you, and receaving letters from you, I should be very much disheart'ned to find that some of mine never came to your hands at all, and some that do come though they are mine, yet they are a kind of reall anagram, and ar so transposed, that what is meant to you is carried into Worcestershire, and that which was directed thether is come to you. But the truth is, though there be an error, yet there is no danger in the mistake. Unless it be you two, there is not a third that I communicat frequently withall; and my letters to you both are commonly of the same argument, for ether we conferr of bookes, or somthing of kindness intervenes, and that doth *implere utramque paginam.* That of yours which concerned the recovery both of your health and of your Ladies', I not onely receaved, but return'd a letter of joy for it. And that which concern'd som sermons that wer com forth, you had not onely my letter, but my judgement of them. Those of that excellent man Bishop Andrews[1], I had not then seen, but deliver'd my sense of them, that ether they wer suppositious, or so imperfect, that when he was alive he did not own them, not because they wer not his, but because, they wer ether embrios, and imperfect conceptions (for no man calls an embrio his child) or there wer such unskillfull midwives (I mean the transcribers) who with the legerdemain of brachygraphy have made what shapes they pleas'd, and what might otherwise have com forth handsomly into the world, they have rend'red with infinite disadvantages, besides the σφάλματα of the printer, which ar more then the new admired romancer[2] hath in his.

And that I may say somthing of him, I am so farr from being taken with him, that though I do not look upon him in his naturall parts as an inconsiderable person, yet certainly he weighes so light in the balance of judgement, that every feather of a new interest will sway him. It fell

---

4 "My Lady Duchess". I suggest that this may well be the Duchess of Richmond (see Letter XXIV and Note).

5 "The maid lately dead." This may well have been Elinor Duppa, a poor relation, who acted as Gentlewoman to Mrs. Duppa. Her will was made on June 7th, 1657, and proved on February 20th, 1658, so that it would exactly fit. In this will Elinor Duppa left money to "Barlavington Sussex where I was born." She mentions her "honoured friend Bryan Bishop of Sarum and honoured mistris, Mistris Duppa." She is described as "of Richmond". The Revd. Henry Duppa, —Rector of Barlavington (1586-1616), was her father (Will,—Chichester Probate Records, M. Dean, 26; Venn).

1 "Bishop Andrews." See Letter XCIX, Note 1.

2 "The new admired romancer." Possibly Harrington is meant. See Letter XCVIII, Note 4.

out very unluckily that this device of his was modell'd when a Republick was in vogue; but the scaene is since like to be alter'd, and now he must repair to Contzen and Machiavell[3] again, and see whether he cannot find somthing for a new romance that may fitt a Monarchy.

Since there was an error committed in bringing you the letter that was directed to Dr. Hammond[4], I am the less sorry for it, because I desire to know how farr you concurr with me, in the counsell that I gave him. But probably I have said too much allready, and therefore to engage you in no farther trouble, I shall content my self in saying no more then that I am,

Your very faithfull freind, and humble servant

BR: S.

Richm: March 2.

LETTER CII

[JUNE 30th.]

Sir, Your ar to expect of your young children that which is observed of new-made instruments, which will be hardly avoided, that they must not often be out of tune. Especially those maladies which you mention ar generally so incident to infants of that age, that there ar few about us escape it. The way of cure of the convulsions is (as I hear) ether by making fontanells or by giving som easy vomits; but I persuade my self that your parts ar not so destitute of learned phisitians but that you have store of counsell, and yet som times som good woman my neighbor, out of the treasure of her experience may tell me more then a whole junto of them. But the advice which I am to give you is of an other nature, and that is, that God having given you an heyre unto your family, you should not sett your heart too much upon it, but look upon it as such a blessing, which must chearfully be parted with when the doner shall call for it, and *quicquid amas cupias non placuisse nimis*[1].

I am very much pleas'd to find by you that after so long durance[2]

[3] "Contzen and Machiavell." Adam Contzen (1573–1635) was a German Jesuit. His chief work was *Politicorum libri decem, in quibus de perfectae reipubl. forma, virtutibus, et vitiis, institutione ciuium, legibus, magistratu ecclesiastico, civili, potentia reipublicae; itemque seditione et bello, ad usum vitamque communem accomodate tractatur*, published in Cologne in 1621. The B.M. copy has the arms of James I stamped on the binding. Contzen had considerable contemporary fame, as he was quoted by Bishop Williams at his trial, against Kilvert. (See App. A under Margaret Kilvert). Machiavell, is, of course, Niccolo Machiavelli, the Florentine historian and philosopher, author of *The Prince*. (For Contzen, see *Allgemeine Deutsche Biographie*; for Machiavelli, Hallam, *Literature of Europe* (1854), Vol. I, pp. 401–8, Encycl. Brit., etc.)

[4] "Dr. Hammond." After his release from detention in Bedfordshire, Hammond went to live with Sir J. Packington of Westwood, Worcestershire (*Walker Revised*), where he died just before the Restoration, on April 25th, 1660. For Hammond see Letter XIX, Note 5.

[1] *Quicquid amas*, etc. "However much you love, don't try to indulge it too much." Martial, *Epigr.* VI, 29, 8.

[2] "Long durance." Towards the end of April, 1658, Sir Justinian was arrested, and taken to Northampton by orders of Major-General Butler. In answer to a letter from Sir Francis Gardiner dated March 29th, 1658, proposing a marriage between his son and Elizabeth Isham, Sir Justinian drafted a reply that he was "at present some few hours since your son's coming to mee ordered amongst divers other gent: of these parts to be secured at Northampton towne under a guard of soldiers, not yet knowing anything of the business or occasion" (I.C. 459). For the reasons for this arrest, see the Introduction to this year. On May 13th Theodore Greene, the lawyer, wrote "I heare that most of the West Country gent. who were imprisoned are dismissed, and sent home to their houses. . . that now the plott is discovered, and the guilty shall receive their doome, the innocent shalbe no further troubled" (I.C. 459a). However this was over-optimistic, and Sir Justinian was still at Northampton at the end of June.

(which nether you nor any of your freinds can give a reason for) you ar now in som hopes of som near approach of your freedom. And it is happier to be so in an ordinary course, then to be obliged to freinds for their mediation in it. My neighbor in the Park[3] purposely made a journey about it, and though she return'd *re infecta*, yet she made this discovery that the man *a secretis* hath so much a pike against you that there is no favor to be expected for at his hands, but what your unquaestionable innocence may plead for you. Why he stands thus averse, you may better guess then I who know nothing of him at all. But what ever it is, your warynese must be the greater, and your prayer must be the more frequent that God may deliver you from every malitious, and cruell man.

Sir, you ar seldom out of my thoughts, and non shall pray more earnestly and long more passionately for the happyness of you and yours, then

Your most faithfull freind, and humble servant

B.S.

June 30.

Letter CIII

[July 26th.]

Sir, It is som kind of liberty not to be confined, though absolutely free I cannot call you, as long as you are driven to draw your chain after you. For the clause of being ready upon call, signifies no less. But the hope is that time and patience may work out that too, *et dabit Deus his quoque finem*[1].

That your sweet child is in so good a way of recovery, I do both bless God with you, and for you, and I doubt not but that He who gave you this blessing, will contrive it to you that you may leave one behind you to inherit not onely your fortunes but your virtues, which your example, and your care of him in his education may so happily convey to him.

And that I may give you som account of my self since you ar pleas'd to own me as yours, I am to accquaint you that being now ent'red upon David's grand criticall year, I begin daily to find many effects and symptomes of it, but more especially of late in frequent *deliquiums* and failings of my spirits, which many times bring me so low, that I cannot for a time determine of my self, whether I am among the living or the dead. And these I look upon, as God's gentle warnings, that I may not be surpris'd when

---

[3] "My neighbor in the Park" etc. This phrase elsewhere, as we have seen, refers to the Carliles of Petersham. The Carliles, much as they were associated with both King Charles I and Queen Henrietta Maria, were not ejected from their position at Petersham during the Commonwealth, where their lodgers were all persons obnoxious, for one reason or another, to the Government.
Lady Dysart—surely the "good lady in my neighbourhood" whom, in 1655, Duppa had suggested as a possible intercessor for Justinian when he was incarcerated—is a more likely person to "have made a journey" to Cromwell's Court, with a chance of success (Letter LXVIIA and Note 1).

But Mrs. Carlile was connected with John Thurloe, the Secretary of State, who is obviously the man *a secretis* mentioned by Duppa, who had a "pike" against Sir Justinian. For Anne Litcott, Thurloe's second wife, was a first cousin once removed of Mrs. Carlile, through the Overburys (see Letter XV, Note 3).

Thurloe had at one time been in the service of Oliver St. John, the Cromwellian jurist, who, soon after 1650, built Thorpe Hall near Peterborough. Thurloe's opinion had possibly been derived from St. John. *Re infecta* = nothing accomplished. *Servus a secretis* = secretary.

[1] *Et dabit Deus his quoque finem.* "From these troubles also will God one day give you peace." Virgil, *Aeneid*, I, 199. Sir Justinian has evidently been released, but must be "ready upon call".

the last minute comes, and by often dying make death the less terrible to me. But that I may not be wanting to my self, I am advised to use cordialls, and particularly alkermes[2], which is yet a stranger to me. But I must now venture on. But what ever becomes of me whether living or dying I shall not forgett ether you, or yours, who am very faithfully

Your tru freind, and servant

BR: SARUM.

Richm: July 26.

[ENDORSED REPLY OF SIR JUSTINIAN]

My Lord, I wish I had the same account of your Lordship's sickness and recovery together as I praise God I can now give of mine, some of my family with my selfe falling ill together of a violent flux with some vomittings, were doubtfull whether it might proceede from diet or otherwise. But at length it falling upon others in the towne's neighborhood, none of my little children escaping it, we only tooke some cordialls at the begining not daring any way to stop what Nature (though very violently) drave forth; which after 3 or 4 dayes abated though not quite gon in some till 9 or 10. Of my wife's condition[3] I was most sollicitous, having now her midwife with her as shortly expecting her delivery, but although she hath had many gripings at times in her stomach and bowells, after the manner of us who were ill, yet I praise God no violent flux, which in all probabilitie must have bin very dangerous to her.

My son and dau[ghter] Carew hasted from hence the sooner to Beddington, where they now are, and will some of them I beleive waite on your Lordship ere long. I wish I could with as much conveniency performe it my selfe, especially at this tyme of your Lordship's indisposition, and truly the rather that I might still learn of your Lordship, being able to contribute nothing to you but to offer you my praiers, which also have received life from my converse with your Lordship, and therefore most justly to be powred forth for the preservation of your life.

LETTER CIV

[AUGUST 16th.]

Sir, This day shall be signed by me *meliore lapillo*, for in the morning I was chear'd up by my fellow servant Osbolston, who lately return'd from you as an ey wittness of the voice of joy and health restored to your family. And that this joy might be the fuller, I receaved your second letter on the same day, of the happy delivery of your excellent good Lady[1]. Your feares made you sollicitous what might be the event of it, but God's goodness to you both hath scatter'd those feares, and hath now given you a double evidence of his favor to you, and stored you with such olive branches, that if one should fail, you may have the comfort to say, *ramus non deficit alter.*[1a] But the more of these blessings you receave, the more I am persuaded your heart is inflamed to a greater degree of thankfullness, to that good God of yours, who though He hath embitter'd som

---

[2] "Alkermes." "In Medicine, a term borrowed from the Arabs, denoted a celebrated remedy . . . whereof the Kermes berries are the basis". Samuel Johnson's *Dictionary* (1755).

[3] "My wife's condition." Vere Isham was expecting the birth of her second son. See Letter CIV, Note 1.

[1] "The happy delivery." Justinian II was born on August 11th, 1658.

[1a] *Romus non deficit alter.* "Another branch takes its place". Virgil, *Aeneid*, VI, 137, 143.

of your dayes, yet when the account is made, you will find at the foot of it, *vicit candida turba nigriorem*[2].

And as for my own particular (who onely valew my self because I see you ar concern'd in me) I am for the present qualified to make up one of the quire, the *chorus laudantium*; for the distempers, and the frequent *deliquia* which I suffered under, ar by God's infinite blessing to me so well past over, that I begin to lay my cordialls aside, and to look onely to that hand from Heaven, which hath so often recover'd me, and by these essaies hath taught me how easy a thing it will be to dy, when He shall call me to it.

Your son and daughter at Bedington have don me the favor to send to me, but the distance of ten miles hath not suffer'd me yet to wait upon them. Besides I beleive that their tenant[3], who had so great a hand in putting all things out of order, hath not taken much care of leaving Bedington as he should do, which will require som time before it be don. Could I see you once again in these parts, I should the more chearfully say my *Nunc dimittis*: but the times are not yet seasonable for it, and therefore I shall moderate my longings. My poor wife is a very passionat servant to you both, and can want no comforts, as long as she sees you have store of them, which that God may daily multiply to you is the ioint prayer of us both, and the daily task of

Your most faithfull and affectionat freind to serve you
BR: SAR:

Richm: Aug. 16.

LETTER CV

[NOVEMBER 3rd.]

Sir, Though Lucian be very bitter upon Pindar for saying Ἄριστον μὲν ὕδωρ[1], yet I shall give more credit to your experience then to his witt, not that I beleive that Pindar commended it for a diet, but for those other necessary uses that we have of that element; for possibly he himself rather made use of such Greek wines which wer as parable to him as water, or else his freind Horace would have given him a more dilute commendation. But the greatest honor to water as a diet is given in these later times, where in the midst of so much debauchery, truth hath so far praevail'd, that severall phisitians of eminency have praescribed it for the praeserving of health, and for the curing of severall diseases. And to name no more then Vander Heidin[2], the old phisitian of Gaunt, who, among the *Parabiles Medicinae* which he recommends as of soveraigne use both for rich and poor, omitts not water, which he highly magnifies ether inwardly taken, or outwardly applied. I onely fear that as to my own particular, seventy yeares of age may keep me from being his disciple. But your condition is different, both in respect of yeares and temper, and till you find som notable inconvenience in it, I can be none of those that shall dissuade you from it.

---

[2] *Vicit candida turba nigriorem.* "The white lettered days have prevailed over the black ones." Martial, *Epigr.*, XII, 34, 7. An allusion to the Roman system of marking in their calendar the happy anniversaries in white.

[3] "Their tenant." This was Robert Rich, 2nd Earl of Warwick, whose grandson married Cromwell's daughter Elizabeth. He died on May 18th, 1658. See Letter LXXI, Note 3.

[1] "Ἄριστον μὲν ὕδωρ" "Water is best." Pindar, *Olymp.*, I, 1.

[2] "Vander Heidin." John Van der Heyden, of Belgian origin, was a doctor in Cologne in 1497 (Chevalier, *Répertoire des Sources Historiques du Moyen Age* (1905)).

The catalogue which you mention of Dr. Dee's[3] books was sent me printed at the same time that I receaved his *Life* written by Merick Casaubon, and, as I conceave will be printed with it. Unless you have som other corrispondent to furnish you from hence with bookes of this nature, I have great reason to serve you in it.

I am troubled to hear that the sickness of your family continues; but it is an epidemick evill, and nether good aire nor diet is a sufficient fence against it. We wer wont to magnify the aire of Richmond, and the Parke was look'd upon as one of Nature's peculiars, exempt from sickness. But in this fatall autumne[4], no place can hold out against that strange ague, which hath not yet gott a denomination, but beginns doubtfully, and the phisitians ar posed how to call it, but commonly ends in a quartan, that formerly call'd *opprobrium medicorum*, but never so convincingly as at this time, for it is not simply a quartan, but doubles and trebles upon the patient. And as it is a strange disease, so the best remedy (as they say) against it, is a powder that is brought from China, which for the more credit of it is call'd the Jesuits' Powder, who first brought it from thence, and ar now as famous for the good use of this powder, as they were formerly infamous for a powder of an other nature. Among others, Dr. Sheldon[5] (a freind whom I could ill have lost in these times), being surprised at the Park (where he soiourn'd for a time) by this destroying ague,

---

[3] "Dr. Dee's books". Dr. John Dee (1527–1608), mathematician and astrologer, was a great traveller, and intimate of Royal persons. Queen Mary, Queen Elizabeth, Maximilian II, Rudolph II were at various times visited by him, and shown his magic glass, etc. He vainly asked James I to clear him from the imputation of being a magician (D.N.B.). At Lamport there is an important unpublished letter addressed to "Mr. Aldrich" (see Letter I, Note 2) from Arthur Dee, his son, dated December 15th, 1649 from Norwich, giving details of John's life, which differs in some respects from the published sources. Arthur Dee says that he was born on June 12th, 1522, in London, in St. Dunstan's in the East. "He was a great traveller into most partes of Christendom, and well known to forrain Princes and most learned men in Europe, with whom he had correspondency. He was much favoured by Queen Elizabeth to whom he read the Latine and Greek." He died, according to this letter, at Mortlake in 1609. Sir William Boswell (see Letter III, Notes 1 and 11) was possessed of most of his written books, "whom", says Arthur Dee, "I have sollicited for many yeares, but to no purpose" (I.C. 272). Meric Casaubon (see Letter LXX, Note 4) wrote *A True and Faithful Relation of what passed for many years between Dr. J. Dee . . . and some spirits.* This work (a copy of which is at Lamport) was not published till 1659, but the Bishop had no doubt seen the MS. as on January 5th, 1659, he reverts to the subject, as also to Sir Justinian's water diet. He here speaks of Casaubon's book as something not yet printed. Casaubon was an early critic of the Royal Society. (See R. H. Syfret, "Some Early Critics of the Royal Society", *Notes and Records of the Royal Society of London*, Vol. 8, No. 1 (October 1950)).

[4] "This fatall autumne" had already claimed Cromwell and his daughter as victims.

[5] "Dr. Sheldon." Gilbert Sheldon (1598–1677), Fellow (1622) and Warden of All Souls College, Oxford (1626–1648), was with Charles I in the Isle of Wight. He was imprisoned in 1648, and lived mainly in the Midlands after his release at the end of the year till the Restoration. In the autumn of 1658 he had evidently been lodging with the Carliles at Petersham Lodge ("the Park"). He was a frequent correspondent of Duppa, Hammond and Morley, during the Interregnum. At the Restoration he was made Bishop of London, where his influence in Church affairs was paramount. He was thus the natural successor to Juxon in the See of Canterbury on the latter's death in 1663. Indeed, owing to the age and infirmity of Juxon, he had virtually been Primate since the Restoration. This testimony of Duppa's to the value which he placed on Sheldon is important, since Sheldon can fairly be described as the architect of the Restoration settlement of the Church. (D.N.B., *Walker Revised*, Bosher, *The Making of the Restoration Settlement* (1951)). The "Jesuits' powder" is an "old name for powdered Peruvian bark" (quinine) introduced into Europe by the Society of Jesus (O.E.D.).

was rescued by this powder, and for the present hath 'scaped his fitts, and whether this recovery be perfect som few dayes more will shew. *Mens sana in corpore sano*[6], is the great blessing of this life, and that it may never be wanting to you or yours is the prayer of

Your most affectionat faithfull freind,
BR: SAR:

Richm: Novem: 3.

LETTER CVI

[NOVEMBER 28th.]

Sir, My letters come slowly, for I am frozen up with a double winter, the one from without me, and the other from within. Against the former I make use of good fires as long as I am able, but against the latter there is no fence but from Heaven, and I must fetch my fire from thence. And that is my business, even to direct all my thoughts thether, when there is any damp upon me. We ar here near to the forge where all irons ar heated, and what thunder bolts may be produced from thence we know not. Only this I know from our old freind Horace, *Justum, et tenacem propositi virum, non civium ardor prava jubentium mente quatit solida*[1].

I confess I have many sad thoughts when I look about me, but when I turn my prospect upward, I am at quiet. And yet I cannot chuse but be sollicitous for our freinds at Bedington, which makes me very busy in enquiring after them, though I am not in a condition to visit them. There is a cloud, I hear, hangs over them, but there is hope it may be dissipated before any danger com from it. And that the voice of health and peace may continue in your dwellinge is the hearty prayer of

Your most affectionat tru freind,
BR: SAR:

Richm: Nov: 28.

LETTER CVII

[DECEMBER 7th.]

Sir, I gett as close to the fire side as I can, that I may find warmth enough to write to you; not that I can want it in my affection, for no frost can benumm me there, but that the wether at this time is really so bitter to me, that *neque pes neque manus libenter officium suum faciunt*[1]. But nothing must keep me from the pleasure I have in writing to you, for I beleive I should venture to do it though I wer under the Pole.

And now I must acknowledge that had not your letter come to me at this season, when it finds me suffering under a double winter, the one without me, and the other within me, you have so pow'rfully argued for your water diet, that I should have been more easily convinc'd by you, then by Sir H.

[6] *Mens sana*, etc. "A sound mind in a sound body." Juvenal, *Sat*. x, 356.

[1] *Justum, et tenacem propositi virum*, etc. "The passion of citizens demanding a depraved way of life does not shake a man who is fair and of firm purpose." Horace, *Odes*, III, 3, 1-2, 4.

The handwriting of this letter is shaky, and might belong to 1659. The death of Cromwell in September left the future government uncertain. London, "the forge where all irons ar heated", was both prize and key.

[1] *Neque pes neque manus*, etc. "Neither hand nor foot does its duty willingly". The quotation is from Terence, *Eunuchus*, IV, 5, 3, but Terence applies it to a drunken man, unable to stand up, *neque pes neque mens satis suum officium facit*.

Blunt's example[2], who putts the same liquor into his bookes, as he doth into his belly. But I am heartily glad, that water agrees so well with you, onely I could wish, that you would not so pertinaciously adhaere to it, as not to admitt of a warmer diet, when your stomack may require it. I would say more to you, wer I not barr'd by a trembling hand, particularly I should tell you what I thought of the legend of Dr Dee[3], but I must deferr it till I can find a milder season.

It can be no newes to you that we ar to have one Parlament more[4]; but should I say that there would be first an Act of Amnesty past, which should make all persons of all parties aequally eligible, I should say more then I beleive, though not more then is spoken. But I can hardly hold my pen any longer, and therefore, without adding more, give me leave in all wethers heartily to subscribe my self

Your most affectionat tru freind, and servant,

BR: SAR:

Richm: December 7.

---

[2] "Sir H. Blunt's example." Sir Henry Blount (1602–82), of Trinity College, Oxford and Gray's Inn, was a traveller. He wrote *A Voyage into the Levant* (1636), described by Lowndes as "of little value or authority." He was a Gentleman Pensioner to King Charles I. He was knighted in 1640, and sided with the Royalists in the war. He attended the King at the battle of Edgehill, where he was in charge of the young Princes, and afterwards at Oxford. But he does not seem to have been out of favour with the Republican Governments. He was one of the Commissioners for reforming the criminal law, and he was a member of the Court appointed by Cromwell to try Don Pantaleone Sa. Dr. Turner was also a member of this Court, and Duppa may have derived information from him. He rebuilt Tyttenhanger House, Herts, to which he succeeded on the death of his brother Thomas in 1654, and he spent his latter years there. Blount was considered a sceptic, and his better known son, Charles Blount (1654–93), was a Deist, who committed suicide because he was forbidden to marry his deceased wife's sister. (D.N.B., F. Inderwick, *The Interregnum* (1891), H. Avary Tipping, *English Homes and Gardens*, Stuart Period, Vol. IV, (1929)).

[3] "Dr. Dee." See Letter CV, Note 3.

[4] "One Parlament more." "His [Cromwell's] death was a momentous event . . The Royalists took heart, for they had regarded the Protector as their chief oppressor; but they were far too weak to move, so long as their enemies, who still retained exclusive possession of political power, remained united." (Ranke, Vol. III, Preface to Book XIII). Richard Cromwell, the new Protector, and his adherents insisted on the calling of Parliament and "took every precaution to secure the return of desirable candidates." But, as Duppa has noticed, "a free Parliament" was once more a political possibility.

1659

This was a critical year in national history. Oliver's title of Protector had descended quietly to his son Richard, and Royalist hopes of an immediate revolution had receded. But Richard Cromwell, though he had good advice, proved unable to rule, because he was not strong enough to support his friends. He bowed to Fleetwood, and the Council of Officers, who might have allowed him to continue with the empty title of Protector, had not the inferior officers and the rest of the Army objected. Accordingly, the Rump was re-established in power. These quarrels encouraged the Royalists, and a rising was planned for July on a more ambitious scale than the Hewett–Slingsby affair of 1658. The rising failed, because the plans became known to the Council of State. Only in Cheshire and Lancashire was any success achieved, but the Parliament sent Lambert and an army, which easily crushed the rebellion in August.

Simultaneously, another project miscarried. Sir Edward Hyde now Chancellor, made a fresh effort to goad the surviving Bishops in England to perpetuate their order. The Bishops agreed to act, but they undoubtedly hoped that the success of the rebellion would make action unnecessary. When the rising failed, they were more nervous than ever. Bishop Duppa relates how his house at Richmond was searched, and his papers ransacked (Letter CXII). He was the man most trusted by Hyde and the King, most active (despite his years) of his order, and not unnaturally an object of suspicion to the Government. The searching of his house seems to have put a stop to the Bishops' endeavours, and Duppa himself wrote on November 16th to Sheldon to complain that Hyde did not, from his distance from the scene, understand the difficulties of their position. "When I met with the expression of his being amazed that there is so little care taken of our great business [i.e. consecrating new Bishops], I must impute it to the distance of place which is between us, . . . for otherwise if all difficulties and circumstances were made known to him, he might pity some of us, but there would be no place for wonder left." (Tanner MSS. 51, f.159v).

It was unfortunate for Duppa that the soldiers found a letter from Lord Bruce about the recognition of souls after the Resurrection, matter for serious alarm, since Lord Bruce was one of the conspirators who failed to act in the July rebellion (Letter CXII).

Sir Justinian, for once, was not troubled, but he must have been apprehensive. On April 27th 1659, Sir Charles Compton of Grendon, brother of the 3rd Earl of Northampton, who like all his family had fought for the King, wrote to Sir Justinian an enigmatic letter apparently about some property near "Wooleston" [Wollaston] which he intended to purchase. However, in view of the extreme secrecy enjoined, and the mention of "my cousin Elizabeth Mordaunt," who was the wife of the principal conspirator, it is possible that the letter was "cover" for some action relating to the rising. In any case "the enclosed paper", which Sir Charles enjoined should not "be perused by any other," no longer exists, so it is impossible to say. Charles Compton himself was engaged in the conspiracy, and (with Lord Bruce) was blamed by Mordaunt for the failure of the "easterne and northern engagements" (I.C. 488; *Mordaunt Letter-Book*, No. 93, p.67; for Sir Charles Compton see William Bingham Compton, 6th Marquess of Northampton, *The History of the Comptons* (printed for private circulation, 1930), p.118). Had Lamport been searched, the letter might well have "exercised the inquisitors."

On the back of the letter, Sir Justinian has written, after his manner, a draft letter, not to Compton, but evidently to Dr. Thorndike regarding his book *An Epilogue to the Tragedy of the Church of England* which was troubling Anglicans at that time, and which is mentioned by Duppa in Letter CVIII. Compton's letter is worth quoting:—

> "Sir, I have here enclosed sent you the ptlr [particular] you desired. When you please to goe, if you doe make use of my name to my Couzen Elizabeth Mordaunt whoe lives there, you may receive what sattisfaction in the thing you can desire, and if you agree I am assured that the title willbe made good. It is desired you will not acquaint any one whose it is, nor take notice so much as to any of the servants there that you are upon any treaty for it; as times goe, some prejudice may be if it should be divulged; the reasons I suppose I did partly acquaint you of. This is all I shall at present trouble you with, but doe desire if in this or any other waies I may be serviceable to you, that you will let me receive your commands and they shall be very punctually observed by, Sir,
>
> your friend and servant,
>
> CHA: COMPTON
>
> I desire you will not let this enclosed paper be perused by any other, if in case you doe not proceede, but be returned after you have done with it to me; the place is within a mile of Wooleston towne. April 27, 1659."

Domestically, the year was a quiet one. Lady Isham had another son, christened John after his grandfather. This boy, after unsuccessfully trying for Parliament, became Under-Secretary of State under Lord Nottingham, and lived to the advanced age of eighty-seven.

Even in this confused year, the Bishop and Sir Justinian had time to discuss books, and the passages relating to Dr. John Dee (Letter CVIII) are specially interesting.

LETTER CVIII

[JANUARY 5th.]

Sir, the last week was taken up in performing the duties belonging to the time, which we have fully observed here without any interruption, though there was such severity used in the City in prohibiting the worship of God on those dayes, that som begin to doubt whether they shall be suffer'd to be Christians any longer or no. But the disciples of Hobbs are secure, who if they ar putt to it, ar taught to gratify authority by denying Christ with their tongue, as long as they retain him in their heart, for which you must take their own words, for no outward act of theirs can witness for them.

The more I consider the legend you mention, the more I am in a maze, whether this unhappy man[1] were voluntaryly deluded, or whether the cunning of Kelly[2] had inevitably ensnared him. For what can we think of the carriage of that business, wherein all the credit of it lies upon the skryer (as he calls him), Dee himself nether seeing nor hearing any thing but by his eyes and eares, unless in som very few instances, which might very well be delusions too. And whether this will satisfy the new Sadduces of the time who beleive nothing of spirits, I cannot tel, unless Kellie's own spirit be sufficient to resolve their beleife into. There is onely one thing that may possibly clear the business, and that is som ingenuous testimony from Arthur Dee[3] (if he be yet alive), of what he saw and heard after he was initiated into the mystery of being a skrier. But I find by his letter (which I have sent you back) that being so vaen as to beleive his father's universal medicine, and those admirable effects of his chrysopoea, as the multiplying of one dram to so many thousand thousands (both he and his father still remaining miserably poor), his word is not likely to go for much. For his being a good mathematician you can bear him wittness, but for the rest, it might be said of him that would gather votes for him, *Circuit, & fatuos non invenit.*[4]

The last elaborate peice of Mr. Thorndike's[5] was sent me by him self, and as yet lies by me, but to give any character of it, I dare not yet adven-

---

[1] "This unhappy man." This is Dr. Dee for whom see Letter CV, Note 3.

[2] "Kelly." Edward Kelley, alias Talbot (1555–95), twenty-eight years younger than Dee, was a rather sinister occultist who, in 1582, became associated with Dee in the raising of spirits, admitting, later, that he was sent to Dee at Mortlake to trap him into an admission that he had dealings with the devil. Kelley was paid £50 per annum for his services as "skryer" or seer to Dee. Kelley accompanied Dee on his journeys to Bohemia, Poland, and Germany, but they quarrelled and parted in 1589. (D.N.B.).

[3] "Arthur Dee." For Arthur Dee see Letter III, Note 11 and Letter CV, Note 3. He was with his father and Kelley in their travels. He returned to London in 1592, and was, though unqualified, recommended to the Tsar by James I as a physician. He was a friend of (Sir) Thomas Browne, and died at Norwich (D.N.B.). Sir Justinian had evidently sent the letter of Arthur Dee to the Bishop to peruse (see Letters cited above). Chrysopoea = gold-making.

[4] *Circuit, & fatuos non invenit.* "He canvassed and did not find the fools (to trust him)." Juvenal, *Sat.* IX, 8.

[5] Herbert Thorndike's *An Epilogue to the Tragedy of the Church of England* in three books was published in 1659. The book maintained that the way to raise the Church from ruins was drastically to reconstruct its constitution along more primitive and Catholic lines. It caused much criticism. Sir Edward Hyde wrote (May 1659) "I pray tell me, what melancholy hath possessed poor Mr. Thorndike? His name and reputation in learning is too much made use of, to the discountenance of the poor Church" (Bosher, *The Making of the Restoration Settlement*, p. 93). In the Isham Correspondence are several letters that passed between Sir Justinian and Dr. Thorndike after this book came out, in which Sir Justinian expressed doubt on some passages in it. There is a detailed analysis of the book in T. A. Lacey' *Thorndike*, pp. 83–109.

ture. Without all quaestion he hath excellent notions, but they ar *veritates in puteo*, and (as you very well say) he must digge deep that findes them. He that reades must not onely read but study him, which I shall do before I venture to give a censure of him.

I am really joyfull to hear from you that your new diet agrees so well with you, and would my freinds about me suffer me, I have a great mind to follow you. Many yeares of happyness may you and your good Lady have together, for all my New Year gifts are prayers, and none can be more liberall of them for you then,

Sir, Your most affectionat freind, and humble servant

BR: SARUM

Richm: Jan: 5.

LETTER CIX

[FEBRUARY 1st.]

Sir, I am not in any way displeas'd, that I do not find your name in the catalogue of elections[1], which is som advantage in the condition of a delinquent (for so we have the luck to be call'd *qui ipsa rerum nomina perdimus*). Wer there any good to be don, I should wish such a publick sowl as yours among them; but since there is no such thing to be hoped for, and the very bottom of Pandora's box hath no such reserve left, the best satisfaction that an honest soul can have is *stare gratis cum silentio*[2]. And in that quiet of mind, I am willing to leave you.

But in this coniuncture of time, when there is a fermentation (such as the phisitian you speak of is not concern'd in his art to speak of) of hott and contrary humors, so passionately different one from the other, and of such divided interests, the polititians of this time ar at such a loss that they cannot guess what the result will be, but watch carefully where the advantage may ly, that they may steer them selves accordingly. Onely the innocent, and pious Christian is at rest, who being cast into a bark, where being nether assured of the pilot's skill, nor the marriners' obedience, committs himself to the bottom of the ship, and waites with patience how Providence will dispose of him.

But [this is] but a πάρεργον, and was never intended to be the argument of this letter. Our converse is of another nature, such as was in Tullye's time, *Si vales bene est*: *ego quidem valeo*[3]. The health of the publick (though we cannot but be concern'd in it) is out of the sphaere we move in; and therefore to revert to your ψυχροποσία, your drinking of cold water, I am very well pleas'd to find so frequent continuation of the good effects of it in your severall letters, as being fitted to allay the boiling and fermenting of bloud, which you being of a sanguine constitution, might otherwise be liable to. But yet still, though it may be useful in one particular, yet it may praeiudice you in som other, and therefore in the *reglement* of health, there must be a comprehensive care, and all particulars must be look'd to. And who am I who should tell you this, when your own experience must be

---

[1] "Elections." Richard Cromwell opened Parliament with traditional state on January 27th, 1659. Papists and Royalists were, of course, excluded from the list of candidates (Ranke, Vol. III, p. 226). *Qui ipsa rerum nomina perdimus*. "We who forget the very names of things."

[2] *Stare gratis cum silentio*. "To rest without reward with silence." This is an echo of Martial, x, 3, 12, which, freely translated, would read: "Why should I toil for an evil reputation, when it costs me nothing not to be notorious?"

[3] *Si vales bene est*: *ego quidem valeo*. "All is well if you are well; I certainly am (if all is well with you)." The valedictory ending to Cicero's Letters. See Letter XXI, Note 1.

the guide to lead you? But there it must be such an experience, as must have length of time to ripen it. And wherefore all this? Not that I am against the diet, but that I would have you wary in the continuing of it, least you should be surpris'd by custom and not know how to leave it, when possibly it may concern you. But this impertinence of mine may be the easier pardon'd when you consider it comes from him who prayes heartily for you, and yours, and faithfully continues,

Sir, Your most affectionat freind, and humble servant,

BR: SARUM.

Richm: Febr: 1.

LETTER CX

[JUNE 7th.]

Sir, To recompense the stay which my last letter made (though how occasion'd I know not), I make the more hast with this. Not that any new occurrents here require it[1] (for we ar still in the same eddy of confusion, whirl'd about as in a great fall of waters, and which way they may settle their course we know not), but upon the old score of pleasing my self with writing to you as often as I can have any hint to do it. You could hardly have express'd more love to me (though you may find many wayes to do it) then to reioice with me for the recovery of *animae dimidium meae*.[1a] And yet the joy is not full, for there ar still some relicks and dregs of the distemper hanging about her, which (though much against my will) brings me to London to have the best advice I can procure for her. But when all this is don, how uncertain is the tenure we hold by? Our recoveries ar but as short repreives, and the *statutum est* must at last be executed, and nether youth, nor honor, nor riches can prevent it, of which we have a sad instance in the death of my Lord Mansfeld[2], who died at

---

[1] Richard Cromwell, failing to stand up to Fleetwood and the Council of Officers, was forced to dissolve Parliament on April 22nd. After that "nobody resorted to him, nor was the name of the Protector afterwards heard of but in derision" (Clarendon, Book XVI, § 11). On May 6th, in the room of the vacuum which they had created, the Army leaders issued a declaration to restore the Long Parliament. The excluded members tried to take their seats, but were prevented, so the Rump ruled as a restored Republic. But the problem of the Army and its influence remained.

[1a] *Animae dimidium meae*. "The half of my soul." Horace, *Odes* III, 8.

[2] "Death of my Lord Mansfeld." In Otterden Church, Kent, is a monument to Sir Justinian Lewyn, uncle to Sir Justinian Isham, who died in 1620, aged 34. The monument shows his wife, Elizabeth Capel, sister of Arthur, 1st Lord Capel of Hadham (1610?–1649) and a single sorrowing daughter. This daughter married, according to the notes of Sir Justinian Isham, 5th Bart (I.L. 3997), Richard Rogers of Brianston [sic], Dorset. King Charles I stayed at the house of Mr Rogers at "Brianstone" for four nights on October 10th, 1644. (*Iter Carolinum*). Their daughter, Elizabeth, "your young kinswoman" here mentioned, married first Charles Cavendish, Viscount Mansfield, eldest son of the Royalist general, the Marquess of Newcastle. He died, as noted here, in 1659. The actual date was May 31st. Bishop Duppa was right, she did not long remain a widow, but married about the middle of 1660, Charles Stuart, Earl of Lichfield, who on August 10th, 1660, succeeded as 6th Duke of Lennox and 3rd Duke of Richmond. (*Archaeologia Cantiana*, Vol. XI, pp. 253–5, and Clarendon, Book VII, § 95). She died in childbed on April 21st, 1661. *The Complete Peerage* gives the mother of Elizabeth, Duchess of Richmond, as Ann, daughter of Sir Thomas Cheeke, but it appears that this is a mistake, and that her mother was the daughter of Sir Justinian Lewyn, and she was thus a first cousin once removed of Sir Justinian Isham. Otterden Place in Kent, which the Lewyns acquired in Queen Elizabeth's reign, passed to her two husbands, and after her death was sold to Sir George Curtis. (Harris, *History of Kent*, Vol. I (1719)). See Letter XLVII, Note 1 for the connection of the Lewyns and the Capels. See also Table C.
(T. E. Watson, *History and Pedigree of the Family of Lewin*, p. 7, agrees with the account given here of the descent of Elizabeth Rogers (see App. A).

Bolsever of a dead palsy the last of May, so that your young kinswoman, the very good Lady, is become an early widow before she could bring forth an heir to him. I heartily wish that her next choice (for she is young enough to chuse again) may be as happy as her former.

I am very much ioy'd at the quiet which you possess, and so much the more, that you rather immediatly ow it to Providence then to a supercilious Secretary. And I trust that the good angel which hath hetherto kept you, will not leave you in the midst of all the confusions, which ether ar or shall be, for the wheel is still in motion, and cannot stop till God shall please to fasten it with that nail which He hath praedetermin'd. And that the same God may keep you and yours from all the evil of the times, is the prayer of

Your most truly affectionat and humble servant,

BR: S.

Sir, I am now going to London, and shall carry this letter my self, that I may be the surer that it shall not loyter by the way.

JUNE 7.

LETTER CXI

[August 3rd.]

Sir, What quiet there is about you I know not, but *apud nos omnia in turbido*. God send a calme, or else these stormes will ruin all. I had not wrott at this time (for *inter arma silent literae*)[1], but that by frequency of writing I have gott such an habit towards you, that I know not how to break off, especially when you require me to return my opinion in the particular proposed by you. The passage mention'd by you, I confess I had not mett with, for commentaries ar not books alwayes read through, but occasionally consulted with. But finding it as you say, I am absolutely of your judgement, that this learned freind of ours[2] is in an error to conceave that the Israelites did not pass through the sea from one side to the other, for besides the novelty of it (*quae mihi semper suspecta est*) it is not onely contradicated by all maps, but it seems to be contrary to reason, that they who fled from a pursuing enemy, having ent'red the sea should not rather make their march in a direct line, then reflect back again to the same coast they fled from. The onely argument that may make any shew

---

[1] *Inter arma silent literae*. "In the clash of arms, literature is dumb." This is an adaptation of Cicero, *Pro. Milone*, 4. *Silent enim leges inter arma*. The Royalists, encouraged by the conflict among their enemies, planned a widespread rising for the middle of July, 1659. The Government, however, learnt of the conspiracy, according to the *Gazette*, quoted by Ranke, through the treachery of Lady Mary Howard, but, according to Clarendon, through Sir Richard Willis. As a result "many persons of Honour and Quality [were] committed to several Prisons throughout the kingdom, before the day appointed" (Clarendon, Book XVI, § 36), but the enterprise of seizing strong places everywhere failed, except in Cheshire and Lancashire, where Sir George Booth secured Chester. When Bishop Duppa wrote this letter, Lambert, whom the Parliament sent against Booth, had not yet defeated his forces and captured him (Winnington Bridge, August 19th).

[2] "This learned freind of ours." This is Dr. Hammond. In his notes on I Corinthians Cap. X in *A Paraphrase and Annotations upon all the Books of the New Testament* (1653), Hammond (Note a, p. 576) has an elaborate commentary on "and all passed through the sea," beginning "For it must be remembered first that the *Israelites* past not so through the *Red-sea*, as to go *over* it." When annotating Hebrews Cap. XI, Hammond returns to this theme apropos of v. 29: "By faith they passed through the Red Sea as by dry land" (Note e, p. 801). But as he here does not mention Etham (see Letter CXII) it is clear that it is the Corinthians passage which was discussed by Sir Justinian and Bishop Duppa.

for it is, that the way from Aegipt to Canaan led them not cross the Red Sea. But whether he can make it good or no, I know not; or if he can it will not necessarily follow, that they being in danger of so violent an enemy, might not probably be forced to divert from the ready way and to take any course to avoid him. But when I write to him next, I shall tempt him to discover farther what he hath to say for it. He is a person of great ingenuity as well as knowledge, and if he be once convinced that he is in an error, he will not be unwilling to confess it.

I am very glad to hear that your constant use of drinking water agrees so well with you, but you must give me leave to fear somtimes where no fear is. We heartily pray here that your wife and your daughter may have a happy delivery[3]. But for your comming into these parts, I cannot yet *rebus sic stantibus* have any hope for. We ioyn with you in that part of the Collect[4], for never wer there more changes or chances and never had we more need of that prayer. I must say no more; for Angerona, and Sigaleon bid me cease[5].

From your faithfull, and most humble servant
S.

Aug: 3.

Letter CXII

[September 20th.]

Sir, Your letters, dated the 29th of August, came not to my hands till the 16th of this present September. But their slow pace in coming was abundantly recompenced in the reading of them, for not daring to write my self, nor expecting to hear from you as long as these troubles continued,[1] I was surprised with the joy of it; for the truth is I did infinitely long to hear from you though I durst not break the ice, or ford a passage toward it. And this I did the rather forbear, because my house and study was lately search'd, and my papers and letters ransack'd, and among them one of yours was mett with[2] that treated upon the passage of the Israelites

[3] "That your wife and daughter may have a happy delivery." A third son, John, was born to Lady Isham on August 4th, 1659. He lived to be eighty-seven. Susan Carew's eldest child, Susan, was buried December 28th, 1659 (see Carew pedigree in Manning and Bray, *History and Antiquities of Surrey*, Vol. II (1809), opp. p. 523). She was baptised August 28th, 1659 (*Beddington Registers*).

[4] "The Collect." The prayer to which the Bishop refers is the first Collect "to be said after the Offertory, when there is no Communion" in the Book of Common Prayer. It contains the phrase "all the changes and chances of this mortal life."

[5] "Angerona, and Sigaleon." Angerona was a Roman Goddess, to whom sacrifice was offered in the temple of Volupia, in which stood a statue of Angerona with a finger on her mouth, which was bound and closed (Encycl. Brit.). Sigaleon (recte, Sigalion), is the name used with the epithet Aegyptius to describe the Egyptian God Harpocrates or Horus the younger, who is represented with his finger on his lips as the God of Silence. Lewis and Short quote a passage in Letter XXV of Ausonius (to Pontius Paulinus), in which there is an allusion to "Sigalion Aegyptius" as sealing the lips. (Note based on information from Miss Margaret Toynbee).

[1] "As long as these troubles continued." For the political situation see the last letter (CXI, Note 1). The disturbed state of the country no doubt delayed letters.

[2] "One of yours was mett with." This is Sir Justinian's letter alluding to the commentary in Hammond's *Paraphrase and Annotations* on the Passage of the Red Sea (see Letter CXI, Note 2). Apart from his known relation to the Royalists, and the nervousness of the Government, there seems to have been no reason why Bishop Duppa should have been searched at this moment. It is quite true that Chancellor Hyde had sent John Barwick to England to urge the Bishops still surviving to consecrate new Bishops, and a special charge was laid on Duppa. It is conceivable that the Republican Government may have become aware of traffic

through the Red Sea. The letter was long studied on, and read over more then once, imagining (as I conceaved) that there was some notable Cabala in it, and taking the Red Sea, and the wilderness of Etham, to be as hieroglyphicks relating to som present matters then in action. But the riddle (had there been any) being not to be unriddled, the innocent paper was laid down again. An other letter that exercised the inquisitors was a letter written three yeares past by my Lord Bruce[3], who consulted with me (as he used to do somtimes in som things out of the ordinary road) whether the soules of freinds departed ioyn'd to their bodies at the Resurrection, should ether know one the other, or have any mutuall complacence, in seeing the relations which they own'd on Earth, possess'd of the same joyes in Heaven with them. But this being a speculation of concernments in an other world, was not much insisted on; the things of this world, being the onely things they look'd after. But not to trouble you longer with any more περιαυτολογία, I must hartily congratulate with you, that your family is a kind of Goshen, where you enioy health, though you ar surrounded with sickness, and an happy quietness though noise and trouble hath been round about you.

As for the latter part of your letter, I must take *diem ad deliberandum* before I answer it. Onely I must say that your affection to me, I find, dazles you, and makes you see me at a false light, for the argument which you would recommend to me is of that height, that if there wer a Junto of all the politick witts that ar left, if there be any left (which the variation of so many scaenes, and the giddy carriage of the affaires among us may make us beleive there is not), it wer enough to pose them all. There be few Inigoes[4] to raise up materiall buildings, but rationall, and morall buildings, will meet with greater difficulties.

I have not told you any thing of my health, which I enioy for the

---

between Richmond and the exiled Court in Brussels, if not of its exact nature. But the Bishops were apprehensive as it was, and this searching of Duppa's house seems to have "put the seal on the hesitations and fears of the aged prelates" (Bosher, *The Making of the Restoration Settlement*, p. 96).

John Mordaunt specially noted the searching of "Dr. D's house" (*Mordaunt Letter-Book* No. 55, p. 32). On August 5th, President Whitelock ordered Major Audley "On information received Council desires you to go or send to the Countess of Devonshire's house at Roehampton and search for suspected persons, papers, and arms etc. The like for Dr. Dupper's house at Richmond, and all suspected places near. You are to secure what you find, and take the Doctor's examination concerning his knowledge of persons who have discussed with him the present designs of the enemy, and take his security for his good behaviour and his abiding at his own house, or otherwise secure him at his house." (C.S.P. Dom. 1659-60, p. 76). It will be noticed that Duppa's friend, Lady Devonshire (who is also, mentioned in the *Mordaunt Letter-Book* No. 29, p. 17 and No. 54, p. 30) had her house searched at the same time as Duppa's (see Letter xxxv, October 19th, 1653 Note 1a).

[3] "Lord Bruce." Robert, Lord Bruce of Whorlton, son of the 1st Earl of Elgin in the peerage of Scotland, succeeded his father in 1663. There was some reason to scan a letter from him, as not only were his sympathies Royalist, but in May 1659, he had actually been in touch with Sir George Booth, whose capture had ended the revolt. Lord Bruce did not rise in August, but was arrested (*Mordaunt Letter-Book*, No. 23, p. 15). After the Restoration, which he assisted, he brought in a bill in May 1663 for settling all offices, civil and military, on such as had been "loyal and conformable to the Church." He was created Earl of Ailesbury in 1664, and after being made Lord Chamberlain, died in 1685 (D.N.B., Feiling, *A History of the Tory Party*, p. 107, G.E.C., *Complete Peerage*). Anthony Wood described him as "a learned person, well versed in history and antiquities" (*Fasti*).

[4] "Inigoes." This is an allusion to Inigo Jones (1573–1652), Surveyor General of the Works to King James (1615) and King Charles, and the architectural genius of England in the first half of the 17th century. (See J. A. Gotch, *Inigo Jones*).

present farr beyond ether what I deserved, or expected. But my dear wife on whom my health very much depends, is so often and so variously infirme, that I have great feares for her. She hath had a present given her from the East Indies which may be usefull when the cold wether comes in.[5] Whether you or your very good Lady (to whom we both desire to have our service rememb'red) shall please to make use of it, she shall think her self the happier that any thing which she can offer to you may serve you.

And thus having said too much for one letter, I shall reserve the rest for the next, and with many prayers for you and yours rest

Your most affectionat true freind,

BR: SAR: Sept: 20.

LETTER CXIII

[DECEMBER 20th.]

Sir, I do not find by this return that you receaved the last which I sent you; but there will be nether loss, nor danger in it, for it contain'd onely the complaints of old age, and cold wether. This brings with it somthing more, which I would not willingly have miscarry, and that is two little tracts[1] lately printed. The one is a seasonable paraenesis to the corrupted gentry by an anonymous author, but for the matter and the stile (if I can judge of it) excellently drawn up, and usefull for these times; the other concerning the education of children (an argument which you so often enquire after) is St. Chrysostome's (though not to be found in any of our printed editions), translated by a gentleman of this county, with a praeface where he gives an instance, a child of his own. And the reading of it pleas'd me so well, that I could not forbear the imparting of it to you.

The lady which you mention[2] hath nether been in these parts, nor have I ether heard of her, or from her. She is certainly of a sweet and gentle disposition, but this virtu of hers may possibly expose her, and make her the more easy to be seduced in her second choice. It had been very happy for her, if she had taken you in her way, whose counsell might have arm'd her against the snares that ar likely to be laid for her. If I hear any thing concerning her I shall not keep it from you. For the present I shall say no more but wish this solemn time now drawing on may be happy to you. I rest,

Your most affectionat freind, and humble servant,

BR: SAR: Decem: 20.

---

[5] "A present from the East Indies." We last heard of a present from the East Indies for Mrs. Duppa, sent to Lady Isham, on March 1st, 1658, in Letter C. It is permissible to wonder who it was that sent Mrs. Duppa these gifts.

[1] "Two little tracts." The two books mentioned are:

(a) *The Gentleman's Calling* by the author of *The Whole Duty of Man*. This is mentioned again (more fully) in Letter CXIV; see Note 1.

(b) The book on the education of children translated "by a gentleman of this county", must be St. John Chrysostom's *Golden Booke concerning the education of children, translated by John E.*, published in London in September, 1659. "John E." is John Evelyn, the diarist, who was born at Wotton House, near Dorking, Surrey, in 1620. From 1652 to 1694, he lived at Sayes Court, at Deptford. He then returned to live at Wotton with his brother, whom he succeeded there in 1699. He died at the age of 85 in 1706. He spent much of the Interregnum abroad. (Lowndes, and Ponsonby, *English Diaries* (1923)). Oddly enough, in his *Diary* Evelyn gives the date of the publication of his translation as September 1658. The child described in the Preface is Richard Evelyn, who died, aged 5, on January 27th, 1657/8.

[2] "The lady which you mention." This is probably Justinian's cousin, the widowed Viscountess Mansfield. See Letter CX, Note 2.

1660

The first thing that strikes the reader of these letters in the early part of this year is how unconscious the writers seem of their approaching deliverance. General Monk's march from Scotland, and his entry into London on February 3rd, might mean anything, but the depressed tone of the Bishop's letters suggests that the Royalists expected little. Sir Justinian, in his reply to the Bishop's letter of February 27th, indeed, was logical in suggesting that Presbyterianism might be the outcome, since Monk himself was thought to favour that course. It is not till March 27th, that Bishop Duppa speaks confidently: "If the voice of the people be an oracle to be heark'ned after, it never spake lowder, nor better."

Lambert's escape and appearance in arms at Daventry was a serious threat to the expected settlement. On his capture, the last obstacle to the Restoration was removed, and the Convention Parliament invited the return of the King. Some measure of the economic situation that rendered this necessary can be gathered from Pepys' remark (April 27th) that the Exchequer was so low that there was not even £20 to pay the messenger that brought the news of Lambert's capture. But at the news of the capture, Pepys notes (April 24th): "things now very open and safe. And every man begins to be merry and full of hopes."

There can be no doubt that both the Bishop and Sir Justinian had every reason to be glad at the Restoration. For the latter, it meant an end of "tedious imprisonments," and a promise of useful service to his county and country, which the Republican Governments had barred, and for the former, it gave at least the promise of the Restoration of the Church. This was not accomplished till 1661. The Restoration of the Monarchy in 1660 left the ecclesiastical settlement in doubt, and Bishop Duppa's anxieties are expressed in his letters in the summer of 1660.

Lord Sandwich's opinion, expressed to Pepys on April 26th, that in the elections to the Convention Parliament, "the Cavaliers have now the upper hand clear of the Presbyterians," was sound enough, but the young squires went off to their estates, leaving in August, a Presbyterian majority in the Commons. Charles II resorted to the expedient of a recess, so that the Bishops could be consecrated without the embarrassing presence of Parliament. On October 28th, the first post-Restoration consecration of Bishops took place in King Henry VII's chapel at Westminster. Under mandate from the aged Archbishop Juxon, Duppa, now Bishop of Winchester, acted as chief consecrator. His friends, all mentioned in these letters, were consecrated to the most important Sees, Sheldon to London, Henchman to Salisbury, and Sanderson to Lincoln. (*Mercurius Publicus*, 1660, No. 44, p.693). But Duppa himself was feeling a great strain. His infirmities increased. His writing becomes shaky. Press of business on an old sick man must have told heavily. On October 3rd, Richard Chaworth wrote to Sir Justinian: "My Lord of Winton (upon his old account though upon his new title) presents his service to you, and desyres to be excus'd from writing this tyme which hee was going to doe, but hee had a comaund to come to Court to the K[in]g upon business. This is all I shall trouble you with at present, but the service of my Aunt Duppa to your selfe and Lady" (I.C. 500). It is perhaps not surprising that no more letters were sent to Lamport from Richmond after 1660. For one thing, in the early part of the next year, Sir Justinian, now a magistrate and a deputy-lieutenant, was fully occupied with the rising of the sectaries, and in April he was elected to the Cavalier Parliament as knight of the shire for Northamptonshire; in London, he was near the Bishop, and could meet him in person, and not merely by letters.

In this year, public affairs for the first time take up most of the letters. Lady Isham's confinement, the marriage of his daughter Elizabeth – these affairs still occupy their place in Sir Justinian's correspondence, but they find no echo in the letters that passed between Richmond and Lamport. No doubt Sir Justinian felt that the public cares pressed so heavily on the ageing Bishop that it was not right to trouble him with such things. But as a picture of Royalist and Anglican sentiment in the year of the Restoration, these letters are probably unsurpassed in interest.

It was perhaps a happy thing for Bishop Duppa that he did not live to see the full establishment of a Court so unlike that which he remembered and loved. But it would be churlish to judge him for the tears of joy that overflow in his letter of May 8th; "The King so long laid aside, is now proclaimed the headstone of the corner. Never was there so miraculous a change as this, nor so great things don in so short a time. But *a Domino factum est istud*; no human wisdome can claime a share in it."

LETTER CXIV

[JANUARY 10th.]

Sir, You see what a stranger I am to Paul's Church yard, by sending to you books of an old date, as if they had been newly printed. But being my self taken with the argument of them both, who have no children to breed up, and not knowing whether you had seen them, or no, I could not forbear the sending them to you. That concerning *The Gentleman's Calling*[1] was presented to me as from the author, but who the author is

[1] *The Gentleman's Calling. By the author of* "*The Whole Duty of Man*" [*i.e. Lady D. Pakington? or Archbishop Sterne?*] (*Private Devotions*) *with a prefatory epistle signed H.H.* (*i.e. Dr. Humphry Henchman*) 8vo, was published in London in 1660 (B.M. Catalogue).

There is an unpublished letter in the Bodleian Library addressed to Dr. Sheldon on the subject of this book, dated November 7th, 1659: "I make bold to send you a little new book viz. *The Gentleman's Calling*. I have I think now in some sort obeyed you, for you bade me get the Author of *The Whole Duty of Man* to come to the press again, and you would be sure to know him then, and now you have him. You will find your friend Dr. Henchman's Epistle before it. Tim Garthwaite."

I cannot yet learn, but as I conceave it much differs in the sprightfullness of the stile, from that of *The Whole Duty of Man.* In my judgement, it is excellently well written, and very pertinently in relation to the education of the gentry of these times. He is censured by som who feel themselves touch'd to be too satyricall. But the truth is that in this argument *difficile est satyram non scribere.*[2] Causinus[3] hath done very good service in his way, and as farr as I have mett with his writings, there is nothing of his but deserves an *euge.*[4] As for my own particular, the longer I live, the more I dislike all that I ether do in this kind, or have done. I have had so many sad impressions upon me, that all that I can do, is to keep my self from a deiected mind, wherein your freindship to me doth very much contribute. The inclosed note is sent and satisfied. But how to satisfy you I know not. Unless this may in part satisfy you, that this kindness of yours cannot be lost upon me, who make it my earnest sute, that when it shall prove a burthen to you, you would *claudere rivos*[5], for I never yet knew how to love my self so much, as to do it to my freinds' disadvantage. This extreme cold wether, makes writing a penance to me, and therefore having no better things to say, I shall favor my self and say no more, but reserve the rest in my prayers for you, who most faithfully am,

Your most affectionat freind,
BR: SARUM

Richm: Jan: 10.

[ENDORSED REPLY OF SIR JUSTINIAN]

My Lord, Your Lordship's of Jan. the 10th, meeting with some stop by the way, came not to mee till yesterday. In it I am sorry to find that any sad impressions upon your Lordship's spirit should prevaile so far as to give you a dislike of anything your Lordship hath formerly writt, being confident that nothing hath passed your Lordship's pen upon any argument but would be very acceptable to all men of piety and knowledge, and indeed had much rather your Lordship's exercise in that kind might divert your sadder apprehensions then your giving way to them should hinder any thing of so great use both to your selfe and others. 'Tis true we have seen so many revolutions, and so suddaine, that it was never better instanc'd unto us then now how all sublunary things are *tenui*

(Tanner MSS. 51, f. 158). Timothy Garthwaite was a London bookseller who flourished from 1650 to 1669, in which year he died. He dealt chiefly in theological literature. (H. R. Plomer, *Dictionary of Booksellers . . . 1641 to1667*, Bibliographical Soc. (1907)). *The Whole Duty of Man* ran to 18 editions before 1861; was translated into Latin, French and Welsh; and has been attributed to nine different authors, including three future Archbishops, Sancroft, Frewen and Sterne. This letter suggests that it was an Oxford man, well known to Sheldon, and Dr. Richard Allestree (1619–81) would seem to be a likely candidate (Lowndes).

[2] *Difficile est*, etc. "It is difficult not to write a satire." Juvenal, *Sat.* I, 30.

[3] "Causinus." R. P. Nicholas Caussin, S. J., who was Confessor to Louis XIII, was known as Causinus. For Caussin, see *Biographie Universelle.* The B.M. Catalogue contains the following entry under Caussin's works: *The Unfortunate Politique (or the Life of Herod) First written in French by C.N. (the Judicious and eloquent Causinus). Englished by G.P.* [Extracted from "La Cour Sainte"] pp. 218, L. Lichfield for Joseph Godwin, Oxford 1638 8°. The fact that this work and others by this French Jesuit were translated into English, and published openly, is adduced by Godfrey Davies in support of his view of the tolerance of Catholics in England, under Charles I's personal government (*The Early Stuarts*).

[4] "An *euge.*" A bravo.

[5] *Claudere rivos.* This is an adaptation of Virgil, *Eclogues* III, 111, *Claudite iam rivos, pueri; sat prata biberunt.* A shepherd is speaking: "Shut off the streams, my boys, the fields have drunk enough."

pendentia filo[6], but even from thence what argument can a man raise for an absolute dejectedness of minde when the fickle occasion may sooner alter then he be restor'd to clearness of spiritt and health of body which a settled melancholy hath cheated him of upon an unsettled ground.

And although I hope not to want higher cordialls for a fainting spiritt, yet sometimes find that things even liter then cork or bladders may keepe one from sinking sooner then weighty arguments, and do even now, when the folly and madness of the age would over-sett a man with greife, rather then too much torment my selfe, represent the mutabilitie of it to my children who cannot yet read, but see in a peice of paper lapt into severall formes, now a cap, then a boat, then a cock, and all in an instant, as 'twere with a puff, and yet the same paper still. But this paper to your Lordship bearing none of those various shapes doth in the old constant fold conclude mee,

Your,

LETTER CXV

[JANUARY 24th.]

Sir, If my last letter hath fall'n into any other hands then your own, the loss will not be great nor any other secret reveal'd, but such as I am willing should be made known, viz. that I have receaved from your brother[1] what you directed for me and return you a very thankfull heart for the continuance of your freindship toward me. If you would know in what condition we ar here, I know not how to tell you, for fame was never more busy then now, *dum vanis rumoribus oppida pulsat.*[2] Never was more said, and less known. What may be the event of all Θεῶν ἐν γούνασι κεῖται[3], and upon this alone I sett my rest. There was never more need of mutuall prayers, and in that entercourse with Heaven, nothing can hinder us. Let our angle of incidence be there, and then we shall happily meet, what ever becom of our letters. That all peace and happyness may be within your dwellinge is the daily prayer of,

Your most affectionat freind and humble servant,

BR: SAR:

Richm: Jan: 24.

---

[6] *Tenui pendentia filo.* "Hanging by a slender thread." Ovid, *Ex Ponto*, IV, 3, 35. *Omnia sunt hominum tenui pendentia filo.* "All the affairs of mankind hang by a slender thread."

[1] "Your brother." This is Sir Justinian's brother-in-law, Will Garrard, younger son of Sir John Garrard, 1st Bart of Lamer, and brother of Mrs. Jane Isham. His father left him £1,500 and an annuity in his will (dated April 8th, 1637, proved June 21st same year). He was then under age, as his father directed for "my two younger sons William and Charles" to be given "diet lodging and entertainment" "until such time as my overseers hereafter named . . . shall think fit to place them at a university or otherwise." In addition to an eldest brother John (already married in 1637), who became 2nd Bart, five sisters are mentioned in the will. There is no mention of Mrs. Jane Isham, although she did not die till 1638/9. William was a lawyer, and there are many letters from him, dated from London, to Sir Justinian, on legal business, at Lamport. (See also Letter CXXIII, Endorsed Reply).

[2] *Dum vanis rumoribus oppida pulsat.* "While she (Fame) makes towns buzz with empty rumours." Adapted from Petronius, *Fragmenta*, XXVIII, 3.

[3] Θεῶν ἐν γούνασι κεῖται. "Rests on the knees of the Gods." Homer, *Odyssey*, I, 267 and 400. General Monk was on his way to London. He was at Market Harborough on January 23rd and must have passed through Lamport on his way to Northampton (January 25th) and London which he reached on February 3rd. *Clarke Papers*, Vol. IV (1901), pp. xxiii, 259 and 260.

LETTER CXVI

[FEBRUARY 7th.]

Sir, I do not well remember what the particulars of my last letter wer; but it seems by yours that you fast'ned upon som melancholy part of it, which occasion'd you like a very good freind to apply such remedies as might call me to my self again, if I had unhappily wand'red. It is true, I confess, that these times work upon me, and though I take in the best ballast of the mind, which ether reason or religion can afford me, yet they toss, and tumble me, but yet it is a ship that rides at anchor which, though the windes may shake and move, yet remove they cannot as long as the anchor holds. For I know Whom I have trusted, and am every day more and more a proficient in the practise of that great lesson of the Christian, the committing chearfully all that concernes me into the hands of God, as knowing first that nothing is don without Him, and next that whatsoever He will have don, is best. And yet after all this philosophizing, there is still left a *motus trepidationis*, such as of the needle in the compass, which though it looks towards the north, yet hath its quiverings and shakings. But that verse in the Psalmes, "Nevertheless though I am sometimes affraid yet will I putt my trust in him" many times occurs to me, and setts me up again, when I am drooping. I had not troubled you with this solaecisme in conversation, call'd περιαυτολογία, which severe men say makes freinds weary one of the other had not your affectionat expressions towards me, drawn it from me. And therefore that you who give so many comforts to your freinds, may never want any, is a prayer grounded upon such a truth, as I am very confident is heard in heaven for you, as soon as it is breath'd here.

I am infinitely pleas'd, as with all the rest, so with the latter part of your letter, where you let me know what repraesentations you make to your children, not onely of the severall scaenes, and revolutions of the time (which they cannot yet be very sensible of) but of what they in themselves ar being in your hands, just as that paper is, to be folded up and framed into what shapes you please, for *argilla quidvis imitaberis uda*[1]. And that the happyness with which God hath blest you both in your vine, and in your branches may increase to you, is earnestly pray'd for by

Your most affectionat and obliged freind and servant,

BR: SAR:

Richm: Feb: 7.

LETTER CXVII

[FEBRUARY 27th.]

Sir, I write letters to you, as usurers lend their mony, with expectation of interest upon interest, which in your returnes you never fail to pay me; particularly in your last, where for my giving you but a hint of one verse in the Psalme, you have return'd me a full paraphrase. And to say the truth, I have been infinitely pleas'd ever since to find that we are like instruments so tuned, that a touch upon one (though at so great a distance) not onely workes upon the other by a similar motion, but like a multiplying echo returns many sounds for one, and improves every thing I write so much to my advantage.

[1] *Argilla quidvis imitaberis uda.* "When the clay is wet, you can mould it to what shape you will." Horace, *Epist.*, II, 2, 8.

But where ar we all this while, that we have so much leasure to busy our selves in David's Psalmes? Parlaments and Armies, changes and revolutions fill the heads of other men, and we like Archimedes are drawing lines, while Syracuse is taking. But, alass, what is left for us to do? or which way shall we look in such a storm, when as Homer saith τὰ δ' ὑπέρτερα νέρτερα θήσει Ζεὺς ὑψιβρεμέτης[1]? can we have a better prospect then to turn to David's Psalmes again? and when we find that *Dominus regnavit*, "The Lord is king, be the people never so impatient, He sitts between the Cherubins, be the Earth never so unquiet," what is there that can any way shake, or discompose us? And with this charme I every night lay my head upon my pillow, and (I bless God for it) sleep quietly after it. The good Marquess of Hartford[2] the last time I saw him, told me with a great deal of chearfullness, what comforts he found when he repeated the 57th Psalme, particularly in those words, "Under the shadow of thy wings shall be my refuge, till this tyranny be overpast." And it is well that these evil times have that good influence upon us as to reduce that primitive usage which St. Paul mentions, that every one had his Psalme, for we never had more need of it.

The lady whom you mention hath not been yet seen by me, as being out of my reach. I allwaies look'd upon her as of a very gentle, and soft temper, fitted to receave all good impressions, but the danger is that even these good qualities may expose her the easier to be wrought upon to her disadvantage. I heartily wish that she may light upon a good guide, for nothing else can secure her. God guide us all, for "All the earth is full of darkness, and cruell habitations."

Sir, you ar in the heart, and in the prayers of,

Your most faithfull, and affectionate freind and servant,

BR: SAR:

Richm: Febr: 27.

---

[1] τὰ δ' ὑπέρτερα νέρτερα θήσει Ζεὺς ὑψιβρεμέτης. "When Zeus, the high Thunderer has turned everything upside down." Aristophanes, *Lysistrata*, 772-3.

[2] "The good Marquess of Hartford." This is William Seymour, 1st Marquess of Hertford (1588–1660). He married the King's cousin, Lady Arabella Stuart, in 1610, which caused them both to be imprisoned. In 1621, he succeeded his grandfather as Earl of Hertford; he bore St. Edward's Staff at Charles I's coronation; and in 1640 he was created Marquess of Hertford. He was Governor to the Prince of Wales 1641–3 when Duppa, as the Prince's tutor, must have known him well, and, in the Civil War, was Lieutenant-General of the Royal forces in the West. He was one of the four peers who asked to be allowed to suffer in place of the King, when sentence was passed on Charles I. When his first wife died "distracted" in prison, he married Lady Frances Devereux, daughter of the 2nd Earl of Essex. In 1660 he was restored as 2nd Duke of Somerset, but died a month later, on Oct. 24th, 1660. (G.E.C., *Complete Peerage*). His son, Henry, Lord Beauchamp, was the father of the 3rd Duke of Somerset. Lord Beauchamp's death was noted by Duppa on April 11th, 1654. See Letter XLVI, Note 3.

As has already been mentioned, the composition of the office for King Charles, Martyr, in the Prayer Book has been traditionally ascribed to Duppa. Some support for this is found in Duppa's use of the verse from the 57th psalm here. Did he have this saying of Lord Hertford in mind when he wrote the prayer (collect) in "The Order for Morning Prayer" for "the Thirtieth of January, being the Day of the Martyrdom of the Blessed King Charles the First"? These words occur "Thou didst not leave us for ever, as sheep without a shepherd; but by Thy gracious providence didst miraculously preserve the undoubted Heir of his [Charles I's] Crowns, our then gracious Sovereign King *Charles* the Second, from his bloody enemies, hiding him under the shadow of Thy wings, until their tyranny was overpast."

[ENDORSED REPLY OF SIR JUSTINIAN]

Your Lordship's favourable acceptance of whatsoever I write, as it may make mee the more confident, so, I think, the more cautious, as being the higher crime to abuse so much goodness, then to give trouble to a less. The truth is 'tis now the spring and I fancie there is something growing in men's heads (as elsewhere), that usually putts them upon straines and actions too more then at other seasons. And this may be somewhat to those revolutions your Lordship mentions, as wel as to my scribling, and whether this various and windy weather about the aequinox hath not influence over our affairs. We read of *texti doctrinarum*, we have lately had as many several doctrines as there are points on the compass, that they having now gon around they begin Presbiterian againe, and who knowes not wither this dance may not like others end in the same measure they began, and then men come to be restor'd to their witts again, when the biting of this cursed tarantula is wrought out by those various and violent motions.[3]

However, 'tis now tyme for mee to rest, and doe rest,

My Lord, etc.

LETTER CXVIII

[MARCH 27th.]

Sir, I would willingly say somthing to you, but nether are letters good conveyors of it, nor is our spring of hopes so forward, but winds, and frosts may blast it. And the truth is we have been so often deluded with expectation (that all stormes wer over), that every sunshine is suspected by me. Should I tell you all I hear, I should rather amuse you then satisfy ether you, or my self. But if the voice of the people be an oracle to be heark'ned after, it never spake lowder, nor better.[1] The patience of waiting what a few dayes will produce will sufficiently settle us, and point out the center we ar to rest in. In the mean time, I think my self to be in such a dream as David mentions when God turn'd away the captivity of Sion. But because none can tell his dream, unless he wer perfectly awake, I shall stay till this pleasing slumber be over. What ever the event may be, I shall praepare to receave it as com from Heaven without consulting Artemidorus or any of the oneirocriticks for it.[2]

[One line carefully cut from the MS.]

Your most faithfull, and humble servant,

B. S. March 27.

---

[3] "Various and violent motions." On February 21st, 1660, the members ejected from Parliament in December 1648, were restored to their seats, with a consequent strengthening of the Presbyterian party, which Monk, at this time, favoured. "The Presbyterian party had once more the upper hand, and was fully determined to keep it." (Ranke, Vol. III, p. 292)

[1] "The voice of the people." On March 25th the City of London presented a memorial to the Council of State, asking for an invitation to be sent to Charles II, requesting him to return and exercise his kingly functions. (See Ranke, Vol. III, p. 295). Pepys (March 16th) records that "one came with a ladder to the Great Exchange, and wiped with a brush the inscription that was upon King Charles [*Exit tyrannus, Regum ultimus, anno libertatis Angliae, anno Domini* 1648 *Januarie* XXX] and . . . there was a great bonfire made in the Exchange, and people called out 'God bless King Charles the Second'."

[2] "Artemidorus." Artemidorus was a soothsayer and interpreter of dreams, who flourished in the second century A.D. during the reigns of Hadrian and the Antonines. His 'Ονειροκριτικά, or interpretation of dreams, was translated into English by Robert Wood (4th ed. 1644). The 5th edition, newly corrected, appeared in 1656.

Letter CXIX

[April 23rd.]

Sir, Having not heard from you after three returnes of the carrier, I was in some feares, that ether you wer not well, or letters had miscarried, or som troubles had been in those parts that might have hind'red you, but your letters which I receaved on Saterday last have scatter'd all those feares and satisfied me that there was no other cause of the failing, but your too much care, in trusting your freind with it rather then your carrier; by which I gain this instruction, that when the ordinary way may probably serve, we commonly loose by it if we lay hold on any thing in stead of it.

It is yet standing water with us, we nether flow nor ebbe; how farr the near approaching Parlament[1] may ether advance, or drive us back I know not. But we hope the best. Many machinations there ar, plots under ground and above, to praevent any settling at all, but God keepes His counsells apart and unless our ruin be irreversibly decreed, will at last happily finish what He hath so wonderfully begun. But the hott breathings of vindictive spirits, must be first better allai'd; some good essaies have been made toward it, by noble and good persons of severall counties, and I should be pleased to see some such express from Northamptonshire for your sake.

I did not intend to trouble you to turn over the leafe, but having written thus farr, and being ready to subscribe, there was newes brought that there was *turba gravis paci*[2], which being drawn into a body to obstruct the expected settlement wer happily routed and scatter'd, and som of the cheif leaders seas'd on; which if it be true, we may live to see the comforts of a sunshine after so many stormes. Your country was the scaene of our ruin in the defeat at Naseby, and this action done about Daventry,[3] though by smaller numbers, may be of as great importance for the better. We ar all here in great expectation, and if the end answers these blessed

---

[1] "Approaching Parlament." Monk encouraged the Long Parliament to dissolve, which it did on March 16th after appointing "a Council of State, consisting of many sober and honest gentlemen, who had never wished the King ill." (Clarendon Book XVI, § 135). Writs were issued for a new Parliament to meet on April 25th. Those who had borne arms against the Parliament were nominally excluded from the Convention Parliament, but the qualification was little observed, and many who had borne arms for the King became members. (Ranke, Vol. III, p. 301).

[2] *Turba gravis paci.* The "grave threat to peace" (Martial, *Epigrammaton Liber* or *Liber Spectaculorum* I, 4, 1) was Lambert's rising. Ranke (Vol. III, p. 302) explains that "The Republicans and Anabaptists found themselves virtually excluded in the new elections. Hitherto they had kept in their own hands the two great keys of power, the majority in Parliament, and the command of the army. They were now deprived of both . . . The defeated party had no thoughts of abandoning their cause at once; they hoped to save themselves by one determined effort. In every county they rose in arms. Lambert, who had succeeded in escaping from his confinement in the Tower, appeared soon after at Daventry, at the head of some troops devoted to their general. His force consisted of four squadrons of regular cavalry and a few irregular bands of separatists . . . his secret hope was to find partisans in the rest of the army who would declare for him." This hope was disappointed, and on April 22nd Lambert's troops were dispersed by Colonel Ingoldsby, and he himself was made prisoner and brought back to the Tower.

[3] "This action done about Daventry." According to Clarendon (Book XVI, § 147) Lambert had four troops under him (two of which deserted, one before and one after the skirmish), and Ingoldsby had Monk's own Regiment of Horse, and "a good Body of Foot under Colonel Streater." Monk's swiftness in sending Ingoldsby was fortunate, as "the ways were full of soldiers endeavouring to repair to them [Lambert's force]: so that if they had not been crushed in that instant, they would, in very few days, have appeared very formidable." (Clarendon).

beginnings, we may be once more an happy people; and to this we have all great reason to say, Amen.

From your very affectionat, and faithfull freind,

BR: SAR: Richm: St. George's Day.

[ENDORSED REPLY OF SIR JUSTINIAN]

My Lord, I hope mine writt on Aester day to your Lordship miscarried not, having recieved your Lordship's writt the day after. But this week's votes[4] succeeding that action, we hope very shortly to see the fruits of them. And all men that see it shall say: "This hath God don, for they shall percieve that it is his worke: The righteous shall rejoyce in the Lord and put his trust in him, and all they that are true of heart shall be glad". Mee thinks I see your Lordship welcoming your King with teares of joy, and even ready with old Simeon to say *nunc dimittis*, etc. But God I hope will yet reserve you to be a maine instrument of good to this afflicted Church and State. Some pillars are lately fallen,[5] and I know very much doth rest upon your shoulders who remaine. I beseech God praeserve the King, and such about him as may counsell him for the best, and therein (I think) we also pray for our selves and ours, who I hope shall reape the fruits of his happie reign over us.

My Lord, I know the multitude of business and care will now be upon you. If I may have the favor by letter but sometimes, to tender my humble service in very free lines *cum tot sustineas et tanta negotia*.[6] I shall not so much offend in *publica commoda* as to be long (I dare not say tedious), nor can I expect such frequent returnes from your Lordship's owne hand as formerly, only I still begg my place in your heart and praiers as being, My Lord,

Your most humble and faithfull servant

J.I.

---

[4] "This week's votes." Lambert was brought a prisoner to London on April 24th, and the next day, Parliament met and voted the recall of the King, both Houses sending deputations to The Hague to invite him back.

[5] "Some pillars are lately fallen." Thomas Morton, Bishop of Durham, died on September 22nd, 1659, at Easton Mauduit, Northants, where he had lived with the Yelverton family since 1652, converting the son, Sir Henry Yelverton, 2nd Bart (succeeded 1654), to Anglican principles. Sir Henry was elected to the Convention Parliament as one of the Knights of the Shire for Northamptonshire. Morton might well be described as a "pillar", but he was rather an ancient one, being 95. (Murray's *Handbook to Northamptonshire*, 2 edn. (1901), p. 26, *Northants and Rutland Clergy*; *Walker Revised*). Ralph Brownrigg, Bishop of Exeter, was buried in the Temple Church, London, December 17th, 1659. Brownrigg was a friend of Seth Ward, but can hardly be described as a pillar of the Church. He never entered his diocese of Exeter, to which he was appointed in 1642. But probably Sir Justinian had in mind a more considerable pillar than either of these prelates. Dr. Henry Hammond died at Westwood, Worcestershire, on April 25th, 1660. (See Letters XIX, Note 5, and CI, Note 4). Apart from Duppa (Salisbury), the following Bishops survived till the Restoration; Juxon (London), Wren (Ely), Frewen (Coventry and Lichfield), Skinner (Oxford), Warner (Rochester), Piers (Bath and Wells), King (Chichester). Of these, Juxon and Frewen became Archbishops of Canterbury and York, and Duppa Bishop of Winchester. The others, though restored to their Sees, were not promoted, perhaps because of their failure to perpetuate their order as required by Chancellor Hyde. Luckily, there were many able men, ready to be made Bishops, and take the lead. Sheldon (London), Henchman (Salisbury) (both mentioned in these letters), Morley (Worcester) and Cosin (Durham) all had far more influence than the survivors from Charles I's time with the exception of Duppa himself. Morley and Cosin had spent the Interregnum abroad.

[6] *Cum tot sustineas et tanta negotia*. "When you are burdened with such multitudinous and weighty business." Horace, *Epist.* II, 1, 1.

[May 8th.]

Letter CXX

Sir, The month hath produced happy things: and this day is a day of joy, for the King so long laid aside, is now proclaimed the headstone of the corner.[1] Never was there so miraculous a change as this, nor so great things don in so short a time. But *a Domino factum est istud*; no human wisdome can claime a share in it. Who the persons are, that have the honour to attend the King, and emploi'd to invite him over, you will find by this note enclosed. Your son Carew now a military leader of a troop in the behalfe of his county was with mee this last evening, and is praeparing himself to accompany my Lord Barkley[2] in this journey. All countries have of late emptied themselves into London and now London is as busy to empty itself into Holland. And can you contain your self at Lamport? But probably you are no lover of crowds, and will stay the time, when the throng is over. I have not leasure to say more, being overlaid with visitants, for now every man visits every man, and I am not at quiet, for the *percontantores* will not be satisfied. Our letters onely ar the thinges that make no noise, and that this entercourse may continue between us is the hearty desire of your most affectionat tru freind and servant,

Br: Sarum

[Endorsed reply of Sir Justinian]

My Lord, I am still obliged to your Lordship for your kind letters notwithstanding the multitude of business and many visitants I feare overlaying you. There are scarce any left in the country to proclaim the King, most gent: gone hence for London and many further. I did see it performed at Northampton yesterday, where I had a fall from my horse overborne by others ill managed at the going of the guns, acclamations, etc: but I hope no further harme then a little paine this day. Your Lordship is not mistaken to thinke mee no lover of crowds, and truly I conceive a decent distance in my attendance upon His Majestie be best, not to forbare so long as to shew a neglect of duty, nor so suddaine as to make it troublesome, believing indeed there be som cause of restraint of multitudes flocking about him this hott season, many doing it rather to satisfy their curiosity and some to take off their former XXXX [*sic*][2a] by their new Hosannas then for the performance of any real service. But I hope not to bee long from attending your Lordship, where I may deliver my selfe more freely; as indeed I heare nothing of the Dukes come into England as yet, nor do I mervaille at his Majestie's not coming to Whitehall. King James refused to see Fotheringay Castle in this country[3], or any other place (as I have heard) where his mother was prisoner.

[1] "The King . . . is now proclaimed." On May 8th, King Charles was proclaimed in London, "with a great deal of pomp" according to Pepys.

[2] "Lord Barkley." This is George, 2nd Lord Berkeley of Berkeley Castle (1628–98), who was one of the six Peers sent by the House of Lords to The Hague (Clarendon, Book xvi, § 239). He was created Viscount Dursley and Earl of Berkeley in 1679. His seat was at Durdans, near Epsom, Surrey, so he was a "countryman" of Nicholas Carew of Beddington, soon to be knighted. (D.N.B.).

[2a] "XXXX" perhaps meaning "treason."

[3] The Stuarts had a close if rather unhappy association with Northamptonshire. Mary Queen of Scots was beheaded at Fotheringay and buried at Peterborough; King James was fond of the county for hunting, and frequently stayed at Apethorpe, while his Queen stayed at Pytchley in 1608 with Sir Euseby Isham. Queen Anne of Denmark was given Holdenby House by James; after his surrender by the Scots in 1647, this was the prison of Charles I. Charles II, however, had no scruples about Whitehall, and though he never rebuilt it, as at one time he intended, he lived and died there.

Letter CXXI

[August 7th.]

Sir, I have been of late so uncertain in the place of my abode,[1] having divided my self between London and Richmond, that the letters of my freinds do not readily find me. But I have (though with the loss of som time) happily mett with both yours. And out of them could extract a quintessence of better counsells, then the Court *alembiques* as yet seem ether to promise, or afford. I treasure them up, and wait for the time when I may produce them to the best advantage. But my frequent infirmities keep me at such a distance, that I cannot easily watch for those *mollia tempora*[2], when truths may be best said to Princes. Could I see you in some nearness of place to him, whose good you so passionately and really affect, I should say my *Dimittis*, with a great πληροφορία[3], and confidently expect that our many little confusions at Court, would at last settle in such an order as might assure us of more happyness then the tottering condition which for the present we are in, can suddainly promise us.

Sir, I have not leasure allow'd me to say more, then that I am

Your most faithfull, and most affectionat freind and servant

B: S.

Richm: Aug: 7.

Letter CXXII

[August 27th.]

Sir, I am still detain'd in the place where I am wearied out with impertinencies more then business. But I am now in hope to retire once more to my beloved Richmond, which his Majestie's favor hath this last week, made part of my Diocese, by translating me to Winchester.[1] Mr Vaughan,[2] whom you recommend to me, hath not observed Hippocrates his aphorisme, who saith that a phisitian should be ἐπικαιρολάτος[3] which serves as well for seeking of praeferments, as for curing of diseases. For though I have not the trouble of disposing of them commited to me, yet I find upon enquiry that the places which he looks after ether ar all-

---

[1] "Uncertain in the place of my abode." On July 7th "the place of Lord Almoner was conferred on that most pious and reverend Brian, Lord Bishop of Salisbury, who was his majesty's Tutor when Prince of Wales." (*Mercurius Publicus*, 1660, No. 28, p. 442.)

[2] *Mollia tempora*. Ovid, *Tristia*, IV, 8, 31-2. Duppa, on August 11th, told Sheldon that, at the King's request, he had moved from Richmond "that I might be more useful to him," but "have not found opportunity given me, wherein I might be serviceable." The uneasiness reflected in this letter finds an echo in a further remark to Sheldon: "You are the only person about his Majesty, that I have confidence in, and I persuade myself that as none hath his ear more, so none is likely to prevail in his heart more, and there was never more need of it, for all the professed enemies of our Church look upon this as the critical time to use their dernier resort to shake His Majesty's constancy." (Tanner MSS. 49, f. 17).

[3] πληροφορία. Assurance.

[1] "Translating me to Winchester." According to the *Register and Chronicle* of Bishop White Kennet (1728), p. 253, Duppa was elected to the See of Winchester on September 10th, 1660.

[2] "Mr. Vaughan." For Edmund Vaughan see Letter XIX, Note 4. He was restored to his living at Pitsford in 1660, and enjoyed it for ten years. He had lived at Kingsthorpe during the Interregnum. His living was worth £70 a year. (*Walker Revised*).

[3] ἐπικαιρολάτος. Perhaps ἐπικαιρότατος is meant = "opportunist." It will be recalled that Edmund Vaughan had given the Ishams medical advice.

ready actually disposed of,[4] or there is (for som other reason) a bar upon them to keep all suters off from looking after them. I am very much a freind to the person both for his own sake and yours, and shall be willing at any time to assist him to my power.

We grow weary here of the Parlament[5], for we find that our best freinds have left us and gon after their pleasures, and the tartar onely is left in the bottome. But let us never grow weary of our freindship, which I look upon as part of my happyness, and shall still begg the continuance of that title in your esteem of being

Your most affectionate true freind,

BR: SAR:

St. Martin's Lane. Aug: 27.

[ENDORSED REPLY OF SIR JUSTINIAN]

My Lord, Having a good while since made returne to your Lordship's last of Aug: 27, and now understanding that the solemnities of your Lordship's translation were perform'd on Monday last,[6] as my Lord Archbishop's of Canter[bury] were the weeke before; I cannot but with many other sons of the Church who honour both your function and persons joyne in that Song of Degrees, and (as Dr. Hammond observes) the last of those which were accomodated to the returne from the captivity, *Ecce nunc benedicite Domino*, etc. But here (as I doubt in many other places), some peevish spiritts there are who will ever have (I can hardly say so wel as) a Chappel wherever God hath a Church and yet who expect a large dispensation from his Majestie's goodness and lenitie. But if I mistake not he hath amongst many others those 2 great requisites of a Prince, calmeness and courage, the best though not so usuall composition: *Peragit tranquilla potestas, quod violenta nequit fortius mandataque urget imperiosa quies*[7], and truly to speak my sense where there is roughness to

[4] "Places disposed of." "By neglecting to fill most of the 18 out of 27 vacant sees till October and December 1660, the King kept in his hands enormous patronage, which is well shown by extracts from the Presentations on the Patent Rolls 1660–1685" (Appendix I to the 46th *Annual Report* (1886) of the Deputy Keeper of the Public Records).

[5] "We grow weary here of the Parlament." Dr Bosher explains that as the Convention Parliament went on sitting through the summer of 1660, the young Anglican squires drifted away from the capital, and the Presbyterians regained control. "It is clear that from the beginning of August to the adjournment in September, the Church Party lost control in Parliament" (*Making of the Restoration Settlement*, p. 172). Anti-Presbyterian amendments to the Bill for settling Ministers were defeated on August 21st, and the Presbyterians succeeded on August 22nd and 23rd in carrying their own motions, restricting the clergy to one benefice, and exempting incumbents from further payments of fifths to sequestered ministers (p. 175). So serious did the anti-episcopal trend of Parliament become that the King ordered a recess from September 8th to November 6th, on the ground that many members desired "leave to go into the country."

[6] "The solemnities of your Lordship's translation." "The solemnities of the Translation of the Rt. Reverend Father in God, Brian Lord Bishop of Winchester, were performed on Monday [September 24th] to the great joy and comfort of many Lords and Gentlemen, as well as the Reverend Clergy, who all have a deep sense and memory of the prudence and piety of that eminent Prelate, to whom the whole Nation owes a lasting tribute, not only for his great example of virtue and godliness, but for those excellent seeds and principles so happily laid in the youth of our Sovereign Lord the King, when he was Prince of Wales and under his Lordship's tuition" (*Mercurius Publicus*, 1660, No. 40, p. 625).

[7] *Peragit tranquilla potestas quod violenta nequit mandatque fortiter* [recte, *fortius*] *urget imperiosa quies.* "Calm power achieves what a violent cannot and an imperious quietness strongly urges its commands." Claudian, XVII, 239-41 (*Panegyricus dictus Manlio Theodoro consuli*).

be us'd, as sometymes it must be, I think it may be better express'd by those who act under his authority then by himselfe.

If the King bear with the humor of a Quaker so farr as to suffer him to speake to him with his hatt on, so let it be; but as I lately told some of that rabble, if they come cover'd before mee as a Justice of Peace, or acting by and under the King's authority, I ought to be jealous of the King's honour, and shall bind them to their good behaviors, let their religion or fancie rather be what it will. Last weeke at our Quarter Sessions some of them in the behalfe of a brother committed to the gaole not only refus'd to put off their hatts before the bench but upon question, began their canting and making strange faces. I freely told them they were much mistaken, for they were now under a lawfull and no mountebank Government, and so indeed put some of them besides their triks, but most of all when being offer'd the Oaths of Supremacy and Allegiance they were all committed to the gaole for refusing them. Their cheife speaker confes'd he had travell'd and bin amongst the Turkes where he was pittied, but here ensnar'd with oathes. The answer was easie; but I question whether he had not bin train'd up amongst the Jesuits[8].

I desire that these little accounts in a large letter may not invite your Lordship to anything of trouble in writing to mee againe more then desiring your Lordship's secretarie sometymes to acquaint mee with your and your Ladie's good health so heartily wish'd and prayed for by,

My Lord,

I am bould to acquaint your Lordship with so much of my particular business, that the Lord Mandeville[9], being indebted to mee about 3,000 li, hath desired to pay it in contrary to our first agreement suddenly within less than a month. If his Lordship holds to pay, I am to seeke how to dispose of the money at present. If your Lordship knows of any lands belonging to the Church in these parts or neere Richmond that are out of lease and now to be let, I shall desire to be tenant, upon notice from Dr. Chaworth[10] or whom your Lordship shall apoint. I heare the Dean and Chapter of Peterborough and some others have already lett.

---

[8] "Train'd up amongst the Jesuits." It was a common mistake to suppose that the Quakers were Jesuits in disguise. But the term "Quaker" was very loosely applied. and many of the fanatic party spoke rudely to the magistrates, with their hats on, Sir Justinian's reaction to the Quaker should be compared with Evelyn's (*Diary*, July 8th, 1656): "I had the curiosity to visit some Quakers . . . in prison: a new fanatic sect, of dangerous principles, who show no respect to any man, magistrate, or other, and seem a melancholy, proud sort of people, and exceedingly ignorant."

Bunyan, who cannot be accused of Cavalier views, ascribed strange doctrines to the Quakers in his *Grace Abounding*. Dr. Thorndike, from whom Sir Justinian may have derived information, was likewise bitterly opposed to Quakerism, denying its exponents the title of Christians. The whole passage is interesting, moreover, as it shows the magistracy's important part in the enforcing of the new settlement. The rising of the fanatics of 1661 was to lead to even worse times for the Quakers.

[9] "Lord Mandeville." This is Robert Montagu, son and heir of Edward, 2nd Earl of Manchester, styled Viscount Mandeville 1642–71. In May 1660 he went with the Commons deputation to The Hague to invite Charles II to return. In 1670 he sold the original Montagu estate in Northamptonshire at Hanging Houghton to Sir Justinian. He succeeded his father as 3rd Earl of Manchester, and died in 1682.

[10] "Dr Chaworth." He was Chancellor of the Dioceses of London and Chichester. See Letter II, Note 3.

LETTER CXXIII

[OCTOBER 9th.]

Sir, It wer a fairer way to forbear the committing a fault, then to apologize for it afterward. The truth of it is, that I look upon my self as a very guilty person, and if you have not charity enough to forgive me, I have nothing to say for my self but to plead multiplicity of business, and being overwhelmn'd with visits, and many impertinencies which ar never more troublesome, then when they light upon us as flies, and ar every way as importunat and surprise us commonly when we have least leasure to drive them away.

But I am confident, that whether I write, or not, you ar so fully assured of the integrity of my heart toward you, that nothing can render me in any ill character. For beleive it, there is no person living whom I have greater affection for, and more truly grounded upon the principles of worth, then I have for you. I am now for som few days gott to my cottage at Richmond, which I look upon as my cheif Palace, the rest which I should enjoy as Bishop of Winchester being for the most part so demolish'd, that of 4 houses[1] I have not the 4th part of one left to shelter me. As for my self, I am under the danger of a sore legg, which being cured (as I thought) twenty yeares past, breakes forth again. And I pray God, our publick sores do not do so too. My hope is that you, and yours enioy health and happyness, which is the daily prayer of

Your most true, and affectionat freind to serve you,
BR: WINTON

Richm: Oct: 9.

[ENDORSED REPLY OF SIR JUSTINIAN]

My Lord, I suppose mine by Mr. W. Garrard came to your Lordship's hands but very little after your Lordship's was sent to mee, for which I humbly thanke your Lordship with the many assurances of your Lordship's favour. I doubt not of your Lordship's taking the best advise for your sore leg. My Lord Brudenell[2] my very good neighbor had lately one, and cured (as 'twas thought) ower suddenly, that upon the stopping of the humor which had recourse to that part he was taken with a numness on that side, so that since he hath bin at the Bath and advised to an issue to prevent a palsy. For the publick sores I hope some remedy hath bin lately taken, though as in other diseases a little bleeding[3] at first prevents more than a great deale after. Pernicious flies and waspes have bin executed but the scorpions yet remaine, and some say are likely to do so. God direct all for the best.

---

[1] "4 houses." The "Palaces" of the Bishops of Winchester were Wolvesey House, Winchester, Farnham Castle, Southwark, and Waltham Park. They were all in a dilapidated condition. Wolvesey was rebuilt by Duppa's successor, Bishop Morley. Surrey was at that time part of the Diocese of Winchester.

[2] "Lord Brudenell." Thomas Brudenell of Deene, Northants, who was created in 1628 Baron Brudenell, was "a zealous loyalist, suffering much in the Royal cause, for which he was imprisoned in the Tower of London." He was a fellow prisoner of Sir Justinian in 1658 in Northampton (see Introduction to 1658). He was created Earl of Cardigan in 1661, and died aged "80 and upwards" in 1663. (G.E.C., *Complete Peerage*, Joan Wake, *The Brudenells of Deene* (1953)).

[3] "A little bleeding." On October 9th, 1660, the trial of the Regicides was opened in Hicks Hall before the Grand Jury of Middlesex. Ten of them were executed at Charing Cross, including Hugh Peters, the Preacher, who "lost all fortitude" and whose death was greeted with shouts of applause, on October 13th. The Act of Indemnity for all except the Regicides, was thought by many to err on the side of clemency. (Ranke, Vol. III, pp. 328–30).

[DECEMBER 12th.]

LETTER CXXIV

Sir, I have now newly crawl'd out of my chamber, to which the infirmities of my legs had for many dayes confined me. I cannot yet say that I am well, and it is held out as a probleme by my phisitians, whether it be fitt I should be so or no. But I incline to the favorable part, and if without other applications Nature shall heal it, I shall not willingly call in Art to make me worse.

Whilest this accident was sharp upon me, not onely my feet, but my hands so farr suffer'd by it, that I found as much difficulty to write as to walk, but having now gott into my closet, I shall by degrees hope for a recovery of both.

My greatest trouble for the present is, to answer the importunities of some unreasonable men who haunt me to do that which I am not able to do. For the King by his letters, having commanded that not onely old tenancy should be regarded, but that new purchasers should be satisfy'd, hath so tied up our hands, that though I infinitely long after it, I cannot find anything so free to me as to dispose of it where I please, which hath made me incapable of answering a clause of a former letter of yours. But if any thing worthy of you shall fall under my discovery, you shall quickly hear of me.[1]

In the mean time, I have an 100 [li] ready, to pay where you shall direct me, for though I receaved your bounty formerly as your gift, I must now look upon it under an other notion, as a debt which with many thankes I am to return to you. And when I have don all I can, I shall still be an everlasting debtor to you for all your acts of freindship shewn to

Your very faithfull freind, and humble servant,

BR: WINTON

Westm: Dec: 12.

[ENDORSED REPLY OF SIR JUSTINIAN]

I doubted the infirmitie in your Lordship's leggs would not so suddainly pass off, which made me lately enquire by an other of your Lordship's health, and now I perceive what I writt to your Lordship concerning the ill accident that followed Lord Brudenell's suddain cure of his sore legg,[2] is taken into consideration by your carefull physitians, who will rather attend Nature then over violently check her. And indeed my Lord, if I mistake not, your Lordship may be the best physitian by your selfe, by keeping a carefull diet, as forbearing salt and high season'd meats, etc. But with these infirmities of body, your Lordship acquaints mee with other molestations which I know are impossible to avoid, and as menstruall[2a] so most irksome to a man indispos'd or in yeares.

So that it ought to be the especiall care of some prudent and diligent persons about your Lordship to ease and keepe off as much as may be what is

[1] Some details about the leases of the Church lands are given in W. R. W. Stephens and F. T. Madge, *Documents relating to the History of the Cathedral Church of Winchester in the Seventeenth Century*, especially pp. 115–16 (Hants Record Society, 1897). "The bishops were obviously put in a very difficult position in 1660-1 by the King's commands neither to disregard the claims of old tenants nor to ignore recent purchases . . . The Church was suffering not for the first time from the King's desire to strengthen his position politically." (Note by Miss Whiteman).

[2] For Lord Brudenell see Letter CXXIII, Note 2.

[2a] "Menstruall". Bacon uses this of parts of the body; produced from the menstrual blood of the mother as opposed to spermatical (O.E.D.).

troublesome or impertinent, of which I am the more sensible, even by the honour I have to be so wel knowne to your Lordship, and upon that score have bin buffeted by I know not how many to moove your Lordship in severall things which I think not fitt, as but in one instance, and to save my promise in only mentioning it. My cosen Lane,[3] Mr. Walsh's son was importunate with me to recommend a brother of his to your Lordship's service in what quality your Lordship might thinke him fitt. I know him indeed to be a proper gentleman and have heard no ill of him, but now I have sayd all, and leave your Lordship to your owne freedome, beseeching thus much (once for all) that whatever I mention for my freinds or selfe, your Lordship never proceede beyond your owne good liking, not knowing that thing in the whole world for which I would attempt to abate or soure in the least that nobler freindship I have so long enjoy'd from your Lordship and ever since accounted as the very oyle and balsame of my life.

For what your Lordship is pleased to say is ready to be paid over where I shall appoint, I beseech your Lordship not to think at all of it, your Lordship I know being never the richer by it, nor my selfe poorer for not having it: and now make an open profession to your Lordship how God hath bless'd mee, and I veryly believe much the more for your Lordship's good praiers since I have had the happiness to be knowne to you.

Of honour and place I confess it was never in my nature to be ambitious, but alwaies desirous if it might so please God not to be the last of my family, there remaining not so much as one of my name, with whom I could bestow my daughters, having then no son. But since my tedious imprisonment and the death of my eldest and dearest daughter, God hath now given mee foure sons,[4] having formerly (as your Lordship knowes) had boyes only in picture.[5] Thus I acquaint you with my private comforts as heretofore with my afflictions, but now all overway'd with the publick blessing of seeing our King and religion I may now say re-restor'd.

---

[3] "My cosen Lane." Anne Isham, daughter of John Isham of Pytchley by Anne Fitzwilliam, was born June 13th, 1604. She married after 1620 William Lane of Horton and Glendon. Her father did not approve of this, as he had arranged a marriage for her with Isaac Johnson, son of the founder of Uppingham School. William and Anne Lane had four sons and four daughters: Francis (baptised January 15th, 1626/7), Ralph, William and Edward were the sons, one of whom is the man now recommended to Bishop Duppa. William Lane, the father, died on November 21st, 1637, and his widow then married Pierce Walsh, an Irishman, who was still alive in 1673, when he visited Lamport on July 17th (Thomas Isham's *Journal*).

Anne Isham, the wife of William Lane and later of Pierce Walsh, was a third cousin of Sir Justinian, being the great-granddaughter of Gregory Isham of Braunston, older brother of John Isham of Lamport, the ancestor of the baronets. They were both citizens and Mercers of London. Her grandfather, Sir Euseby Isham, inherited Pytchley on the death of his uncle Gyles, without male issue, in 1559. Sir Euseby Isham built the splendid Elizabethan house at Pytchley, which she and her husband (Lane) sold in 1632 to Francis Downes. After passing through the Washbourne and Knightley families, it became the headquarters of the Pytchley Hunt. It was pulled down in 1829 by George Payne of Sulby, Master of the Pytchley, and a famous gambler. A road now passes over the site. (Barron, *Northamptonshire Families*, V.C.H. (1906), T.G.F. Paget, *History of the Althorp and Pytchley Hunt 1634–1920* (where there is a plate of the old Hall at Pytchley) (1937)).

[4] "God hath now given mee foure sons." A fourth son, Charles, was born November 18th, 1660. The family was completed with the births of Ferdinando on April 18th, 1663, and Henry on September 17th, 1668.

[5] "Boyes only in picture." An allusion to the Infants Christ and St. John by Vandyck (see Letter XXIII, Note 7).

The scorpions I lately writt of were yet remaining, having now their stings discovered; and I hope to give sufficient warning for the future, that such are no way to be dealt with but one.

Next to the seal, Sir Justinian has written a memorandum:

"Gates to be mended, some walled up, warrants for foot and horse scouts to be sent abroad".

This, no doubt, has reference to his duties as deputy-lieutenant. In this capacity, in 1662, he was in charge of the demolition of the walls of Northampton and the Castle.

APPENDIX A

THE FAMILY CONNECTIONS OF BISHOP DUPPA

1. FATHER.

JEFFREY DUPPA, the father of Brian Duppa, had Herefordshire connections, especially, it would appear, with Pembridge, where he endowed a charity, which his sons enlarged. This "charitable work begun by Jeffrey Duppa esq. . . . for the support and maintenance of six poor people" was in 1637 augmented by his eldest son James Duppa, who granted certain named trustees a rent-charge of 40s per annum. Brian Duppa, the Bishop, by an indenture dated October 15th, 1661, further settled and increased the charity, which, administrated by the Rector and Churchwardens of Pembridge, in 1830 supported five old widows and an infirm old maid in an almshouse of six tenements, each with two rooms and a small garden. (*Charity Commissioners' Report on the Duppa Charity at Pembridge*). The almshouses are a range of six tenements on the west side of Bridge Street. They are illustrated (Plate 161) and briefly described in the *Royal Commission on Historical Monuments, Herefordshire*, Vol. III, p.163. It has been conjectured that Jeffrey's father may have been the David Duppa of Kington who is mentioned in the will (proved 1560) of John Duppa, also of Kington. That Jeffrey Duppa possibly had links with Kington is suggested by the fact that on two occasions at least his affairs came within the orbit of Dame Margaret Hawkins, the second wife of Sir John Hawkins, who was herself a native of Kington. In 1607 the fee of a parcel of ground in East Greenwich was conveyed to Jeffrey Duppa, and the name of Thomas Sheffield, a legatee under Lady Hawkins' will, occurs in the transaction (Hasted, *History of Kent*, Part I, *The Hundred of Blackheath*, ed. Henry Drake (1886), p.252). In 1609 Jeffrey Duppa brought an action in Chancery against Edward Scrivener of Frodesley in regard to money lent to him in 1607 on the security of his estates. Scrivener had fraudulently conveyed the property to Dame Margaret Hawkins and others (*Miscellanea Genealogica et Heraldica*, 4th Series, Vol. II (1906–7), p.41). Duppa was, however, of Lewisham, Kent, when he married on December 4th, 1580, Lucrece Marshall (the name is variously spelt) at St. Mary's Church there. He later moved to Greenwich: his daughter Alice is described as of East Greenwich at the time of her marriage in 1613/14.

Jeffrey Duppa, described as "Gentleman" (*Lewisham Parish Registers*), was Purveyor of the Buttery to Queen Elizabeth, and King's Brewer to King James I—positions, one might suppose, not without profit. Moreover, he held these positions for a long time. He was supervisor of malt deliveries to the Court as early as 1574; supplanted the Court brewing contractors in 1592, and kept the contract till the Queen's death. Early in the 17th century "he constructed a court brewhouse in Cambridgeshire" (Allegra Woodworth, *Purveyance from the Royal Household in the Reign of Queen Elizabeth* (Philadelphia (1945), p. 58). This brewhouse was at Newmarket, and was built "for H.M.'s better service and the ease of the country there and H.M.'s other places of abode on his winter journeys . . . upon often proof that both hath been made of his sufficiency . . .

[the Lord Steward orders Jeffrey Duppa] to undertake the charge of brewing ale and beer there and in all other places (to which H.M. journies) till by cause given . . . to the contrary he shall be discharged" (P.R.O., LS 13/168, f. 183; for this reference, and the next, I am indebted to Miss Woodworth). The brewhouse was finished in 1618 when an agreement was made on March 27th allowing Jeffrey Duppa and James Baldwin to "enjoy the use of H.M. Brewhouse lately built in the county of Cambridge at Newmarket without paying any rate or duty for the same" (LS 13/168, f. 193). An additional interest attaches to the brewhouse, in that it was one of the now vanished additions and alterations to the royal manor house at Newmarket carried out by Inigo Jones, then newly appointed to the office of Surveyor-General of the King's Works. They are described in James Lees-Milne's recent work *The Age of Inigo Jones* (1953), pp. 64-5.

By 1625, Jeffrey Duppa was evidently in somewhat reduced circumstances, for in this year the State Papers Domestic record that he and his wife received an annuity of £100 and a grant of a further £100 for their necessities. He died the same year and was buried at Greenwich on November 2nd (*Greenwich Parish Registers*, 1615–1636/7).

2. MOTHER.

LUCRECE MARSHALL (or MARESALL) was almost certainly the daughter of Godfrey Marshall (Mariscall, or Marishall) of the parish of St. Catherine Cree, who died about 1578, by his wife Margaret, whose maiden name is unknown (see G. W. Marshall, *Miscellanea Marescalliana*, Vol. I (1883), p.329, and *Registers of St. Mary, Lewisham*, 1558–1750, p.207. A Godfrey Marshall, or Marischall figures in the State Papers Domestic in 1568). Mrs. Marshall's second husband was Henry Brooke, mercer, of London and Lewisham, from whose will (proved December 2nd, 1595) much of our knowledge of the family of his wife by her first husband is derived: e.g. "To my son-in-law Mr. Jeffrey Duppa a ringe of the valewe of £3". He also mentions his "daughters-in-law Mary Turke and Lucrece Duppa" to whom he left £10. (They were really step-daughters).

3. BROTHERS.

The greater part of the Parish Registers of St. Mary, Lewisham were destroyed by fire in 1830, but from notes made by Lysons in1795, we know that the baptisms of seven Duppa children were recorded there, including those of three boys. There was another son, John, of whose baptism at Lewisham there is no record.

(*a*) JAMES DUPPA, baptised on November 19th, 1581, at Lewisham. He is mentioned in the will of his grandmother's second husband Henry Brooke, made in 1586 and proved in 1595. He was a "Sea-Captain", whose activities may be followed in some detail in the State Papers Domestic, and he is described as Captain James Duppa in the will (1632) of his nephew by marriage, Sir William Smith, of Hill Hall, Essex, to whom he was executor. He appears to have inherited his father's position of Royal Brewer, but his seafaring probably meant that he was unable to supervise the brewing of beer, and there is an entry under date April 8th, 1623, in the *Calendar of State Papers Colonial* (*America and West Indies, 1574–1660*):

> "Newport News. The country will be pleased to hear that revenge has been taken on Dupper for his stinking beer, which has been the death of 200 persons".

James Duppa "more fully settled" the charity begun by his father at Pembridge, "by indenture dated May 15th, 1637" (*Charity Commissioners' Report on the Duppa Charity at Pembridge*).

James Duppa married twice. His first wife was Anne, daughter of Sir Roger Jones, alderman and sheriff of the City of London, by his wife Anne, daughter of Thomas Hackett, whom he married at the Church of St. Michael, Paternoster Row, on February 19th, 1606/7. Anne Duppa was a niece of Thomas Jones (1550?–1619), Archbishop of Dublin and Lord-Chancellor of Ireland (see *Visitation of London* 1634). By this marriage James Duppa had two daughters. His second wife was Margaret Bourne, whom he married at Lewisham on August 3rd, 1637, and by whom inference shows that he had two daughters. He was still alive on February 17th, 1644/5, as on that day "They [i.e. the Lords] have likewise sent the petition of James Duppa which they hold very reasonable; and consent unto it, and desire your concurrence" (*Journals of the House of Commons*, Vol. IV, p. 51).

(*b*) MICHAEL DUPPA, baptised on September 24th, 1594, at Lewisham. He made a will on September 12th, 1621 (P.C.C. Byrde 17), mentioning "£125 in the hands of Sir John Wolstnam in England". This must be a reference to Sir John Wolstenholme, a rich Merchant Adventurer, Commissioner for Virginia, and an early member of the East India Company. Perhaps Michael Duppa's connection with him was in Virginia. Michael died abroad unmarried and administration (with will annexed) was granted to his brother John on February 6th, 1623/4.

(*c*) JOHN DUPPA. The date of his baptism is not given at Lewisham. His burial is recorded in the *Greenwich Parish Registers* as having taken place on April 3rd, 1626, five months after that of his father. However, in the letters of administration of John Duppa, it is shown that Herbert Croft was the son of his sister. (This is one of the links that enabled Miss Margaret Toynbee to unravel the exact relationship of Anne Croft (afterwards Lady Salter) to Bishop Duppa (see below under "Sisters").)

John Duppa accompanied as a civilian the expedition sent by James I to Algiers in 1620–1 against pirates. The fleet of "18 sayle" was commanded by Sir Robert Mansell (1573–1656) as Admiral, and the Vice-admiral was Sir Richard Hawkins, with whose family, as already stated under Jeffrey Duppa, the Duppas had been in touch for many years. Duppa's mission was to ransom English slaves from Barbary, and from Cadiz he reported to Lord [Buckingham (?)] on July 10th, 1622, complaining that he had "received no recompense for his work", but his recompense would be further employment to be a "comfort to those who in the country [Morocco] are in misery of his Ma:ts. subjects". He had succeeded in arranging with the Muccaden of Tetuan for the exchange of eight English slaves, and in securing an undertaking that no more British subjects should be sold (MS. Clarendon State Papers, 3, ff. 139–40). The expedition was described in *Algiers Voyage in a Journall or Briefe Reportary . . . the Accidents of every particular moneth by one that went along in the Voyage* (1621). There are several references to John Duppa in this work. (For this information I am indebted to Miss Margaret Toynbee.)

4. SISTERS.

(*a*) ANN, baptised on December 11th, 1582, at Lewisham. She is mentioned in the will of Henry Brooke. She married Edward Croft of Wigmore, Herefordshire, and had, with other issue, two daughters, Anne and Mary, both of whom are of some concern to us, and who appear below under "Nieces".

(*b*) MARGARET, baptised on July 23rd, 1584, at Lewisham, and buried there in 1592: "dau . . . Jeffrey Dupper, gen. . . . ." She is mentioned in Henry Brooke's will.

(*c*) MARY, baptised on January 4th, 1585/6, at Lewisham, and buried there in 1593: "daugh . . . Duppa was b . . . plague." She is mentioned in Henry Brooke's will.

(*d*) ALICE, baptised on October 11th, 1590, at Lewisham. In the *Visitation of Kent* 1619, it is recorded that William Smith of Greenwich, Serjeant-at-Law, married Alice, daughter of Jeffrey Duppa and (a later insertion) sister of the Bishop of Salisbury. It may be noted that the parcel of ground in East Greenwich, the fee of which was conveyed to Jeffrey Duppa in 1607, is described as "abutting south on the lands of William Smith, Esq.", presumably the father of Alice Duppa's husband. The elder William Smith is called "of Greenwich, sergeant at arms," in the *Visitation of Kent* 1619: he died in 1621. *The Visitation of Kent* 1663, describes the younger William Smith of Greenwich as "Serjt. at Armes to King Charles the first". Of this marriage, which took place on March 7th, 1613/4 at the Church of St. Margaret, Lee, Kent, there were numerous children (see under "Nephews" and "Nieces")*. William Smith made a will on October 29th, 1629, which was proved in March 1633/4 (P.C.C. Seager 26). He made his "loving wife" Alice Smith sole executrix. He bequeathed property in East Greenwich, and to his daughter Mary Smith (afterwards Mrs. Pett) he left "all my part, right, property and interest that I have or ought to have in the good shipp called the Negar [*sic*] and in the tackling, munitions and furniture to the said shipp." He does not, in this will, clear up the obscurity regarding his profession, but this interest in the good ship Negar shows that he was maritime in outlook. Alice Smith married John Bettenham of Pluckley as her second husband.

(*e*) MARGARET. Her baptism is not recorded at Lewisham, but she was presumably born after the death of the first Margaret and probably before the birth of her brother Michael in 1594. On February 20th, 1614/5 she married Richard Kilvert at the Church of St. Christopher near the Stocks, London. She is the most interesting of Duppa's sisters, and Miss Margaret Toynbee has written an account of her (*Notes and Queries*, September 2nd, 1950). Here it is sufficient to note that in 1638 she was a servant of Charles I's daughter, the Princess Elizabeth. She remained with the Princess through the dark days, and was not dismissed until June, 1649, much to her charge's grief. That she was not removed before, was probably due to her lawyer husband having turned his coat, and given evidence against his old master, Archbishop Laud (*Notes and Queries*, September 15th, 1951). Kilvert had been employed by Laud as prosecutor against Bishop John Williams, and Hacket, Williams' biographer, quotes Williams' description of him as "One that would undertake any Office to serve Greatness, and would preserve their Favour that kept him upon any Conditions . . . whose Description I cut off with that which *Cutzen* the Jesuit said of *Illyricus* . . . a vitiated Leper in his whole Substance" (John Hacket, *Scrinia Reserata* (1693), Part II, p.116).

It is satisfactory to note that James, Duke of York (one of whose attempts at escape Mrs. Kilvert had assisted in 1648, at much personal

* The entry in the Register at Lee has been altered, at some period, to "Humphrey" Smith. Information from Rector 13.1.52.

danger), at the Restoration granted her an annuity of £120 and made her (honorary) sub-governess to his children, the Princesses Mary and Anne, afterwards Queens of England, and their short-lived brothers. She died in 1674/5 and was buried on March 6th in the church of St. Martin-in-the-Fields. Bishop Duppa left her £100 in his will, and Mrs. Duppa £200 "to my sister Mistris Margaret Kilvert" (will P.C.C. Hyde 139, proved November 9th, 1665). One of Cromwell's spies reported that a Madame Kilvert (possibly Margaret) was in Bruges in January 1657 in the service of the Royalist Duchess of Richmond: perhaps this was one of the reasons for the search of her brother the Bishop's house in 1659. The Bishop, himself, was evidently friendly with the Duke and Duchess of Richmond (see Letter XXIVA, July 29th, 1652 and Note 1).

5. NEPHEWS AND NIECES.

(A) DUPPA, daughters of Captain James Duppa.

First marriage:

1. ANNE, married William Viner of London. Mrs. Duppa left her "cousin Mistris Viner, widowe, and to her son, Master James Viner" £40 each. Bishop Duppa left James Viner £200.

2. LUCRETIA, married Salomon Smith, who is probably to be identified with the Solomon Smith who was appointed Marshal of the Admiralty in 1635 after serving for sixteen years as the Marshal's deputy.

Second marriage:

3. ELIZABETH, married George Parry. In Bishop Duppa's will there is a bequest to Bryan Parry (£100). He was evidently a son of this marriage. Mrs. Duppa left £40 to Elizabeth Parry.

4. MARGARET, married (1) Rev. Lambrock Thomas, D.D., Vicar of Pevensey 1642–72, Chancellor of Chichester 1660–72, and Dean of Chichester in 1672. He died November 27th, 1672. (2) Before June 30th, 1675, Thomas Briggs, LL.D. (1669), Vicar-general of the Bishop of Chichester in 1702, and, as his monument at Chichester records, for more than forty years Chancellor of the diocese. He died in 1713 in his eighty-first year. (M.I. Chichester Cathedral). As "Margaret Thomas" the Bishop left her £100 and Mrs. Duppa £40. Briggs' second marriage, to Elizabeth Stapley, took place at Ringmer, Sussex on August 30th, 1684, by which time his first wife Margaret must have been dead. (Information from Archivist, Diocesan Record Office, Chichester, 2.1.52.).

(B) CROFT, children of Ann (Duppa) and Edward Croft of Wigmore.

5. HERBERT.

6. ANNE. She married first Sir William Smith of Hill Hall, Essex, who on his death in 1632 left his wife Ann Smith all his possessions including the manor of Ankerwyke. Captain James Duppa was one of his executors. By his previous marriage to Helegonway Conway, Sir William Smith was the father of an only son and heir, Edward, who "at the age of 15 served under Prince Rupert, in the civil wars, where he gained great reputation: he died aged twenty-two." Sir William Smith had an interesting connection with Northampton, since he inherited the "capital messuage and site of the priory of *St. Andrew*, with all the demesne lands and manors thereunto belonging", granted to his ancestor Sir Thomas Smith by Edward VI. On November 25th, 1631, he sold these possessions to Sir

Francis Crane, the builder of Stoke Bruerne Park (John Bridges, *Hist. and Antiq. of Northamptonshire*, Vol. I, p. 455). His widow Anne, "descended from the ancient Family of Croft in Herefordshire", erected a monument to him at Theydon Mount (Wotton's *Baronetage*).

Anne's second husband was Sir William Salter of Richings, Bucks, Royal Carver, who died in 1643. During the Commonwealth, at her house at Richings, Lady Salter entertained various Anglican clergy, including Henry King, Bishop of Chichester, and John Hales, "the ever-memorable", when he was ejected from Eton. He was tutor to her son, the "blockhead" William. Bishop Duppa left her £500 in his will, and Mrs. Duppa left her "my best diamond ring". Miss Margaret Toynbee has written an account of her (*Notes and Queries*, September 15th, 1951).

Of Lady Salter's children: (1) William the "blockhead" was given, in Duppa's will, the "benefit of the overplus of profitts if any be" of the manor of Pottherne (now spelt Potterne), Wilts., of which £200 yearly income was left to Dr. Chaworth, in whose name the manor's lease was. William Salter had a son, Bryan, who died in 1663. (2) Margaret, who was left £200 in the Bishop's will, and £40 in Mrs. Duppa's, married in 1666 Dr. George Stradling, Dean of Chichester 1672–88 (died 1688), and had two sons, Gilbert and George; she died in 1681. (3) Briana, who married Sir Charles Cleaver, was left £200 in the Bishop's will and also the house at Richmond, after the death of Mrs. Duppa and Dr. Chaworth. Mrs. Duppa left her "my second dyamond ring". Lucy, married to Thomas Breton, and Ursula, were two other children.

7. MARY. She was the first wife of (Sir) Richard Chaworth (1598–1672), brother of George, first Viscount Chaworth, who is so often referred to in this correspondence as "my nephew Chaworth". She died at Oxford and was buried in Christ Church Cathedral (November 25th 1645). Miss Margaret Toynbee discovered her existence from the Christ Church Registers (see Wood MS.F. 4., f.79, in the Bodleian Library, and *Life and Times*, Vol. I, p.125). Chaworth's second wife was Lady Sophia Bertie, fourth daughter of Robert, 1st Earl of Lindsey, but as she is nowhere mentioned in this correspondence, it would appear that she married him after the Restoration. She is not mentioned in Bishop Duppa's will, but Mrs. Duppa left her "my emerald ring", from which it may be deduced that the marriage took place between the making of the two wills, i.e. February 4th, 1661/2 and October 15th, 1664. This conjecture would appear to be confirmed by the fact that the Parish Church of Richmond possesses a silver-gilt cup inscribed under the foot "Ex dono Dnae Sophiae Chaworth 1663" (*Surrey Archaeological Collections*, Vol. XIII (1897), pp.63–4). Her brother, the 2nd Earl of Lindsey, was in correspondence with Sir Justinian in 1655 and does not allude to her. She died at Richmond on December 20th, 1689, and was buried there on January 1st, 1689/90. (M.I. and *Parish Registers*).

Dr. Chaworth was one of the Bishop's three executors, and he was left £200 per annum "out of the profitts" of the lease of the manor of Pottherne in Wiltshire, which manor's lease was to "continue in Dr. Chaworth during his life".* The house at Richmond "purchased in Sir Justinian Isham's name" was left to Mrs. Duppa for her life, then to Dr. Chaworth

* *Note*. In Bishop Ward's "Notitia", ii, f. 47, the tenant of this manor, which belonged to the Bishopric of Salisbury, is given as Sir Richard Chaworth c. 1670. The lease dated from c. 1640 and was perhaps put in Chaworth's name, when, in 1641, Duppa became Bishop of Salisbury.

for his life, and after the death of both of them to Lady Cleaver. He was one of Mrs. Duppa's three executors. In Chaworth's will (P.C.C., Pye 90, 1673) he left "my dear sister, the Ladie Salter, tenn pounds for a ringe, as a memoriall of our old freindshipp". He also mentions "my noble freind and nephew, Lord Viscount Chaworth," and his niece Mrs. Dorothy Long. He was buried at Richmond, November 16th, 1672. Aubrey in his *Natural History . . . of Surrey* (1718), pp. 70 and 81, records the inscriptions on two (now vanished) memorials to Chaworth in Richmond Church and Churchyard. The latter gave the date of his death (not elsewhere recorded) as November 12th, 1672.

8. It seems practically certain that Edward and Ann Croft had A THIRD DAUGHTER who was the first wife of Francis Sheldon, Clerk of the Check in Woolwich Dockyard. In his will, proved in 1646, Sheldon left a legacy to his "sister Lady Salter", and his son Charles was left £100 in Bishop Duppa's will.

(C) SMITH, children of Alice (Duppa) and William Smith of Greenwich.

9. WILLIAM, aged five in 1619 (*Visitation of Kent* 1619). Educated at Westminster (K.S. 1630); matriculated from Christ Church, Oxford, July 17th, 1635.

10. FRANCIS, baptised on January 24th, 1616/7 at Greenwich.

11. JOHN, baptised on November 28th, 1623 at Greenwich, mentioned in his father's will 1629.

12. THOMAS, baptised on April 4th, 1626 at Greenwich, mentioned in his father's will 1629. According to the *Visitation of Kent* 1663, he married Katherine, daughter of William Bates, and had a son and heir Bryan, aged three in 1663. The Bishop left "Captaine Thomas Smyth" £300 in his will and Mrs. Duppa left him £40.

13. BRIAN, baptised on June 21st, 1627 at Greenwich, mentioned in the will of his sister Elizabeth Hanbury, proved 1709.

14. MARY, baptised on May 7th, 1618 at Greenwich, became the second wife of Peter Pett, one of the Commissioners of the Navy, frequently mentioned in Pepys' *Diary*. Her father's legacy to her of his interest in a ship has already been noted. See §4(*d*) above. On January 14th, 1660/1 Pepys says: "After dinner Mrs. Pett lent us her coach, and carried us to Woolwich". On June 17th, 1667, Peter Pett was committed to the Tower, "which" says Pepys, "puts me into a fright, lest they do the same with us as they do with him."

Mrs. Pett was left £50 in the Bishop's will, and as "Mary Pitt" £40 by Mrs. Duppa. She was named in her husband's will, made in 1663, and left "two necklaces of pearles . . . one dymond ring" and other jewels and furnishings. But she died on January 28th, 1664/5, and on December 11th, 1665, her husband married (for the third time) Elizabeth, daughter of George Pitt, and relict of Sir Henry Hatton of Mitcham. His will was proved in 1672 (P.C.C. Eure 153). He was unfortunate in being made the scapegoat of the Dutch raid into the Thames. His house and gardens were famous and their rarities viewed by both Pepys and Evelyn. (Pepys' *Diary*; "The Builders of the Navy", *The Ancestor*, Vol. x (July 1904); *Miscellanea Genealogica et Heraldica*, 4th Series, Vol. I (1905/6), pp.214, 216 and 249).

15. LUCRECIA, baptised on June 16th, 1619, at Greenwich, mentioned in her father's will 1629.

16. KATHERINE, baptised on January 31st, 1620/1 at Greenwich, not mentioned in her father's will, as are his other four daughters, which

suggests that she might have been dead by 1629.

17. FRANCES (Fraunce) baptised on May 6th, 1622, at Greenwich, mentioned in her father's will 1629.

18. ELIZABETH, whose baptism is not recorded at Greenwich, but who is mentioned last of the four daughters in her father's will of 1629, married as the first of her three husbands William Acworth, store-keeper at Woolwich Dockyard, whose first wife Avice Cole had been a sister of Peter Pett's first wife Catherine, and whose second wife Elizabeth was the widow of a "soldier of fortune and no estate" named William Mundy. (*The Ancestor*, Vol. XII (January 1905), p. 195.)

The writer of the articles in *Miscellanea Genealogica et Heraldica* (4th Series, Vol. II, pp. 40–43 and 54–56) noted that a number of gold jacobus were "concealed in the dress of a Mrs. Ackworth, while riding through O. Cromwell's Army", and three of these it is conjectured were left to her first cousin once removed, Margaret Salter, who became Mrs. Stradling. It was suggested that these coins were sent by Bishop Duppa for the use of Charles II in his exciting escape after the battle of Worcester. Some colour is lent to this suggestion by these letters, in which the friendship is established between Bishop Duppa and Dr. Henchman, who played a prominent part in the escape of the King. It was Dr. Henchman who arranged for Charles' concealment at the secluded house of his friend, Mrs. Hyde of Heale near Salisbury, and, with Colonel Phelips, planned his subsequent journey to the Sussex coast, and so to France and safety. (Allan Fea, *The Flight of the King*, 2nd edn. (1908)). Mrs. Acworth's exploit would be quite in keeping with the character of the courageous women of her family, Margaret Kilvert and Anne Salter. She and her husband also occur in Pepys' *Diary* after the Restoration, for he describes a dinner at Mrs. Acworth's on January 15th, 1660/1 as a "good dinner and very handsome". Although Pepys' opinion of William Acworth was unflattering (he calls him "a very knave"), he describes his wife as a "very proper lovely woman". When her brother-in-law Peter Pett was committed to the Tower in 1667, Mrs. Acworth obtained a warrant to visit him (State Papers Domestic). William Acworth, however, was evidently a Royalist, and in 1647 he warned Charles I, then a prisoner at Hampton Court, that Colonel Rainsborough, who was sailor as well as soldier, was plotting to kill the King (*A Narrative by John Ashburnham*, Vol. II, p.107).

After her first husband's death (which probably took place about 1670) Elizabeth Acworth made two further marriages, first, to Robert Foley of Stourbridge, then to Capel Hanbury.* In her will of 1709

* *Note.* The writers in *The Ancestor* give the name of Elizabeth Acworth's second husband as Robert Tobey of Stourbridge, but in Nash, *Collections for the History of Worcestershire*, Vol. II (1782), p.464a, there is a pedigree of the Family of Foley, ironmasters of Stourbridge, in which it is stated that "Elizabeth . . . relict of William Ackworth" was the second wife of Robert Foley, J.P., who died aged fifty on November 19th, 1676, "sometime high sheriff of the county of Worcestershire". He was a younger brother of Pepys' friend Thomas Foley (D.N.B.). In the same pedigree Elizabeth Acworth's third husband is stated to be Capell Hanbury of Whorston near Bewdley. For Capel Hanbury see A. A. Locke, *The Hanbury Family* (Two volumes, 1916), Vol. I, pp. 148–51. In the account of Capel Hanbury's father it is stated that he was, like the Foleys, interested in iron, being a "dealer in merchandise of iron". Elizabeth Foley was Capel Hanbury's third wife, and they were married at the Church of St. Martin, Worcester, on August 6th, 1682. He died at Hoarstone (Nash's "Whorston") on January 14th, 1704/5 and was buried in Kidderminster Church.

(P.C.C. Lane 1) she mentions "her loving kinswoman Elizabeth Pett" and her grandson-in-law (i.e. step-grandson) Jacob Acworth, afterwards knighted and for many years Commissioner of the Navy. (*The Ancestor*, Vol. XII (1905), p.195). Duppa left "Mrs. Ackworth for Bryan her sonne, £100", and Mrs. Duppa left £40 to her and to three other nieces of her late husband, Margaret Thomas, Elizabeth Parry and Mary Pitt (Pett), as mentioned above.

(D) KILVERT, children of Margaret (Duppa) and Richard Kilvert.

19. ROBERT. He matriculated from Christ Church, Oxford, aged sixteen on November 10th, 1637. He was in about 1640 appointed "quarter waiter" in the Royal Household, and he "served and suffered in the King's cause in the late wars", as he explained in a petition to Charles II in 1660. Robert Kilvert, "the sonne" of Mrs. Kilvert, was left £100 by Bishop Duppa, and Mrs. Duppa left her "cousin, Robert Kilvert" £40. He had a son to whom the Bishop left £100.

20. A DAUGHTER, whose husband's name was Thornton. Bishop Duppa left £100 to Mrs. Thornton "for her daughter" and Mrs. Duppa left her £40, as "Mistris Thornton".

21. MARY (Jackson) is mentioned in the schedule of legacies attached to Bishop Duppa's will thus: "Mrs. Jackson for her daughter £100". Miss Toynbee suggests that her husband was possibly the Jackeson whom Princess Elizabeth mentioned on his dismissal from her service, wishing him "good fortune" in a letter of June 29th, 1649. Mrs. Duppa describes her as "Mistris Mary Jackson" sister of Mrs. Thornton (No. 20), and also left her £40.

22. JANE. Mrs. Duppa left £100 to "my neece and Godaughter Mistris Jane Smith wife of Master Miles Smith".* Her marriage must have taken place between the making of Bishop Duppa's will (February 4th, 1661/2) and Mrs. Duppa's (October 15th, 1664) as in the Bishop's will she appears as Jane Kilvert, to whom a legacy of £300 was left.

Miles Smith (c.1618–1671/2) was an Oxford man ("servitour" at Magdalen in 1634–5) who, on the outbreak of the Civil War, adhered to the King's side and was made B.C.L. on August 4th, 1646. After the Restoration, he entered the service of Gilbert Sheldon, Bishop of London, and became his secretary, when Sheldon was made Archbishop. He died on February 17th, 1671/2, and was buried at St. Mary's Church, Lambeth (M.I. which, however, has disappeared).† Jane Kilvert's marriage to Miles Smith was yet another connection with the ecclesiastical lawyers. There was a son of the marriage, undergraduate at Trinity College, Oxford, who died on October 17th, 1682, aged 18 (Foster, Wood, *Life and Times*, III, 28).

The authorities for this list of relations (where not specially given) will be found in Miss Margaret Toynbee's two articles on Margaret Kilvert and

* That this Miles Smith was the Miles Smith who was Sheldon's secretary is proved by an entry (p.308) in the *Act Books of the Archbishops of Canterbury*, 1663–1859, Part II, L–Z, Index Library, LXIII (1938) (where Jane Smyth, wife of Miles Smyth of Lambeth, Surrey, was licensed to eat flesh meat in Lent 1663/4, and also by the secretary's will.

† For original inscription see *The History and Antiquities of the Parish of Lambeth in the County of Surrey* (1786), See also Appendix No. XXI, Epitaphs at Lambeth, pp. 39–40, and D.N.B., where however, the date of his death is wrongly given as 1670/1, and there is no mention of his marriage; Foster, where he is wrongly stated to have been a son of Miles Smith, Bishop of Gloucester, died 1624. He was, perhaps, a great-nephew. Wood, *Ath. Ox.* III, 951–2, and *Fasti* II, 94 (ed. Bliss), gives an accurate account. Miles Smith's will is in P.C.C. (Eure 34).

Lady Salter in *Notes and Queries* (September 2nd, 1950 and September 15th, 1951)*; two articles in *Miscellanea Genealogica et Heraldica*, 4th Series, Vol. II (1906-7), pp.40–3 and 54–6; J. Challenor Smith, "Bishop Duppa's Wife", *The Genealogist*, New Series, Vol. IV (1887), pp. 116–18.

6. OTHER CONNECTIONS.

It remains to comment on some of the connections mentioned in the notes.

First, Mrs. Jeffrey Duppa's family (the Marshalls) are the key to Bishop Duppa's relationship to the Lewyns, with whom Sir Justinian was connected through his mother. Lucrece Marshall (Mrs. Jeffrey Duppa), the Bishop's mother, had a sister Mary, who occurs in the will of her step-father Henry Brooke as "Mary Turke" (see §2 above). Her husband was John Turke, an attorney at law, of Wrotham, Kent, and Staple Inn, Holborn, and they had, with other issue, a daughter Susan (born 1588), who married on August 21st, 1610 at the Church of St. Olave, Hart Street (*Parish Registers* 1563–1700: they contain many Turke and Lewyn entries) Daniel Lewyn of Gerpins, Essex. Daniel and Susan were the parents of "our little cousin", John Lowen, who occurs several times in the letters and is mentioned in Mrs. Duppa's will. This Daniel Lewyn was a second cousin of Judith Lewyn, who married Sir John Isham.

Secondly, Mrs. Jane Duppa's family (the Killingtrees) explain another complicated problem relating to the letters,† the marriage of Franck (Frances) Marsh and Dr. William Turner. Nicholas Killingtree, Jane Duppa's father, had, with other issue, a daughter Elizabeth, who was the second wife of Dr. James Marsh, Archdeacon of Chichester (1639), and a Royal Chaplain. She occurs in Bishop Duppa's will as "Mrs. Elizabeth Marsh", and he left her £100. Mrs. Duppa also left "my sister, Mistris Elizabeth Marsh, Widowe", £1,000 and an annuity of £200. She was one of Mrs. Duppa's three executors. She was buried at Richmond on September 24th, 1680 (*Parish Registers of Richmond, Surrey*). The exact date of Dr. James Marsh's death is not known, but it must have been between 1644 and 1646. (He was still alive in 1643/4 (*Walker Revised*, p.54), but dead by August, 1646, when William Killingtree's sisters obtained administration of his will, and Elizabeth Marsh is described as "widow"). Frances Marsh, though described in "Bishop Duppa's Wife" as a niece of the Duppas, was, however, only the step-daughter of Mrs. Elizabeth Marsh. Her mother was the first wife of Dr. James Marsh, Elizabeth, daughter of Sir John Davis of Pangbourne. She died on November 21st, 1634 and was buried at Hurst, Berks. (M.I.). (See "Some Notice of Various Families of the Name of Marsh" printed at the end of *The Genealogist*, New Series, Vol. XVI (1899–1900), p. 5). Frances Marsh's civil marriage to Dr. William Turner took place on February 19th, 1654/5, "by John Bentley, esquire" (*Parish Registers of Richmond*, Vol. I (1903), p.149). This was followed by the religious ceremony in Duppa's house performed by the Bishop on February 25th (Quinquagesima Sunday). She was his second wife. They had a son Bryan, born on September 21st, 1660 (*Richmond Registers*), who was left £100 in the Bishop's will and

* When she wrote her article on Margaret Kilvert, Miss Toynbee had not seen the full text of Mrs. Duppa's will. This mentions "Mistris" (not Margaret) Thornton, and proves that the conjecture that Mrs. Jackson was another daughter of Mrs. Kilvert was correct.

† *Note.* See Letter LXIV, February 21st, 1654/5, and Note.

£50 by Mrs. Duppa, who describes him as "my late husband's Godsonne". He was buried on August 2nd, 1687 (*Richmond Registers*). There was also a daughter Frances, born on June 10th, 1662 (*ibid.*), who was left £20 by Mrs. Duppa.

Although there is no direct allusion to it in the letters, one other important connection of Mrs. Jane Duppa's family should be noted. In her will, she made her first cousin once removed, Henry Mallory, her residuary legatee and left him £1,500 (see Note A at end). He was one of the three persons who proved her will in 1665. She also mentions her cousins John and Richard Mallory, to whom she left legacies. These were, perhaps, Henry's brothers. Another brother, Anthony, was buried at Richmond on January 14th, 1640/1. His sisters "Barbarah Cooke wife of John Cooke Chirurgion" and "Mistris Wiseman" are separately mentioned. Mrs. Duppa's father, Nicholas Killingtree, had married Jane, daughter of William Mallory of Papworth, Hunts (where Mrs. Jane Duppa was born). This William Mallory died in 1585: he had a son William (brother of Mrs. Jane Killingtree), who had a son Sir Henry Mallory, and Henry Mallory was the latter's son. He has a special interest, in that he was involved in the Hewett-Slingsby conspiracy against Cromwell in 1658. He was then of Preston, Sussex (Thurloe, *State Papers*, Vol. VII, p.74). He was drawn into the conspiracy by John Stapley of Patcham, who offered Mallory a commission as major in his regiment. John Stapley's father Anthony (a regicide) had a sister, Grace, who married, as his second wife, Thomas Shirley of Preston, the uncle of Henry Mallory, whose mother was Judith Shirley. Incidentally, Anthony Shirley, Thomas Shirley's grandson by his first wife, was another of the 1658 conspirators. This Sussex conspiracy by men all nearly related, and all connected with Mrs. Duppa, must have made 1658 a worrying year for the Bishop and his wife. Bishop Duppa left Henry Mallory £20 in his will. (For Mallory see Thurloe, Vol. VII, pp.88, 194, 220, 622; Clarendon, Book XV; and C. Thomas-Stanford, *Sussex in the Great Civil War and the Interregnum, 1642–1660* (1910)).

CONCLUSIONS

Although it will be seen that only a few of these relations are mentioned in the present correspondence, they have a certain importance for the understanding of the Bishop's family background. The following conclusions may be drawn:

1. The Bishop's own family were intimately connected with the Court as Royal servants.
2. The Bishop himself was very much the great man of the family, and one sister and nearly all the nephews and nieces called children after him, e.g. Bryan Acworth, Bryan Salter, Bryan Turner, Bryan Parry, Brian and Bryan Smith, and even "Briana" Salter!*
3. Mrs. Duppa's family connections were even more "Royalist" than the Bishop's, and through Henry Mallory she was connected with a formidable group of Royalist conspirators.
4. Apart from Royal servants, the family connections appear to have favoured the legal profession, e.g. William Smith, Richard Chaworth, Richard Kilvert, John Lowen, Thomas Briggs and Miles Smith; and the

* *Note.* In the schedule attached to Bishop Duppa's will, Bryan Reeves is left £50. His name occurs between those of Mrs. Pett and Mrs. Thomas. He may be another great-nephew, possibly the son of Lucrecia or Frances Smith, of whom we know nothing after 1629 when they were aged ten and seven.

Navy, e.g. besides James Duppa himself, Solomon Smith, Peter Pett, William Acworth and Francis Sheldon. John Duppa, perhaps the youngest brother, although not actually a sailor, went, as we have seen, on a naval expedition. Bishop Duppa himself seems to have taken a lively interest in sea-travel and exploration. Richard Ligon in dedicating to the Bishop his *True and Exact History of the Island of Barbados* (1657) states that Duppa had made enquiries regarding the Island, and given encouragement to the publication "for the common benefit of those, who intend to spend their times, and venture their fortunes upon such undertakings"; and Duppa in a letter accepting the dedication (printed in the volume), urges him, however, "to look over your Catalogue of Friends; and, though you cannot finde one that loves you better, yet to make choice of him, that can protect you better"; an allusion to the fact that the dedication (July 12th, 1653) was written from the Upper Bench Prison.

One of the few clergymen that occur has a Court connection, i.e. Dr. James Marsh. There is also a connection with Chichester, where Duppa was Bishop 1638–41. Dr. Marsh was Archdeacon and Chancellor of Chichester; Margaret Duppa, the Bishop's niece, married Lambrock Thomas, the Vicar of Pevensey, also, for a short time, Dean of Chichester; and another Dean, George Stradling, married a great-niece Margaret Salter (see §5B). Richard Chaworth and Margaret Thomas' second husband, Thomas Briggs, were also successively Chancellors of the diocese of Chichester.

Note A. On April 3rd, 1666, Sir Richard Chaworth wrote to Sir Justinian regarding his Aunt Duppa's death. This letter mentions Mrs. Elizabeth Marsh, Mrs. Duppa, and Captain Mallory. The text is as follows:—

(I. C. 581).

"This to the much honour'd Sir Justinian Isham, Baronett, at Lamport in Northampton shr,—present." "pd. 6d."

Sir,

I presume you have heard of the sad mischance of my aunt Duppa, who dyed by a fall in her garden last October, who has left the residue of her estate (after many legacyes to her kindred and friends) to Cap[tain] Mallory; her house now falls to me, if yu pleas to depute Mr. Chabnor according to the inclosed to surrender your right to the court for my admittance, and to returne it sign'd and seal'd to mee at my lodging at Mrs. Seyles ovr agt. St. Dunstan's Fleet street, as soon as my admission is over (which wilbe in Easter weeke or the weeke after) I shall transmitt under your hand and seale of 230*li.* which I here acknowledge to be delivered unto yu upon my admission, so I shall deliver it to any you shall name, or inclose it in a letter to your cuncell. My Aunt Duppa left about 8000*li.* which Mrs. Marsh thought all hers, but has but about 1000*li.* and 200*li.* per ann. for her life but the interest of soe much as must not be called in as long as she lives, shee has left yu 10*li.* for a ring, but I shall not trouble you with more particulars but with my humble service to your selfe and your noble Lady, remayne

Your very humble and obliged servant,

RICH. CHAWORTH.

London, Fleet Street. April the 3rd, '66.

On June 5th, 1666 at a "special Court Baron of the very noble Edward Villiers Esq. Lord of the Manor of Richmond . . . Justinian Isham by John Chabnor his attorney surrendered" the Richmond property "to the use of Richard Chaworth Knt his heires and assigns forever." At Sir Richard Chaworth's death in 1672, the property passed to his nephew and heir-at-law Patrick, Viscount Chaworth, who surrendered it at the Manorial Court in 1685. "Marsh widow" is mentioned as a tenant with Sir Richard Chaworth at the Court Baron in 1666. (Court Rolls of the Manor of Richmond; transcripts at Richmond Public Library.)

APPENDIX B

UNDATED LETTERS

There are eleven letters which cannot be positively dated owing to the lack of internal evidence. With the exception of I(D)133 March 15th (1658?), they are not of great importance. A Calendar of these letters follows. They are catalogued in the Isham MSS. as I(D)123 and 125–134.

BRIAN DUPPA TO SIR JUSTINIAN ISHAM

1. I(D)123. April 12th. [After 1653 (allusion to "your good Lady")].

"Had not Seneca told his good friend Lucilius *satis magnum theatrum. Sumus tu et ego*[1], we might possibly be at a loss what to write one to the other: for the things without us ar so unpleasant, and so unfitt for letters, that wer it not for the mutuall enquiring about each other's health, we might spare the carrier the labor of being the instrument of continuing this intercourse between us. But the acts of freindship admitt of no long pauses and intermissions."

Duppa alludes to the healthy winter, and his own freedom from gout, stone, and colds, but says there is a "murain among horses" which threatens a plague among men, and it is said that it is begun already (though concealed) in Poneropolis, "where the chair of wickedness imagins mischief as a law."[2] Adds a postscript: "My wife returns her humble thanks to your self and your good Lady,[3] who hath so kindly remembered her."

2. I(D)125. May 15th. [After 1651. Justinian already a Baronet.]

A short letter in which the Bishop complains of "sore eyes".

3. I(D)126. February 3rd. [After 1653.]

Has been visiting London, to "assist a dying person, and so noble a freind to me, that unless it be yourself I have not such an other left me." While in London was "full of doubts and fears, concerning that excellent lady the Countess of Devonshire (who all that while lay languishing under God's hands, expecting with great patience the minute of her dissolution). Your letter brought me the unwellcom news of your own sickness, and your Ladie's which laid more load upon me." But, luckily Lady Devonshire is better, thanks to "God's favor to her, who having brought her to the gates of death, hath stop'd there at least if He hath not brought her back again." Hopes to hear of the recovery of Sir Justinian and his wife.

---

[1] See Letter XLII, February 1st, 1654.

[2] 1657 and 1658 were the years of the "new disease". See Letter XCIII, October 14th, 1657, Note 1. But there was a horse disease in Suffolk in April 1659, so the letter may belong to that year (I.C. 487). Poneropolis, "the city of wickedness", is Duppa's synonym for London.

[3] The marriage to Vere Leigh took place in 1653. Sir Justinian succeeded to the baronetcy, July, 1651.

Duppa mentioned Lady Devonshire living at Roehampton, November 1st, 1653. (See Letter XXXV, Note 3). She was then apparently quite well. She did not die till 1674. The illness must have been after 1653. These "distempers" might place the letter either in 1657 or 1658.

4. I(D)127. May 10th. [1653?]

Sir Justinian has had a "feaver," but the news of his recovery followed close on the news of an illness. Is glad to think of the "care and art of your phisitian, which hath not onely been happy in curing your disease, but in praeventing that of your daughter in whom you have so much comfort." Hopes to see him in London or Richmond. "I must say nothing of our present alterations, for though som look upon them as wonders, I should rather look upon it as a wonder if they were not." Adds that "this conversing by letters is apt to deceave me. . . I am willing to beleive that it is no trouble to read what otherwise I should have said, had you been with me on the seat, on the top of the Hill, where we wer wont to see the glory of the world, and despise it when we had don."

The daughter referred to is presumably Jane Isham, who kept house for Sir Justinian before his second marriage. This places the letter either in 1652 or 1653. The "present alterations" may refer to the expulsion of the Long Parliament in April, 1653 and the establishment of the Council of State on April 29th (Gardiner Vol. II, p.273). There is a gap in the letters in that year, March 29th to June 9th, which this letter may fill.

5. I(D)128. October 8th. [After 1650.]

Duppa is anxious because he did not hear, as he expected, from Sir Justinian, so he writes again, "Freindship is a kind of spirituall fire, and may be kept alive without any such paper and mutuall pair of bellows", i.e. their correspondence. (A short letter).

6. I(D)129. [After 1653.]

Dated only "Monday morning". Sir Justinian has brought his wife on a visit to the Bishop, and taken her "for such a walk that unless you have used her to it nearer your own home, she might possibly receave som praejudice by it." Hopes they will return soon—"your departure was so suddain." "On that solemn day which is now so near approaching, you may here privately receave the Holy Sacrament."

7. I(D)130. March 14th. [1655?]

A letter of the Bishop's has miscarried: "there was nothing in it either of old or new treasons (and consequently no danger in the miscarriage)." Is sending this letter "by the very honest hands of Mr. Adler."

This may be the letter referred to by Mr. Adler in his letter to Sir Justinian of April 5th, 1655: see Letter LXIII, Note 5.

8. I(D)131. February 12th. [After 1651.]

Is worried at not having heard from Sir Justinian. "I shall begge a letter from you upon the next return . . for God hath so order'd it, that I must ether joy or mourn with you." Later, "I am as yet in health, and as yet in liberty." (A short letter).

9. I(D)132. November 30th. [After 1651. Possibly 1657.]

Thanks for "your kind token to my wife, and your charitable contribution to that deserving person whose book I sent you came safe to us." He signs himself unusually "Your many wayes obliged freind and humble servant."

Sir Justinian made Bishop Duppa the distributor of his charity to the sequestered clergy. In 1657, Bishop Duppa sent Anthony Farindon, silenced Minister of St. Mary Magdalen, Milk St, 40*s* through the hands of Mr Adler. This was the year Farindon published his first volume of sermons. It is possible that this book and this episode may be linked with this letter. See Letter XCIX Note 3.

10. I(D)133. March 15th. [After 1653. 1658?]

"This superfoetation [the formation of a second foetus in a uterus already pregnant] and latter birth of winter is so sharp and bitter to me, that it confines me to the chimny corner, where though I can take a book in my hand, and please my self with reading, yet when I come to the writing part, my hand shakse and my benumbed fingers do it very untowardly. But whatever it is, or may be, you must not 'scape the trouble of my letters, for should I faile once in that tribute I should deserve to be posted up as a bankrupt in freindship, the onely thing left me to be rich in."

He mentions having read the reply Sir Justinian has mentioned to some work, finds some "delight for the manner of writing it, but the argument in itself is taedious to me. . . Replyes of this nature ar seldom better then coleworts [cabbages] twice boil'd." But a political argument of this kind "will little concern us on ether side. The grand result of the quaesion is expected from somthing else, and it is an oracle of power, and not of witt that must determine it. In the meane time, you ar safe in your oeconomicall government, where none quaestions your power, and the onely ballance is the religious care of the parents and the complying of all your relatings in obedience to you. But I am driven to turne againe to the fireside, and shall reserve the rest till a warmer season day." His wife insists on presenting her service "to your very good Lady."

This is the most interesting letter of the series. In his draft reply to Bishop Duppa's letter of July 29th, 1657, Sir Justinian Isham mentioned Matthew Wren's *Considerations on Mr. Harrington's Oceana*. On September 9th, Bishop Duppa mentioned having read the book with approval, and added: "the *Reply* I as yet hear nothing of, and when I do I shall not much long after it." It is, therefore, quite likely this *Reply* of Harrington's, which was published in 1658, that Duppa has just read, and this letter then belongs to that year.

11. I(D)134. June 29th. [1652?]
Asks for a letter. "Onely let me not be a stranger to you, for with out courting or flattering you . . . I have built up much of the comforts of my short remainder of this life upon your freindship, which, I am persuaded, is no hollow ground." Has no great hopes of seeing Sir Justinian. "There is a long and it may be an everlasting vacation coming on, when London shall be no longer the *Medius Terminus* to bring freinds together, for the Reformation holds forth to you that Law (and somthing else with it) shall be brought home to your own dores."

In January, 1652, a Committee was appointed (with Matthew Hale at its head) "to remove the inconveniences of the existing law." In March, 1652 it forwarded the draft of several bills to Parliament. One of them provided for district registries for wills, deeds, and letters of administration in every county in England. Bishop Duppa may be referring to this legal "Reformation", and the letter, therefore, be assigned to 1652. But this is such a "lean" year for correspondence, that there is little to check this guess. The draft legislation of the Hale Committee was considered by Parliament in January, 1653, but none of it was ever passed owing to the turning out of the Long Parliament in April, 1653. Hale was one of Selden's executors, and Duppa does not seem to trust him. See Letter LXI, Note 2. (F. Inderwick, *The Interregnum* (1891), for legal reforms in this period, also Gardiner, Vol.II, p.82.)

APPENDIX C

ADDENDA TO THE FOOTNOTES

(i. Referring to the Memoir of Bishop Duppa)

P. xx—Duppa as Dean of Christ Church.

Among the learned men, whom Duppa encouraged as Dean of Christ Church, was John Gregory (1607–1646), the orientalist, whom he made Chaplain of the Cathedral at Oxford, and, on his elevation to the episcopate, his own domestic chaplain.

Gregory's *Notes and Observations upon some Passages of Scripture* (1646) was dedicated to Brian Duppa (D. N. B.). The Rev. John Gregory is not to be confused with a man of the same name who was a contemporary, and a Strand barber and wig-maker, of whose curious epitaph at St. Clement Danes a copy is preserved at Lamport (I.L.4335).

P. xxii—Duppa's edition of *Jonsonus Virbius*.

Brian Duppa had a posthumous connection with another famous Johnson. As Mr. Lindsay Fleming has recently shown, Samuel Johnson made extensive use of Duppa's *Holy Rules and Helps to Devotion* when compiling his Dictionary. In his copy of this book, Dr. Johnson marked in pencil passages to illustrate 84 words (Lindsay Fleming "Dr. Johnson's use of Authorities in compiling his Dictionary of the English Language" in *Notes and Queries*, June, July and August, 1954 (New Series, Vol.I, No. 6, 7 and 8)).

Duppa's *Holy Rules and Helps to Devotion* was used by others besides Dr. Johnson. The book "was greatly admired and constantly used by one who in depth of piety and learning and in soundness of churchmanship was, to say the least, not a whit behind the author – Walter Farquhar Hook, sometime dean of Chichester". (W. R. Stephens, *Memorials of the South Saxon See and Cathedral Church of Chichester* (1876), p. 281. I am grateful to Mr. Lindsay Fleming for drawing my attention to this work).

P. xxix—Duppa's Charity at Richmond.

Regarding Duppa's Almshouses, Miss Kathleen Courlander, in her recently published *Richmond* (1953) records a tradition retailed by the old people in Richmond (p. 65):

> "Noticing that he was followed by soldiers, Duppa rushed into a cottage and begged the housewife to hide him. She made him get into a bed and cover himself with clothes, contriving to get rid of the men when they knocked at the door, on the pretext that she had a sick daughter. The grateful prelate vowed he would repay her kindness."

P. xxx—Duppa's literary work.

Although the Life of Archbishop Spotiswood prefixed to his *History of the Church of Scotland* (1655), in the previously quoted MS. at Corpus Christi College, Oxford, is said to be by Brian Duppa, the preface of this work by the Publisher states "What the Life of the Author was, has been diligently and faithfully collected by a Reverend Person of that Nation, who out of the midst of the Ruines of his Church, hath gather'd out of the Rubbige of it, the substance of these following Particulars". It is possible that Alexander Ross was the Scotsman who collected the materials for Spotiswood's life, and that Duppa used these in the writing of the Archbishop's brief Life. There is nothing in the text to connect it with Duppa, but the style and sentiments are similar and there are some characteristic words and phrases, e.g., "sword-men". The publisher (Royston) also published some work by Alexander Ross.

(ii. Referring to Letters II, III, XII, XV, XXXV, XCVI, XCIX and CII).

P. 5, Letter II, Note 3.

Foster states that Chaworth sat for Midhurst in Parliament from January 6th to February 15th 1640/1. But according to the Commons' *Journals*, of the three elected in 1640 (May, Cawley and Chaworth) only the two former were duly declared elected on February 15th, 1640/1, so that presumably Chaworth did not sit after that time (*Accounts and Papers, Members of Parliament*, Part I (1878), p. 495, Note 1).

P. 8, Letter III, Note 1.

Margaret, Lady Boswell, was also a notable benefactress to Sevenoaks. In addition to the two Sir William Boswell Scholarships of £12 a year for boys from Sevenoaks School (or failing them from Tonbridge School) to go to Jesus College, Cambridge, she left money for the education of fifteen poor children by a schoolmaster. The Lady Boswell School at Sevenoaks still exists.

In 1692, ten years after her death at the age of 87, a monument was erected to her memory in St Nicholas' Church at Sevenoaks, where she is shewn kneeling between two angels (Inscription recorded in Rawlinson MSS., D.682, ff. 56 and 56 v.)

P. 10, Letter III, Note 11.

In view of Justinian's allusion to papers of Bacon as well as Dee, in Sir William Boswell's hands, it is worth noting that there is a letter in the Bodleian Library (Rawlinson MSS., D. 391, f. 101) from Isaac Gruter to (Sir) Thomas Browne, in Latin, dated June 24th, 1651, in which Gruter says that during the past few weeks he has acquired some manuscripts of Bacon *ab ipso authore emendata, partim politica, et moralia, partim physiologica* from the library of Sir William Boswell.

P. 29, Letter XII.

"Your pastry man, though he hath not so many languages as Mr. Boncle . . . ." Mr. Boncle must be John Boncle (Bunckley) created M.A. in 1652, by virtue of a letter of Cromwell as Chancellor of Oxford University. He was master af the Charterhouse school in 1653, then a fellow of Eton, and headmaster in 1654, from which posts he was ejected at the Restoration. In July, 1660, he petitioned Charles II, claiming that he had been sent to serve the Royal children, but had been dismissed by the Parliament. He was accordingly made master of the school in the Mercers' Chapel in London, where he was living in 1673 (Foster; Wood, *Fasti*, ed. Bliss, Vol. II, p. 174; C.S.P. (Dom) 1660-61, p. 166; H. C. Maxwell Lyte, *A History of Eton College* (1875)).

P. 33, Letter XV, Note 3.

A further proof of the connection between the Duppas and the Carliles is furnished by the will of Mrs. Duppa, in which she left to "Mistris Joane Carlile my greate Maudlin Silver cupp". A maudlin cup was used for mead (maudlin=metheglin). (Will proved November 9th, 1665).

P. 57, Footnote.

For the Pelhams, see Mrs. A. Pelham and David McLean *Some Early Pelhams* (1931), *Visitation of Sussex, 1633*, Harl. Soc. Vol. LIII (1905) and *Visitation of Sussex, 1632*, Harl. Soc. Vol. LXXXIX (1937).

P. 70, Letter XXXV, Note 2.

Dorothy Osborne also read "the Story of China written by a Portugese, Fernando Mendez Pinto", and comments on it in Letter 59. G. C. Moore Smith in his note (p. 277) suggests that she probably read it in the French version (1628 and 1645), but she may well have read Cogan's translation in English, which he wrongly states did not appear till 1663. It came out in 1653, and her letter is dated February 19th (1653/4).

Dorothy was certainly acquainted with Cogan's work as a translator, as in Letter 40, she mentions his translation of *Ibraham ou L'illustre Bassa* which appeared in 1652. She was not impressed with his work, and says "I have noe Patience neither with these translatours of Romances", who disguised the originals, and used so many French words and phrases, "that twas impossible for one that understood not French to make any thing of them". In the same letter she mentions that she had had "but one letter from Sir Jus: but twas worth twenty of any body's else to make me sport". One wonders if in this letter, he mentioned *Ibraham*, as the subject of de Scudéry's book would have been particularly appropriate to his purpose; the romance of a certain Justinian of the age of Charles V, who, after many adventures, won the hand of a noble Italian lady.

P. 147, Letter XCVI, Note 2.

Sir Justinian was certainly acquainted with Thomas Stanley who was a neighbour of the Garrards in Hertfordshire, and who married Dorothy, sister of Katherine Enyon, the daughter of Sir James Enyon, Bart., of Flore, Northants. Katherine Enyon became the wife of Sir George Buswell, Bart., of Clipston, Northants. There is a draft letter (I.C. 602) of Sir Justinian at Lamport to Thomas Stanley on the subject of Buswell's will and the remarriage of his widow to Justinian's nephew, John Garrard; also an undated letter from Stanley himself to Sir Justinian, entirely concerned with his bad state of health (I.C. 3043). Thomas Isham in his *Journal* (1875) records the visit on two successive days of "Mr. Stanley" (September 23rd, and 24th, 1672) accompanied on the first occasion by "Mr. Garrard" his neighbour, and Sir Justinian's nephew, and, on the second, by his wife, son and daughter, and his sister-in-law, Lady Buswell.

P. 155, Letter XCIX, Note 3.

The quotation from Tanner MSS. 52, f. 207v. is given in modernised spelling from a transcript of Dr. Bosher. The reply is given in the original spelling.

P. 159, Letter CII, Note 3.

Lady Dysart cannot have been the person to have interceded for Sir Justinian in 1658, as she was in France at the time, and did not return to England until Cromwell's death. (Major-General E. D. H. Tollemache, *The Tollemaches of Helmingham and Ham* (1949), p. 57). The suggestion in this note that it was Mrs. Carlile, who performed this office, is therefore much strengthened.

LIST OF AUTHORITIES AND AUTHORS CITED

(The dates of publication given are those of the edition consulted; where two editions had been used, both are given, and this is explained in the footnotes).

MANUSCRIPTS

Drake, Revd. Richard, Diary; MSS. Rawl. D. 158 (Bodleian Library).
Harleian MSS., British Museum.
Isham Correspondence; also Isham (Lamport) Collection of MSS. (Northants. Record Office, Lamport Hall).
Lamport Library Catalogue, compiled by Charles Edmonds (1880).
Rawlinson MSS., (Bodleian Library).
Richmond, Court Rolls of the Manor of, (Public Record Office; also transcripts at the Public Library, Richmond, Surrey).
Tanner MSS., (Bodleian Library).
Ward, Seth, *Notitia*. (Salisbury Diocesan Archives).
Wills (P.C.C.) proved in the Prerogative Court of Canterbury (now at Somerset House).
Wills (Archd. North'ton) proved in the Archdeaconry of Northampton (now at Birmingham).

PRINTED BOOKS AND ARTICLES

Act Books of the Archbishop of Canterbury (1938).
Algiers Voyage in a Journal or Briefe Reportary . . . by one that went along in the Voyage (1621).
Allegemeine Deutsche Biographie, 56 vols. (1875-1912).
The Ancestor.
Annual Reports of the Deputy Keeper of the Public Records (Published as Parliamentary Papers up to 1915).
Ashburnham, John, A Narrative by John Ashburnham (1830).
Ashley, Maurice, Oliver Cromwell (1937).
Archaeologia Cantiana.
Aubrey, John, Brief Lives, ed. A. Clark (1898);
—— Natural History . . . of Surrey (1718).
Augustine, Saint, *De Civitate Dei* (Trans. Dodds, 1871).
Bacon, Francis, *Instauratio Magna* (1620) (The *Novum Organum* is the second part of this work).
Barker, G. F. R. and Stenning, A. H., The Record of Old Westminsters (1928).
Barksdale, Clement, A Remembrance of Excellent Men (1670).
Baronetages, see Cokayne and Wotton.
Beck, Cave, The Universal Character etc. (1657).
Beckett, R. B., Lely (1951).
Bodleian Library Record.
Boscobel Tracts, ed. J. Hughes (1857).
Bosher, Revd. Dr. R. S., The Making of the Restoration Settlement (1951).
Boswell, James, Life of Samuel Johnson, ed. G. B. Hill (1887).
Bridges, John, The History and Antiquities of Northamptonshire (2 vols. 1791).
Browning, G. A., Thomas Osborne, Earl of Danby (1951).
Bryce, Viscount, The Holy Roman Empire (new edn. 1922).
Bunyan, John, Grace Abounding to the Chief of Sinners (1666).
Burke, Sir J. Bernard, General Armory (1878);
—— Extinct and Dormant Baronetcies (1844);
—— Dormant and Extinct Peerages (1883);
—— Vicissitudes of Families (new edn. 2 vols.) (1883).
Burghclere, Winifred Lady, George Villiers, Second Duke of Buckingham (1903).
Burton, Robert, Anatomy of Melancholy (1621) (by "Democritus Junior").
Calendars:
Calendar of Clarendon State Papers (IV vols. 1872-1932).
Calendar of the Committee for Advance of Money (1642-1656) ed. Mrs. Everett Green (III Parts).
Calendar of the Committee for compounding with Delinquents etc. (1643-1660) ed. Mrs. Everett Green (V Parts).
Calendar of State Papers, Domestic esp. Charles I (XXIII Vols.) The Commonwealth ed. Mrs. Everett Green (XIII Vols.).

Calendars (continued):
Calendar of State Papers, Colonial esp. 1574-1660 Vol. I (1860).
Cammell, C. R., The Great Duke of Buckingham (1939).
Cardano, Girolamo (Cardan) *De Consolatione* (Trans. Thomas Bedingfield, 1573).
Carlyle, Thomas, Oliver Cromwell's Letters and Speeches (3rd edn. 1849).
Cartwright, Julia, *Sacharissa* (1893).
Casaubon, Meric, A True and Faithful Relation of what passed for many years between Dr. John Dee and Some Spirits (1659);
—— Treatise concerning Enthusiasme etc. (1655);
—— The Vindication (1624).
Caussin, Revd. Nicholas [Causinus or C.N.], The Unfortunate Politique (or the Life of Herod). Englished by G.P. (1638).
De La Chambre, M. C., The Characters of the Passions (1650).
Chancellor, E. Beresford, The History and Antiquities of Richmond (1894).
Charity Commissioners Reports.
Chevalier, C.U.P., *Répertoire des Sources historiques du Moyen Age* (1905).
The Clarke Papers, ed. C. H. Firth (1891-1901).
Cloria and Narcissus (1653) and (1661).
Cogan, Henry, Translations: *Gioralamo Lunadoro, Relatione della Corte di Roma* (1635);
—— Fioravante Martinelli's addition to Lunadoro's book (1650);
—— The Court of Rome (1654);
—— The Voyages and Adventures of Fernand Pinto a Purtugal; During his Travels . . . in the Kingdoms of Ethiopia, China . . . Japan. Done into English by H. C. Gent (1653).
Cokayne, G. E., The Complete Baronetage (6 vols. 1900-6).
Complete Peerage, The, G. E. Cokayne (1887-98), also the new edn. (in progress) by G. E. Cokayne, Vicary Gibbs and others.
Courlander, Kathleen, Richmond (1953).
The Court and Times of Charles I, ed. R. F. Williams (1848).
Coxe, H. O., Catalogue of Oxford College MSS., 2 vols. (1852).
Dart, John, History and Antiquities of Westminster (1742).
Davenant, Sir William, Gondibert. An Heroic Poem (1651); with a Preface addressed to Thomas Hobbes (1651).
Davies, Godfrey, The Early Stuarts (1937).
Descartes, René, The Passions of the Soul (trans.) (1650).
Dictionary of National Biography.
Digges, Leonard, Pantometria, dedicated to Sir Nicholas Bacon (1571).
Dircks, H., A Biographical Memoir of Samuel Hartlib (1865).
Drinkwater, John, Mr. Charles, King of England (1926).
Duppa, Brian, Holy Rules and Helps to Devotion (1675).
Eachard, Lawrence, History of England (1718).
Eikon Basilike, (1649).
Encyclopaedia Britannica, ed. Walter Yust (1947).
Esdaile, Katherine A., English Church Monuments (1946).
Evelyn, John, Diary, ed. A. Dobson (1908);
—— St. John Chrysostom's Golden Booke concerning the education of Children (trans.) (1659).
Fea, Allan, The Flight of the King (2nd edn. 1908).
Feiling, Keith, History of the Tory Party, 1640-1718 (1924).
Ferne, Dr. Henry, Pian Piano etc. (1656).
Firth, Sir C. H., The Last Years of the Protectorate, 1656-1658, 2 vols. (1909);
—— Acts and Ordinances of the Interregnum, 1642-1660, 3 vols. ed. by C. H. Firth and R. S. Rait, (1911).
Foss, Edward, Judges of England (1848-64).
Foster, Joseph, *Alumni Oxonienses* (1891).
Fuller, Revd. T., The Worthies of England (1672).
Gardiner, S. R., Constitutional Documents of the Puritan Revolution (1906);
—— History of the Commonwealth and Protectorate (4 vols.) (1913).
The Genealogist (New Series).
Gooch, G. P., Political Thought from Bacon to Halifax (1914).
Gotch, J. A., Inigo Jones (1928);
—— The Old Halls and Manor Houses of Northamptonshire (1936);
—— "Some newly found Drawings and Letters of John Webb", R.I.B.A. Journal 3rd Series, Vol. XXVIII, No. 10.
Gramont Memoirs (2 vols.) ed. Vizetelly (1889).
Green, Mrs. M. A. E., Lives of the Princesses of England, Vols. V and VI, (1849-55).
Hacket, John (Bishop of Coventry and Lichfield), *Scrinia Reserata* (1693).

Hallam, Henry, Literature of Europe (3 vols.) (4th edn. 1854).
Halliwell, J. O., Autobiography of Sir Simonds D'Ewes (1845).
Ham House, A Guide (1951).
Hammond, Dr. Henry, An Answer to the Animadversions [of J. Owen] on the dissertations touching Ignatius' Epistles etc. (1654).
—— *Dissertationes quatuor, contra sententiam D. Blondelli et aliorum* (1651).
—— A Paraphrase and Annotations upon all the Books of the New Testament (1653).
Harleian Society Publications; (for Parish Registers publ. by, see Parish Registers).
(1) Visitation of Cheshire, 1616, ed. Armytage (1909).
(2) „ „ Kent, 1619, ed. Hovenden (1898).
(3) „ „ Kent, 1663, ed. Armytage (1906).
(4) „ „ London, 1633, ed. Howard and Chester (1883).
(5) „ „ Northamptonshire, 1681, ed. Longden (1935).
(6) „ „ Nottinghamshire, 1614, ed. Marshall (1871).
Harrington, James, Commonwealth of Oceana (1655);
—— Prerogative of Popular Government (1658);
—— Reply to Matthew Wren's Considerations (1658).
Harris, Dr. John, History of Kent (1719).
Hasted, Edward, History of Kent, ed. Drake (1886).
Heber, R., Life of Jeremy Taylor (revised Eden, 1854).
Hobbes, Thomas, Leviathan (1651). See also Index of Persons.
Hopley, Revd. A., Guide to Westham Church (1905).
Hutchinson, Lucy, Memoirs of the Life of Colonel Hutchinson (1845).
Hutton, Revd. William, Laud (1895).
Hyde, Edward 1st Earl of Clarendon, History of the Rebellion, ed. W. D. Macray (6 vols. 1888).
Inderwick, F. A., The Interregnum (1891).
Isham (Sir) Thomas, Journal, trans. Revd. Robt. Isham; ed. Walter Rye (1875).
Isham, Sir Gyles, All Saints Church, Lamport (1950);
Articles in The Reports and Papers of the Northamptonshire Architectural and Archaeological Society (1952);
—— "The Architectural History of Lamport";
Northamptonshire Past and Present (1948);
——"The Historical and Literary Associations of Lamport";
Christ's College Magazine (1927);
—— "The connection of the Isham Family with Christ's College".
Iter Carolinum (1660) (Anon.).
Johnson, Samuel, Dictionary, 2 vols. (1755).
Ben Jonson, ed. C. H. Herford and Percy Simpson (1925).
Jonsonus Virbius, ed. Brian Duppa (1638).
Journals of the House of Lords, vols. ii–x.
Journals of the House of Commons, vols. i–viii.
Pauli Jovii, *Historia sui temporis* (1556).
Kennet, Bishop White, A Register and Chronicle ecclesiastical and civil etc. (1728).
King, Henry, Bishop of Chichester, A Sermon, preached at the Funeral . . . of . . . Bryan Lord Bp. of Winchester etc. (1662).
The Knyvett Letters, ed. B. Schofield, Norfolk Record Society (1949).
Lacey, Revd. T. A., Herbert Thorndike (1929).
The History and Antiquities of the Parish of Lambeth in the County of Surrey (1786).
The History of the Troubles and Tryal . . . of William Laud etc. (1695).
Lees-Milne, James, The Age of Inigo Jones (1953).
Le Neve, John, *Monumenta Anglicana*, 5 vols. (1717-19).
Lewis, Samuel (the elder), Topographical Dictionary of England, 4 vols. (5th edn. 1842).
Ligon, Richard, True and Exact History of the Island of Barbadoes (1651).
Locke, A. A., The Hanbury Family (1916).
Longden, Revd. H. I., Northamptonshire and Rutland Clergy from 1500. 15 vols. 1938-1942 with Index, etc. Vol. 16, 1952.
Lowndes, William Thomas, The Bibliographer's Manual, revised by H. G. Bohn. 4 vols. (1857-64).
Lysons, Daniel, The Environs of London, 4 vols. (1792-6).
Lysons, Daniel and Samuel, *Magna Britannia*, vols. 1-6 (1806-22).
Madan, Francis F., A New Bibliography of the *Eikon Basilike* (1950).
Magna Britannia (1731).
Manning, Owen and W. Bray, History and Antiquities of Surrey, 3 vols. (1804-14).
Marshall, G. W., *Miscellanea Marescelliana* (1883).
Masson, David, Life of Milton etc. 6 vols. (new edn.) (1881-96).
Matthews, A. G., Walker Revised (1948).

Mayne, Revd. Jasper, Certain Sermons and Letters of Defence and Resolution to some of the late Controversies of Our Times (1653).
Mercurius Politicus.
Mercurius Publicus.
Milton, John, Judgement of M. Bucer concerning Divorce printed in Works, ed. J. Mitford Vol. 4 (1851).
Miscellanea Genealogica et Heraldica.
Montagu Musters Book, ed. J. Wake, Northants. Record Society, Vol. VII (1935).
Montagu, Bishop Richard, *Analecta Ecclesiasticarum Exercitationum* (1622).
—— (For his edition of Photius' Letters see under Photius (Biblical, Classical and Patristic Authors).
Letter Book of John Mordaunt, ed. Mary Coate (Camden Society, 1945).
More, Henry, A Modest Enquiry into the Mystery of Infinity (1644);
—— *Conjectura Cabbalistica* etc. (1653).
Morley, John, Cromwell (1900).
Murray, Handbook to Northamptonshire, 2nd edn. (1901).
Nash, Joseph, Mansions of England in the Olden Time (1869-72).
Nash, Treadway, R., Collections for the History of Worcestershire (1782).
Nelson, Sir T. J., Richmond Park (1883).
Nichols, John, History and Antiquities of the County of Leicester, 4 vols. (1795-1815).
Nightingale, J. E., The Church Plate of the County of Wilts (1891).
Norfolk Antiquarian Miscellany.
Northampton, William Bingham, 6th Marquess of, The History of the Comptons (printed for private circulation, 1930).
Northamptonshire Notes and Queries.
Northamptonshire Past and Present.
Quarter Sessions Records of the County of Northampton, ed. J. Wake, Northants. Record Society, Vol. I (1924).
Victoria County History of Northamptonshire, 4 vols.
—— Genealogical Volume (Northamptonshire Families) by Oswald Barron (1906).
Notes and Queries.
Northamptonshire. See Harleian Society; Longden; Parish Registers.
Oman, Carola, Henrietta Maria (1936).
Letters of Dorothy Osborne, ed. Moore Smith (1928).
Oswald, Arthur, Articles in Country Life on Lamport Hall, September 26, 1952, October 3, 1952 and October 10, 1952.
Parish Registers,
Greenwich (Transactions Greenwich and Lewisham Antiq. Soc., 1920);
Lamport, see below, Northamptonshire;
Lee, St. Margaret's, 1579-1754 (1888);
Lewisham, St. Mary's (ed. Duncan, 1891);
London. St. Dionis, Backchurch, (Harl. Soc. 1878); St. Martin-in-the-Fields, Part II, 1619-36, ed. J. V. Kitto, (Harl. Soc. 1916); St. Olave's, Hart Street (Harl. Soc. 1916); Westminster Abbey, (Harl. Soc. 1876);
Northamptonshire Parish Registers, ed. Phillimore and Longden (1909);
Richmond, Surrey, ed. J. Challenor-Smith (1903).
Paget, Major T. G., History of the Althorp and Pytchley Hunt (1927).
Pascal, Blaise, Provincial Letters (trans. from *Les Lettres provinciales*, 1657).
Patterson's Roads, 18th edn. (1829).
Peile, John, Biographical Register of Christ's College (1918).
Pell Records, Issues of the Exchequer during the reign of James I, ed. Fredk. Devon (1836).
Pepys, Samuel, Diary, ed. H. B. Wheatley, 9 vols. (1893-9).
Petrie, Sir Charles, The Letters, Speeches and Proclamations of King Charles I (1935).
Piper, A. Cecil, History of Richmond Parish Church (1947).
Plomer, H. R., Dictionary of Booksellers 1641 to 1667 (1907).
Ponsonby, Arthur, English Diaries (1923).
—— More English Diaries (1927).
Poole, Mrs. Reginald Lane, Catalogue of Oxford Portraits (1925).
Power, D'Arcy, William Harvey (1897).
Prynne, William, *Histrio-Mastix*, The Players Scourge: or, Actors Tragoedie (1633).
Ranke, Leopold von, History of England, principally in the 17th century (trans.), 6 vols. (1875).
Requeste, Procès Verbaux . . . faits à la diligence du Recteur et par l'ordre de l' Université etc. Paris (1644).
Roberts, B. Dew, Mitre and Musket (1938).
Ross, Alexander, Some Animadversions and Observations upon Sir Walter Raleigh's Historie of the World (1653);

—— Sir Walter Raleigh's History of the World . . . now abbreviated (1650);
—— *Virgilius Evangelizans* (1634).
Royal Commission on Historical Monuments, Reports of the
Royal Society, Notes and Records.
Salmasius, C. (Claude Saumaise), *Defensio regia pro Carolo I* (1649).
Scott, Eva, The Travels of the King (1907).
Semedo, Alvarez de, The History of the Great and Renowned Monarchy of China, trans. into English from Italian (1655).
Selden, John, Table Talk, (1689);
—— Titles of Honour (1631);
—— Theanthropos, or God Made Man (1661).
Smith, Logan Pearsall, The Life and Letters of Sir Henry Wotton (1907).
Spotiswoode, Archbishop John, History of the Church of Scotland (1655).
Stanford, C. Thomas-, Sussex in the Great Civil War and Interregnum (1910).
Stanley, Thomas, Lives of the Philosophers, 4 vols. (1655-62).
Stephens, Revd. W. R., Memorials of the South Saxon See and Cathedral Church of Chichester (1876).
Stopford-Sackville, Nigel, Drayton House (privately printed 1939).
Stoughton, Revd. John, Ecclesiastical History of England: Opening of Long Parliament to death of Oliver Cromwell, 2 vols. (1867).
—— The Church of the Restoration, 2 vols. (1870).
Strawley, Revd. J. H., Michael Honywood (Lincoln Minster Pamphlets, No. 5, 1950).
Surrey Archaeological Collections.
Surrey: Victoria County History.
Tatham, G. B., The Puritans in Power (1912).
Taylor, Revd. Jeremy, Real Presence and Spiritual of Christ, etc. (1653).
—— *Unum Necessarium* (1654).
Thompson, Revd. Henry L., History of Christ Church (Oxford) (1900).
Thorndike, Revd. H., An Epilogue to the Tragedy of the Church of England (1659).
Thurloe, John, Collection of the State Papers of, ed. Birch, 7 vols. (1742).
Trevelyan, G. M., England under the Stuarts (rev. edn. 1908).
Trevor-Roper, H. R., Archbishop Laud (1940).
Trollope, Anthony, Framley Parsonage (1867).
Turnbull, G. H., Samuel Hartlib; a Sketch of his Life etc. (1920);
—— Hartlib, Dury and Comenius (1947);
—— ed. by G. H. Turnbull, J. A. Comenius, Two Pansophical Works (1951).
Universal Library or Compleat Summary of signs, containing above 60 treatises, 22nd edn. (1722).
Vaughan, Thomas (*Eugenius Philalethes*), *Anthroposophia Theomagica* (1650).
Venn, J. A., *Alumni Cantabrigienses* (1922-7).
Verney Family, Memoirs of the,
Verney, Parthenope Lady, The Civil War, Vol. I and II (1892);
Verney, Margaret Lady, Restoration to Revolution, Vol. III and IV (1894-99).
Wake, Joan, The Brudenells of Deene (1953).
Walker, Rev. J., The Sufferings of the Clergy (1714); (also Matthews, A. G., Walker Revised).
Walpole, Horace, Anecdotes of Painting (ed. R. Wornum), 3 vols. (1888).
Walton, Brian, *Biblia Sacra Polyglotta*, 6 vols. (1654-57).
Walton, Isaac, The Compleat Angler (1653) and (1655); ed. John Buchan (1901).
—— "Life of Dr. John Donne" in Lives of Donne, Wotton, Hooker and Herbert (1670).
Ward, Rev. Seth, *Vindiciae Academiarum* etc. . . . by H. D. . . . (Oxford, 1654).
Watson, T. E., History and Pedigree of the Family of Lewin (1919).
Whole Duty of Man, Author of the (? Dr. R. Allestree), The Gentleman's Calling (1660).
Documents relating to . . . the Cathedral Church of Winchester, in the seventeenth century, ed. W. R. Stephens and F. T. Madge (Hants. Record Society, 1897).
Wolf, Lucien, Menasseh Ben Israel's Mission to Oliver Cromwell (1901).
Wood, Anthony à, Athenae Oxonienses } 2 vols. (1721).
Fasti ,, }
—— Ath. Ox. with Fasti, ed. F. Bliss, 4 vols. (1813-20).
—— The Life and Times of, ed. Andrew Clark, (1891-1900).
Woodworth, Allegra, Purveyance for the Royal Household in the Reign of Queen Elizabeth (Philadelphia, 1945).
Wotton, Thomas, Baronetage of England, 5 vols. (1741).
Wren, Matthew, Considerations on Mr. Harrington's Commonwealth of Oceana (1657).
Wright, T., History and Topography of the County of Essex (1836).
Young, G. M., To-day and Yesterday (1948).

INDEX OF
BIBLICAL, PATRISTIC & CLASSICAL AUTHORS, ETC.

References to quotations are indicated by cit. = cited.

INDEX OF PLACES

The abbreviations of the names of counties are those used by the Place-Name Society.

INDEX OF PERSONS

INDEX OF SUBJECTS

(Trades and occupations will be found all together under that heading)

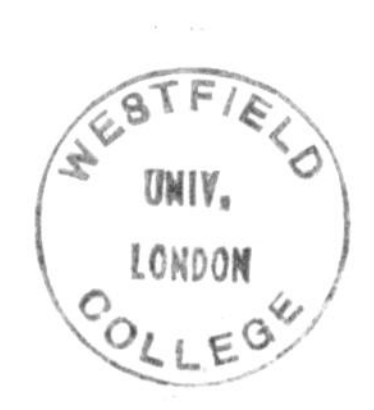

VYN

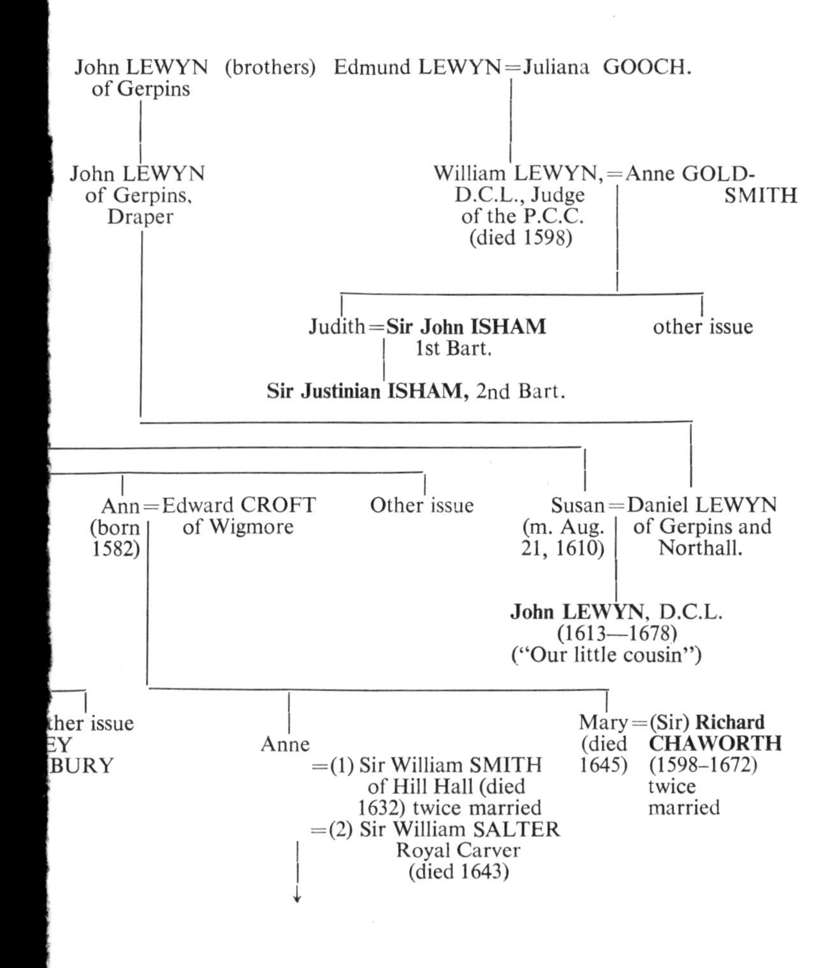

John LEWYN of Gerpins
(brothers)
Edmund LEWYN = Juliana GOOCH.
John LEWYN of Gerpins, Draper
William LEWYN, D.C.L., Judge of the P.C.C. (died 1598) = Anne GOLDSMITH
Judith = Sir John ISHAM 1st Bart.
other issue
Sir Justinian ISHAM, 2nd Bart.
Ann (born 1582) = Edward CROFT of Wigmore
Other issue
Susan (m. Aug. 21, 1610) = Daniel LEWYN of Gerpins and Northall.
John LEWYN, D.C.L. (1613—1678) ("Our little cousin")
ther issue
EY
BURY
Anne
=(1) Sir William SMITH of Hill Hall (died 1632) twice married
=(2) Sir William SALTER Royal Carver (died 1643)
Mary (died 1645) = (Sir) Richard CHAWORTH (1598–1672) twice married

TABLE A.— FAMILIES OF MALLORY, DUPPA, MARSHALL AND LE

(*Persons mentioned in the Duppa-Isham Correspondence are indicated by heavy type*)

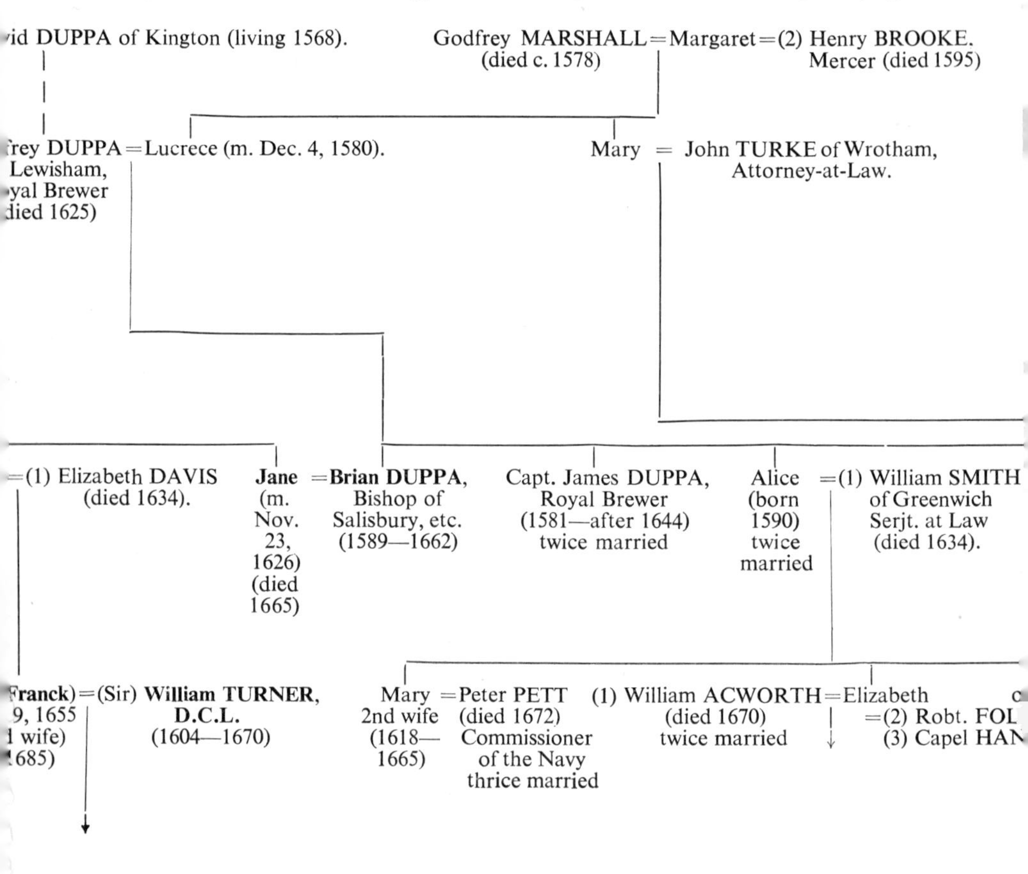

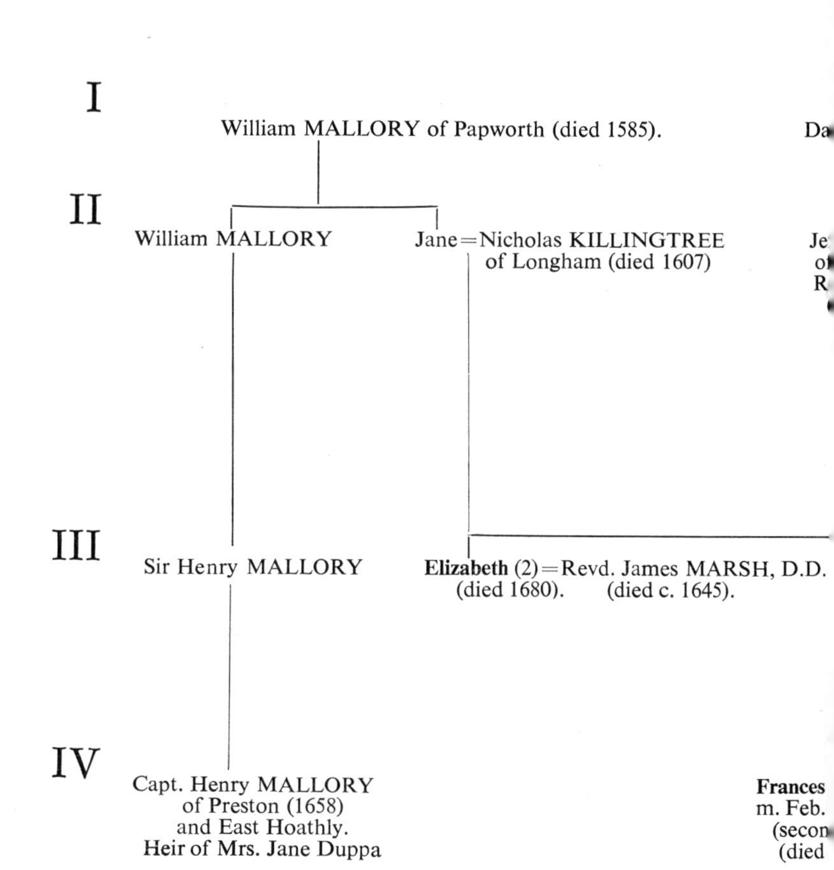
I
William MALLORY of Papworth (died 1585).
II
William MALLORY
Jane=Nicholas KILLINGTREE
of Longham (died 1607)
III
Sir Henry MALLORY
Elizabeth (2)=Revd. James MARSH, D.D.
(died 1680).
(died c. 1645).
IV
Capt. Henry MALLORY
of Preston (1658)
and East Hoathly.
Heir of Mrs. Jane Duppa
Frances
m. Feb.

(c) Jane = John ARDYS
(1586–1612) of Renhold (Ronhall)
(Living 1621)

25)

Judith
(1610–1636)

Thomas ARDYS
mentd. in his grandmother
ISHAM'S Will, 1621

h TURNOR,
3 died 1713)

Charles ISHAM,
(1660–1671)

Mary = (Sir) Marmaduke DAYRELL
(1654–1679) of Castle Camps (died 1729)
1st wife twice married, issue by 2nd wife

Vere
(1654–1674)

t

John ISHAM,
Under-Secretary of State
(1659–1746)

other issue

TABLE B.—THE ISHAMS OF LAMPORT (*a*)

(*Persons mentioned in the Duppa-Isham Correspondence are indicated by heavy type*)

Thomas ISHAM = Elizabeth NICHOLSON
of Lamport (1555–1606) (m. 1576 died 1623)
"The Blind Squire"

usanna
(1581–1653)
2nd wife

Sir John ISHAM, = Judith LEWYN
1st Bart. (1582–1651) (m. 1607 died 16

.E (*d*)
aw

(1) Jane GARRARD = **Sir Justinian ISHAM** = (2) **Hon. Vere LEIGH**
(m. 1634 died 1639) 2nd Bart. (1611–1675) (m. 1653 died 1704)

Elizabeth
(1609–1654)

:STRANGE, **Susan** = (Sir) **Nicholas CAREW**
art. of Beddington
ged 37) (1635–1688)

(Sir) **Thomas ISHAM,**
3rd Bart.
(1657–1681)

(Sir) **Justinian ISHAM,** = Elizabe
4th Bart. (1658–1730) (m. 168

Susan (*f*)
(born and died 1659)

Baronets
of Beddington

Baronets of Lampo

ne Pedigree
mptonshire,
amptonshire

gister).

I

II

(1) Sir Anthony DENTON = **Elizabeth** = (2) Paul D'EWES
of Tonbridge (died 1615) / Gentleman Pensioner / to Queen Elizabeth I
Elizabeth ("Lady Denton") (1578–1662)
(2) Paul D'EWES of Stowlangtoft (died 1631) 2nd wife, issue by both wives

Sir Martin STUTEVILLE (*b*) =
of Dalham (died 1631, aged 62) twice married, issue by both wives

III

Five Daughters

John STUTEVIL
Barrister at
(1609–1671)

IV

John (born 13 Feb. bur. 25 Feb. 1639)

(*e*) **Jane** eldest daughter (1635-1655)

Judith twin with Elizabeth (1636–1679)

Elizabeth = Sir Nicholas I
(m. 1662) (1636–1689)
2nd
(died 1669,

V

Baronets of Hunstanton

(*a*) Apart from the corrections and additions noted below, this Table is based o[n]
compiled by the late Revd. H. I. Longden, appended to *The Visitation of Nor[…]*
1681 (Harl. Soc. Vol. LXXXVI (1935). For earlier generations, see *No[…]*
Families (V.C.H. (1906)), p. 141.

(*b*) "As a young man went to America with Francis Drake" (M.I. at Dalham).

(*c*) Jane Isham m. John Ardys of Renhold, was bur. there 7 Oct. 1612 (*Parish R[…]*

(*d*) Born 16 Oct. 1609, bur. 5 May 1671 (Parish Register at Dalham).

(*e*) Born 19 Aug. 1635 (Note by her father in his copy of Ussher's *Annals*).

(*f*) Bapt. 28 Aug. 1659 (Beddington *Parish Registers*).